W9-CHJ-739

INSTRUCTOR'S ANNOTATED EDITION

Evergreen

WITH READINGS

INSTRUCTOR'S ANNOTATED EDITION

Evergreen

WITH READINGS

A Guide to Writing

FOURTH EDITION

Susan Fawcett
Alvin Sandberg

Houghton Mifflin Company ▪ Boston
Dallas ▪ Geneva, Illinois ▪ Palo Alto ▪ Princeton, New Jersey

Sponsoring Editor: Mary Jo Southern
Senior Development Editor: Barbara Roth
Senior Project Editor: Barbara Roth
Assistant Design Manager: Karen Rappaport
Production Coordinator: Frances Sharperson
Senior Manufacturing Coordinator: Marie Barnes
Marketing Manager: Diane Gifford

Printed in the U.S.A.

Student Edition ISBN: 0-395-59183-X

Instructor's Annotated Edition ISBN: 0-395-59184-8

BCDEFGHIJ-WC-95432

Acknowledgments

Illustration Credits

Cover illustration by Dorothea Sierra, 1991.

We are grateful to the following individuals for permission to reproduce their photographs in this text: p. 38—Albright-Knox Art Gallery, Buffalo, N.Y. Bequest of A. Conger Goodyear, 1966; page 47—Jaye R. Phillips/The Picture Cube; page 79—George Mars Cassidy/The Picture Cube; page 90—Frank Siteman/Stock, Boston; page 91—© Jon Nickson; page 95—Grant Heilman Photography; page 104—Cynthia W. Sterling/The Picture Cube; page 125—Heath Paley/The Picture Cube; page 130—Deborah Kahn Kalas/Stock, Boston; page 131—© Jon Nickson; page 212—Ed Carlin/The Picture Cube; page 229—Art Resource/Hirshhorn Museum and Sculpture Garden, Smithsonian Institution.

Text Credit

Page 67—"The Silver Horn": © 1944 Harper's Magazine Company, renewed 1971. Reprinted with permission.

Pages 468–473—"Beauty: When the Other Dancer is the Self" from IN SEARCH OF OUR MOTHERS' GARDENS, copyright © 1983 by Alice Walker, reprinted by permission of Harcourt Brace Jovanovich, Inc., and David Higham Associates Limited.

Acknowledgments continue on page 520.

Contents

Preface xi

Suggestions for the Teacher of Writing xv

Suggestions for Using *Evergreen with Readings* xxi

UNIT 1 Getting Started 1

1 Exploring the Writing Process 2

Part A The Writing Process 2
Part B Subject, Audience, and Purpose 3

2 Gathering Ideas 5

Part A Freewriting 5
Part B Brainstorming 8
Part C Clustering 9
Part D Asking Questions 10
Part E Keeping a Journal 13

UNIT 2 Discovering the Paragraph 15

3 The Process of Writing Paragraphs 16

Part A Defining and Looking at the Paragraph 16
Part B Narrowing the Topic and Writing the Topic Sentence 22
Part C Gathering Ideas for the Body 27
Part D Selecting and Dropping Ideas 29
Part E Arranging Ideas in a Plan 30
Part F Writing and Revising the Paragraph 31
Checklist: The Process of Writing Basic Paragraphs 39

4 **Achieving Coherence**   40

Part A   Coherence Through Order   40
Part B   Coherence Through Related Sentences   51

UNIT 3   Developing the Paragraph   63

5 **Illustration**   64

Checklist: The Process of Writing an Illustration Paragraph   71
Suggested Topic Sentences for Illustration Paragraphs   72

6 **Narration**   73

Checklist: The Process of Writing a Narrative Paragraph   79
Suggested Topics for Narrative Paragraphs   80

7 **Description**   81

Checklist: The Process of Writing a Descriptive Paragraph   89
Suggested Topics for Descriptive Paragraphs   90

8 **Process**   92

Checklist: The Process of Writing a Process Paragraph   100
Suggested Topics for Process Paragraphs   101

9 **Definition**   102

Part A   Single-Sentence Definitions   102
Part B   The Definition Paragraph   107
Checklist: The Process of Writing a Definition Paragraph   112
Suggested Topics for Definition Paragraphs   113

10 **Comparison and Contrast**   114

Part A   The Contrast and the Comparison Paragraphs   114
Checklist: The Process of Writing a Contrast or Comparison
Paragraph   125
Suggested Topics for Contrast or Comparison Paragraphs   126
Part B   The Comparison-Contrast Paragraph   127
Working Through the Comparison-Contrast Paragraph   130
Suggested Topics for Comparison-Contrast Paragraphs   131

11 **Classification**   132

Checklist: The Process of Writing a Classification Paragraph   139
Suggested Topics for Classification Paragraphs   140

12 Persuasion   141

Checklist: The Process of Writing a Persuasive Paragraph   154
Suggested Topics for Persuasive Paragraphs   154

UNIT 4   Improving Your Writing   157

13 Revising for Consistency and Parallelism   158

Part A   Consistent Tense   158
Part B   Consistent Number and Person   163
Part C   Parallelism   169
Part D   Consistent Quotations   175

14 Revising for Sentence Variety   181

Part A   Mix Long and Short Sentences   181
Part B   Use a Question, Command, or Exclamation   183
Part C   Vary the Beginnings of Sentences   185
Part D   Vary Methods of Joining Ideas   190
Part E   Review and Practice   208

15 Revising for Language Awareness   213

Part A   Exact Language: Avoiding Vagueness   213
Part B   Concise Language: Avoiding Wordiness   219
Part C   Fresh Language: Avoiding Triteness   223
Part D   Figurative Language: Similes and Metaphors   225

16 Putting Your Revision Skills to Work   230

Writing Sample 1   231
Writing Sample 2   232

UNIT 5   Writing the Essay   237

17 The Process of Writing an Essay   238

Part A   Looking at the Essay   238
Part B   Writing the Thesis Statement   242
Part C   Gathering Ideas for the Body   246
Part D   Ordering and Linking Paragraphs in the Essay   253
Part E   Writing and Revising Short Essays   260
Checklist: The Process of Writing an Essay   267
Suggested Topics for Essays   267

18   Types of Essays   269

Part A   The Illustration Essay   269
Part B   The Narrative Essay   271
Part C   The Descriptive Essay   274
Part D   The Process Essay   276
Part E   The Definition Essay   278
Part F   The Comparison or Contrast Essay   281
Part G   The Classification Essay   283
Part H   The Persuasive Essay   285

19   The Introduction, the Conclusion, and the Title   289

Part A   The Introduction   289
Part B   The Conclusion   293
Part C   The Title   294

20   The Essay Question   297

Part A   Budgeting Your Time   297
Part B   Reading and Understanding the Essay Question   300
Part C   Choosing the Correct Paragraph or Essay Pattern   303
Part D   Writing the Topic Sentence or the Thesis Statement   305
Checklist: The Process of Writing the Essay Question   309

UNIT 6   Reviewing the Basics   311

21   The Simple Sentence   312

Part A   Defining and Spotting Subjects   312
Part B   Spotting Prepositional Phrases   313
Part C   Defining and Spotting Verbs   315

22   Coordination and Subordination   318

Part A   Coordination   318
Part B   Subordination   321
Part C   Semicolons   325
Part D   Conjunctive Adverbs   327
Part E   Review   328

23   Avoiding Sentence Errors   334

Part A   Avoiding Run-Ons and Comma Splices   334
Part B   Avoiding Fragments   338

24 Present Tense (Agreement)   346

Part A   Defining Subject-Verb Agreement   346
Part B   Three Troublesome Verbs in the Present Tense: *To Be, To Have, To Do*   348
Part C   Special Singular Constructions   351
Part D   Separation of Subject and Verb   352
Part E   Sentences Beginning with *There* and *Here*   353
Part F   Agreement in Questions   354
Part G   Agreement in Relative Clauses   355

25 Past Tense   358

Part A   Regular Verbs in the Past Tense   358
Part B   Irregular Verbs in the Past Tense   360
Part C   A Troublesome Verb in the Past Tense: *To Be*   363
Part D   Troublesome Pairs in the Past Tense: *Can/Could, Will/Would*   364

26 The Past Participle   368

Part A   Past Participles of Regular Verbs   368
Part B   Past Participles of Irregular Verbs   369
Part C   Using the Present Perfect Tense   374
Part D   Using the Past Perfect Tense   375
Part E   Using the Passive Voice (*To Be* and the Past Participle)   376
Part F   Using the Past Participle as an Adjective   378

27 Nouns   382

Part A   Defining Singular and Plural   382
Part B   Signal Words: Singular and Plural   385
Part C   Signal Words with *Of*   386

28 Pronouns   389

Part A   Defining Pronouns and Antecedents   389
Part B   Making Pronouns and Antecedents Agree   390
Part C   Referring to Antecedents Clearly   394
Part D   Special Problems of Case   397
Part E   Using Pronouns with *-Self* and *-Selves*   401

29 Prepositions   405

30 Adjectives and Adverbs   409

Part A   Defining and Using Adjectives and Adverbs   409
Part B   The Comparative and the Superlative   411
Part C   A Troublesome Pair: *Good/Well*   414

31 The Apostrophe 417

Part A   The Apostrophe for Contractions   417
Part B   The Apostrophe for Ownership   419
Part C   Special Uses of the Apostrophe   421

32 The Comma 423

Part A   Commas for Items in a Series   423
Part B   Commas with Introductory Phrases, Transitional Expressions, and Parentheticals   424
Part C   Commas for Appositives   426
Part D   Commas with Nonrestrictive and Restrictive Clauses   427
Part E   Commas for Dates and Addresses   429
Part F   Minor Uses of the Comma   430

33 Mechanics 433

Part A   Capitalization   433
Part B   Titles   435
Part C   Direct Quotations   437
Part D   Minor Marks of Punctuation   439

Appendix 1 Spelling 443

Appendix 2 Look-Alikes/Sound-Alikes 454

Reading Selections 467

Beauty: When the Other Dancer Is the Self   *Alice Walker*   468
In Search of Bruce Lee's Grave   *Shanlon Wu*   474
A Brother's Murder   *Brent Staples*   477
One More Lesson   *Judith Ortiz Cofer*   480
How to Get the Most out of Yourself   *Alan Loy McGinnis*   485
Hunger of Memory   *Richard Rodriguez*   489
Two Views of the River   *Mark Twain*   493
How to Put Off Doing a Job   *Andy Rooney*   495
Some Thoughts About Abortion   *Anna Quindlen*   497
On Kids and Couples   *Francine Klagsbrun*   501
Do You Know Who Your Friends Are?   *Larry Letich*   505
Living with My VCR   *Nora Ephron*   508
A Life Defined by Losses and Delights   *Nancy Mairs*   512
Three Types of Resistance to Oppression   *Martin Luther King, Jr.*   516

Index   521

Rhetorical Index   529

Preface

Evergreen with Readings combines in one book the new Fourth Edition of our popular college writing text *Evergreen* and fourteen professional reading selections. Based on our classroom experience at Bronx Community College of the City University of New York, *Evergreen* was designed for students who need to improve the writing skills so necessary to success in college and in most careers. Its clear, paced lessons, plentiful practices, and engaging writing assignments have guided hundreds of thousands of students through the process of writing effective paragraphs and essays, from prewriting to final draft. Now those instructors who wish to include reading in their writing classes may choose from richly varied and provocative reading selections by such writers as Alice Walker, Richard Rodriguez, Anna Quindlen, and Martin Luther King. Each selection is accompanied by a headnote, glosses, comprehension questions, and writing assignments.

Features of *Evergreen with Readings*

- **Fourteen Reading Selections.** Ranging from two to six pages, these essays represent a variety of authorial voices, subjects, and styles. The selections include examples of each rhetorical mode taught in the text. Each reading selection is followed by four discussion and writing questions and three suggested writing assignments.

- **New Continuous Discourses, Paragraphs, and Essays for Proofreading.** Nearly seventy practices have been replaced with continuous discourses (sequential sentences that explore one topic), paragraphs, and short essays for proofreading and other tasks. High-interest topics include Maya Lin's creation of the Vietnam War Memorial, rap music, recovery from addiction, improving study skills, sports greats who overcame disabilities, the Regent Diamond, and surgeon Daniel Hale Williams. These exercises motivate students to read while improving their writing skills.

- **New and Revised Model Paragraphs and Essays.** We have replaced and enriched many written models, aiming for compelling subject matter and thorough development.

- **New Chapter 1, "Exploring the Writing Process."** This chapter gives an overview of the writing process and introduces audience and purpose.

- **New Material on Clustering.** Clustering has been added to the prewriting techniques in Chapter 2, "Gathering Ideas."

- **New Chapter on Narration.** Unit 3 now includes a chapter on narration, and the narrative essay is presented in Chapter 18, "Types of Essays."

- **Increased Peer Editing Coverage.** Suggested questions to guide peer editors now appear in Chapter 17, "The Process of Writing an Essay."

- **New Chapter on Prepositions.** Geared especially to ESL students, Chapter 29 presents a list of fixed expressions containing prepositions.

- **New Spelling and Look-Alikes/Sound-Alikes Placement.** This material has been moved to two appendixes; instructors may assign it or not, as they choose.

- **Extensive Ancillary Package.** Available upon adoption of the text, the following ancillaries provide the instructor with support material and expand teaching options. New to this edition of *Evergreen with Readings* is Evergreen Editing Exercises, a software program containing supplementary paragraph- and essay-length proofreading exercises.

  Evergreen Editing Exercises
  Instructor's Annotated Edition
  Instructor's Resource Manual
  Test Package
  Computerized Diagnostic/Mastery Tests
  Test Bank Data Disk

- **Choice of Binding.** *Evergreen with Readings* is available in spiral binding or in Otabinding, a new paperback process that allows the book to lie flat when open.

  Also Available

- *Evergreen*, Fourth Edition, without the reading selections.

Organization of the Text

Evergreen with Readings begins with an overview of the writing process, audience, and purpose and then introduces five prewriting techniques. Unit 2 guides students through the paragraph-writing process: planning, writing topic sentences, developing ideas, organizing, making smooth transitions, and revising. Unit 3 moves on to the rhetorical modes most often required in college writing (illustration, narration, description, process, definition, comparison/contrast, classification, and persuasion). Unit 4 covers the more subtle skills of sentence variety and language awareness. In Unit 5, the techniques of paragraph writing are applied step by step to the process of writing essays and to answering essay examination questions. Unit 6 thoroughly reviews basic grammar, highlighting such major problem areas as verbs, punctuation, and mechanics; two appendixes cover spelling and homonyms. The final section, Reading Selections, consists of essay-length reading selections, discussion questions, and writing assignments.

Evergreen with Readings, with its full range of materials and flexible organization, adapts easily to almost any course design and to a wide range of student needs. Since each chapter is self-contained, the text also works well for tutorials and self-teaching.

Acknowledgments

We wish to thank those people whose thoughtful comments and suggestions helped us develop the Fourth Edition:

Nancy Barlow, Brookhaven College, TX

Francine L. DeFrance, Cerritos College, CA

Edwin L. Demerly, Henry Ford Community College, MI

Elaine Denman, Terra Technical College, OH

Anne M. Fitts, Concordia College, AL

Sandra Sellers Hanson, LaGuardia Community College, NY

Roslyn J. Harper, Trident Technical College, SC

Judith Harway, Milwaukee Institute of Art and Design, WI

Susan D. Huard, Manchester Community College, CT

Reginald A. Jenkins, University of the District of Columbia

Steven Katz, State Technical Institute at Memphis, TN

Irma Luna, San Antonio College, TX

D. Michael Nifong, Georgia College

Bonnie Orr, Wenatchee Valley College, WA

Carolyn Russell, Rio Hondo Community College, CA

Eugene Shiro, University of the District of Columbia

Eileen M. Ward, College of DuPage, IL

Russ Ward, Aims Community College, Greeley, CO

Our editor Barbara Roth was a vigilant, patient, and invaluable participant in the process of creating *Evergreen with Readings*. In addition, we
owe a special debt to Barry Kwalick, whose research and fine writing provided a number of the excellent new practices in this edition. Thanks also
to Troy Bethune for letting us adapt his poem.

Susan Fawcett especially thanks her husband, Richard Donovan, for
nearly twenty years of deepening love built on shared values; she con-
fesses that any sports examples in *Evergreen with Readings* revealing
sophistication and panache were contributed by him. She would also like
to embarrass David Fawcett by saying how grateful she is to have such
a handsome, intelligent, and funny brother. Alvin Sandberg would like to
thank Beth Levenstein, whose love and support made this book possible
and whose encouragement was the necessary ingredient for its completion. He would also like to thank Miriam Levenstein, whose careful reading of the manuscript provided numerous suggestions and emendations
that ultimately found their way into this printed text. And of course we
thank our students, who daily teach us the power of words.

Susan Fawcett and Alvin Sandberg

Suggestions for the Teacher of Writing

Student Attitude and Motivation

The students in a basic writing course usually represent a mix of levels, ages, and, perhaps, ethnic groups—a pool of varied experience that can be used to good purpose in class. Many of these students, however, may enter the classroom with negative attitudes about writing and about themselves as writers. Past experience may have convinced them that writing is a magical ability one either does or does not possess and that writing courses are ipso facto painful, frustrating ordeals in which only the teacher knows the rules. They may fear that any attempt at writing will provoke a volley of red marks.

Fortunately these attitudes can be dealt with and even converted to positive motivation if only the writing instructor is aware of them and designs strategies that take them into account. Writing students can be motivated (or not) by a number of factors that the instructor can to some extent control. Very important are the instructor's own attitudes and expectations. Conveying by actions as well as words the belief that students can and will improve their writing will affect student performance positively. Students are also motivated by a learning environment that encourages mutual support. The instructor can set the tone for constructive peer criticism and help create an atmosphere in which everyone works together to solve writing problems and build writing skills.

The effectiveness of books and materials can also spark or squelch motivation; a textbook that addresses students on their terms and really teaches what they need to know cannot help but motivate them. And at the heart of any writing course are the writing assignments themselves, their subject matter, wording, and so forth.

Perhaps the strongest motivator is the student's own belief in good writing skills as an attainable source of personal power. Again, the student's fear, plus inaccurate perceptions of his or her capabilities, may block this belief. Usually, however, as the term progresses and students are helped to see improvement, their inner motivation will grow. You can use class discussions and writing assignments to point out the importance of writing skills to their daily survival as students, employees, consumers, and concerned citizens.

In the paragraphs that follow, these factors will be discussed in more depth and illustrated with suggestions and exercises from our classroom experience.

The First Weeks of Class

One of the most important tasks facing the writing instructor during the first weeks is the creation of an effective learning environment. We try to create a writers' community based on sharing, discussion, and group activities.

Consider spending the entire first class getting to know one another. One exercise that students enjoy is Sixty-Second Autobiographies. Break the class into groups of four or five students, making sure that someone in each group has a watch with a second hand. Have each group member in turn tell as much about himself or herself as possible in one minute; you can demonstrate (while a student times you) speaking as fast as you can and setting the tone for participation. Such activities, if you feel comfortable with them, are great icebreakers and can legitimize risk taking and even acting a little foolish—both possible assets in a writing course.

Another get-acquainted exercise involves short writings. Go once around the room, having each person say the name by which he or she would like to be called. Then ask the students to write for five minutes about their own names—whether they like them or not, where their names came from, and so forth. Let volunteers read some or all of what they have written. Often such sharing is contagious, but at this point it should be optional. Assure the students before they write that papers will be ungraded.

In general, the more students write, the better. Frequent in-class writings are especially useful early in the term, since they dispel fears about writing and provide you with an accurate picture of student performance in a controlled setting. Because paragraphs and short assignments are less intimidating to write and to read aloud than longer essays, they can be assigned almost daily. We have had good luck with topics like "A Career Dream," "A Valued Possession," and "Why I Like (or Dislike) My Job."

Early on, as an introduction to the writing process, we have the class try freewriting and focused freewriting. We explain that writing requires two different skills—*creative* and *critical*—best used at different phases of the writing process. Freewriting is a creative, or idea-generating, method. Later, the writer can go over a freewriting with a critical eye, selecting good ideas, rearranging, rewriting. (For more on using and processing freewriting, see the notes for Chapter 2, "Gathering Ideas.")

After a paper is read aloud in class, encourage students to say what they liked about it, being as specific as possible. In this way, the class can begin to build its own definition of "powerful writing." From the very start, guided discussions of student work (and later, written models) can give students an idea of what to aim for as writers and how to respond critically as readers.

Consider returning the first few papers with comments but no grades. Some instructors grade no papers at all for the first one or two weeks, preferring to comment fully and specifically, especially pointing out an individual's strengths. In any case, these early papers will help you ascertain the level of the class so you can select the appropriate textbook chapters and sequence of lessons.

Reproducing and Discussing Student Work

We find it worthwhile to reproduce student work, either by retyping and photocopying it or by using an overhead projector. Basic writing students need practice in *seeing* and paying close attention. Furthermore, students usually love to see their work in print, and successful peer writings are a great inspiration to the whole class.

Always choose papers that are good in some way and whose strengths and weaknesses relate to the current lesson. Ask students to underline sections that seem especially strong or confusing and to give specific reasons for their opinions. *What words* make this line so vivid? Just *why* is this paragraph so moving? *Why* is this conclusion unclear? Stress effect rather than correctness.

In-class revising sessions are very helpful to students, who, like all of us, spot errors and awkwardness more easily in other people's work and can sharpen their own sense of correctness and style by suggesting changes. Approach in-class revision in the spirit of shared problem solving. Let the class argue the merits of any suggested change. The important point for students to grasp is that the writer needs to make reasoned choices.

In these discussions, you should model and reinforce good editing skills. Through questions and discussion, help students avoid the "hasty closure" that often characterizes basic-skills learners—that is, their tendency to rush through uncomfortable new tasks.

Writing Exercises and Assignments

Seek a variety of writing topics and assignments. Clearly, not every student will be inspired by every topic, and different approaches give all students a chance to perform well. At the same time, students should be reminded that good writing can be done on just about any subject; we use focused freewriting, collaborative brainstorming, series of questions, and so forth to show students how to direct a topic toward areas that interest them. *Evergreen with Readings* and the notes to the instructor suggest a number of paragraph and essay assignments. You will no doubt have others.

You will probably assign more personal topics early in the course, as students often write most easily about their own lives. As the term progresses and more formal topics are assigned, you may need to spend extra class time making sure that students grasp particular modes of organization or relationships between ideas. Unused to thinking and writing in an orderly way, many students at first have trouble here. Class analysis of written models and discussion of relevant practices in the text can be invaluable. Further, ask the author of a successful paper to share with classmates how he or she "got it."

Occasionally link writing assignments to techniques you are teaching—consistency, parallelism, and so forth—urging students to pay attention to one or two techniques and marking papers with an eye to these techniques. In addition, combine grammar review and paragraph writing. For example, if you have just reviewed verb agreement, assign a five- or ten-minute writing exercise. Place a student in front of the class and ask the other students to create a verbal portrait in the present tense. ("Wanda shifts from side to side and pops gum. Every time she catches my eye, she grins and turns away. . . .") Have volunteers read their paragraphs while the class listens for the verbs and checks verb agreement.

As you move into more abstract assignments, students' enjoyment need not fade. Have them classify the people they are dating, or urge them to define a term that matters to them. To relate thinking and writing skills to the real world, bring in sets of facts about American eating habits, teen-age suicide statistics, a collection of advertisements. Have the students analyze these, looking for and articulating patterns. Government publications can be wonderful resources for the writing instructor: the *Statistical Abstract of the United States*, the survey on women and work by the National Commission on Working Women, and so on. A useful book that will help students find information on nearly any topic is Robert I. Berkman's *Find It Fast: How to Uncover Expert Information on Any Subject* (Harper and Row, 1990). Introduce your students to almanacs, reference books, and sources of entertaining or bizarre information, like Charles Panati's *Panati's Extraordinary Origins of Everyday Things* (Houghton Mifflin, 1987).

There has been much interesting discussion about the importance of writing assignments to the learning process and the haphazard way in which these writing assignments are sometimes constructed. Erika Lindemann's *A Rhetoric for Writing Teachers* (Oxford University Press, 1982) contains a thought-provoking list of questions to guide instructors as they create writing assignments. See also "Current Research and Unanswered Questions in Writing Assessment" by Gordon Brossell in *Writing Assessment: Issues and Strategies*, edited by Greenberg, Wiener, and Donovan (Longman, 1986).

Writing in Groups

The writing process lends itself to collaboration. We use an approach that takes advantage of the full class as a group to provide an audience beyond the teacher, to inspire by example, to model and practice the writing process, to hone reading and speaking skills, to build team skills, and so forth. We use small peer groups in our writing classes as well. Small groups of five or six students, established early in the term, serve as a home base for developing writers, a place to get air time, test early written drafts, and collaboratively brainstorm or edit. One way to balance democracy with quality control in peer group feedback is to use a Peer Feedback Sheet, a page of questions that each group member fills out and hands to the author of the draft under discussion.

Some instructors use small groups occasionally, after full-group discussions have trained students' critical eyes and ears. Other instructors base the entire class on small peer groups. For more information on writing in groups, see Kenneth Bruffee's "Collaborative Learning and the Conversation of Mankind" in *College English*, November 1984.

Evaluation

Balancing writing-process instruction and grammar work, the basic writing teacher tries to encourage students and yet realistically assess their written performance. However, many students enter our classes unwilling to write much for fear of leaving what Mina Shaughnessey in her classic book *Errors and Expectations* (Oxford University Press, 1977) called "a trail of errors." We have found it effective to note strengths as well as weaknesses throughout the term, pointing out what the student does particularly well or what has improved, not just what is still wrong. Responding to content as well as to error helps keep a balance.

Even with this approach, a developing writer will be overwhelmed by receiving a paper covered with red marks. Ellery Sedgwick writes in the *Journal of Developmental Education*, "A considerable body of research indicates that intensive marking of most or all errors is at least inefficient and quite possibly counterproductive" ("Alternatives to Teaching Formal, Analytical Grammar," January 1989). He cites both Shaughnessey and George Hillocks' *Research on Written Composition* (NCRE/ERIC, 1986). Consider marking errors and problem areas cumulatively, adding one or two at a time as the term progresses and new material is taught. Stress writing itself as the context for grammar instruction. Whatever your system, explain it clearly to your students so they will not be surprised when you mark errors that you did not mark before. Help students see their individual writing patterns; have them chart the errors made in each paper and review the chart before revising. Use instructor-student conferences to teach writing skills, evaluate students' work, and apprise them of their progress.

Suggestions for Using
Evergreen with Readings

Organization of the Text

Evergreen with Readings moves from an overview of the writing process and a presentation of prewriting techniques in Unit 1 to the basics of writing and organizing paragraphs in Unit 2. Unit 3 presents more sophisticated modes of development, whereas Unit 4 teaches the skills of revising for consistency, parallelism, sentence variety, and language awareness. Unit 5 applies these principles of good writing and the developmental modes to the essay and the essay examination question. Unit 6 and the Spelling and Look-Alikes/Sound-Alikes appendixes provide grammar and spelling review with abundant practices. Fourteen professional Reading Selections conclude the text, each accompanied by discussion questions and writing assignments.

The organization of the text suggests one possible way to structure a course in basic composition. However, because chapters and units are self-contained, they can be taught in any order that suits the individual instructor and the needs of a particular class. Within the text, on-page cross-references direct student and instructor to relevant material in other chapters. A very complete table of contents and index further expand options.

We focus on the paragraph as a model and move later to a discussion of the full-length essay, but if you wish to do so, you can teach the essay early in the course, since the modes of development presented in Unit 3 are specifically applied to essays in Unit 5; in fact, Chapter 18 contains a sample essay, instruction, and practice for each mode taught in Unit 3. Unit 1, "Getting Started," and Unit 4, "Improving Your Writing," work equally well for paragraphs and essays.

Whatever order is followed in the course, we suggest that the chapters in Unit 3, "Developing the Paragraph," not be taught straight through but integrated with the material in Units 4, 5, and 6. Likewise, the chapters in Unit 6, "Reviewing the Basics," and the appendixes, "Spelling" and "Look-Alikes/Sound-Alikes," should be assigned as needed. We find it most effective to weave the Reading Selections throughout the course, perhaps as follow-up for related chapters. Work on process, for example, might be followed by a process essay by Andy Rooney or Larry Letich. Because varying the activities of any class works best, you could balance the introduction of one type of paragraph or essay by assigning a short in-class writing exercise on one day, group work on grammar or a problem of style on the next, and a reading selection and writing activity on the third.

Organization of Each Chapter and Appendix

In general, each chapter of *Evergreen with Readings* moves from simple to more difficult material. Each lesson consists of examples, explanations, and practices that reinforce each skill taught and always move toward the writing of paragraphs or longer compositions. Depending on the level of the class, you may wish to assign all the practices in a particular chapter or assign them selectively. Many of the practices make effective and enjoyable full-class exercises. A checklist for writers concludes most of the chapters in Units 2, 3, and 5; you may find it useful to have students turn in checked checklists with their written assignments. Because of their carefully paced progression, most chapters work well for tutorial sessions and even self-teaching.

The Readings

These fourteen essays provide a variety of authorial voices, subjects, and written models for instructors who wish to incorporate reading into their writing classes. At least one example of each rhetorical mode taught in this book is included; see the rhetorical index to the readings for guidance.

You may wish to follow certain chapters in the text with readings—for example, follow work on narration with Brent Staples' "A Brother's Murder," or exact language with Alice Walker's "Beauty: When the Other Dancer Is the Self" or Judith Ortiz Cofer's "One More Lesson." If your class is poorly prepared for reading, you might consider using prereading strategies to help them gain access to an essay. Short writings or small group discussions on a topic relevant to the essay work well.

As an aid to comprehension, you may wish to have students keep a journal, perhaps a double-entry journal in which one column is devoted to notes and queries about the material they are reading, and another is devoted to the student's own reactions and questions. Having students briefly summarize an essay is another excellent technique; precise writing teaches important skills and improves comprehension. Small group discussions, perhaps guided by one or more of the Discussion and Writing Questions, will help students make sense of what they have read.

Some instructors will assign essays individually, and others may wish to use clusters or thematically linked groups. Having students apply the ideas or style in one essay to those in another builds thinking skills and promotes a conversation of ideas. Try having students write dialogues between themselves and an author or between one author and another. Consider such clusters as these: male roles and relationships (Staples, Wu, Letich); dealing with loss (Mairs, Quindlen, Klagsbrun, Walker, Staples); success and failure (McGinnis, Ortiz Cofer, Walker, Staples); multicultural or minority experience and self-esteem (Ortiz Cofer, Rodriguez, King, Staples, McGinnis); work and careers (Rooney, Twain, Rodriguez, Ortiz Cofer).

Encourage students to apply themes and ideas from a reading selection to current articles from newspapers or magazines or to a film. This exercise will help them connect their reading to the "real world."

For in-depth discussion of each chapter and reading selection in *Evergreen with Readings,* please see the Notes on the Chapters and Appendixes and the Notes on the Readings in the *Evergreen with Readings* Instructor's Resource Manual.

Unit 1

Getting Started

1

Exploring the Writing Process

PART A The Writing Process
PART B Subject, Audience, and Purpose

This chapter will give you a brief overview of the writing process, which is explored in greater depth throughout this book. By surveying the steps that many writers take and some of the factors they consider, you will see that writing is not a magic ability some are born with, but a skill—the result of planning, hard work, and a positive attitude.

The Writing Process

Many people have the mistaken idea that good writers simply sit down and write out a perfect letter, paragraph, or essay from start to finish. In fact, writing is a **process** consisting of a number of steps:

1. Thinking about a topic
2. Freely jotting down ideas about the topic
3. Narrowing the topic and writing it in one sentence   } prewriting
4. Selecting and dropping ideas
5. Arranging ideas in a plan
6. Writing a first draft   } writing
7. Rethinking and rewriting as necessary
8. Writing one or more new drafts   } revising and proofreading
9. Proofreading for errors

Not all writers perform all the steps in this order. Actually, writing can be a messy process of thinking, writing, reading what has been written, and writing again. Some steps overlap or must be repeated. The important thing is that writing the first draft is just one stage in the process. "I love being a writer," jokes Peter De Vries. "What I can't stand is the paperwork."

Before they write, good writers spend time **prewriting**—thinking and planning on paper. Steps 1 through 5 above are prewriting steps. Here the writer thinks, lets his or her imagination run free, jots down ideas, decides which ideas to use, and comes up with a plan for writing. Many beginning writers get into trouble by skipping the prewriting phase. They don't realize that doing this early work saves time and frustration later and usually creates a much better piece of writing than just sitting down and starting to write.

Next comes **writing** the first draft. If the writer has planned ahead, he or she is now free to concentrate on writing the best possible draft. The focus is on presenting ideas, feelings, and experiences as convincingly as possible.

The next phase of the process—and one that many writers rush through or omit altogether—is **revising.** Steps 7 and 8 are revising steps. Experienced writers do not accept the first words that flow from their pens; they are like sculptors, shaping and reworking rough material into something meaningful. Writers do this by letting the first draft sit for five minutes, an hour, or a day. Then they read it again with a fresh, critical eye and rewrite—adding, dropping, or rearranging ideas; changing words to achieve more clarity and punch; and so on. Many writers revise two or three times until they get it right—until their writing says clearly and effectively what they want it to say. Finally, they **proofread** for grammar and spelling errors, so that their writing seems to say, "I am proud to put my name on this work."

PART B

Subject, Audience, and Purpose

Early in the prewriting phase, writers should give some thought to their subject, audience, and purpose.

Whenever possible, choose a **subject** that you know and care about: waitressing, life in Wichita, working with learning disabled children, repairing motorcycles, overcoming shyness, watching a friend struggle with drug addiction, succeeding in college. You may not realize how many subjects you do know or have strong opinions about. What special experience or expertise do you have? What angers you, inspires you, saddens you? What do you love to do? The answers to these questions will suggest good subjects to write about. In college courses, your instructor often will assign you a broad subject. Try to direct this subject toward some aspect that intrigues you. If you have interest, energy, and passion about a topic, then probably your readers will too.

Just how you approach your subject will depend on your readers—your **audience.** Ask yourself just who these readers are: your classmates, your professor, other students at your college, your boss, youngsters in your community, people who probably agree with you, people who don't? Keeping your audience in mind will help you know what information to include and what to leave out. For example, if you were writing about rap music for an audience of middle-aged parents, you would explain your subject differently than you would to an audience of eighteen-year-old rap fans. What do your readers already know about your subject? What might they need or want to learn?

Next you will want to think about your **purpose** in writing. Do you want to explain something to your readers, persuade them that a certain view is correct, entertain them, tell a good story, or some combination of these? Keeping your purpose in mind will help you write more effectively. For example, if your purpose is to persuade your company to recycle its paper and glass, you might want to write about ways that recycling would benefit the company: Recycling could earn or save money, improve the company's image, or make employees proud to work there.

PRACTICE 1   List five subjects about which you might like to write. For ideas, reread the list of possible subjects and the questions in Part B, page 3.

1. _____

2. _____

3. _____

4. _____

5. _____

PRACTICE 2   Jot down ideas for these three assignments, by yourself or with a group of classmates. Notice how your ideas and details differ, depending on the audience and purpose.

1. You have been asked to write a description of your college for local high school students. Your purpose is to explain what advantages the college offers its students. What kinds of information should you include? What will your audience want to know?

2. You have been asked to write a description of your college for the governor of your state. Your purpose is to persuade her or him to spend more money to improve your college. What information should you include? What will your audience want to know?

3. You have been asked to write a description of your college for your best friend, who attends a college out of state. Your purpose is to share your personal impressions and experiences. What information should you include? What will your audience want to know?

2

Gathering Ideas

PART A   Freewriting
PART B   Brainstorming
PART C   Clustering
PART D   Asking Questions
PART E   Keeping a Journal

This chapter presents five effective prewriting techniques that will help you get your ideas onto paper and overcome the "blank page jitters" that many people face when they sit down to write. Try all five and see which ones work best for *you*, alone or in combination.

PART A

Freewriting

Freewriting is an excellent method that many writers use to warm up and get ideas. These are the guidelines: for five, ten, or fifteen minutes, write rapidly, without stopping, about anything that comes into your head. If you feel stuck, just repeat or rhyme the last word you wrote, but *don't stop writing.* And don't worry about grammar, logic, complete sentences, or grades.

The point of freewriting is to write so fast that ideas can flow without comments from your inner critic. The *inner critic* is the voice inside that says, every time you have an idea, "That's dumb; that's no good; cross that out." Freewriting helps you tell this voice, "Thank you for your opinion. Once I have lots of ideas and words on paper, I'll invite you back for comment."

After you freewrite, read what you have written, underlining any parts you like.

Here is one student's first freewriting, with his own underlinings:

> Boy I wish this class was over and I could go home and get out of this building, boy was my day miserable and this sure is a crazy thing to do if a shrink could see us now. My I just remember I've got to buy that cassette my my my I am running out of stuff to write but dont worry teach because this is really the nuttiest thing but lots of fun you probably like reading this mixed up thing That girl's remark sounded dumb but impressing. You know this writing sure puts muscles in your fingers if I stop writing oh boy this is the most incredible assignment in the world think and write without worrying about sentence structure and other English garbage to stall you down boy that guy next to me is writing like crazy so he looks crazy you know this is outrageous I'm writing and writing I never realized the extent of mental and physical concentration it takes to do this constantly dont mind the legibility of my hand my hand oh my hand is ready to drop off please this is crazy crazy and too much work for a poor fellow like myself. Imagine me putting on paper all I have to say and faster than a speeding bullet.

■ This example has the lively energy of many freewritings. Why do you think the student underlined what he did? Would you have underlined other words or phrases? Why?

Freewriting is a powerful tool for helping you turn thoughts and feelings into words, especially when you are unsure about what you want to say. Sometimes freewriting produces only nonsense, but often, freewriting can help you zoom in on possible topics, interests, and powerful writing you can use later.

PRACTICE 1

1. Now, set a timer for ten minutes or have someone time you. Freewrite without stopping for the full ten minutes. If you get stuck, repeat or rhyme the last word you wrote until words start flowing again but *don't stop writing!*

2. When you finish, write down one or two words that describe how you felt while freewriting.

   Sample answers: excited, liberated, creative, intense
   _____

   _____

3. Next, read your freewriting. Underline any words or lines you like—anything that strikes you as interesting, powerful, worthwhile, or funny. If nothing strikes you, that's okay.

PRACTICE 2   Try three more freewritings at home—each one ten minutes long. Do them at different times of day or night when you have a quiet moment. If possible, use a timer. Set it for ten minutes; then write fast and freely until it rings. Later, read over your freewritings and underline any striking lines or ideas.

Focused Freewriting

In **focused freewriting,** you simply try to focus your thoughts on one subject as you freewrite. The subject might be one assigned by your instructor, one you choose, or one you have discovered in unfocused freewriting. The goal of most writing is a polished, organized piece of writing, and focused freewriting can help you generate ideas or narrow a topic to one aspect that interests you.

Here is one student's focused freewriting on the topic *someone who strongly influenced you:*

underline appealing lines

> Gran, you started me in music. Indian cheekbones, dark skin, she took me in in in in. Lived for her albums, trophies and plaques, photos in robes and flowery dresses, Gran turning the pages she taught me to believe in myself, to reach for my dream— my music—gospel was her thing and her voice rocked the church on Sundays, navy dress, white hat, head thrown back she belted out the glory of the lord, she sang and sang till the power fell down, she prayed and prayed till she began to moan. Then the singing stopped, the turning stopped, I saw her last on a bed of lace in a box.

- This student later used her focused freewriting—its vivid details about Gran and her influence—as the basis for a strong paper. Underline any words or lines *you* find especially striking or appealing. Be prepared to explain why you like what you underline.

PRACTICE 3   Do a three-minute focused freewriting on each of these words:

highway	red
success	grandfather (or grandmother)
rain	friendship

Underline as usual. Did you surprise yourself by having a lot to say about any one word? Perhaps this is something you would like to write more about.

PRACTICE 4

1. Read over your earlier freewritings and notice your underlinings. Would you like to write more about any underlined words or ideas? Write two or three such words or ideas here:

Sample answers:

Sometimes I feel closer to my grandfather than to my parents.

I'm often most content on a rainy day.

2. Now choose one word or idea. Focus your thoughts on it and do a ten-minute focused freewriting. Try to stick to the topic as you write but don't worry too much about that; just keep writing.

PART B

Brainstorming

Another prewriting technique that may work for you is **brainstorming,** or freely jotting down ideas about a topic. As in freewriting, the purpose is to get lots of ideas on paper so you have something to work with and choose from. Write down everything that comes to you about a topic—words and phrases, ideas, details, examples.

After you have brainstormed, read over your list, underlining interesting or powerful ideas you might develop further. As with freewriting, many writers brainstorm on a general subject, underline, then brainstorm again as they focus on one aspect of that subject to write about.

Here is one student's brainstorm list on the topic *computers:*

> They're everywhere
>
> Advertisements in the paper daily
>
> Words I don't understand—*bytes, RAM, modem*
>
> Ron and Wanda have a computer
>
> Computers scare me
>
> In the bank, at work, hospital, learning center
>
> My little brother knows more than I do
>
> Classes for kids
>
> He's not afraid—loves problems to solve, games
>
> Whole different generation
>
> Kids get used to the keyboard, the screen—to them, it's a game
>
> All kids should learn young

As he brainstormed, this writer moved toward a more focused topic—*All kids should learn young.* Once he had discovered a topic about which he had something to say—that all children should receive computer training when they are young—the writer could brainstorm again for more reasons, details, and examples to support this idea.

PRACTICE 5 Choose one of the following topics that interests you and write it at the top of your paper. Then brainstorm. Write anything that comes into your head about the topic. Just let ideas pour onto paper!

1. a place I never want to go back to   4. a lesson

2. an unforgettable movie character   5. my best/worst job

3. dealing with difficult people   6. dating

Once you fill a page with your list, read it over, underlining the most interesting ideas. Draw arrows to connect related ideas. Is there one idea that might be the subject of a paper?

PART C

Clustering

Some writers use a third method—called **clustering** or **mapping**—to get their ideas onto paper. To begin clustering, simply write an idea or topic, usually one word, in the center of your paper. Then let your mind make associations, and write these ideas down, branching out from the center.

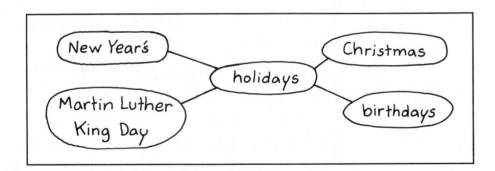

When one idea suggests other ideas, details, and examples, write these around it in a "cluster." After you finish, pick the cluster that most interests you. You may wish to freewrite for more ideas.

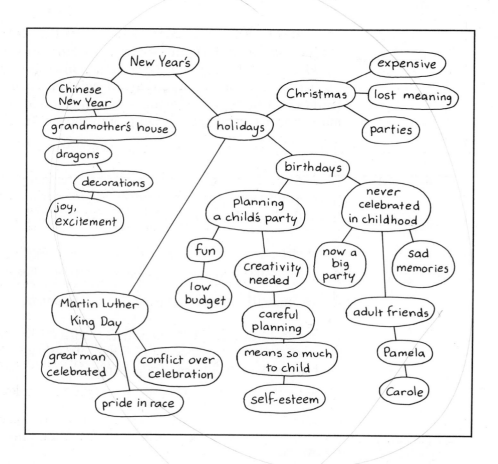

PRACTICE 6 Choose one of these topics or another topic that interests you. Write it in the center of a piece of paper and then try clustering. Keep writing down associations until you have filled most of the page.

1. heroes   4. inspiration

2. holidays   5. a dream

3. jobs   6. cars

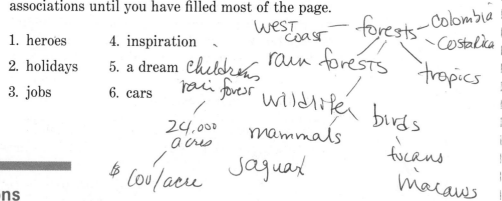

Asking Questions

Many writers get ideas about a subject by asking questions and trying to answer them. This section describes two ways to do so.

The Reporter's Six Questions

Newspaper reporters often answer six basic questions at the beginning of an article: **Who? What? Where? When? Why? How?** Here is the way one student used these questions to explore the general subject of *sports* assigned by his instructor:

Who?	Players, basketball and football players, coaches, fans. Violence—I'm tired of that subject. Loyal crazy screaming fans—Giants fans.
What?	Excitement. Stadium on the day of a game. Tailgate parties. Cookouts. Incredible spreads—Italian families with peppers, stuff to spread on sandwiches. All day partying. Radios, TVs, grills, Giants caps.
Where?	Giants Stadium parking lot. People gather in certain areas—meet me in 10-B. Stadiums all over the country, same thing. People party on tailgates, in cars, on cars, plastic chairs, blankets.
When?	People arrive early morning—cook breakfast, lunch. After the game, many stay on in parking lot, talking, drinking beer. Year after year they come back.
Why?	Big social occasion, emotional outlet.
How?	They come early to get space. Some stadiums now rent parking spaces. Some families pass on season tickets in their wills!

Notice the way this writer used the questions to focus his ideas about tailgate parties at Giants Stadium. He has already come up with many interesting details for a good paper.

Ask Your Own Questions

If the reporter's six questions seem too confining, just ask the questions *you* want answered about a subject. Let each answer suggest the next question.

Here is how another student responded to the subject of *teen-age marriage:*

What do I know about teen-age marriage? I saw my sister's plans cut short by early marriage. She won high school fashion design award, was spunky, full of fun. Now, two kids to raise. He left three years later. She never went to college, works in a diner to make ends meet.

[handwritten margin note:] the basic 6 to make sure you've addressed all details

[handwritten margin note:] use the basic 6 to answer about "recycling"

What would I like to know? What is the biggest reason kids marry young—especially females? Romantic view of marriage? Desire to escape parental control? Pregnancy? The desire to be taken care of? To care for others and not take care of themselves?

Where can I find out why teen-age girls marry? Guidance counselors in my old high school. Planned Parenthood. From my girl friends, my sister—interview them!

What would I like to focus on? What interests *me*? I'd like to know what pressures, fears, and hopes teen-age girls feel that make them choose marriage when the odds are so against it working out.

What is my point of view? I wish teen-age girls would explore a wider range of choices about their futures—and have support to make their own decisions.

Who is my audience? I'd like to write for teen-age girls—to help them see the problems of early marriage and explore other options.

PRACTICE 7 Answer the reporter's six questions on one of the following topics or on a topic of your own choice.

1. drug addiction
2. sports
3. career goals
4. coping with stress
5. music
6. family get-togethers
7. replacing negatives with positives
8. choosing a major or concentration

PRACTICE 8 Ask and answer at least five questions of your own about one of the topics in Practice 7. Use these questions if you wish: What do I know about this subject? What would I like to know? Where can I find answers to my questions? What would I like to focus on? What is my point of view about this subject? Who is my audience?

PART E

Keeping a Journal

A journal can be another excellent source of writing ideas. Get yourself an attractive notebook or journal with 8½-by-11-inch paper. Every night, or at least several nights a week, write for ten or fifteen minutes in your journal. Don't just record the day's events ("I went to the store. It rained. I came home."). Instead, write in detail about what really got to you that day.

Carry journal paper with you during the day for "fast sketches," and jot down moving or funny things that catch your attention: a man playing a banjo in front of the bank, a compliment you received at work, something your child just learned to do.

Write about what you know and care about—motorcycles, loneliness, working in a TV repair shop, family relationships, turkey farming, ending or starting a friendship. You might have to think twice to realize just how much you do know. Write; think; write some more. Aim to capture your truth so exactly that someone reading your words could experience it too.

In your journal, you may wish to record quotations or facts that spark your interest. Suppose you read Abe Lincoln's statement that "Most folks are as happy as they make up their minds to be," and you like that thought. Write it down. Later, thinking and writing about that one statement could produce a whole paragraph or theme. Or note facts that impress you—the average American child watches 18,000 TV murders before he or she graduates from high school! Analyzing that one fact could produce a good paper.

Mostly, your journal is for you—the place where you record your experiences and your inner life, the place where, as one writer says, "I discover what I really think by writing it down."

PRACTICE 9   Get an 8½-by-11-inch loose-leaf notebook for your journal. Write in it for at least fifteen minutes five times a week.

At the end of each week, reread what you have written, underlining sections or ideas you like and putting a check next to subjects you might like to write more about.

Unit 2
Discovering the Paragraph

3

The Process of Writing Paragraphs

PART A   Defining and Looking at the Paragraph
PART B   Narrowing the Topic and Writing the Topic Sentence
PART C   Gathering Ideas for the Body
PART D   Selecting and Dropping Ideas
PART E   Arranging Ideas in a Plan
PART F   Writing and Revising the Paragraph

This chapter will guide you step by step from understanding to writing basic paragraphs. The paragraph makes a good learning model because it is short and yet contains many of the elements found in longer compositions. Therefore, you easily can transfer the skills you gain by writing paragraphs to longer essays, reports, and letters.

In this chapter, you will first look at finished paragraphs and then move through the process of writing paragraphs of your own.

PART A

Defining and Looking at the Paragraph

A **paragraph** is a group of related sentences that develops one main idea. Although there is no definite length for a paragraph, it is often from five to twelve sentences long. A paragraph usually occurs with other paragraphs in a longer piece of writing—an essay, article, or letter, for example. Before studying longer compositions, however, we will look at single paragraphs.

A paragraph looks like this on the page:

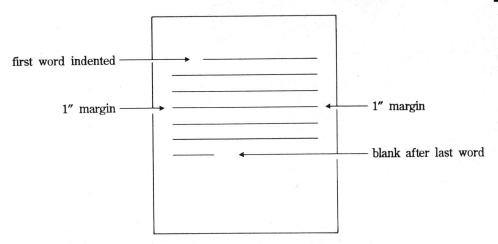

- Clearly **indent** the first word of every paragraph about 1 inch or five spaces on the typewriter.

- Extend every line of a paragraph to the right-hand margin.

- However, if the last word of the paragraph comes before the end of the line, leave the rest of the line blank.

Topic Sentence and Body

Most paragraphs contain one main idea to which all the sentences relate.

The **topic sentence** states this main idea.

The **body** of the paragraph develops and supports this main idea with particular facts, details, and examples:

> I allow the spiders the run of the house. I figure that any predator that hopes to make a living on whatever smaller creatures might blunder into a four-inch-square bit of space in the corner of the bathroom where the tub meets the floor, needs every bit of my support. They catch flies and even field crickets in those webs. Large spiders in barns have been known to trap, wrap, and suck hummingbirds, but there's no danger of that here. I tolerate the webs, only occasionally sweeping away the very dirtiest of them after the spider itself has scrambled to safety. I'm always leaving a bath towel draped over the tub so that the big, haired spiders, who are constantly getting trapped by the tub's smooth sides, can use its rough surface as an exit ramp. Inside the house the spiders have only given me one mild surprise. I washed some dishes and set them to dry over a plastic drainer. Then I wanted a cup of coffee, so I picked from the drainer my mug, which was still warm from the hot rinse water, and across the rim of the mug, strand after strand, was a spider web.
>
> —Annie Dillard, *Pilgrim at Tinker Creek*

- The first sentence of the paragraph above is the **topic sentence.** It states the main idea of the paragraph: that the spiders are allowed *the run of the house.*

- The rest of the paragraph, the **body,** fully explains and supports this statement. The writer first gives a reason for her attitude toward spiders and then gives particular examples of her tolerance of spiders.

The topic sentence is more *general* than the other sentences in the paragraph. The other sentences in the paragraph provide specific information relating to the topic sentence. Because the topic sentence tells what the entire paragraph is about, *it is usually the first sentence,* as above. Sometimes the topic sentence occurs elsewhere in the paragraph, for example, as the second sentence after an introduction or as the last sentence. Some paragraphs contain only an implied topic sentence but no stated topic sentence at all.

As you develop your writing skills, it is a good idea to write paragraphs that *begin* with the topic sentence. Once you have mastered this pattern, you can try variations.

PRACTICE 1   Find and underline the **topic sentence** in each paragraph below. Look for the sentence that states the **main idea** of the entire paragraph.

Paragraph a: The summer picnic gave ladies a chance to show off their baking hands. On the barbecue pit, chickens and spareribs sputtered in their own fat and in a sauce whose recipe was guarded in the family like a scandalous affair. However, every true baking artist could reveal her prize to the delight and criticism of the town. Orange sponge cakes and dark brown mounds dripping Hershey's chocolate stood layer to layer with ice-white coconuts and light brown caramels. Pound cakes sagged with their buttery weight and small children could no more resist licking the icings than their mothers could avoid slapping the sticky fingers.

—Maya Angelou, *I Know Why the Caged Bird Sings*

Paragraph b: Health care will continue to be one of the most important groups of industries in the economy in terms of job creation. Employment in the health services industries is projected to grow from 8.2 to 11.3 million. New technology and a growing and aging population will increase the demand for health services. Because of the rapid expansion of health care employment, 7 of the 10 fastest growing occupations between 1988 and 2000 will be health related.

—*Occupational Outlook Handbook, 1990–91*

Paragraph c: Eating sugar can be worse than eating nothing. Refined sugar provides only empty calories. It contributes none of the protein, fat, vitamins or minerals needed for its own metabolism in the body, so these nutrients must be obtained elsewhere. Sugar tends to replace nourishing food in the diet. It is a thief that robs us of nutrients. A dietary emphasis on sugar can deplete the body of nutrients. If adequate nutrients are not supplied by the diet—and they tend not to be in a sugar-rich diet—they must be leached from other body tissues before sugar can be metabolized. For this reason, a U.S. Senate committee labeled sugar as an "antinutrient."

—Janice Fillip, "The Sweet Thief,"
Medical Self-Care

Paragraph d: Memphis in the late forties and early fifties was a seed-bed of musical activity. Never really much of a center for commercial country music, it had a raw hillbilly style and a distinguished blues tradition that went back to the twenties. In 1950 Howlin' Wolf and Sonny Boy Williamson were broadcasting on station KWM from West Memphis; WDIA, the Mother Station of the Negroes, and the first black-operated radio outlet in the South, featured B. B. King and Rufus Thomas spinning records and performing daily. On Beale Street you were likely to run into such prominent figures as one-man-band Joe Hill Louis, veteran bluesman Frank Stokes, the famous Beale Streeters. In W. C. Handy Park you might hear a free concert by the legendary white blues singer and medicine show entertainer, Harmonica Frank Floyd. And at 706 Union Avenue, Sam Phillips had opened the Memphis Recording Service "for Negro artists in the South who wanted to make a record [but] just had no place to go," an enterprise which would evolve in 1952 into the Sun Record label. In the meantime, though, a quiet revolution had begun to take place. Many of the small independent record producers were becoming aware of it, and in Memphis, where there had long been a relaxed social, as well as musical, interchange between black and white, it was particularly noticeable. White kids were picking up on black styles—of music, dance, speech, and dress.

—Peter Guralnick, "Elvis Presley and the
American Dream," *Lost Highway*

PRACTICE 2   Each group of sentences below could be unscrambled and written as a paragraph. Circle the letter of the **topic sentence** in each group of sentences. Remember: the topic sentence should state the main idea of the entire paragraph and should be general enough to include all the ideas in the body.

Example   a. Rubies were supposed to stimulate circulation and restore lost vitality.
b. Clear quartz was believed to promote sweet sleep and good dreams.
c. For centuries, minerals and precious stones were thought to possess healing powers.
d. Amethysts were thought to prevent drunkenness.
(Sentence C includes the ideas in all the other sentences.)

Bo Jackson won the Heisman Trophy, the top prize in college football, while he attended Auburn University.
When he graduated, the Kansas City Royals drafted him as an outfielder.
In 1987, Jackson became a star running back for the L.A. Raiders.
After two years in the big leagues, he made the daring decision to play pro football as well as pro baseball.
In 1989, he played with the Royals in the All-Star Game.
Bo Jackson is the first athlete in modern times to win recognition as an all-star in both professional football and professional baseball.

The better skaters played tag or crack the whip.
Every winter, the lake was the center of activity.
People talked and shoveled snow, exposing the dark, satiny ice.
Children on double runners skated in the center of the cleared area.
Dogs raced and skidded among the skaters.

Albert Einstein, whose scientific genius awed the world, could not speak until he was four and could not read until he was nine.
Inventor Thomas Edison had such severe problems reading, writing, and spelling that he was called "defective from birth," taken f school, and taught at home.
famous people have suffered from learning disabilities.
pic diving champion Greg Louganis was teased and laughed r his speech delay, stutter, and perceptual problems.

at Kensington College, without our student numbers, we ld hardly exist.
must display our student numbers and IDs just to get onto npus.
e must pencil our student numbers on computer cards in order register for courses.
When our grades are posted, the A's and F's go not to Felicia Watson and Bill Jenkins, Jr., but to 237-002 and 235-1147.

Today Americans live longer than ever before.
Statistics show that forcing a person to retire can actually impair his or her emotional and physical health.
Research indicates that workers aged sixty-five to seventy-five perform as well as younger workers in all but heavy physical jobs.
Forced retirement according to age does not make sense when we examine the facts.
Older workers tend to be more stable than younger workers.

Annie Oakley could riddle a playing card with bullet holes before it fell from someone's hand to the ground.

b. From 1869 to 1875, as a poor child in Ohio, she paid off the family's mortgage by hunting and selling wild game.

c. In her teens, she competed against Frank Butler, a famous marksman who came to town, and beat him by one point.

d. European kings and queens loved to watch her perform, and she once shot a cigarette from the lips of the future Kaiser Wilhelm II of Germany.

e. Years later, Annie married Butler and joined Wild Bill's Wild West Show, where she was the star.

f. Annie Oakley was one of the best sharpshooters of all time.

7. a. In Mexico the folk arts are still thriving.

b. Beautiful bowls and trays made of papier-mâché are widely available.

c. Hand-embroidered dresses of pure cotton are common.

d. Throughout the country, pottery making and the fiber arts are alive and well.

e. Every town has its market glittering with hand-wrought silver jewelry.

8. a. Maggie throws her head back and slaps her thigh.

b. The most amazing thing about Maggie is her laughter.

c. When something strikes her as funny, she first lets out a shriek of surprise.

d. Then she breaks into loud hoots.

e. When the laughter stops, she shakes her head from side to side and says, "Lord have mercy."

9. a. At the University of Michigan, he helped develop a flu vaccine.

b. He served as a consultant to the World Health Organization, a branch of the U.N. that brings medical help to developing countries.

c. Dr. Jonas Salk has contributed much to the cure of disease.

d. After years of research, he finally created the first effective polio vaccine.

e. Dr. Salk is now racing against time to make an AIDS vaccine.

10. a. Believe it or not, the first contact lens was drawn by Leonardo da Vinci in 1508.

b. However, not until 1877 was the first thick, glass contact actually made by a Swiss doctor.

c. The journey of contact lenses from an idea to a comfortable, safe reality took nearly five hundred years!

d. In 1948, smaller, more comfortable plastic lenses were introduced to enthusiastic American eyeglass wearers.

e. These early glass lenses were enormous, covering the whites of the eyes.

f. Today, contact lens wearers can choose ultra-thin, colored, or even disposable lenses.

Narrowing the Topic and Writing the Topic Sentence

A writer can arrive at the goal—a finished paragraph—in several ways. However, before writing a paragraph, most writers go through a process that includes these important steps:

1. Narrowing the topic

2. Writing the topic sentence

3. Gathering ideas for the body

4. Selecting and dropping ideas

5. Arranging ideas in a plan

The rest of this chapter will explain these steps and guide you through the process of writing basic paragraphs.

Narrowing the Topic

As a student, you may be assigned broad writing topics by your instructor—success, drug use in the schools, a description of a person. Your instructor is thereby giving you the chance to cut the topic down to size and to choose one aspect of the topic *that interests you.*

Assume, for example, that your instructor gives this assignment: "Write a paragraph describing a person you know." The challenge is to pick someone you would *like* to write about, someone who interests you and would probably, therefore, interest your readers.

Giving some thought to your *audience* and *purpose* may help you narrow the topic. In this case, your audience probably will be your instructor and classmates; your purpose is to inform or perhaps entertain them by describing someone.

Now think about the people you know, and freewrite, brainstorm, or ask yourself questions. For example, you might ask yourself, "What person do I love, hate, or admire?" "Is there a family member I would like to write about?" "Who is the funniest, most unusual, or most talented person I know?"

Let's suppose you choose Pete, an unusual person and one about whom you have something to say. But Pete is still too broad a subject for one paragraph; you could probably write pages and pages about him. To narrow the topic further, you might ask yourself, "What is unusual about him? What might interest others?" Pete's room is the messiest place you have ever seen; in fact, Pete's whole life is sloppy, and you decide that you could write a good paragraph about that. You have now narrowed the topic to just one of Pete's qualities: *his sloppiness.*

Writing the Topic Sentence

The next important step is to state your topic clearly *in sentence form.* Writing the topic sentence helps you further narrow your topic by forcing you to make a statement about it. The simplest possible topic sentence about Pete might read *Pete is sloppy,* but you might wish to strengthen it by saying, for instance, *Pete's sloppiness is a terrible habit.*

Writing a good topic sentence is an important step toward an effective paragraph since the topic sentence will determine the direction and scope of the body. The topic sentence should be *complete* and *limited.*

The topic sentence must be a **complete sentence.** It must contain a subject and verb and express a complete thought. Be careful not to confuse a **topic** or **title** with a **topic sentence.** *A view of my grandmother,* for example, could not be a topic sentence because it is not a complete sentence but a fragment.* However, *A View of My Grandmother* could be a title† because topics and titles do not have to be sentences.

Here are some possible topic sentences for a paragraph entitled *A View of My Grandmother:*

> 1. My grandmother was a courageous woman.
>
> 2. I have always loved looking at my grandmother's face.
>
> 3. At sixty-five, my grandmother remains an active sportswoman.

- Each topic sentence is a *complete sentence* that focuses on one particular view of the woman.

- Since there are as many possible topic sentences for any topic as there are writers, creating a topic sentence forces the writer to focus clearly on one aspect of the topic. If you were assigned the topic, *a view of my grandmother,* what would your topic sentence be?

  Sample answer: My grandmother has the special ability to understand other

  people's feelings.

PRACTICE 3   Put a check beside each possible topic sentence below. Remember, a topic sentence must be a grammatically complete thought. Rewrite any fragments into possible topic sentences.

*For more practice in correcting fragments, see Chapter 23, "Avoiding Sentence Errors," Part B.

†For practice in writing titles, see Chapter 19, "The Introduction, the Conclusion, and the Title," Part C.

Examples ✔ Some folk remedies really work.

Rewrite: _____

_____ A four-day work week.

Rewrite: _Linear Graphics Company should adopt a four-day work week._

1. _____ The worst class I ever had.

   Rewrite: _Accounting 102 was the worst class I ever had._

   _____

2. ✔ When it comes to selecting audio equipment, Roscoe is a perfectionist.

   Rewrite: _____

   _____

3. _____ Helping a child learn to read.

   Rewrite: _The highlight of my student teaching was helping children learn to_

   read.

4. _____ Police officers who take bribes.

   Rewrite: _Police officers who take bribes undermine the morale of the entire_

   department.

5. ✔ The moon cast a silver glow over the empty street.

   Rewrite: _____

   _____

6. _____ Why I volunteer at a shelter for the homeless.

   Rewrite: _Volunteering at a shelter for the homeless makes me feel that I'm_

   helping less fortunate people in our city.

7. _____ The difficult social life of a single parent.

   Rewrite: _A single parent must juggle schedules, pay baby sitters, and_

   overcome exhaustion in order to have a social life.

8. _____ Some remarkable episodes of "Star Trek."

   Rewrite: _In some episodes of "Star Trek," humor is the main ingredient._

   _____

The topic sentence should be **limited.** It should be carefully worded to express a limited main idea. As a rule, the more limited the topic sentence, the better the paragraph. Which of these topic sentences do you think will produce the best paragraphs?

> 4. Five wet, bug-filled days at Boy Scout Camp made my son a fan of the great indoors.
>
> 5. America today has problems.
>
> 6. Norine is a very intelligent basketball player.

- Topic sentences 4 and 6 are both limited enough to provide the main idea for a good paragraph. Both are carefully worded to suggest clearly what ideas will follow. From topic sentence 4, what do you expect the paragraph to include?

  The paragraph will probably describe how weather and insects ruined the young

  man's week.

- What do you expect paragraph 6 to include?

  The paragraph will probably include examples of Norine's intelligent basketball

  playing.

- Topic sentence 5, on the other hand, is so broad that the paragraph could include almost anything. *Who* or *what* has problems? A school in Topeka? Hospital workers in Chicago? The average consumer? In other words, focus on just one specific problem for an effective paragraph.

PRACTICE 4   Put a check beside each topic sentence that is limited enough to allow you to write a good paragraph. If a topic sentence is too broad, narrow the topic according to your own interests and write a new, limited topic sentence.

Examples   ✔ Keeping a journal can improve a student's writing.

Rewrite: _____

_____ This paper will be about my family.

Rewrite: My brother Mark has a unique sense of humor.

1. ✔ Eugene's hot temper causes problems at work.

Rewrite: _____

_____

2. ___ This paragraph will discuss study techniques.

Rewrite: _Organizing my study time has been difficult for me to achieve._
_____

3. ___ Things are better today.

Rewrite: _Because of both technology and legislation, cars are safer today than_
they were thirty years ago.

4. ✔ Many blue jeans commercials on TV imply that wearing designer jeans will improve your social life.

Rewrite: _____
_____

5. ___ Child abuse is something to think about.

Rewrite: _Child abuse is more common than was once thought._
_____

6. ✔ Tournament prize money in international tennis should be the same for women and men.

Rewrite: _____
_____

7. ✔ Learning karate increased my self-confidence.

Rewrite: _____
_____

8. ✔ A stroll through the park calms my nerves.

Rewrite: _____
_____

PRACTICE 5   Here is a list of broad topics. Choose three that interest you; then narrow each topic and write a topic sentence. Make sure that each topic sentence is a complete sentence and limited enough for you to write a good paragraph.

Overcoming fears	Drug use in your community
A supportive mate	A time you were in (or out of) control
An experience of success	A person you like or dislike
The value of humor	

Sample answers:

1. Topic: __Overcoming Fears__

   Narrowed topic: __Overcoming fear of flying__

   Topic sentence: __Overcoming his fear of flying boosted Daryl's career and__

   __calmed his nerves.__

2. Topic: __A Person You Like or Dislike__

   Narrowed topic: __I dislike Tom__

   Topic sentence: __I dislike Tom because he talks behind people's backs.__

3. Topic: __Being a Parent__

   Narrowed topic: __Learning things with your children__

   Topic sentence: __As the parent of a seven-year-old, I have learned a lot about__

   __natural history.__

PART C

Gathering Ideas for the Body

One good way to generate ideas for the body of a paragraph is **brainstorming**—freely jotting down anything that relates to your topic sentence: facts, details, examples, little stories. This step might take just a few minutes, but it is one of the most important elements of the writing process. Brainstorming can provide you with specific ideas to support your topic sentence. Later you can choose from these ideas as you compose your paragraph.

Here, for example, is a possible brainstorm list for the topic sentence *Pete's sloppiness is a terrible habit:*

1. His apartment is carpeted with dirty clothes, books, candy wrappers

2. His favorite candy—M & Ms

3. He is often a late-comer or no-show

4. He jots time and place information for dates and appointments on scraps of paper that are tucked away and forgotten

5. Stacks of old newspapers on chair seats

6. Socks bake on lampshades

7. Paper for classes wrinkled and carelessly scrawled

8. I met Pete for the first time in math class

9. His sister is just the opposite, very neat

10. Always late for classes, out of breath

11. He is one messy person

12. Papers stained with Coke or M & Ms

Instead of brainstorming, some writers freewrite or ask themselves questions to generate ideas for their paragraphs. Do what works best for you. If you need more practice in any of these methods, reread Chapter 2, "Gathering Ideas."

PRACTICE 6   Choose the topic from Practice 5 (in Part B) that most interests you. Write that topic and your topic sentence here.
Sample answers:
Topic: __A Supportive Mate__

Topic sentence: __My husband helps and encourages me as a college student.__

Now brainstorm. Write anything that comes to you about your topic sentence. Just let your ideas pour onto paper.

1. __Encouraged me to apply to college__

2. __Washes dishes so I can study__

3. __Tells me to try things even if I might not be successful__

4. __Suggested I take calculus__

5. __Now I might major in calculus__

6. __Reads my papers__

7. __Understands when I stay up late studying__

8. __Came to my favorite class__

9. __Met my calculus professor__

10. __Will help me give a class party__

11. _____

12. _____

13. _____

14. _____

15. _____

and more . . .

PART D

Selecting and Dropping Ideas

Next simply read over what you have written, **selecting** those ideas that relate to and support the topic sentence and **dropping** those that do not. That is, keep the facts, examples, or little stories that provide specific information about your topic sentence. Drop ideas that just **repeat** the topic sentence but add nothing new to the paragraph.

If you are not sure which ideas to select or drop, underline the **key word** or **words** of the topic sentence, the ones that indicate the real point of your paragraph. Then make sure that the ideas you select and drop are related to those key words.

Here is the brainstorm list for the topic sentence *Pete's sloppiness is a terrible habit*. The key word in the topic sentence is *sloppiness*. Which ideas would you keep? Why? Which would you drop? Why?

1. His apartment is carpeted with dirty clothes, books, candy wrappers

2. His favorite candy—M & Ms

3. He is often a late-comer or no-show

4. He jots time and place information for dates and appointments on scraps of paper that are tucked away and forgotten

5. Stacks of old newspapers on chair seats

6. Socks bake on lampshades

7. Papers for classes wrinkled and carelessly scrawled

8. I met Pete for the first time in math class

9. His sister is just the opposite, very neat

10. Always late for classes, out of breath

11. He is one messy person

12. Papers stained with Coke or M & Ms

You probably dropped ideas 2, 8, and 9 because they do not relate to the topic—Pete's sloppiness. You should also have dropped idea 11 because it merely repeats the topic sentence.

PRACTICE 7   Read through your own brainstorm list in Practice 6 (in Part C). Select the ideas that relate to your topic sentence and cross out those that do not. In addition, cross out any ideas that just repeat your topic sentence. Be prepared to explain why you drop or keep each idea.

PART E

Arranging Ideas in a Plan

Now you must choose an **order** in which to arrange ideas. First, group together ideas that have something in common, that are related or alike in some way. Then decide which ideas will come first, which second, and so on. You might wish to number the ideas on your list.

Here are the ideas for a paragraph about Pete arranged in one possible way:

Topic sentence: Pete's sloppiness is a terrible habit.

His apartment is carpeted with dirty clothes, books, candy wrappers

Stacks of old newspapers on chair seats

Socks bake on lampshades

He jots time and place information for dates and appointments on scraps of paper tucked away and forgotten

He is often a late-comer or no-show for appointments

Always late for classes, out of breath

Papers for classes are wrinkled and carelessly scrawled

Papers are stained with Coke or M & Ms

- Do you see the logic in this arrangement? How are the ideas in each group above related?   Each group includes examples of Pete's sloppiness in one area of his life.

- Does it make sense to discuss Pete's apartment first, his appointments second, and classes third? Why?   Yes. The order goes from his home outward and from the personal to the social.

- Once you complete this step, you should have a clear **plan** from which to write the paragraph.*

PRACTICE 8   On notebook paper, arrange the ideas from your brainstorm list according to some plan. First, group together related ideas; then decide which ideas will come first, which second, and so on.

Keep in mind that there is more than one way to group ideas. Think about what you want to say; then group ideas according to what *your* point is.

PART F

Writing and Revising the Paragraph

Writing the First Draft

The first draft should contain all the ideas you have decided to use in the order you have chosen in your plan. Be sure to include your topic sentence. Try to write the best, most interesting, or most amusing paragraph you can, but avoid getting stuck on any one word, sentence, or idea. If you are unsure about something, put a check in the margin and come back to it later. Writing on every other line will leave room for later corrections.

Once you have included all of the ideas from your plan, think about adding a concluding sentence that summarizes your main point or adds a final idea. Not all paragraphs need concluding sentences. For example, if you are telling a story, the paragraph can end when the story does. Write a concluding sentence if it will help to bring your thoughts to an end for your reader.

If possible, once you have finished the first draft, set the paper aside for several hours or several days.

Revising

Revising means rethinking and rewriting your first draft and then making whatever additions or corrections are necessary to improve the paragraph. You may cross out and rewrite words or entire sentences. You may add, drop, or rearrange details.

As you revise, keep the *reader* in mind. Ask yourself these questions:

- Can a reader understand and follow my ideas?

- Is my topic sentence clear?

*For more work on order, see Chapter 4, "Achieving Coherence," Part A.

- Does the paragraph follow a logical order and guide the reader from point to point?

- Will the paragraph keep the reader interested?

In addition, check your paragraph for adequate support and unity, characteristics that we'll consider in the following pages.

Revising for Support

As you revise, make sure your paragraph contains excellent **support**— that is, specific facts, details, and examples that fully explain your topic sentence.

Be careful, too, that you have not simply repeated ideas—especially the topic sentence. Even if they are in different words, repeated ideas only make the reader suspect that your paragraph is padded and that you do not have enough facts and details to support your main idea properly.

Which of the following paragraphs contains the most convincing support?

Paragraph a: (1) Our run-down city block was made special by a once-vacant lot called The Community Garden. (2) The lot was planted with all sorts of plants, vegetables, and flowers. (3) There was a path curving through it. (4) We went there to think. (5) The Community Garden made our block special. (6) Though our neighborhood was known as "tough," no one ever vandalized the garden.

Paragraph b: (1) Our run-down city block was made special by a once-vacant lot called The Community Garden. (2) I'm not sure who first had the idea, but the thin soil had been fertilized, raked, and planted with a surprising assortment of vegetables and flowers. (3) Anyone interested in gardening could tend green pepper plants, string beans, fresh herbs, even corn. (4) Others planted flowers, which changed with the seasons—tall red dahlias, white and purple iris, and taxi-yellow marigolds to discourage the insects. (5) A narrow path curved gracefully among the plants, paved with bricks no doubt left over from the building that once stood here. (6) The Community Garden was our pride, the place we went to think and to be still. (7) Though the neighborhood was known as "tough," no one ever vandalized the garden.

- *Paragraph a* contains general statements but little specific information to support the topic sentence.

- *Paragraph a* also contains needless repetition. What is the number of the sentence or sentences that just repeat the topic sentence?

Sentence 5

- *Paragraph b,* however, supports the topic sentence with specific details and examples: *thin soil, fertilized, raked and planted, green pepper plants, string beans, fresh herbs, corn, red dahlias.* What other specific support does it give?

It states that others planted white and purple iris, taxi-yellow marigolds; it

describes in detail the curving path of brick and explains why people went

there.

_____

_____

Remember: A good paragraph must adequately support and explain its topic sentence.

PRACTICE 9   Check the following paragraphs for adequate support. As you read each one, decide which places need more or better support—specific facts, details, and examples. Then rewrite the paragraphs, inventing facts and details whenever necessary and dropping repetitious words and sentences.

Paragraph a: (1) My uncle can always be counted on when the family faces hardship. (2) Last year, when my mother was very ill, he was there, ready to help in every way. (3) He never has to be called twice. (4) When my parents were in danger of losing their little hardware store because of a huge increase in rent, he helped. (5) Everyone respects him for his willingness to be a real "family man." (6) He is always there for us.

Paragraph b: (1) The overrated television show "The Simpsons" makes heroes out of ignorant, antisocial people. (2) I don't like this show at all. (3) Bart Simpson is stupid and proud of it. (4) His parents are just as stupid as he is. (5) They all do dumb things, and it's supposed to be funny. (6) Americans are wasting their hard-earned money on Bart Simpson tee shirts because they love him. (7) I don't see why.

Revising for Unity

It is sometimes easy, in the process of writing, to drift away from the topic under discussion. Guard against doing so by checking your paragraph for **unity;** that is, make sure the topic sentence, every sentence in the body, and the concluding sentence all relate to one main idea.*

*For more work on revising, see Chapter 16, "Putting Your Revision Skills to Work."

This paragraph lacks unity:

> (1) A. Philip Randolph, the great African-American champion of labor and civil rights, led confrontations with three very popular presidents. (2) Mr. Randolph called for a march on Washington by thousands of African-Americans on July 1, 1941, if President Roosevelt would not take action to end discrimination in defense industries during World War II. (3) Mr. Randolph was born in Florida. (4) After much delay, the president met with Randolph and one week later, opened many defense jobs to black workers. (5) A few years later, in 1948, Mr. Randolph threatened mass civil disobedience if President Truman did not end segregation against African-Americans in the military. (6) On July 26, Truman approved the order that integrated the armed services. (7) The last confrontation was with John F. Kennedy, who sought to stop the 1963 civil rights March on Washington. (8) Mr. Randolph led the historic march on August 28; it featured Martin Luther King's unforgettable "I Have a Dream" speech and led to the Civil Rights Bill of 1964.

- What is the number of the topic sentence in this paragraph?

  Sentence 1

- Which sentence in the paragraph does *not* relate to the topic sentence?

  Sentence 3

This paragraph also lacks unity:

> (1) Quitting smoking was very difficult for me. (2) When I was thirteen, my friend Janice and I smoked in front of a mirror. (3) We practiced holding the cigarette in different ways and tried French inhaling, letting the smoke roll slowly out of our mouths and drawing it back through our noses. (4) I thought this move, when it didn't incite a fit of coughing, was particularly sexy. (5) At first I smoked only to give myself confidence on dates and at parties. (6) Soon, however, I was smoking all the time.

- Here the topic sentence itself, sentence 1, does not relate to the rest of the paragraph. The main idea in sentence 1, that quitting smoking was difficult, is not developed by the other sentences. Since the rest of the paragraph *is* unified, a more appropriate topic sentence might read, *As a teen-ager, I developed the bad habit of smoking.*

PRACTICE 10   Check the following paragraphs for **unity**. If a paragraph is unified, write *U* in the blank. If not, write the number of the sentence that does *not* belong. If the topic sentence does not fit the rest of the paragraph, write *T* in the blank and write a more appropriate topic sentence for the paragraph.

Paragraph a: __6__ (1) At Paradise Produce, attractive displays of fruit and vegetables caught my eye. (2) On the left, oranges, lemons, and apples were stacked in neat pyramids. (3) In the center of the store, baskets of ripe peaches, plums, and raspberries were grouped in a kind of still life. (4) On the right, the leafy green vegetables had been arranged according to intensity of color: dark green spinach, then romaine lettuce and parsley, next the lighter iceberg lettuce, and finally the nearly white Chinese cabbage. (5) On the wall above the greens hung braided ropes of garlic. (6) Some nutritionists believe that garlic prevents certain diseases.

Paragraph b: __3__ (1) Speed and excitement make the Indianapolis 500 one of the world's most popular auto races. (2) Every Memorial Day weekend, thirty-three of the world's fastest cars compete in this 500-mile race around the oval track at the Indianapolis Motor Speedway. (3) Racing cars can be divided into six types. (4) Speeds have increased almost every year since the track opened in 1909. (5) The first winner, Ray Harrowiz, drove his Marmon Wasp an average speed of 74.59 miles per hour. (6) In 1990, Arie Luyendyk won in his Lola-Chevrolet with an average speed of 185.98. (7) Today the Indy 500 draws 200,000 fans each year, making it the best-attended sporting event on the planet.

Paragraph c: __T__ (1) Turquoise is mined in the Southwest today much as it was mined in prehistoric times. (2) Turquoise was the Native American's bank account. (3) It was given as pawn in exchange for staple items that he or she needed. (4) It was a status symbol. (5) In addition, turquoise was considered a sacred presence and was often a part of religious offerings. (6) Turquoise was an important part of life for Native Americans in the Southwest.

Paragraph d: __5__ (1) Dr. Jerome Bach believes that children may play certain roles in the family depending on their birth order. (2) The first child, who usually identifies with the father, takes on the family's more obvious social and career goals. (3) The second child is tuned in to the family's emotional requirements and may act out the hidden needs of others, especially the mother. (4) The behavior of the third child often reflects what is going on between the parents; for instance, if eating is the only thing the parents enjoy doing as a couple, the third child may be overweight. (5) In general, families today have fewer children than in the past.

Writing the Final Draft

Finally, recopy your paper. If you are writing in class, the second draft will usually be the last one. Be sure to include all your corrections. Write neatly and legibly—a carelessly scribbled paper seems to say that you don't care about your own work. When you finish, **proofread** for grammar and spelling. If you are unsure about spelling, check a dictionary. Pointing to each word as you read it will help you catch errors or words you have omitted. Make neat corrections in pen.

Here is the final draft of the paragraph about Pete's sloppiness:

> Pete's sloppiness is a terrible habit. He lives by himself in a one-room apartment carpeted with dirty clothes, books, and crumpled candy wrappers. Stacks of papers cover the chair seats. Socks bake on the lampshades. When Pete makes a date or appointment, he may jot the time and place on a scrap of paper that is soon tucked into a pocket and forgotten, or—more likely—he doesn't jot down the information at all. As a result, Pete is often a latecomer or completely forgets to appear. His grades have suffered, too, since few instructors will put up with a student who arrives out of breath ten minutes after the class has begun and whose wrinkled, carelessly scrawled papers arrive (late, of course) punctuated with Coca-Cola stains and melted M & Ms. The less Pete controls his sloppiness, the more it seems to control him.

- Note that the paragraph contains good support—specific facts, details, and examples, that explain the topic sentence.

- Note that the paragraph has unity—every idea relates to the topic sentence.

- Note that the final sentence provides a brief conclusion so that the paragraph *feels finished.*

Writing Assignments

The assignments that follow will give you practice in writing basic paragraphs. In each, aim for (1) a clear, complete, and limited topic sentence and (2) a body that fully supports and develops the topic sentence.

Remember to **narrow the topic, write the topic sentence, freewrite or brainstorm, select,** and **arrange ideas** before you write. Rethink and **revise** as necessary before composing the final version of the paragraph. As you work, refer to the checklist at the end of this chapter.

Paragraph 1: Discuss an important day in your life. Think back to a day when you learned something important, preferably outside of school. In the topic sentence, tell what you learned. Freewrite or brainstorm to gather ideas. Then describe the lesson in detail, including only the most important steps or events in the learning process. Conclude with an insight.

Paragraph 2: Describe a room you have strong feelings about. Close your eyes and visualize this room in detail. Notice the color of the walls, the furniture, the objects, and the feeling of the room. In the topic sentence, name the mood of the room in one word: *warm, colorful, drab, sterile,* and so on. Freewrite or brainstorm, then select and arrange details that develop your topic sentence and show the mood of the room. In your paragraph, try to capture the room in words.

Paragraph 3: Interview a classmate about an achievement. Write about a time your classmate achieved something important, like winning an award for a musical performance, getting an *A* in a difficult course, or helping a friend through a hard time. To gather interesting facts and details, ask your classmate questions like these and take notes: *Is there one accomplishment of which you are very proud? Why was this achievement so important?* Keep asking questions until you feel you can give the reader a vivid sense of your classmate's triumph. In your first sentence, state the person's achievement—for instance, *Being accepted in the honors program improved Gabe's self-esteem.* Then explain specifically why the achievement was so meaningful.

Paragraph 4: Choose an ideal job. Decide what kind of job you are best suited for and, in your topic sentence, tell what this job is. Then give three or four reasons that will convince readers of the wisdom of your choice. Discuss any special qualifications, talents, skills, or attitudes that would make you an excellent _____. Revise your work, checking for support and unity.

Paragraph 5: Describe a meeting place. Many towns, neighborhoods, and colleges have a central place where people gather to chat and review the day's experiences—a park, restaurant, and so on. If you know such a place, describe it. Explain who goes there, what they do there, and what they talk about.

Paragraph 6: Discuss your ideal vacation day. Present your ideal vacation day from morning to night. Do *not* tell everything, but highlight the four or five most important moments or activities of the day. As you jot down ideas, look for a pattern. Are the activities you choose all physical and active or lazy and slow? Is your day spent alone, with others, or both? In your topic sentence, state the pattern that includes all the activities or moments discussed in the paragraph.

Paragraph 7: Discuss a childhood experience. Choose an experience that deeply affected you. First tell exactly what happened, giving important details. Then explain the meaning this experience had for you.

Paragraph 8: Describe a portrait. Look closely at this self-portrait by the Mexican painter Frida Kahlo. Notice her mouth, eyes, eyebrows, hair, and other important details. Then write a paragraph in which you describe this picture for a reader who has never seen it. In your topic sentence, state your overall impression of the picture. Support this impression with details.

Checklist: The Process of Writing Basic Paragraphs

_____ 1. Narrow the topic in light of your audience and purpose.

_____ 2. Write a complete and limited topic sentence. If you have trouble, freewrite or brainstorm first; then narrow the topic and write the topic sentence.

_____ 3. Freewrite or brainstorm, gathering facts, details, and examples to develop your topic sentence.

_____ 4. Select and drop ideas as you plan the body of the paragraph.

_____ 5. Arrange ideas in order. Decide which ideas will come first, which will come second, and so forth.

_____ 6. Write the best first draft you can.

_____ 7. Conclude. Don't just leave the paragraph hanging.

_____ 8. Revise as necessary, checking your paragraph for support and unity.

_____ 9. Proofread for grammar and spelling errors.

4

Achieving Coherence

PART A   Coherence Through Order
PART B   Coherence Through Related Sentences

Every composition should have **coherence.** A paragraph *coheres*—holds together—when the sentences are arranged in a clear, logical *order* and when the sentences are *related* like links in a chain.

PART A

Coherence Through Order

An orderly presentation of ideas within the paragraph is easier to follow and more pleasant to read than a jumble. *After* jotting down ideas but *before* writing the paragraph, the writer should decide which ideas to discuss first, which second, which third, and so on, according to a logical order.

There are many possible orders, depending on the subject and the writer's purpose. This section will explain three basic ways of ordering ideas: **time order, space order,** and **order of climax.**

Time Order

One of the most common methods of ordering sentences in a paragraph is **time,** or **chronological, order,** which moves from present to past or past to present. Most stories, histories, and instructions follow the logical order of time.* The following paragraph employs time order:

*For work on narrative paragraphs, see Chapter 6, "Narration," and for work on process paragraphs, see Chapter 8, "Process."

> (1) It was the most astonishing strikeout the fans had ever seen. (2) It *began* in the top of the seventh inning, when Big Fred Gnocchi came up to bat. (3) He took a few practice swipes to loosen up the power in his shoulders and back. (4) *Then* the catcher signaled, the pitcher nodded, and a steaming fast ball barreled toward Big Fred. (5) He watched it pass. (6) The umpire called a strike. (7) *Next* came a curve ball and another strike as Fred swung and missed. (8) Angry and determined, Fred dug in at the plate, spat, and gritted his teeth. (9) *Again* the pitcher wound up and delivered—a slow ball. (10) Gnocchi swung, realized he had moved too soon, swung again, and missed again. (11) That may have been the first time in baseball history that a batter took four strikes.

- The events in this paragraph are clearly arranged in the order of time. They are presented as they happened, *chronologically.*

- Throughout the paragraph, key words like *began, then, next,* and *again* emphasize time order and guide the reader from event to event.

Careful use of time order helps to avoid confusing writing like this: *Oops, I forgot to mention that before Fred swung and missed the last time, he had already swung and missed, and before that....*

Occasionally, when the sentences in a paragraph follow a very clear time order, the topic sentence is only implied, not stated directly, as in this example:

> (1) [Harriet] Tubman was born into slavery, escaped to the North in 1849, and established the "underground railroad" from which she "never lost a single passenger." (2) Tubman led over three hundred men, women, and children from slavery into freedom during the 1850's, risking her freedom nineteen times on her trips into the slave states. (3) Called "Moses," she became a legendary figure, and a reward of forty thousand dollars was offered for her capture. (4) During the Civil War, she worked as a spy, a scout, a nurse, and a commander of both black and white troops for the Union Army.... (5) Tubman spread her beliefs in freedom and liberty by speaking, organizing, and inspiring others. (6) In her later years, she attended women's suffrage conventions and helped organize the National Federation of Afro-American Women (1895).
>
> —Judy Chicago, *The Dinner Party: A Symbol of Our Heritage*

■ Time order gives coherence to this paragraph. Sentence 1 tells us the beginning of Harriet Tubman's career as a fighter against slavery. However, it does not express the main idea of the entire paragraph.

■ What is the implied topic sentence or main idea developed by the paragraph? <u>Harriet Tubman dedicated her life to fighting slavery and inequality.</u>

_____

_____

■ The implied topic sentence or main idea of the paragraph might read, *Harriet Tubman devoted much of her life to the cause of freedom.*

■ Because the writer arranges the paragraph in chronological order, the reader can easily follow the order of events in Tubman's life. What words and phrases indicate time order? Underline them and list them here: <u>in 1849; during the 1850's; during the Civil War; in her later</u>

<u>years; (1895)</u>

_____

PRACTICE 1   Arrange each set of sentences in logical time order, numbering the sentences 1, 2, 3, and so on, as if you were preparing to write a paragraph. Underline any words and phrases, like *first*, *next*, and *in 1692*, that give time clues.

1. __2__ <u>First,</u> turn off the appliance that caused the fuse to blow.

   __5__ <u>Finally,</u> replace with a new fuse of the same amperage.

   __4__ To remove the blown fuse, turn it from right to left.

   __1__ Changing a fuse is not difficult.

   __3__ <u>Then</u> identify the blown fuse by its clouded glass cap.

2. __5__ The judge <u>later</u> deeply regretted his part, but this sorry chapter in American history has never been forgotten.

   __2__ Two books "proving" that witches existed by the famous Puritan ministers Increase Mather and his son Cotton Mather further fanned the hysteria <u>in 1693.</u>

   __3__ The stage was set for the terrible Salem witch trials.

   __4__ Nineteen so-called "witches and wizards" were hanged, and one was pressed to death.

   __1__ <u>In 1692,</u> when two girls in Salem Village, Massachusetts, had fits, they blamed the townspeople for bewitching them.

3. __4__   She started her new work with the poor by teaching the street children of Calcutta arithmetic and reading.

   __1__   Mother Teresa has rightly and lovingly been named the "Saint of the Gutters."

   __3__   After several years at the school, she decided that her calling lay with the poor.

   __7__   After her efforts in India, she aided relief agencies in Lebanon and Ethiopia, caring for the displaced and the starving.

   __6__   With help from local authorities, she opened and staffed free clinics in the worst sections of Calcutta.

   __5__   Soon she realized that what these poor people needed most was adequate medical facilities.

   __2__   She began her career working at a Catholic school for the wealthy in Calcutta.

Writing Assignment 1

As you write each paragraph below, compose a topic sentence, freewrite or brainstorm to gather ideas, and then arrange them *chronologically*. You may wish to use transitional words and phrases like these:*

first	after that
then	soon
next	while
during	moments later
before	finally

Paragraph 1: Narrate the first hour of your average day. Start with when you get up in the morning and continue describing what you do for that first hour. Record your activities, your conversations, if any, and possibly your moods as you go through this hour of the morning. As you revise, make sure that events clearly follow time order.

Paragraph 2: Record an unforgettable event. Choose a moment in sports or in some other activity that you vividly remember, either as a participant or as a spectator. In the topic sentence, tell in a general way what happened. (*It was the most exciting touchdown I have ever seen*, or *Ninety embarrassing seconds marked the end of my brief surfing career.*) Then record the experience, arranging details in time order.

*For a more complete list, see the section on transitional expressions, pages 58–59.

Paragraph 3: Relate an accident or close call. Focus on just a few critical moments of an accident or close call that you experienced or witnessed, depicting the most important events in detail. Try to capture your thoughts and perceptions at the time as honestly and exactly as possible. Arrange them in time order.

Space Order

Another useful way to arrange ideas in writing is **space order**—describing a person, a thing, or a place from top to bottom, from left to right, from foreground to background, and so on. Space order is often used in descriptive writing because it moves from detail to detail like a movie camera's eye:*

> (1) We lived on the top floor of a five-story tenement in Williamsburg, facing the BMT elevated train, or as everyone called it, the El. (2) Our floors and windows would vibrate from the El, which shook the house like a giant, roaring as if his eyes were being poked out. (3) When we went down into the street, we played on a checkerboard of sunspots and shadows, which rhymed the railroad ties above our heads. (4) Even the brightest summer day could not lift the darkness and burnt-rubber smell of our street. (5) I would hold my breath when I passed under the El's long shadow. (6) It was the spinal column of my childhood, both oppressor and liberator, the monster who had taken away all our daylight, but on whose back alone one could ride out of the neighborhood into the big broad world.
>
> —Philip Lopate, *Bachelorhood: Tales of the Metropolis*

- This paragraph uses space order.

- Sentence 1 clearly places the scene: on the *top floor* of a tenement, *facing* the elevated train.

- In sentences 3 and 4, the paragraph moves *downstairs*, from the apartment to the street. These sentences describe the pattern made by the sun through the tracks overhead.

- Sentence 5 moves directly *under* the railroad. Note how words and phrases like *on the top floor, facing, down into the street, above our heads,* and *passed under* help locate the action as the paragraph *moves* from place to place.

*For more work on space order, see Chapter 7, "Description."

Some paragraphs, clearly arranged according to space order, have only an implied topic sentence:

> (1) On my right a woods thickly overgrown with creeper descended the hill's slope to Tinker Creek. (2) On my left was a planting of large shade trees on the ridge of the hill. (3) Before me the grassy hill pitched abruptly and gave way to a large, level field fringed in trees where it bordered the creek. (4) Beyond the creek I could see with effort the vertical sliced rock where men had long ago quarried the mountain under the forest. (5) Beyond that I saw Hollins Pond and all its woods and pastures; then I saw in a blue haze the world poured flat and pale between the mountains.
>
> —Annie Dillard, *Pilgrim at Tinker Creek*

- The main idea of this paragraph is *implied*, not stated by a topic sentence. What is the main idea? <u>Standing on the hill, I had a broad view of</u>

  <u>the surrounding countryside.</u>

- The implied topic sentence or main idea of this paragraph might read, *This is the scene all around me.* Because the paragraph is so clearly arranged according to space order, the reader can easily follow it.

- Transitional phrases like *on my right* and *on my left* guide the reader from sentence to sentence. What phrases in sentences 3, 4, and 5 help

  guide the reader? <u>before me; beyond the creek; beyond that</u>

PRACTICE 2 Arrange each group of details here according to **space order,** numbering them 1, 2, 3, and so on, as if in preparation for a descriptive paragraph. Be prepared to explain your choices.

1. Describe a science classroom.

   <u>3</u> rows of chairs and counters where students are writing

   <u>1</u> back wall of shelves with jars containing small animals, a human brain

   <u>4</u> on front counter, large plastic model of an eyeball

   <u>2</u> human skeleton hanging on a pole in front of the jars

   <u>5</u> professor in white lab coat explaining the parts of the eye

2. Describe a person.

_2_ intense brown eyes

_5_ faded jeans

_4_ broad shoulders

_3_ two-inch scar on right cheek

_6_ ostrich leather cowboy boots

_1_ rumpled, sandy-colored hair

3. Describe a car.

_1_ painted white

_6_ leopard-print upholstery

_2_ mangled front bumper

_3_ hood ornament, a winged horse

_5_ fuzzy dice hanging from rear-view mirror

_4_ trunk covered with dents

Writing Assignment 2

Use **space order** to give coherence to each paragraph below. Compose a topic sentence, freewrite or brainstorm for details, and then arrange them in space order. Use transitional words and phrases like these if you wish:*

on the left	above	beside	beyond that
on the right	farther out	behind	next to

Paragraph 1: Describe a classroom scene, a person, or a car. Choose one group of details from Practice 2, formulate a topic sentence that sets the scene for them all, and use them as the basis of a paragraph. Convert the details into complete sentences, adding words if you wish.

Paragraph 2: Describe a room in your home. Describe a room in your home that has special meaning to you—the bedroom, the kitchen, a workroom or den. Choose details that capture the special feeling or purpose of the room. Before you write the paragraph, arrange your details in space order.

*For a more complete list, see the section on transitional expressions, pages 58–59.

Paragraph 3: Describe a photograph. Describe this scene captured by photographer Jaye Phillips as clearly and exactly as you can. First, jot down the four or five most important details in the scene. Then, before you write your paragraph, arrange these details according to space order—moving from foreground to background, perhaps, or from left to right.

Paragraph 4: Describe a public figure. Choose someone you admire or like—for example, a person in the news or a television personality. Working from memory or from a photograph, choose five or six striking details to use as the basis of a paragraph that employs space order. Move from head to toe, from face to hands, but follow a logical plan.

Order of Climax

It is sometimes possible to arrange the ideas in a paragraph in the **order of climax,** usually starting with the least important idea and building to a climax at the end of the paragraph. This is an especially effective way to arrange reasons in a persuasive composition or examples that develop a topic sentence.* Paragraphs arranged in the order of climax can have dramatic power:

*See Chapter 5, "Illustration," and Chapter 12, "Persuasion."

> (1) Mrs. Prym, our town's eccentric millionaire, lived and died indulging her whims. (2) Winter or summer, indoors or out, she always wore white gloves. (3) *Another oddity* was her insistence upon a breakfast of freshly laid quail eggs every morning. (4) They say that when Mrs. Prym traveled, she took live quails along. (5) Her burial was *the last extravagant whimsy:* she was lowered into the earth in her silver Ferrari.

- The three whims that develop the topic sentence in this paragraph are discussed in the **order of climax:** from the *least to the most expensive* and from the *least to the most surprising.*

- Demanding quail eggs for breakfast is a stranger and more expensive habit than wearing white gloves. But being buried in a Ferrari is the costliest and oddest whim of all.

- Transitional words like *another* and *the last* help the reader follow clearly from one whim to the next.

As you write, pay attention to the relative importance of ideas. Depending on the subject, there may be a natural order of climax—according to price, size, or importance—that can structure the paragraph. Order of climax can help counter the tendency of some writers to state the best idea first and then let the paragraph dwindle away.

Sometimes, though, it can be effective to reverse the order of climax. Occasionally try beginning with the most important idea and ending with the least important one. In this way, the reader is immediately impressed with the force of your ideas and will want to read on. Be especially careful to begin with the most important idea in business correspondence and on essay exams. In those situations, your reader definitely wants to see the most important points first. Read the following paragraph.

> (1) Louis Pasteur is honored as a great scientist for at least three reasons. (2) Most important, this Frenchman created vaccines that have saved millions of human and animal lives. (3) The vaccines came from his discovery that weakened forms of a disease could be used to prevent that disease. (4) Almost as important was Pasteur's brilliant idea that tiny living beings, and not chemical reactions, spoiled beverages. (5) He therefore developed the process, called pasteurization, that keeps milk, wine, vinegar, and beer from spoiling. (6) Finally, Pasteur found ways to stop a silkworm disease that threatened to ruin France's very profitable silk industry.

■ What three points develop the topic sentence?

(1) Creating vaccines, (2) developing pasteurization, (3) saving France's silk

industry

■ Note how the words *most important, almost as important,* and *finally* guide the reader from one point to another.

PRACTICE 3   Arrange the ideas that develop each topic sentence in the **order of climax,** numbering them 1, 2, 3, and so on. *Begin with the least important* (the smallest, cheapest, or least surprising or severe) and build to a *climax.* Or reverse the order if you think a paragraph would be more effective if it began with the *most* important idea. Be prepared to explain your choices.

1. Cynthia Lopez's first year of college brought many unexpected expenses.

   __2__   Her English professor wanted her to own a college dictionary.

   __4__   All those term papers to write required a new electronic typewriter.

   __3__   She had to spend $90 for textbooks.

   __1__   Her solid geometry class required various colored pencils and felt-tipped pens.

2. Alcoholic beverages should not be sold at sporting events.

   __3__   Injuries and even deaths caused by crowd violence would be eliminated.

   __1__   Fans could save money by buying soft drinks instead of beer.

   __2__   Games and matches would be much more pleasant without the yelling, swearing, and rudeness often caused by alcohol.

3. On January 2, the Waltons returned to find that their home had been robbed.

   __2__   The compact disk player was gone.

   __4__   Some costume jewelry was missing.

   __3__   A portable radio had been taken.

   __1__   Mrs. Walton's mink coat was nowhere to be found.

   __5__   Two cans of noodle soup had been filched.

Writing Assignment 3

Use **order of climax** to give coherence to the paragraphs that follow. Use transitional words and phrases like these to guide the reader along:

first   even more

another   last

next   the most (of all)

Paragraph 1: Discuss a day when everything went right (or wrong). Freewrite or brainstorm to gather ideas. Choose three or four of the day's best (or worst) events and write a paragraph in which you present them in order of climax, from the least to the most important. Try a humorous paragraph if you wish.

Paragraph 2: Describe an unusual person. Choose a person you know whose looks *or* actions are unusual. Write your topic sentence and gather ideas; choose either three to five details about the person's looks or three to five details about the person's actions; arrange these ideas according to order of climax, saving the most unusual for last.

Paragraph 3: Explain why you want something. Write a paragraph that begins, *I want a college education* (or other goal) *for three reasons.* Choose the three reasons that matter most to you and arrange them in order of importance—*either* from least to most important *or* from most to least important.

**PRACTICE 4
Review**

Decide how you would develop each of the following topic sentences into a paragraph and choose an appropriate **order** of ideas. In the blanks, state what order you would use and briefly describe your approach.

There are no "right" answers. Some topics can be developed in several ways, depending on the writer.

Example

The fields behind the barn are vibrant with color.

Order: ___Space___   Approach: ___Describe the colors of the fields___

___from foreground to background.___

Order: ___Time___   Approach: ___Describe the different colors at___

___three different times of day.___

Order: ___Climax___   Approach: ___Describe the details of color from___

___least to most striking.___

1. Paula Abdul gave an exciting performance at Stage Left.

   Order: _____Climax_____ Approach: _____Describe the songs Ms. Abdul

   performed, from the least to the most exciting.

2. The room was filled with unusual objects.

   Order: _____Space_____ Approach: _____Describe the room's contents

   from foreground to background.

3. Three things influenced my decision to major in _____.

   Order: _____Climax_____ Approach: _____Describe the influences, from

   least to most important.

4. During my first term at college, I made four changes in my study habits.

   Order: _____Time_____ Approach: _____Describe the changes in the

   order in which they were made.

5. One look at my dog reveals his mixed heritage.

   Order: _____Space_____ Approach: _____Describe the dog from nose to

   tail.

6. Gregor Mendel, an Austrian monk, performed many experiments before he discovered the laws of heredity.

   Order: _____Time_____ Approach: _____Describe Mendel's early

   experiments, and lead up to his major discovery.

PART B

Coherence Through Related Sentences

In addition to arranging ideas in a logical order, the writer can ensure paragraph coherence by linking one sentence to the next. This section will present four basic ways to link sentences: **repetition of important words, substitution of pronouns, substitution of synonyms,** and **transitional expressions.**

Repetition of Important Words and Pronouns

Link sentences within a paragraph by *repeating important words and ideas.*

> (1) A grand jury is an investigative body composed of members elected from the community. (2) It serves as a buffer between the state and the citizen. (3) The prosecutor, in many cases, brings before the grand jury the evidence gathered on a particular case. (4) The grand jury must then decide if sufficient evidence exists to hand down an indictment—the indictment being a formal charge against an accused person written by the prosecutor and submitted to a court by the grand jury. (5) With the indictment issued, the prosecutor can proceed to the arraignment.
>
> —Ronald J. Waldron et al., *The Criminal Justice System: An Introduction*

- What important words are repeated in this paragraph?

- The words *grand jury* are repeated four times, in sentences 1, 3, and 4. The word *indictment*, introduced near the end of the paragraph, is repeated three times, in sentences 4 and 5. The word *prosecutor* is repeated three times, in sentences 3, 4, and 5.

- Repetition of these key words helps the reader follow from sentence to sentence as these terms are defined and the relationships between them are explained.

Although repetition of important words can be effective, it can also become boring if overused.* To avoid *unnecessary* repetition, substitute *pronouns* for words already mentioned in the paragraph, as this author does:

> (1) The technique of coastal whaling spread to the New World, where in the early 1700's *it* underwent a major change. (2) American whalemen gradually extended their range from coastal waters to the open sea. (3) Later *they* transferred their tryworks—furnaces and iron caldrons in which blubber was reduced to oil—from the shore to the ships themselves.
>
> —William Graves, "The Imperiled Giants," *National Geographic*

- The use of *pronouns* in this paragraph avoids unnecessary repetition. In sentence 1, the pronoun *it* refers to its antecedent,† *the technique of coastal whaling*, already mentioned in the sentence.

---

*For practice in eliminating wordiness (repetition of unimportant words), see Chapter 15, "Revising for Language Awareness," Part B.

†For more work in pronouns and antecedents, see Chapter 28, "Pronouns," Parts A, B, and C.

■ The pronoun *they* in sentence 3 gives coherence to the paragraph by

referring to what antecedent? _____whalemen_____

Use pronoun substitution together with the repetition of important words for a smooth presentation of ideas.

PRACTICE 5   What important words are repeated in the following paragraph? Underline them. Circle any pronouns that replace them. Notice the varied pattern of repetitions and pronoun replacements.

I have always considered my father a very intelligent person. (His) intelligence is not the type usually tested in schools; perhaps (he) would have done well on such tests, but the fact is that (he) never finished high school. Rather, my father's intelligence is (his) ability to solve problems creatively as (they) arise. Once when I was very young, we were driving through the desert at night when the oil line broke. My father improvised a light, squeezed under the car, found the break, and managed to whittle a connection to join the two severed pieces of tubing; then (he) added more oil and drove us over a hundred miles to the nearest town. Such intelligent solutions to unforeseen problems were typical of (him). In fact, my father's brand of brains—accurate insight, followed by creative action—is the kind of intelligence that I admire and most aspire to.

Writing Assignment 4

Paragraph 1: Discuss success. How do you measure *success?* By the money you make, the number or quality of friends you have? Freewrite or brainstorm for ideas. Then answer this question in a thoughtful paragraph. Give the paragraph coherence by repeating important words and using pronouns.

Paragraph 2: Discuss a public figure. Choose a public figure whom you admire—from the arts, politics, media, or sports—and write a paragraph discussing *one quality* that makes that person special. Name the person in your topic sentence. Vary repetition of the person's name with pronouns to give the paragraph coherence.

Synonyms and Substitutions

When you do not wish to repeat a word or use a pronoun, give coherence to your paragraph with a **synonym** or **substitution. Synonyms** are two or more words that mean nearly the same thing. For instance, if you do not wish to repeat the word *car,* you might use the synonym *automobile* or *vehicle.* If you are describing a sky and have already used the word *bright,* try the synonym *radiant.*

Or instead of a synonym, **substitute** other words that describe the subject. If you are writing about José Conseco, for example, refer to him as *this powerful slugger* or *this versatile outfielder.* Such substitutions provide a change from constant repetition of a person's name or a single pronoun.*

Use synonyms and substitutions together with repetition and pronouns to give coherence to your writing:

> (1) On September 10, 1990, *the main building of Ellis Island* in New York Harbor reopened as a museum. (2) Restoration of *the huge red brick and limestone structure* took eight years and cost $156 million. (3) From 1900 to 1924, *this famous immigrant station* was the first stop of millions of newcomers to American shores. (4) *The building* was finally abandoned in 1954; by 1980, *it* was in such bad condition that snow and rain fell on its floor. (5) Today, visitors can follow the path of immigrants: from a ferry boat, through the great arched doorway, into the room where the weary travelers left their baggage, up the stairway where doctors kept watch, and into the registry room. (6) Here questions were asked that determined if each immigrant could stay in the United States. (7) *This magnificent monument to the American people* contains exhibits that tell the whole immigration history of the United States.

- This paragraph effectively mixes repetition, pronouns, and substitution. The important word *building* is stated in sentence 1 and repeated in sentence 4.

- Sentence 4 also substitutes the pronoun *it.*

- In sentence 2, *the huge red brick and limestone structure* is substituted for *building,* and a second substitution, *this famous immigrant station,* occurs in sentence 3. Sentence 7 refers to the building as *this magnificent monument to the American people* and concludes the paragraph.

Sometimes the dictionary lists synonyms. For instance, the entry for *smart* might list *clever, witty, intelligent.* An even better source of synonyms is the **thesaurus,** a book of synonyms. For example, if you are describing a city street and cannot think of other words meaning **noisy,** look in the thesaurus. The number of choices will amaze you.

---

*For more work on exact language, see Chapter 15, "Revising for Language Awareness," Part A.

PRACTICE 6   Read each paragraph carefully. Then write on the lines any synonyms and substitutions that the writer has used to replace the word(s) in italics.

Paragraph 1: Rocky Mountain bighorn sheep use their massive horns as percussion instruments. During the fall rutting season, when hormone changes bring on the breeding urge, 250-pound rams square off in violent, head-butting matches to determine which gains leadership of the herd and pick of the ewes. Duelists rear on hind legs, then drop to all fours and, heads down, charge at full speed.

—National Geographic

Rocky Mountain bighorn sheep are also referred to as ___250-pound___

___rams___ and ___duelists___ .

Paragraph 2: Hollywood has long depended on *publicity stunts* to draw attention to movies and their stars. Movie premieres often have been the settings of elaborate schemes; for instance, only horses and their riders could attend the drive-in premiere of *Blazing Saddles.* The photo opportunity is another kind of attention-grabber; think of the famous picture of Marilyn Monroe with her dress blowing in the breeze. A third favorite strategy is to hold an unusual contest, for example, offering a prize to the woman who most passionately kisses a picture of Tom Selleck or giving free tickets to *Creep Show* to people singled out as creeps by a "creep detector." In one of the wackiest pranks ever, a publicist named Jim Moran promoted *The Egg and I* by sitting on an ostrich egg for forty days until it hatched.

Publicity stunts are also referred to as ___elaborate schemes___ ,

___attention-grabbers___ , ___strategies___ , and

___pranks___ .

Paragraph 3: On April 8, 1982, *Captain Fred Wilson* landed an RF-4 Phantom Jet on short notice. He had been sitting in the back seat of the plane when a bird crashed through the windshield and knocked the pilot unconscious. One year later, the air force veteran had to repeat his performance when once again a bird crashed into the plane in which Wilson was riding. The experienced air hero helped land the plane, assisted by the pilot, who received only minor injuries.

Captain Fred Wilson is also referred to as ___the air force veteran___

and ___the experienced air hero___ .

PRACTICE 7 Give coherence to the following paragraphs by thinking of appropriate synonyms or substitutions for the words in italics. Then write them in the blanks.

Paragraph 1: The story of Arnold Schwarzenegger's success exemplifies the American dream. Called the Austrian Oak when he arrived in the United States in 1968, the eighteen-year-old *muscleman* had only twenty dollars and a gym bag. Within a few years, the __rugged hunk__ won five Mr. Universe and seven Mr. Olympia titles, making him the most famous __strongman__ on earth. Then in the mid-1970s, he was featured in both the book and the movie *Pumping Iron.* Audiences saw that Arnold was not just a __body builder__, but a smart and warm man with a magnetic personality. The __gat-toothed Goliath__ soon became the star of a series of thriller films that have earned him millions of box-office dollars and fans all over the world.

Paragraph 2: Much evidence shows that the urge to take a midafternoon *nap* is natural to humans. Sleep researchers have found that volunteer subjects, kept in underground rooms where they cannot tell the time, need a __sleep break__ about twelve hours after the halfway point of their main sleep. For example, if people sleep from midnight till 6:00 a.m., they'll be ready for a __relaxing doze__ at 3:00 the next afternoon. Other studies show that people have less trouble taking a __snooze__ in the midafternoon than at any other daylight time. In many countries with warm climates, citizens take their daily __siesta__ in the afternoon. Even stressed Americans take an average of two afternoon naps a week.

Paragraph 3: All John ever does is watch *TV.* He comes into the house, clicks on the ___set___ , flops into his chair, and stares glassy-eyed at the screen until he falls asleep. His wife complains that she has been widowed by ___an electronic rival___ ; his kids whimper that Daddy loves ___the tube___ more than he loves them. Yes, John is a ___television___ addict.

Writing Assignment 5

As you do the following assignments, try to achieve paragraph coherence by using repetition, pronouns, synonyms, and substitutions.

Paragraph 1: Discuss an invention. Pick an invention or product that intrigues you—a video game, the miniature cassette recorder, the ballpoint pen—and discuss the ways in which human beings benefit from its use. Or you may do a humorous paragraph, showing how frozen pizza or leather pants have done great things for humankind.

In any case, name the invention in your topic sentence; then give the paragraph coherence by replacing the name of the product with both a pronoun and one or two synonyms or substitutions. For example, you might replace *the miniature cassette recorder* with the pronoun *it* and with such phrases as *this handy little device* or *this revolutionary gadget.*

Paragraph 2: Describe your ideal mate. Decide on three or four crucial qualities that your ideal husband, wife, or friend would possess, and write a paragraph describing this extraordinary person. Use repetition, pronouns, and word substitutions to give coherence to the paragraph. For example, *My ideal husband ... he ... my companion.*

Paragraph 3: Write a horror story. Go wild with synonyms and substitutions. Write a mini-horror story that begins: *Suddenly, the hideous, rubbery creature began to move.* As you write, replace the words *hideous, rubbery creature* with as many vivid substitutions as you can.

Transitional Expressions

Skill in using transitional expressions is vital to coherent writing. **Transitional expressions** are words and phrases that point out the exact relation between one idea and another, one sentence and another. Words like *therefore, however, for example,* and *finally* are signals that guide the reader from sentence to sentence. Without them, even orderly and well-written paragraphs can be confusing and hard to follow.

The transitional expressions in this paragraph are italicized:

> (1) Zoos in the past often contributed to the disappearance of animal populations. (2) Animals were cheap, and getting new ones was easier than providing the special diet and shelter necessary to keep captive animals alive. (3) *Recently, however,* zoo directors have begun to realize that if zoos themselves are to continue, they must help save many species from extinction. (4) *As a result,* some zoos have begun to redefine themselves as places where endangered species can be protected and even revived. (5) The Basel Zoo in Switzerland, *for example,* selects endangered species and encourages captive breeding. (6) If zoos continue such work, perhaps they can, like Noah's ark, save some of earth's wonderful creatures from extinction.

- Each transitional expression above links, in a precise way, the sentence in which it appears to the sentence before. The paragraph begins by explaining the destructive policies of zoos in the past.

- In sentence 3, two transitional expressions of contrast—*recently* (as opposed to the past) and *however*—introduce the idea that zoo policies have *changed*.

- The phrase *as a result* makes clear that sentence 4 is *a consequence* of events described in the previous sentence(s).

- In sentence 5, *for example* tells us that the Basel Zoo is *one particular illustration* of the previous general statement.

As you write, use various transitional expressions, together with the other linking devices, to connect one sentence to the next. Well-chosen transitional words also help to stress the purpose and order of the paragraph.

Particular groups of transitional expressions are further explained and demonstrated in each chapter of Unit 3. However, here is a combined, partial list for handy reference as you write.

Purpose	*Transitional Expressions*
to add	also, and, and then, as well, besides, beyond that, first (second, third, last, and so on), for one thing, furthermore, in addition, moreover, next, what is more

Purpose	*Transitional Expressions*
to compare	also, as well, both (neither), in the same way, likewise, similarly
to contrast	although, be that as it may, but, even though, however, in contrast, nevertheless, on the contrary, on the other hand, yet, whereas
to concede (a point)	certainly, granted that, of course, no doubt, to be sure
to emphasize	above all, especially, in fact, in particular, indeed, most important, surely
to illustrate	as a case in point, as an illustration, for example, for instance, in particular, one such, yet another
to place	above, beside, below, beyond, farther, here, inside, nearby, next to, on the far side, opposite, outside, to the east (south, and so on)
to qualify	perhaps
to give a reason	as, because, for, since
to show a result	and so, because of this, as a consequence, as a result, consequently, for this reason, hence, so, therefore, thus
to summarize	all in all, finally, in brief, in other words, lastly, on the whole, to sum up
to place in time	after a while, afterward, at last, at present, briefly, currently, during, eventually, finally, first (second, and so on), gradually, immediately, in the future, later, meanwhile, next, now, recently, soon, suddenly, then

PRACTICE 8   Carefully determine the *exact relationship* between the sentences in each pair below. Then choose from the list a **transitional expression** that clearly expresses this relationship and write it in the blank. Pay attention to the punctuation and capitalize the first word of every sentence.*

1. No one inquired about the money found in the lobby. __Consequently__, it was given to charity.

*For practice using conjunctions to join ideas, see Chapter 22, "Coordination and Subordination."

2. First, cut off the outer, fibrous husk of the coconut. __Then__ poke a hole through one of the dark "eyes" and sip the milk through a straw.

3. The Women's Studies office is on the fifth floor. __Next__ to it is a small reading room.

4. Some mountains under the sea soar almost as high as those on the land. One underwater mountain in the Pacific, __for example__, is only 500 feet shorter than Mount Everest.

5. All citizens should vote. Many do not, __however__ .

6. Mrs. Dalworth enjoys shopping in out-of-the-way thrift shops. __Furthermore__ , she loves bargaining with the vendors at outdoor flea markets.

7. In 1887, Native Americans owned nearly 138 million acres of land. By 1932, __in contrast__ , 90 million of those acres were owned by whites.

8. Kansas corn towered over the fence. __Beside__ the fence, a red tractor stood baking in the sun.

9. Most street crime occurs between 2:00 and 5:00 A.M. __For this reason__ , do not go out alone during those hours.

10. Dr. Leff took great pride in his work at the clinic. __Nevertheless__ , his long hours often left him exhausted.

11. Few scientists have worked so creatively with a single agricultural product. __Besides__ peanut oil and peanut butter, George Washington Carver developed literally hundreds of uses for the peanut.

12. We waited in our seats for over an hour. __Finally__ the lights dimmed, and the Fabulous String Band bounded on stage.

PRACTICE 9   Add **transitional expressions** to this paragraph to guide the reader smoothly from sentence to sentence. To do so, consider the relationship between sentences (shown in parentheses). Then write the transitional word or phrase that best expresses this relationship.

Since Clyde has been saving money for months, he will __eventually__ (time) be able to afford the vacation of his dreams. He spends enjoyable hours imagining himself on different cruises,

_____such as_____ a boat trip on the Amazon River or a cruise to the Carib-
　　(illustration)

bean. He enjoys looking through the travel section of the newspaper and

reading through tourist brochures. ___Of course___ he does not as
　　　　　　　　　　　　　　　　　(conceding a point)

yet have enough money to go far away. ___Therefore___, he brings
　　　　　　　　　　　　　　　　　　　　　　　(result)

his lunch every day and puts the money in a special vacation fund.

___In addition___, he saves all the cash that comes his way as gifts and
　　(addition)

allows himself very little spending money. It may take a while, but Clyde

___surely___ will take that vacation of his dreams.
　(emphasis)

PRACTICE 10
Review

Most paragraphs achieve coherence through a variety of linking devices: repetition, pronouns, substitutions, and transitional expressions. Read the following paragraphs with care, noting the kinds of linking devices used by each writer. Answer the questions after each paragraph.

Paragraph 1: (1) The blues is the one truly American music. (2) Born in the Mississippi Delta, this twelve-bar cry of anguish found its durable, classic form in the searing soliloquies of poor black men and women who used it to ventilate all the aches and pains of their condition—the great Bessie Smith, Robert Johnson, Ma Rainey, Lightnin' Hopkins and Son House, Mississippi John Hurt, John Lee Hooker and Blind Lemon Jefferson. (3) And, ever since, the blues has served as the wellspring of every major movement in this country's popular music.

—Paul D. Zimmerman with Peter Barnes et al.,
"Rebirth of the Blues," *Newsweek*

1. What important words appear in both the first and the last sentence?

　　the blues

2. In sentence 2, *the blues* is referred to as ___this twelve-bar cry of anguish___

3. What transitional expressions are used in sentence 3? ___and; ever since___

Paragraph 2: (1) Mrs. Zajac seemed to have a frightening amount of energy. (2) She strode across the room, her arms swinging high and her hands in small fists. (3) Taking her stand in front of the green chalkboard, discussing the rules with her new class, she repeated sentences, and her lips held the shapes of certain words, such as "homework," after she had said them. (4) Her hands kept very busy. (5) They sliced the air and made karate chops to mark off boundaries. (6) They extended straight out like a traffic cop's, halting illegal maneuvers yet to be perpetrated. (7) When they rested momentarily on her hips, her hands looked as if they were in holsters. (8) She told the children, "One thing Mrs. Zajac expects from each of you is that you do *your* best." (9) She said, "Mrs. Zajac gives homework. (10) I'm sure you've all heard. (11) The old meanie gives homework." (12) *Mrs. Zajac.* (13) It was in part a role. (14) She worked her way into it every September.

—Tracy Kidder, *Among Schoolchildren*

1. What important words are repeated in this paragraph? __Mrs.__

   Zajac, hands, homework

2. What is the antecedent of *they* in sentences 5 and 6? __hands__

Paragraph 3: (1) More important perhaps than the recipes and ideas that flowed into the home through cookbooks and magazines were the conveniences that began more and more to appear in the kitchen. (2) First it was the icebox. (3) Next it was running hot water, along with the cold. (4) Then it was the gas stove, a frightening apparatus for the uninitiated—and then, just as soon as mastery of its dials and heat had been achieved, along came the electric stove to sow confusion again. (5) The icebox gave way to the refrigerator and the freezer. (6) And out of Clarence Birdseye's observation that Eskimos in Labrador froze their meat and fish evolved the quick-freezing of various foodstuffs, a revolution of the first order in American cooking.

—*Foods of the World/American Cooking,* Time-Life Books Inc.

1. Underline the transitional expressions in this paragraph.

2. What *order* of ideas does the paragraph employ? __time order__

Unit 3
Developing the Paragraph

5

Illustration

To **illustrate** is to explain a general statement by means of one or more specific *examples*.

Illustration makes what we say more vivid and more exact. Someone might say, "My math professor is always finding crazy ways to get our attention. Just yesterday, for example, he wore a high silk hat to class." The first sentence is a general statement about this professor's unusual ways of getting attention. The second sentence, however, gives a specific example of something he did that *clearly shows* what the writer means.

Writers often use illustration to develop a paragraph. They explain a general topic sentence with one, two, three, or more specific examples. Detailed and well-chosen examples add interest, liveliness, and power to your writing.

Topic Sentence

Here is the topic sentence of a paragraph that is later developed by examples:

> Many famous athletes have overcome severe illness or injury.

- The writer begins an illustration paragraph with a topic sentence that makes a general statement.

- This generalization may be obvious to the writer, but if he or she wishes to convince the reader, some specific examples would be helpful.

Paragraph and Plan

Here is the entire paragraph:

> Many famous athletes have overcome severe illness or injury. For example, O. J. Simpson suffered as a child from rickets, a bone disease caused by too little calcium, and had to wear leg braces. After hard work, Simpson came to excel in both college and pro football, setting records for total yards gained and touchdowns scored. Another inspiring example is track great Wilma Rudolph, who had polio as a child and could not walk without braces until she was eight. Twelve years later, she won three gold medals in the 1960 Olympics, taking the 100- and 200-meter dashes and running on the winning 400-meter relay team. At the height of his golf career in 1949, Ben Hogan was badly injured in a car crash, but he fought back and gained even greater glory, winning three out of the four major golf tournaments in 1953. Finally, Joan Benoit took up running in order to get back into shape after she broke a leg while skiing. She became America's top female long-distance runner and has won many marathon races.

■ How many examples does the writer use to develop the topic sentence?

four

■ Who are they?

O. J. Simpson, Wilma Rudolph, Ben Hogan, Joan Benoit

Before composing this illustration paragraph, the writer probably made a plan like this:

Topic sentence: Many famous athletes have overcome serious illness or injury.

Example 1:   O. J. Simpson
—rickets as a child
—came to excel in college and pro football
—records for yards gained and touchdowns

Example 2:   Wilma Rudolph
—polio, walked with braces until age eight
—three gold medals in 1960 Olympics (100- and 200-meter dash, 400-meter relay)

Example 3:   Ben Hogan
—badly injured in car crash in 1949
—recovered to gain greater glory
—won three of four major tournaments in 1953

Example 4:   Joan Benoit
—broke a leg skiing and took up running
—became top U.S. female long-distance runner
—won many marathons

■ Note that each example clearly relates to and supports the topic sentence.

Instead of using three or four examples to support the topic sentence, the writer may prefer instead to discuss one single example:

> Miniaturized versions of many products—from electronic dictionaries to VCRs—are now available to consumers. The pocket television, for instance, is a popular product in the small-scale craze. This tiny TV can be carried in a shirt pocket or purse or worn on a handstrap. Taking up from four to six inches of space, it has a screen the size of a matchbook. It exploits the newest advances in electronics, reproducing images in the same manner as both conventional televisions and digital watches. Although it lacks some of the picture controls of conventional television, the pocket-sized version has all the usual features, including color. Even in noisy public places, it can be heard clearly through its own earphones. With the development of miniature televisions, seasoned travelers may soon automatically pack a television next to their toothbrush.

■ What is the general statement? Miniaturized versions of many products—
from electronic dictionaries to VCRs—are now available to consumers.

■ What specific example does the writer give to support the general statement? the pocket television

The single example may also be a **narrative,** a *story* that illustrates the topic sentence.

*For more on narrative, see Chapter 6, "Narration," and Chapter 18, "Types of Essays," Part B.

> Little things that happened during these years seemed of great importance. I remember that in my first year at camp I wore an ill-fitted Boy Scout hat. One of the counselors, a boy five years my senior who seemed to me to belong already to the grown-up world of brilliance and authority, began, in a pleasant way, to tease me about the hat. Every morning for a week he led us to the abandoned logging road and clocked us as we walked and trotted a measured mile. My hat was anchored down by a heavy chin strap; it flopped and sailed about my head as I ran to the finish line. The boy began to laugh at me. He waved his arms and called out, "Come on, you rookie!" The other kids took it up and Rookie became my first nickname. I loved it. I tingled when someone called it out. I painted it on my belt, carved it on my packing case, inked it into my hatband, and began to sign it to my letters home. Years later when we were grown I knew this camp officer again. The gap between our ages had vanished and in real life now he seemed to me a rather colorless young lawyer. He did not remember about the hat.
>
> —Thomas Sancton, "The Silver Horn," *Harper's*

- What general statement does the story of the hat illustrate? <u>Little things that happened during those years seemed of great importance.</u>

- Note that this narrative follows **time order.***

Transitional Expressions

The simplest way to tell your reader that an example is going to follow is to say so: *"For example,* O. J. Simpson . . ." or "The pocket television, *for instance.* . . ." This partial list should help you vary your use of **transitional expressions** that introduce an illustration:

Transitional Expressions for Illustration

for instance	another instance of
for example	another example of
an illustration of this	another illustration of
a case in point is	here are a few examples
to illustrate	(illustrations, instances)

*For more work on time order, see Chapter 4, "Achieving Coherence," Part A.

■ Be careful not to use more than two or three of these transitional expressions in a single paragraph.*

PRACTICE 1   Read each of the following paragraphs of illustration. Underline each topic sentence. Note in the margin how many examples are provided to illustrate each general statement.

Paragraph 1: Artists, by choice and by repute, are eccentric, sensitive and antisocial. The poet Emile Verhaeren disconnected his door-bell because its ringing caused him pain; Schiller could write only when he soaked his feet in ice water; and Proust lined his study with cork to shut out all distracting noises. Flaubert, Holderlin and Swinburne holed themselves up in isolation, being unable to tolerate the hue and hustle of . . . crowds and barking dogs.

(6 examples)

—Colin Martindale, "What Makes Creative People Different," *Psychology Today*

Paragraph 2: Rulers and governments have a long history of censoring or destroying books and other forms of expression that they find objectionable. A book dictated by the prophet Jeremiah was burned by King Jehoiakim of Judah in 603 B.C.; and in the third century B.C. the Chinese emperor Shih Hwang-ti, who did things in a big way (he built the Great Wall), ordered the burning of *all* books, with the exception of those dealing with science, medicine, or agriculture. Even philosophers have been in favor of censorship: In the *Republic*, Plato proposed to censor "the writers of fiction" in order to keep "bad" works away from children.

(3 examples)

—Arthur Miller, *Miller's Court*

PRACTICE 2   Each example in a paragraph of illustration must clearly relate to and support the general statement. Each general statement in this practice is followed by several examples. Circle the letter of any example that does *not* clearly illustrate the generalization. Be prepared to explain your choices.

Example   The museum contains many fascinating examples of African art.
a. It houses a fine collection of Ashanti fertility dolls.
b. Drums and shamans' costumes are displayed on the second floor.
c. The museum building was once the home of Frederick Douglass.
(The fact that the building was once the home of Frederick Douglass is *not an example* of African art.)

1. Amelia Earhart dared to act beyond the limits of what society thought a woman could or should do.

*For a complete essay developed by illustration, see "Acting to Save Mother Earth," Chapter 18, Part A.

(a.) She saw her first plane at the Iowa State Fair.

b. She became a pilot and mechanic, entering the all-male world of aviation.

c. She presented her new husband with a marriage contract that gave both partners considerable freedom.

2. Every athlete has his or her own way of reacting to success.
   a. Daryl Strawberry celebrates a home run by inventing new versions of the high five.
   (b.) Janet Evans, a champion swimmer, has been an honor student at Stanford University.
   c. After a victory on the court, tennis star André Agassi occasionally peels off his wristband, headband, and even his shirt and hurls them into the screaming crowd.
   d. After making a successful between-the-legs pass, basketball player Mark Jackson spreads his arms and zooms upcourt like an airplane.

3. In the Arizona desert, one sees many colorful plants and flowers.
   a. Here and there are patches of pink clover.
   b. Gray green saguaro cacti rise up like giant candelabra.
   (c.) Colorful birds dart through the landscape.
   d. Bright yellow Mexican poppies bloom by the road.

4. Many people are still lively and creative in old age.
   a. Eighty-seven-year-old Mary Baker Eddy founded *The Christian Science Monitor*, one of the world's great newspapers.
   b. Pablo Picasso was engraving and drawing at ninety.
   c. When she was one hundred years of age, Grandma Moses was still painting.
   (d.) Painting is a fascinating hobby.

5. My boss seems to go out of his way to make me miserable.
   a. He waits until 4:45 P.M. and then runs to my desk with ten letters that "must be out tonight."
   (b.) He golfs every weekend.
   c. Last Friday he backed his car into mine and left with my fender.
   d. He allows me vacation time only in the coldest months of the year.

6. Many conveniences of modern life that we take for granted are less than sixty years old.
   a. It was not until 1969 that the Sony Corporation brought out a video recorder with tape in a cassette, causing a revolution in home viewing.
   b. Aluminum foil, introduced by Richard S. Reynolds in 1947, can now be found in almost every home in America.
   (c.) Hair coloring was first used by the ancient Egyptians.

7. Radio and television announcers sometimes make amusing slips of the tongue when they are on the air.
   a. An early morning talk show host broke for a commercial with "We'll be right back after these words from General Fools."

b. President Bush was once introduced on the evening news as President Botch.
c.) Announcers often earn good salaries.
d. A governor of Illinois was called to the microphone as the "Governor of the United States."

8. Many months in our calendar take their names from Roman gods or heroes.
a. Mars, the Roman war god, gave his name to March.
b. January was named for Janus, the god of doorways, whose two faces looked both forward and back.
c. August honors Augustus, the first Roman emperor and the second Caesar.
d.) December means *ten* because it was the tenth month in the Roman calendar.

PRACTICE 3   The secret of good illustration lies in well-chosen, well-written examples. Think of one example that illustrates each of the following general statements. Write out the example in sentence form (one to three sentences) as clearly and exactly as possible.

1. Many television commercials exaggerate the effectiveness or quality of the products they sell.

    Example: __One commercial for a dish soap claims it will make the user's hands__

    __soft and beautiful.__

    _____

2. In a number of ways, this college makes it easy for working students to attend.

    Example: __The college offers many courses on Saturdays and Sundays.__

    _____

    _____

3. Food prices have risen during the past several years.

    Example: __Five years ago I could buy hamburger for $1.29 a pound; today I__

    __must pay $2.29 a pound.__

    _____

4. Believing in yourself is 90 percent of success.

    Example: __My friend Paco owns a successful restaurant today because his__

    __enthusiasm and confidence attracted investors.__

    _____

5. Our college's food festival featured taste treats from many countries.

   Example: <u>One of my favorites was Jamaican goat curry served with a tangy</u>

   <u>mango chutney.</u>

   _____

6. Growing up in a large family can teach the value of compromise.

   Example: <u>The five Hanson children take turns choosing what game they will</u>

   <u>all play.</u>

   _____

7. Children say surprising things.

   Example: <u>My daughter said that she couldn't sit in her car seat because the</u>

   <u>Wizard of Oz was already sitting there.</u>

   _____

8. _____ is not keeping his (her) campaign promises to the voters.

   Example: <u>Senator Williams promised to fight for more federal funds for street</u>

   <u>repair in our major cities, but he hasn't done anything about that issue since he</u>

   <u>was elected.</u>

Checklist: The Process of Writing an Illustration Paragraph

Refer to this checklist of steps as you write an illustration paragraph of your own.

_____ 1. Narrow the topic in light of your audience and purpose.

_____ 2. Compose a topic sentence that can honestly and easily be supported by examples.

_____ 3. Freewrite or brainstorm to find six to eight examples that support the topic sentence. If you wish to use only one example or a narrative, sketch out your idea. (You may want to freewrite or brainstorm before you narrow the topic.)

_____ 4. Select only the best two to four examples and drop any examples that do not relate to or support the topic sentence.

_____ 5. Make a plan for your paragraph, numbering the examples in the order in which you will present them.

_____ 6. Write a draft of your illustration paragraph, using transitional expressions to show that an example or examples will follow.

_____ 7. Revise as necessary, checking for support, unity, logic, and coherence.

_____ 8. Proofread for errors in grammar, punctuation, sentence structure, spelling, and mechanics.

Suggested Topic Sentences for Illustration Paragraphs

1. A sense of humor can make difficult times easier to bear.

2. In my family, certain traditions (or values or beliefs) are very important.

3. Unfortunately, many great athletes behave in such a way that they are very poor role models for the young people who look up to them.

4. Painful experiences sometimes teach valuable lessons.

5. In many ways, women are not yet treated as men's equals in the workplace.

6. Some enjoyable activities in this area are inexpensive or even free.

7. I do (do not) perform well under pressure.

8. Many musicians have used their talents to support social causes in recent years.

9. Despite the high divorce rate, a few couples seem to know the secret of a wonderful marriage.

10. Some unusual characters live in my neighborhood.

11. Some professors are masters at helping their students learn.

12. The way people dress may reveal their personalities.

13. Films (or television programs) often contain unnecessary violence.

14. Sometimes the best-planned vacations do not work out.

15. Choose one of these sayings (or one of your own favorites). First, state whether you think the saying is true; then use examples from your own experience to support your view.

    a. Beauty is only skin deep.
    b. Honesty is the best policy.
    c. Luck comes to those who earn it.
    d. Necessity is the mother of invention.

6

Narration

To **narrate** is to tell a story that explains what happened, when it happened, and who was involved.

A news report may be a narrative about how Congress voted, what the president did, or how a child was rescued from a burning building. When you read a bedtime story to your children, you are reading them a narrative.

In a letter to a friend, you might want to write a narrative detailing how you were hired for your new job; your narrative could emphasize the fact that your relaxed and confident manner throughout the interview impressed your future employer. Or you might wish to retell what happened on your first skiing trip, when a minor accident proved to you that you prefer tamer recreation.

However, no matter what your narrative is about, it must make a *point:* it must clearly tell what you want your reader to learn or take away from the story.

Topic Sentence

Here is the topic sentence of a **narrative** paragraph:

> Last September, I watched my ten-year-old grandson act like an adult in an emergency.

- The writer begins a narrative paragraph with a topic sentence that tells the point of the narrative.

- What is the point of this narrative?

  to show how the grandson acted like an adult in an emergency

Paragraph and Plan

Here is the entire paragraph:

> Last September, I watched my ten-year-old grandson act like an adult in an emergency. While cleaning the living room carpet, I tripped and fell over the vacuum cleaner hose. At first, I was dazed. Soon I realized that my left arm hurt terribly. I called to my grandson Joel, who was the only other person at home. When Joel saw me on the floor, his face went pale. Then he calmly took charge of the situation. He went to the phone and dialed for emergency help. I heard him give our address, exact details of what had happened, and a description of the position I was lying in. I could tell that he was carefully listening to the instructions he was given. Returning to the living room, Joel covered me with a wool blanket and told me that an ambulance was on its way. He sat by my side in the ambulance and stayed with me while the doctor treated me. My sprained arm bothered me for only three weeks, but I will always feel proud of what my grandson did on that day.

- The body of a narrative paragraph is developed according to time, or chronological, order.* That is, the writer explains the narrative—the entire incident—as a series of smaller events or actions in the order in which they occurred. By keeping to strict chronological order, the writer helps the reader follow the story more easily and avoids interrupting the narrative with, *But I forgot to mention that before this happened. . . .*

- What smaller events make up this narrative?

  I tripped and fell; I called to my grandson; his face went pale; he called for help;

  he covered me; he sat by my side in the ambulance; he stayed with me while I

  was being treated.

  _____

  _____

Before writing this narrative paragraph, the writer probably brainstormed or freewrote to gather ideas and then made a plan like this:

Topic sentence: Last September, I watched my ten-year-old grandson act like an adult in an emergency.

*For more work on time, see Chapter 4, "Achieving Coherence," Part A.

Event 1:   I tripped and fell.
—dazed
—left arm hurt

Event 2:   I called to Joel, my grandson.

Event 3:   His face went pale.

Event 4:   He took charge and called for help.
—provided information
—listened to instructions

Event 5:   He covered me.

Event 6:   He sat by my side in the ambulance.

Event 7:   He stayed with me while I was being treated.

- Note that all of the events occur in chronological order.

- Also note that the first three events provide background information—they tell what led up to the grandson's actions.

- Finally, note that the specific details of certain events (like 1 and 4 above) make the narrative more vivid.

Transitional Expressions

Since narrative paragraphs tell a story in **chronological** or **time order,** transitional expressions that indicate time can be useful.*

Transitional Expressions for Narratives

after	finally	soon
as (soon as)	later	then
before	meanwhile	upon
during	next	when
first	now	while

PRACTICE 1   Read the following narrative paragraph carefully and answer the questions.

Walt Disney might be the only filmmaker who claimed to owe his success to a rodent. At first, Disney was an animator who produced a cartoon

*For a complete essay developed by narration, see "Maya Lin's Vietnam War Memorial," Chapter 18, "Types of Essays," Part B.

series called "Oswald the Rabbit." Then he decided to launch out on his own. Right after he realized that he needed a new animated character, he remembered a friendly mouse from a studio he had once worked in. He decided to name his new character after this old friend, whom he fondly called Mortimer Mouse. Later, he changed the name to Mickey. After a few cartoons appeared, Mickey Mouse fever swept the nation. Soon, he even became an international figure. The French called him "Michel Souris" while the Italians dubbed him "Topolo." During World War II, "Mickey-Mouse" became a secret password in the Allied Command. Disney created many other lovable characters, but none achieved the popularity of that cute little mouse with the white gloves.

■ What is the point of the narrative? _Disney's unusual debt to a mouse_

_____

■ What events make up this narrative paragraph?

List them: _Disney produced "Oswald the Rabbit"; he named his new_

character Mortimer Mouse after a mouse that used to live in his old studio; later

he changed the name to Mickey; after a few cartoons, Mickey Mouse fever

swept the nation; "Mickey-Mouse" became a password during World War II.

_____

_____

_____

PRACTICE 2   Here are three plans for narrative paragraphs. The events in the plans are not in correct chronological order. The plans also contain events that do not belong in each story. Number the events in the proper time sequence and cross out any irrelevant ones.

1. Aesop's fable about a dog and his reflection teaches a lesson about greed.

    _3_   He thought he saw another dog with another piece of meat in his mouth, so he decided to get that one too.

    _5_   Now the dog had nothing at all to eat.

    _1_   A dog was happily carrying a piece of meat in his mouth.

    _____   ~~The dog was brown with white spots.~~

_2_ While crossing a bridge, he saw his reflection in the water of a running brook.

_4_ When he snapped at the reflection, the meat dropped from his mouth into the water and sank.

2. On March 9, 1862, during the Civil War, the first battle between iron-covered ships changed sea warfare forever.

_2_ Two hours later, the *Monitor*, which looked like a prehistoric monster, ran out of ammunition and moved into shallow water in order to reload.

____ ~~The Civil War lasted from 1861 to 1865.~~

_4_ After four hours, the *Merrimac* made her escape from the battle scene because she was leaking and her smokestack was broken.

_3_ When the *Monitor* returned, the *Merrimac*, resembling an iron barn, lured her into deep water, then suddenly swung around and rammed her, barely leaving a dent.

_5_ Neither iron-clad ship had really won the battle, but the wooden fighting ship was now a thing of the past.

_1_ At first, the two strange looking ships—the North's *Monitor* and the South's *Merrimac*—just kept circling each other, firing at close range, but causing no damage.

3. The debut of our singing group at the college talent show last Saturday was a total disaster.

_4_ Halfway through our act, our lead singer's microphone went dead for three minutes.

_1_ Calvin arrived so hoarse that he could hardly sing at all.

____ ~~The theater is in Horace Hall.~~

_2_ The announcer introduced us as the "Huge Notes" instead of the "High Tones."

_5_ All the lights in the theater flashed on and off throughout our last song.

_3_ Starting our first song a half-beat too late, Dina threw the rhythm off for the rest of us.

PRACTICE 3   Here are topic sentences for three narrative paragraphs. Make a plan for each paragraph, placing the events of the narrative in the proper time sequence.

1. When I was _____ , help came from an unexpected source.

_____

_____

_____

_____

_____

_____

2. The first day of being on my own was not what I had expected.

_____

_____

_____

_____

_____

_____

3. Last year, _____ learned something important about himself/herself.

_____

_____

_____

_____

_____

PRACTICE 4   Assume that you are sending the picture on the next page to a close friend and that you are writing a brief letter explaining the narrative behind the photograph. That is, invent a story to go with the photograph. In your topic sentence, state the point of your narrative. Then list all the events of the narrative in chronological or time order. Your narrative can be serious, funny, or informative.

Checklist: The Process of Writing a Narrative Paragraph

Refer to this checklist of steps as you write a narrative paragraph of your own.

_____ 1. Narrow the topic in light of your audience and purpose.

_____ 2. Compose a topic sentence that tells the point of the story.

_____ 3. Freewrite or brainstorm for all of the events and details that might be part of the story. (You may want to freewrite or brainstorm before you narrow the topic.)

_____ 4. Select the important events and details; drop any that do not clearly relate to the point in your topic sentence.

_____ 5. Make a plan for the paragraph, numbering the events in the correct time (chronological) sequence.

_____ 6. Write a draft of your narrative paragraph, using transitional expressions to indicate time sequence.

_____ 7. Revise as necessary, checking for support, unity, logic, and coherence.

_____ 8. Proofread for errors in grammar, punctuation, sentence structure, spelling, and mechanics.

Suggested Topics for Narrative Paragraphs

1. A favorite family story
2. A lesson about life
3. The discovery that a parent is also a friend
4. A laugh at yourself
5. An important decision
6. A breakthrough (emotional, physical, spiritual, and so on)
7. Your or someone else's best (or worst) date
8. A typical morning (workday or weekend)
9. A first day at college (or at a new job)
10. A triumphant (or embarrassing) moment
11. A special event from your childhood
12. A story that ends with a surprise
13. A strange dream
14. Something you dared to do
15. An incident that made you happy (or proud)

7

Description

To **describe** something—a person, a place, or an object—is to capture it in words so others can imagine it or see it in the mind's eye.

The best way for a writer to help the reader get a clear impression is to use language that appeals to the senses: sight, sound, smell, taste, and touch. For it is through the senses that human beings experience the physical world around them, and it is through the senses that the world is most vividly described.

Imagine, for instance, that you have just gone boating on a lake at sunset. You may not have taken a photograph, yet your friends and family can receive an accurate picture of what you have experienced if you *describe* the pink sky reflected in smooth water, the creak of the wooden boat, the soothing drip of water from the oars, the occasional splash of a large bass jumping, the faint fish smells, the cool and darkening air. Writing down what your senses experience will teach you to see, hear, smell, taste, and touch more acutely than ever before.

Description is useful in English class, the sciences, psychology—anywhere that keen observation is important.

Topic Sentence

Here is the topic sentence of a descriptive paragraph:

> On November 27, 1922, when archaeologist Howard Carter unsealed the door to the ancient Egyptian tomb of King Tut, he stared in amazement at the fantastic objects heaped all around him.

use this as an example

- The writer begins a descriptive paragraph by pointing out what will be described. What will be described in this paragraph?

  The writer will describe King Tut's tomb.

- The writer can also give a general impression of this scene, object, or person. What overall impression of the tomb does the writer provide?

The writer gives the impression that the heaps of fantastic objects in King Tut's

tomb were an amazing sight.

Paragraph and Plan

Here is the entire paragraph:

what is described to reinforce idea of amazing?

> On November 27, 1922, when archaeologist Howard Carter unsealed the door to the ancient Egyptian tomb of King Tut, he stared in amazement at the fantastic objects heaped all around him. On his left lay the wrecks of at least four golden chariots. Against the wall on his right sat a gorgeous chest brightly painted with hunting and battle scenes. Across from him was a gilded throne with cat-shaped legs, arms like winged serpents, and a back showing King Tut and his queen. Behind the throne rose a tall couch decorated with animal faces that were half hippopotamus and half crocodile. The couch was loaded with more treasures. To the right of the couch, two life-sized statues faced each other like guards. They were black, wore gold skirts and sandals, and had cobras carved on their foreheads. Between them was a second sealed doorway. Carter's heart beat loudly. Would the mummy of King Tut lie beyond it?

- The overall impression given by the topic sentence is that the tomb's many objects were amazing. List three specific details that support this impression.

1. wrecks of four golden chariots
2. chest painted with hunting and battle scenes
3. gilded throne with cat-shaped legs

- Note the importance of words that indicate richness and unusual decoration in helping the reader visualize the scene.* List as many of these words as you can:

golden, gorgeous, brightly painted, gilded, cat-shaped legs, winged serpents,

animal faces half hippopotamus and half crocodile, treasures, life-sized statues,

gold skirts and sandals, cobras carved on their foreheads

paint a picture

*For more work on vivid language, see Chapter 15, "Revising for Language Awareness."

- This paragraph, like many descriptive paragraphs, is organized according to space order.* The author uses transitional expressions that show where things are. Underline the transitional expressions that indicate place or position.

Before composing this descriptive paragraph, the writer probably brainstormed and freewrote to gather ideas and then made a plan like this:

Topic sentence: On November 27, 1922, when archaeologist Howard Carter unsealed the door to the ancient Egyptian tomb of King Tut, he stared in amazement at the fantastic objects heaped all around him.

1. To the left:	chariots —wrecked —golden
2. To the right:	a gorgeous chest —brightly painted with hunting and battle scenes
3. Across the room:	a throne —gilded —cat-shaped legs —arms like winged serpents
4. Behind the throne:	a couch —decorated with faces that were half hippopotamus and half crocodile
5. To the right of the couch:	two life-sized statues —black —gold skirts and sandals —cobras carved on foreheads
6. Between the two statues:	a second sealed doorway
7. Conclusion:	expectation that King Tut's mummy was beyond the second door

- Note how each detail supports the topic sentence.

Transitional Expressions

Since space order is often used in description, **transitional expressions** indicating place or position can be useful:

*For more work on space order and other kinds of order, see Chapter 4, "Achieving Coherence," Part A.

helps make picture clearer

> ## Transitional Expressions
> ## Indicating Place
>
> | | |
> |---|---|
> | next to, near | on top, beneath |
> | close, far | toward, away |
> | up, down, between | left, right, center |
> | above, below | front, back, middle |

Of course, other kinds of order are possible. For example, a description of a person might have two parts: details of physical appearance and details of behavior.*

PRACTICE 1   Read the following paragraph carefully and answer the questions.

Someone read aloud

> The woman who met us had an imposing beauty. She was tall and large-boned. Her face was strongly molded, with high, almost Indian-looking cheekbones and skin the color of mahogany. She greeted us politely but did not smile and seemed to hold her head very high, an effect exaggerated by the abundant black hair slicked up and rolled on the top of her head. Her clothing was simple, a black sweater and skirt, and I remember thinking that this woman, dressed in showier garments, would have seemed overwhelming.

1. What overall impression does the writer give of the woman?

   ✓   The impression is that the woman had a regal and imposing beauty.

   _____

   _____

✓ 2. What specific details support this general impression?   tall; high

   cheekbones; mahogany skin; head held high; hair piled high on head; unsmiling

   expression

   _____

   _____

✓ 3. What kind of order does the writer use?   space order

   _____

   _____

*For a complete essay developed by description, see "Disney's Perfect World," Chapter 18, Part C.

PRACTICE 2   It is important that the details in a descriptive paragraph support the overall impression given in the topic sentence. In each of the following plans, one detail has nothing to do with the topic sentence; it is merely a bit of irrelevant information. Find the irrelevant detail and circle the letter.

what detail doesn't fit?

1. It was clearly a bird lover's room.
    a. two blue parakeets whistled in a small cage
    b. huge red and yellow parrot on a perch
    c. on sofa, needlepoint pillows shaped like birds
    (d.) birds make interesting pets
    e. pictures of birds on the walls
    f. large book, *Birds of the World*, on coffee table

2. In the photograph from 1877, Chief Joseph looks sad and dignified.
    a. long hair pulled back, touched with gray
    b. dark eyes gaze off to one side, as if seeing a bleak future
    c. strong mouth frowns at the corners
    d. ceremonial shell necklaces cover his chest
    (e.) Nez Perce tribe once occupied much of the Pacific Northwest

3. In my mind's eye is a plan for the perfect workout room.
    a. complete Nautilus set in center
    b. stationary cycle near the door
    c. on shelf above the bike, a color TV
    (d.) exercise helps me think more clearly
    e. hot tub with view of the woods through one-way glass
    f. spotless blue carpet

4. On the plate lay an unappetizing hamburger.
    a. burned bun, black on the edges
    (b.) burger cost two dollars
    c. fat dripping from the hamburger onto the plate
    d. parts of burger uncooked and partially frozen
    e. sour smell of the meat

5. In a field near the edge of town is an illegal dump site.
    a. fifty or more rusting metal drums, some leaking
    b. pools of green-black liquid on the ground
    (c.) in the distance, view of the mountains
    d. wildflowers and cottonwood trees dead or dying
    e. large sign reading "Keep Out—Toxic Chemicals"

PRACTICE 3   Here is a list of topic sentences for descriptive paragraphs. Give five specific details that would support the overall impression given in each topic sentence. Appeal to as many of the senses as possible. Be careful not to list irrelevant bits of information.

Example | Stopped in time by the photographer, my mother appears (confident).

(handwritten: Shows in what way she appears confident*)*

Details: a. her hair swept up in a sophisticated pompadour

b. a determined look in her young eyes

c. wide, self-assured smile

d. her chin held high

e. well-padded shoulders

(These five details support *confident* in the topic sentence.)

1. This was (clearly) a music lover's room. *(handwritten:* Why? *)*

(handwritten: place objects in the room to show how it is a music lover who lives here. *)*

a. a grand piano at one end

b. music stand with flute laid across it

c. shelves of books about music

d. CD player on one shelf with collection of discs

e. stacks of music on a desk

2. The prizefighter looked tough and fearless.

a. bulging muscles in his arms

b. jaws set

c. teeth clenched

d. hair bristling

e. feet firmly on the ground

Show this w/ details;

3. Spaghetti and meatballs were splattered all over the white kitchen.

a. blotches of sauce on wall behind stove
_____

b. pool of sauce on stove top
_____

c. crusted saucepan in sink
_____

d. stray spaghetti noodles hanging off edge of stove
_____

e. plates on counter with leftover spaghetti spilling over them
_____

4. The auto repair shop was alive with activity.

a. a car rising on a hydraulic lift
_____

b. one tired-looking worker hammering out dents on a car
_____

c. two men repainting a green truck
_____

d. one woman checking the exhaust system of a car
_____

e. telephone constantly ringing as customers call for appointments
_____

5. The buildings on that street look sadly run-down.

a. paint peeling from weathered, old buildings
_____

b. some windows broken or covered with cardboard
_____

c. other windows covered with dirt and grease
_____

    d. <u>sagging roofs with loose tiles</u>

    _____

    e. <u>screen doors open or attached by only one hinge</u>

    _____

6. The beach on a hot summer day presented a constant show.

    a. <u>children running and splashing in the water</u>

    _____

    b. <u>sunbathers rubbing lotion on themselves</u>

    _____

    c. <u>dogs chasing sticks and balls</u>

    _____

    d. <u>vendors selling soda and ice cream bars</u>

    _____

    e. <u>sea gulls circling and diving for food</u>

    _____

7. During the first week of classes, the college bookstore is wall-to-wall confusion.

    a. <u>crowds of students pushing to get into the store</u>

    _____

    b. <u>cartons of books clogging the aisles</u>

    _____

    c. <u>spilled piles of books on the shelves</u>

    _____

    d. <u>students shouting out their orders to harried salespeople</u>

    _____

    e. <u>separate, but unmarked, registers for cash, check, or credit card sales</u>

    _____

8. The automobile seemed like something from the twenty-first century.

    a. <u>streamlined body</u>

    _____

b. hidden headlights and wipers
_____

_____

c. complicated instrument control panel
_____

_____

d. a computer voice telling passengers to fasten their seat belts
_____

_____

e. dark tinted windows
_____

_____

PRACTICE 4 Pick the description you like best from Practice 3. Choose a logical order in which to present the descriptive details and make a plan for a paragraph.

PRACTICE 5 On pages 90 and 91 are two photographs. Choose the one that most appeals to you. Then describe the photograph as clearly and accurately as you can, so that a reader who has not viewed it can see it in his or her mind's eye. In your topic sentence, state your overall impression of the person or scene in the photograph. Then develop this impression with details. You may wish to use space order to organize these details, moving from left to right, from top to bottom, and so on.

DO Both photos, cover not just the objects, but the feeling, tone, colours, etc

groups of 2:
Juanita, ~~Cathy~~ + (Brian)
Victor, Danielle Cathy
Robyn, Gregg
Antonette, Hermano
Teresa, Chris
Ray, Erica
Sally, Barry
Alfred, Vincent

Checklist: The Process of Writing a Descriptive Paragraph

Refer to this checklist of steps as you write a descriptive paragraph of your own.

_____ 1. Narrow the topic in light of your audience and purpose.

_____ 2. Compose a topic sentence that clearly points to what you will describe or gives an overall impression of the person, object, or scene.

_____ 3. Freewrite or brainstorm to find as many specific details as you can to capture your subject in words. Remember to appeal to your readers' senses. (You may want to freewrite or brainstorm before you narrow the topic.)

_____ 4. Select the best details and drop any irrelevant ones.

_____ 5. Make a plan for the paragraph, numbering the details in the order in which you will present them.

_____ 6. Write a draft of your descriptive paragraph, using transitional expressions wherever they might be helpful.

_____ 7. Revise as necessary, checking for support, unity, logic and coherence.

_____ 8. Proofread for errors in grammar, punctuation, sentence structure, spelling, and mechanics.

Suggested Topics for Descriptive Paragraphs

1. An unusual man or woman: for example, an athlete, an entertainer, a street person, a waitress, or a teacher you won't forget

2. A public place: emergency room, library, fast-food restaurant, town square, or theater lobby

fish on ice
winter

3. A classmate

4. The face of a criminal or someone in the news

5. A shop that sells only one item: cheese, soap, cowboy boots, car parts, flowers

6. An animal, bird, or insect you have observed closely

7. A possession you value

8. A photograph of yourself as a child

9. A scene of conflict or a scene of peace

10. A room that reveals something about its owner

11. An outdoor scene

12. A friend or someone you know well

13. The ugliest thing you have ever seen

14. A wealthy or a poor neighborhood

15. A bike, car, computer, or piece of machinery

place
smell
protection from
cold
water soaked
wooden trough
middle aged Asian
two man carrying
3 plastic bags-
showing their
contents to the
world

Kung fu
looking
shoes-

Black African perch

finger gestures
to
indicate desire for
fish

8

Process

Two kinds of **process paragraphs** will be explained in this chapter: the how-to paragraph and the explanation paragraph.

The **how-to paragraph** gives the reader directions on how he or she can do something: how to decorate a room, how to get to the airport, or how to plant a garden. The goals of such directions are the decorated room, the arrival at the airport, or the planted garden. In other words, the reader should be able to do something after he or she has read the paragraph.

The **explanation paragraph,** on the other hand, tells the reader how a particular event occurred or how something works. For example, an explanation paragraph might explain how an internal combustion engine works or how trees reproduce. After reading an explanation paragraph, the reader is not expected to be able to do anything, just to understand how it happened or how it works.

Process writing is useful in history, business, the sciences, sports, and many other areas.

Topic Sentence

Here is the topic sentence of a *how-to paragraph:*

> Learning to make a budget is the key to managing your hard-earned money.

- The writer begins a how-to paragraph with a topic sentence that clearly states the goal of the process—what the reader should be able to do.

- What should the reader be able to do after he or she has read the paragraph following this topic sentence?

    The reader should be able to make a budget.

TTh 1050-1205 CA 021

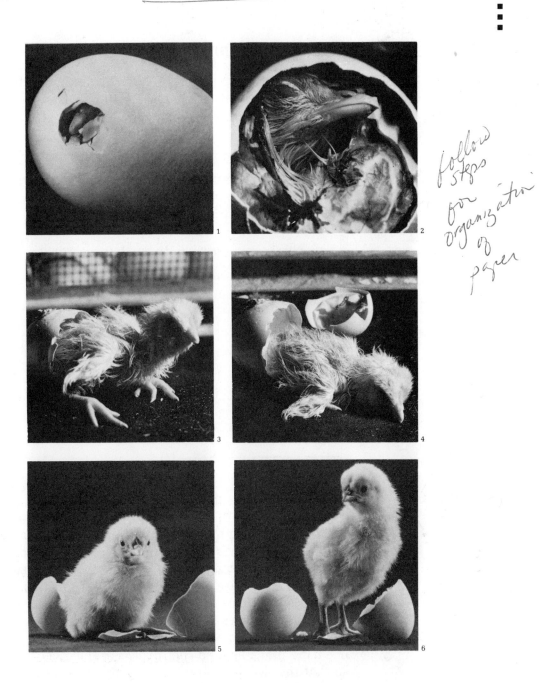

follow steps for organization of paper

✓■ What are they? __(1) deciding to quit, (2) withdrawing from substance, (3)__

__changing one's life, (4) staying off drugs__

■ Make a plan of the paragraph in your notebook.

Just as the photographs on this page show each stage in the process of a chick hatching, so your process paragraph should clearly describe each step or stage for the reader. Before you write, try to visualize the process as if it were a series of photographs.*

*For a complete essay developed by process, see "How to Prepare for a Final Exam," Chapter 18, Part D, and "Bottle Watching," page 241.

Transitional Expressions

Since process paragraphs rely on **chronological order,** or **time sequence,** words and expressions that locate the steps of the process in time are extremely helpful.

look at ✱

Transitional Expressions for Process

Beginning a Process	Continuing a Process		Ending a Process
(at) first	second, third step	when	finally
initially	until	while	at last
begin by	after(wards)	as soon as	
	then	as	
	next	upon	
	later	during	
	before	meanwhile	

PRACTICE 1　Read the following how-to paragraph carefully and answer the questions.

You are sitting in a restaurant quietly having a meal when suddenly a man nearby starts choking on a piece of food lodged in his throat. By using the Heimlich maneuver, you may be able to save this person's life. Your two hands are all you need to perform this lifesaving technique. First, position yourself behind the choking person. Then wrap your arms around the person's midsection, being careful not to apply any pressure to the chest or stomach. Once your arms are around the victim, clench one hand into a fist and cup this fist in the other hand. Now turn the fist so that the clenched thumb points toward the spot between the choker's navel and midsection. Finally, thrust inward at this spot using a quick, sharp motion. If this motion does not dislodge the food, repeat it until the victim can breathe freely.

1. What should you be able to do after reading this paragraph?

   You should be able to perform the Heimlich maneuver.

2. Are any "materials" necessary for this process?　The "materials" are your two hands.

3. How many steps are there in this paragraph? List them.

(1) position yourself behind the choking victim, (2) wrap your arms around the

victim's midsection, (3) clench one fist and cup it with other hand, (4) point

thumb end of fist between navel and midsection, (5) thrust inward here.

PRACTICE 2

√

Here are five plans for process paragraphs. The steps for the plans are not in the correct chronological order. The plans also contain irrelevant details that are not part of the process. Number the steps in the proper time sequence and cross out any irrelevant details.

1. Chewing gum is made entirely by machine.

___3___ Then the warm mass is pressed into thin ribbons by pairs of rollers.

___1___ First, the gum base is melted and pumped through a high-speed spinner that throws out all impurities.

_____ The gum base makes the gum chewy.

___2___ Huge machines mix the purified gum with sugar, corn syrup, and flavoring, such as spearmint, peppermint, or cinnamon.

___5___ Finally, machines wrap the sticks individually and then package them.

___4___ Knives attached to the last rollers cut the ribbons into sticks.

2. These directions will get you to the airport in time for the six o'clock flight to Lockwood.

___2___ When you get off at Woodrow, walk three blocks east on Woodrow to Hanson Place.

_____ The airport is not large enough to accommodate 747s.

___3___ At Hanson Place, catch the number 6 bus marked "City Limits," and take it to the last stop—the airport.

___1___ First, board the "City Square" bus on the corner of 18th Avenue and Gleason Place and go to Woodrow Avenue.

3. Changing the oil in your car is an easy process.

___3___ When the oil stops draining, screw the plug back on and lower the car.

_____ Car supply stores have good sales on oil.

_2_ After placing a plastic catch pan under the drain hole, remove the drain hole plug so all the old oil can pour out.

_6_ Finally, check the oil level and add more oil if the car needs it.

_1_ To drain the old oil, first set the hand brake and jack up the front end of the car.

_5_ Now pour in the fresh oil, and then start the engine and check for leaks.

_4_ Replace the oil filter with a clean one.

4. Robertson got his job through hard work and ingenuity.

_3_ After he got to know the companies thoroughly, he wrote for interviews with all of them.

_2_ Then he read everything he could find about each company, its history, and its prospects for the future.

_4_ During the interviews, he stressed what he could do for the company and played down what the company could do for him.

_____ ~~Robertson has two children, Beth and Joe, Jr.~~

_1_ He began by making a survey of the companies he might like to work for and then chose three that offered the best possibilities for employment.

_5_ A few weeks after the interviews, two of the firms offered him positions.

5. Because turtles are cold-blooded animals, they hibernate during the winter.

_2_ After finding the right place, they dig their winter home, bury themselves in the mud, and fall into a deep sleep.

_1_ As the winter turns cold, turtles begin to seek a spot in the mud near a pond to spend the winter.

_____ ~~Turtles make nice pets.~~

_4_ With the onset of spring, the ice on the pond melts and the thawing mud awakens these buried creatures to new life.

_3_ Throughout the winter, their metabolism remains low.

PRACTICE 3   Here are topic sentences for five process paragraphs. Make a plan for each paragraph, listing in proper time sequence all the steps that would be necessary to complete the process. Answers will vary.

1. Although I'm still not the life of the party, I took these steps to overcome my shyness at parties.

   Two weeks before the party, I told myself that others were as shy as I was.

   One week before the party, I selected clothes I feel comfortable in to wear

   to the party.

   On my way to the party, I rehearsed some conversation topics.

   At the party, I introduced myself to three new people.

   _____

2. Registration was a very complicated (or simple) process this semester.

   I picked the four courses I wanted to take.

   My advisor was in her office when I went to get her signature.

   The line at the registrar's office was short when I arrived.

   None of the courses I wanted was full, so I didn't have to choose   alternatives.

   _____

   _____

3. My morning routine gets me out of the house in twenty minutes.

   Brushing my teeth, shaving, and showering follow each other so quickly that

   they are like one step.

   While toweling off, I decide what I will wear and everything I need to take

   for the day.

   Next, I race to the kitchen to make breakfast and feed the cats.

   I eat breakfast in bits while dressing and packing up my knapsack.

4. Ted learned ____business skills____ in stages over a long period of
   time.

   As a child, he worked in Wertz's Candy Shop after school.

   In high school, he spent afternoons selling shoes at his uncle's store.

   He took several sales and marketing courses in college.

   In his senior year, Ted made excellent money selling health products out of

   his home.

   Finally, he opened his own T-shirt store in the mall after graduation.

5. Let me tell you how I gave up smoking.

I stopped first when I was around a lot of people—in restaurants and at

parties.

A month later, I quit smoking at work.

Next came weekends.

Finally, I stopped having my after-dinner cigarette.

Now I chew on toothpicks when I feel like smoking.

Checklist: The Process of Writing a Process Paragraph

Read these ↓

Refer to this checklist of steps as you write a process paragraph of your own.

_____ 1. Narrow the topic in light of your audience and purpose.

_____ 2. Compose a topic sentence that clearly states the goal or end result of the process you wish to describe.

_____ 3. Freewrite or brainstorm for as many steps as you can think of that might be part of the process. (You may want to freewrite or brainstorm before you narrow the topic.)

_____ 4. Drop any irrelevant information or steps that are not really necessary for your explanation of the process.

_____ 5. Make a plan for your paragraph, numbering the steps in the correct time (chronological) sequence.

_____ 6. Write a draft of your process paragraph, using transitional expressions to indicate time (chronological) sequence.

_____ 7. Revise as necessary, checking for support, unity, logic, and coherence.

_____ 8. Proofread for errors in grammar, punctuation, sentence structure, spelling, and mechanics.

*

Suggested Topics for Process Paragraphs

how to plant a garden

1. How to relax
2. How to prepare for a test
3. How an important discovery was made
4. How to choose a major
5. How to use the card catalogue in the library
6. How a particular machine works
7. How to get the most from your marriage or relationship
8. How to be a good friend
9. How to appear smarter than you really are
10. How a team won an important game
11. How to break up with someone
12. How to build a child's self-esteem
13. How to get somewhere by car or public transportation
14. How to prepare your favorite dish
15. How to _____

Ideas

How does Natural Selection work?
① Explain
② give examples/some historical info
③ summation as related to Now

Here you'll need to write on a Bio topic you know something about.

Describe the stages of the effects of Population growth on the environment.
① CO₂ / people / birth control
② pollution
③ deforestation, etc.

Process of classification

9
Definition

PART A   Single-Sentence Definitions
PART B   The Definition Paragraph

To **define** is to explain clearly what a word or term means.

As you write, you will sometimes find it necessary to explain words or terms that you suspect your reader may not know. For example, *net profit* is the profit remaining after all deductions have been taken; a *bonsai* is a dwarfed, ornamentally shaped tree. Such terms can often be defined in just a few carefully chosen words. However, other terms—like *courage, racism,* or *a good marriage*—are more difficult to define. They will test your ability to explain them clearly so that your reader knows exactly what you mean when you use them in your writing. They may require an entire paragraph for a complete and thorough definition.

In this chapter, you will learn to write one-sentence definitions and then whole paragraphs of definition. The skill of defining clearly will be useful in such courses as psychology, business, the sciences, history and English.

PART A

Single-Sentence Definitions

There are many ways to define a word or term. Three basic ones are **definition by synonym, definition by class,** and **definition by negation.**

Definition by Synonym

The simplest way to define a term is to supply a **synonym,** a word that means the same thing. A good synonym definition always uses an easier and more familiar word than the one being defined.

1. *Gregarious* means *sociable.*

2. *To procrastinate* means *to postpone needlessly.*

3. A *wraith* is a *ghost* or *phantom.*

4. *Adroitly* means *skillfully.*

Although you may not have known the words *gregarious, procrastinate, wraith,* and *adroitly* before, the synonym definitions make it very clear what they mean.

A synonym should generally be the same part of speech as the word being defined, so it could be used as a substitute. *Gregarious* and *sociable* are both adjectives; *to procrastinate* and *to postpone* are verbs; *wraith, ghost,* and *phantom* are nouns; *adroitly* and *skillfully* are adverbs.

5. Quarterback Dan Marino *adroitly* moved his team up the field.

6. Quarterback Dan Marino *skillfully* moved his team up the field.

■ In this sentence *skillfully* can be substituted for *adroitly.*

Unfortunately, it is not always possible to come up with a good synonym definition.

Definition by Class

The **class** definition is the one most often required in college and formal writing—in examinations, papers, and reports.

The class definition has two parts. First, the writer places the word to be defined into the larger **category,** or **class,** to which it belongs.

7. *Lemonade* is a *drink*...

8. An *orphan* is a *child*...

9. A *dictatorship* is a *form of government*...

Second, the writer provides the **distinguishing characteristics** or **details** that make this person, object, or idea *different* from all others in that category. What the reader wants to know is what *kind* of drink is lemonade? What *specific* type of person is an orphan? What *particular* form of government is a dictatorship?

> 10. *Lemonade* is a drink *made of lemons, sugar, and water.*
>
> 11. An *orphan* is a child *without living parents.*
>
> 12. A *dictatorship* is a form of government *in which one person has absolute control over his or her subjects.*

Think of class definitions as if they were in chart form:

Word	Category or Class	Distinguishing Facts or Details
lemonade	drink	made of lemons, sugar, and water
orphan	child	without living parents
dictatorship	form of government	one person has absolute control over his or her subjects

When you write a class definition, be careful not to place the word or term in too broad or vague a category. For instance, saying that lemonade is a *food* or that an orphan is a *person* will make your job of zeroing in on a distinguishing detail more difficult.

Here is a class definition of the animal pictured: A yak is an ox that is large, long-haired, and found wild or domesticated in Tibet.

Besides making the category or class as narrow as possible, be sure to make your distinguishing facts as specific and exact as you can. Saying that lemonade is a drink *made with water* or that an orphan is a child *who has lost family members* is not specific enough to give your reader an accurate definition.

Definition by Negation

A definition by **negation** means that the writer first says what something is not, and then says what it is.

13. A *good parent* does not just feed and clothe a child but loves, accepts, and supports that child for who he or she is.

14. *College* is not just a place to have a good time but a place to grow intellectually and emotionally.

15. *Liberty* does not mean having the right to do whatever you please but carries the obligation to respect the rights of others.

Definitions by negation are extremely helpful when you think that the reader has a preconceived idea about the word you wish to define. You say that *it is not* what the reader thought, but that *it is* something else entirely.

Here is a definition by negation: The grapefruit shield is not just another useless luxury item but a clever device that will allow you to enjoy grapefruit without the mess, sting, and embarrassment of spurting juice.

PRACTICE 1   Write a one-sentence definition by **synonym** for each of the following terms. Remember, the synonym should be more familiar than the term being defined.

1. *irate:* __To be irate is to be angry.__

2. *to elude:* __To elude someone is to keep away from him or her.__

3. *pragmatic:* __To be pragmatic is to be practical.__

4. *fiasco:* __A fiasco is a disaster.__

5. *elated:* __To be elated is to be overjoyed.__

PRACTICE 2   Here are five **class definitions.** Circle the category and underline the distinguishing characteristics in each. You may find it helpful to make a chart.

1. A *haiku* is a Japanese poem that has <u>seventeen syllables</u>.

2. A *homer* is a referee who <u>unconsciously favors the home team</u>.

3. An *ophthalmologist* is a doctor who <u>specializes in diseases of the eye</u>.

4. A *mentor* is a counselor who <u>guides, teaches, and assists another person</u>.

5. *Plagiarism* is stealing <u>writing or ideas that are not one's own</u>.

PRACTICE 3   Define the following words by **class definition.** You may find it helpful

to use this form: "A _____ is a _____
                        (noun)   (class or category)
that _____ ."
                        (distinguishing characteristic)

1. *hamburger:* __A hamburger is a sandwich consisting of a split bun and a ground__

  __beef patty.__

  _____

2. *bikini:* __A bikini is a two-piece swimsuit that is very scanty.__

  _____

  _____

3. *snob:* __A snob is a person who thinks he or she is, and acts as if he or she were,__

  __socially superior to others.__

  _____

4. *high tops:* High tops are sneakers that extend upward to cover and support the ankles.

5. *adolescence:* Adolescence is the period of life between puberty and maturity.

PRACTICE 4   Write a one-sentence definition by **negation** for each of the following terms. First say what each term is not; then say what it is.

1. *bravery:* Bravery is not being fearless; it is acting courageously in spite of fear.

2. *final exam:* A final exam is not just a way to make students suffer but an enforced review of everything learned in the course.

3. *self-esteem:* Self-esteem does not mean conceit but rather a healthy respect for oneself.

4. *intelligence:* Intelligence is not knowledge in a specific area; it is the capacity to acquire and apply knowledge.

5. *freedom of speech:* Freedom of speech is not just a phrase we learn in history class; it is a right guaranteed to each American to express his or her beliefs in public.

PART B

The Definition Paragraph

Sometimes a single-sentence definition may not be enough to define a word or term adequately. In such cases, the writer may need an entire paragraph in which he or she develops the definition by means of examples, descriptions, comparisons, contrasts, and so forth.

Topic Sentence

The topic sentence of a definition paragraph is often one of the single-sentence definitions discussed in Part A: definition by synonym, definition by class, definition by negation.

Here is the topic sentence of a definition paragraph:

> *Ambivalence* can be defined as a feeling or attitude that is both positive and negative at the same time.

- What kind of definition does the topic sentence use?

  class

- To what larger category or class does *ambivalence* belong?

  feeling or attitude

- What are the distinguishing details about *ambivalence* that make it different from all other feelings or attitudes?

  It is both positive and negative at the same time.

Paragraph and Plan

Here is the entire paragraph:

> *Ambivalence* can be defined as a feeling or attitude that is both positive and negative at the same time. For instance, a young woman might feel *ambivalent* about motherhood. She might want to have a child yet fear that motherhood will use up the energy she would like to spend on her career. Or a Michigan man who is offered a slightly higher salary in Arizona might be ambivalent about moving. He and his family don't want to leave their friends, their schools, and a city they love. On the other hand, they are tempted by a larger income and by Arizona's warm climate and clean air. Finally, two people may have ambivalent feelings about each other, loving and disliking each other at the same time. It hurts to be together, and it hurts to be apart; neither situation makes them happy.

- One effective way for a writer to develop the body of a definition paragraph is to provide examples.*

- What three examples does this writer give to develop the definition in the topic sentence?

  young woman ambivalent about motherhood; man ambivalent about moving;

  two people ambivalent about each other

- By repeating the word being defined—or a form of it—in the context of each example, the writer helps the reader understand the definition better: A young woman might feel *ambivalent*, a Michigan man might be *ambivalent*, and two people may have *ambivalent* feelings.

Before writing the paragraph, the writer probably brainstormed or freewrote to gather ideas and then made a plan like this:

Topic sentence: *Ambivalence* can be defined as a feeling or attitude that is both positive and negative at the same time.

Example 1:	A young woman —wants to have a child —yet fears motherhood will use up career energy
Example 2:	Michigan man and his family —don't want to leave friends, schools, city —tempted by income, climate, clean air
Example 3:	Two people —love each other —also dislike each other

- Note that each example in the body of the paragraph clearly relates to the definition in the topic sentence.

Although examples are an excellent way to develop a definition paragraph, other methods of development are also possible. For instance, you might compare and contrast† *love* and *lust, assertiveness* and *aggressiveness,* or *the leader* and *the follower.* You could also combine definition and persuasion.‡ Such a paragraph might begin *College is a dating service,* or *Alcoholism is not a moral weakness, but a disease.* The rest of the paragraph would have to persuade readers that this definition is valid.

There are no transitional expressions used specifically for definition paragraphs. Sometimes phrases like *can be defined as* or *can be considered* or *means that* can help alert the reader that a definition paragraph will follow.§

*For more work on examples, see Chapter 5, "Illustration."
†For more work on contrast, see Chapter 10, "Comparison and Contrast."
‡For more work on persuasion, see Chapter 12, "Persuasion."
§For an entire essay developed by definition, see "Winning," Chapter 18, Part E.

PRACTICE 5   Read the following paragraph carefully and then answer the questions.

A feminist is *not* a man-hater, a masculine woman, a demanding shrew, or someone who dislikes housewives. A feminist is simply a woman or man who believes that women should enjoy the same rights, privileges, opportunities, and pay as men. Because society has deprived women of many equal rights, feminists have fought for equality. For instance, Susan B. Anthony, a famous nineteenth-century feminist, worked to get women the right to vote. Today, feminists want women to receive equal pay for equal work. They support a woman's right to pursue her goals and dreams, whether she wants to be an astronaut, athlete, banker, or mother. On the home front, feminists believe that two partners who work should equally share the housework and child care. Because the term is often misunderstood, some people don't call themselves feminists even though they share feminist values. But courageous feminists of both sexes continue to speak out for equality.

1. The definition here spans two sentences. What kind of definition does

   the writer use in sentence 1? ___definition by negation___

   _____

2. What kind of definition appears in sentence 2? ___definition by___

   ___class___

3. The paragraph is developed by describing some key beliefs of femi-

   nists. What are these? ___equal rights, equal pay for equal work, freedom to___

   ___pursue goals and dreams, working couples should share housework and child___

   ___care___

   _____

4. Which point is supported by an example? ___Feminists have fought for___

   ___equality. Example: Susan B. Anthony___

5. Make a plan of the paragraph.

   ___Topic sentence(s): A feminist is *not* a man-hater, a masculine woman, a___

   ___demanding shrew, or someone who dislikes housewives. A feminist is simply a___

   ___woman or man who believes that women should enjoy the same rights, privileges,___

   ___oportunities, and pay as men.___

   ___—fights for equal rights___

   ___—wants equal pay for equal work___

—wants freedom for women to pursue goals and dreams

—believes working partners should share housework, child care

—some people afraid to call themselves feminists

PRACTICE 6   Read the following paragraphs and answer the questions.

Induction is reasoning from particular cases to general principles, that is, the scientific method: you look at a number of examples, then come to a general conclusion based on the evidence. For instance, having known twenty-five people named Glenn, all of whom were men, you might naturally conclude, through induction, that all people named Glenn are men. The problem with inductive reasoning, however, is Glenn Close, the movie actress.

Deduction is reasoning from the general to the particular. One starts from a statement, known or merely assumed to be true, and uses it to come to a conclusion about the matter at hand. Once you know that all people have to die sometime and that you are a person, you can logically deduce that you, too, will have to die sometime.

—Judy Jones and William Wilson, "100 Things
Every College Graduate Should Know,"
Esquire

1. What two terms are defined? __"induction" and "deduction"__

2. What kind of definition is used in both topic sentences? __class__
   definition

3. In what larger category do the writers place both induction and deduction? __reasoning__

4. What example of induction do the writers give?__Glenn as a man's name__

5. What example shows the *problem* with induction? __Glenn Close is a__
   woman

6. What example of deduction do the writers give? __that every person__
   must die

PRACTICE 7   Here are some topic sentences for definition paragraphs. Choose one that interests you and make a plan for a paragraph, using whatever method of development seems appropriate.

1. An optimist is someone who usually expects the best from life and from people.

2. Prejudice means prejudging people on the basis of race, creed, age, or sex—not on their merits as individuals.

3. A wealthy person does not necessarily have money and possessions, but he or she might possess inner wealth—a loving heart and a creative mind.

4. Registration is a ritual torture that students must go through before they can attend their classes.

5. Pride and vanity are very different character traits.

PRACTICE 8   The Martians have landed. You have been chosen to answer their questions about several things they have noticed on Earth. Since they can read English but cannot speak it, you must write a clear paragraph defining one of the following: *money, clothes, television, cars, the President of the United States.* Begin with a one-sentence definition; then discuss, giving examples and details that fully define the word or term for your Martian readers.

Checklist: The Process of Writing a Definition Paragraph

Refer to this checklist of steps as you write a definition paragraph of your own.

_____ 1. Narrow the topic in light of your audience and purpose.

_____ 2. Compose a topic sentence that uses one of the three basic methods of definition discussed in this chapter: synonym, class, or negation.

_____ 3. Decide on the method of paragraph development that is best suited to what you want to say.

_____ 4. Freewrite or brainstorm to gather ideas that may be useful in your definition paragraph. (You may want to freewrite or brainstorm before you narrow the topic.)

_____ 5. Select the best ideas and drop any ideas that do not clearly relate to the definition in your topic sentence.

_____ 6. Make a plan for your paragraph, numbering the ideas in the order in which you will present them.

_____ 7. Write a draft of your definition paragraph, using transitional expressions wherever they might be helpful.

_____ 8. Revise as necessary, checking for support, unity, logic, and coherence.

_____ 9. Proofread for errors in grammar, punctuation, sentence structure, spelling, and mechanics.

Suggested Topics for Definition Paragraphs

1. Success (or failure)

2. The con artist (or loner, dreamer, big mouth, perfectionist, bully, or party pooper)

3. Country and western music (or hard rock, gospel, rap, or some other type of music)

4. Common sense

5. A good marriage (or a good partner, parent, or friend)

6. The racing car (football, fashion, or other) fanatic

7. A dead-end job

8. An interesting term you know from reading (*placebo, acid rain, apartheid, inflation, hubris,* and so forth)

9. Spring break

10. A racist (sexist, feminist, or other *-ist*)

11. The night person (or morning person)

12. An illness you know about (arthritis, alcoholism, diabetes, etc.)

13. A technical term you know from work or a hobby

14. A slang term you or your friends use

15. A word or term from another language that you know (for example, *machismo* or *déjà vu*)

10
Comparison and Contrast

PART A   The Contrast and the Comparison Paragraphs
PART B   The Comparison-Contrast Paragraph

To contrast two persons, places, or things is to examine the ways in which they are different. To compare them is to examine the ways in which they are similar.

When you go shopping, you often compare and contrast. For instance, you might compare and contrast two brands of frozen foods in order to get the most nutritious meals for your family.

Your employer might ask you to write a comparison and contrast report on two computers, two telephone answering services, or two types of packing crates. Your task would be to gather all the relevant information about these products to show in what ways they are similar and in what ways they are different. Your report may then help your employer choose one product or service over another.

Comparison and contrast, then, helps the reader understand one person, place, or thing (item) in terms of another.

PART A

The Contrast and the Comparison Paragraphs

Topic Sentence

Here is the topic sentence of a contrast paragraph:

> Although black bass and striped bass are two familiar fish in the world of salt water fishing, their habits are altogether different.

- The writer begins a contrast paragraph with a topic sentence that clearly states what two persons, things, or ideas will be contrasted.

- What two things will be contrasted?

  black bass and striped bass

- What word or words in the topic sentence make it clear that the writer will contrast black bass and striped bass?

  altogether different

Paragraph and Plan

Here is the entire paragraph:

> Although black bass and striped bass are two familiar fish in the world of salt water fishing, their habits are altogether different. The black bass feeds steadily on fiddler crabs, mussels, skimmer, and clams, usually staying in one locale and waiting intently for its victims to pass. Building its home in the rocks that lie along the bottom of the ocean wall, the black bass is well protected from the fisherman, whose line will often snag and break before this fish is taken. Still, the best way to catch the black bass is with a hook and sinker. On the other hand, its cousin, the striped bass, feeds on smaller fish, squid, tin cans, or any glittering and wiggly object. The striped bass remains in constant motion, always searching for its prey. Its home is almost anywhere. This fish is usually caught near the surface of the water or several feet from the bottom. Trolling is the best way to catch the striped bass since this fish doesn't remain in one spot for long. Striped bass and black bass, however, do have one thing in common: both make delicious eating after being caught and then fried in an open pan.
>
> —Paul Gazzola (Student)

- The writer first provides information about (A) black bass and then gives contrasting parallel information about (B) striped bass.

- What information about (A) black bass does the writer provide in the first half of the paragraph? The writer discusses the fish's feeding habits, its movements, its home, and the best way to catch it.

- What contrasting parallel information does the writer provide about striped bass in the second half of the paragraph? _The writer discusses_
the same four points.

_____

_____

_____

- Why do you think the writer chose to present the points of contrast in this order? _It makes sense to discuss diet and other habits before discussing_
how best to catch each fish.

_____

_____

_____

Before composing the paragraph, the writer probably brainstormed or freewrote to gather ideas and then made a plan like this:

Topic sentence: Although black bass and striped bass are two familiar fish in the world of salt water fishing, their habits are altogether different.

Points of Contrast	A: Black Bass	B: Striped Bass
1. diet	fiddler crabs, mussels, skimmer, and clams	smaller fish, squid, glittering object, and so on
2. motion	stays in one place	constantly moves
3. home	rocks at bottom	almost anywhere
4. how caught	hook and sinker	trolling

Organized in this manner, the plan for this contrast paragraph helps the writer make sure that the paragraph will be complete. That is, if diet is discussed for black bass, then diet must also be discussed for striped bass, and so on, for all the points of contrast.

Here is another way to write the same contrast paragraph:

> Although black bass and striped bass are two familiar fish in the world of salt water fishing, their habits are altogether different. Staying in one locale and waiting intently for its victims to pass, the black bass feeds steadily on fiddler crabs, mussels, skimmer, and clams. Its cousin, the striped bass, however, remains in constant motion, always searching for its prey. The striped bass feeds on smaller fish, squid, tin cans, or any glittering or wiggly object. The black bass builds its home in the rocks that lie along the bottom of the ocean wall; it is well protected from the fisherman, whose line will often snag and break before this fish is taken. On the other hand, the striped bass makes its home almost anywhere; it is usually caught near the surface of the water or several feet from the bottom. The best way to catch the black bass is with a hook and sinker, whereas trolling is the best way to land a striped bass because this fish does not remain in one spot very long. Striped bass and black bass, however, do have one thing in common: both make delicious eating after being caught and then fried in an open pan.

- Instead of giving all the information about the black bass and then going on to the striped bass, this paragraph moves back and forth between the black bass and the striped bass, dealing with *each point of contrast separately.*

Use either one of these two patterns when writing a contrast or a comparison paragraph:

> 1. Present all the information about **A** and then provide parallel information about **B**:
>
> **First all A:**   point 1
>   point 2
>   point 3
>
> **Then all B:**   point 1
>   point 2
>   point 3

- This pattern is good for paragraphs and for short compositions. The reader can easily remember what was said about A by the time he or she gets to B.

2. Move back and forth between **A** and **B**. Present one point about **A** and then go to the parallel point about **B**. Then move to the next point and do the same:

First A, point 1;   **then B,** point 1

First A, point 2;   **then B,** point 2

First A, point 3;   **then B,** point 3

- The second pattern is best for longer papers, where it might be hard for the reader to remember what the writer said about *A* by the time he or she gets to *B* a few paragraphs later. By going back and forth, the writer makes it easier for the reader to keep the contrasts or comparisons in mind.

What you have learned so far about planning a contrast paragraph holds true for a comparison paragraph as well. Just remember that a **contrast** *stresses differences*, whereas a **comparison** *stresses similarities*.

Here is a comparison paragraph:

Although separated by many years in age, Carolyn's father and her son are remarkably similar. A gray-haired elderly gentleman, Carolyn's father always carefully selects his clothing before he steps into the public view. His greatest treat is to browse through encyclopedias, dictionaries, and almanacs to absorb scraps of knowledge, minute facts, and out-of-the-way statistics. At dinner, he enjoys surprising his family with the annual rainfall of Australia or the average length of the tiger shark. Billy, Carolyn's seven-year-old, also carefully surveys his clothing each morning to see what would best suit his mood. He too loves to read, but he confines himself to children's books on exotic lands. Just like his grandfather, at mealtime he parades his store of odd facts before the family, relishing the surprised looks on their faces. Maybe the old saying should be "Like grandfather, like grandson."

- What words in the topic sentence does the writer use to indicate that

a comparison will follow? ___remarkably similar_____

- In what ways are Carolyn's father and son similar? ___Both carefully___

choose what they will wear, both love to read, and both entertain the family at

dinner with what they have read.

- Which pattern of presentation does the writer use? _The writer_

  presents all the information about the grandfather first and then all parallel

  information about the grandson.

  _____

- What transitional expressions stress the similarities? _also; too; just_

  like

- Make a plan of this comparison paragraph.

Transitional Expressions

Transitional expressions in contrast paragraphs stress opposition and difference:

Transitional Expressions for Contrast	
although	on the other hand
whereas	in contrast
but	while
however	yet
conversely	unlike

Transitional expressions in comparison paragraphs stress similarities:

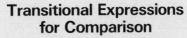
read aloud

Transitional Expressions for Comparison	
in the same way	just as . . . so
and, also, in addition	similarly
as well as	like
both, neither	too
each of	the same

As you write, avoid using just one or two of these transitional expressions. Learn new ones from the list and practice them in your paragraphs.*

PRACTICE 1   Read the following paragraph carefully and answer the questions.

Two different groups of black musicians grew up in New Orleans. The first of these, the slaves, brought with them the music of Africa and the influences of Caribbean music. Denied education and opportunity by slavery, they improvised, making instruments from gourds, bamboo, and bone. They created songs charged with emotion: work songs, chants, and spirituals. In contrast to the slaves, the "free men of color" were raised as Creoles. Formally educated and sometimes sent to European schools, they were well versed in classical music, and they played classical instruments. During the Reconstruction period, these two groups of musicians were flung together. The brilliant child of this unlikely union was jazz.

1. How can you tell from the topic sentence whether a contrast or a comparison will follow? The word *different* suggests a contrast.

2. What two groups are being contrasted? black slave musicians and Creole musicians

3. What information does the writer provide about the slaves? They were uneducated; they fashioned makeshift musical instruments; they created emotional work songs, chants, and spirituals.

4. What parallel information does the writer provide about the "free men of color"? They were formally educated and were trained in classical music; they played classical instruments.

5. What pattern does the writer of this paragraph use to present the contrasts? The writer presents all the information about slave musicians and then the contrasting information about the Creole musicians.

*For an entire essay developed by comparison-contrast, see "Two Childhoods," Chapter 18, Part F.

6. What transitional expression does the writer use to stress the shift from A to B? _____in contrast to_____

PRACTICE 2   The next paragraph is hard to follow because it lacks transitional expressions that emphasize contrasts. Revise the paragraph, adding transitional expressions of contrast. Strive for variety. Answers may vary.

Mexico City is a fascinating mixture of modern and traditional ways of life. The city boasts sleek skyscrapers, such as the famous Latin America Tower. ~~It~~ However, it also proudly displays its graceful Spanish colonial palaces and public buildings, many of which are three hundred years old. Glittering stores line the main shopping streets, offering the latest in international styles of clothing and house furnishings. ~~Old-fashioned~~ On the other hand, old-fashioned street markets fill the city, from the great food market of the Merced to stalls in small plazas selling such items as piñatas and paper Christmas decorations. Huge modern factories in the northern section turn out most of Mexico's clothing, steel, cement, appliances, and electrical supplies. ~~Craftspeople~~ In contrast, craftspeople line the city's streets with their handmade baskets, pottery, metalwork, and textiles.

PRACTICE 3   Below are three plans for contrast paragraphs. The points of contrast in the second column do not follow the same order as the points in the first column. In addition, one detail is missing. First, number the points in the second column to match those in the first. Then fill in the missing detail.

1. **Shopping at a Supermarket**   **Shopping at a Local Grocery**

   1. carries all brands   __4__ personal service

   2. lower prices   __3__ closed on Sundays

   3. open seven days a week   __2__ prices often higher

   4. little personal service   __1__ doesn't carry all brands

   5. no credit   __5__ credit available for steady
                                                customers

2. **My Son**

1. fifteen years old

2. likes to be alone

3. reads a lot

4. is an excellent cook

5. wants to go to chef school

My Daughter

__4__ good at making minor household repairs

__2__ likes to be with friends

__3__ doesn't like to read

__5__ expects to attend a technical college

__1__ seventeen years old

3. **Job A**

1. good salary

2. office within walking distance

3. two-week vacation

4. work alone

5. lots of overtime

6. no health insurance

Job B

__3__ three-week vacation

__4__ work on a team with others

__2__ one-hour bus ride to office

__6__ health insurance

__5__ no overtime

__1__ good salary

PRACTICE 4   Here are five topics for either contrast or comparison paragraphs. Compose two topic sentences for each topic, one for a possible contrast paragraph and one for a possible comparison paragraph. Answers will vary.

Topic	Topic Sentences
Example Two members of my family	A. My brother and sister have different attitudes toward exercise.
	B. My parents are alike in that they're both easygoing.
1. Two friends or coworkers	A. Tom Bogyo and Amanda Gill have very different attitudes towards success.

B. Although Sylvia and Miako excel

at different sports, both are

talented athletes.

2. Two kinds of music or dancing   A. Jazz and classical music are

performed in very different ways.

_____

B. Appalachian folk songs and

Protestant hymns have several

common features.

3. You as a child and you as an   A. I am less selfish than I was as a
   adult

child.

_____

B. As an adult I have some of the

same dislikes I had as a child.

_____

4. Two vacations   A. Some people like to relax on

vacation, but others like to spend

most of their time sightseeing.

_____

B. My vacations in both Barbados

and Sun Valley included miles of

walking.

5. Two teachers   A. Mr. Larkin tends to be friendly

towards his students while Mr.

Jordan is a bit standoffish.

B. Professors Hazard and Jodice

both involve their classes in lively

discussions.

PRACTICE 5   Here are four topic sentences for comparison or contrast paragraphs. Pick just one point of comparison or of contrast that interests you and write a few sentences explaining that particular comparison or contrast. Use a transitional expression wherever you feel it is necessary to show similarities or differences. Answers will vary.

1. When it comes to movies (TV shows, books, entertainment), Demetrios and Arlene have totally different tastes.

    Demetrios loves action and violence, whereas Arlene will leave the theater at

    the first sight of blood on the screen.

    _____

    _____

2. A compact car and a limousine have little in common except that they both have four wheels.

    A compact car is obviously relatively small, whereas a limousine is large. A

    compact comfortably seats three people. A limousine, on the other hand, holds

    as many as six.

    _____

3. Although there are obvious differences, the two neighborhoods (blocks, homes) have much in common.

    The large house has an extensive and beautiful garden. The smaller house also

    has a garden, less extensive but equally colorful.

    _____

    _____

4. Paying taxes is like having a tooth pulled.*

    Both are painful. It hurts to write that tax check and to have that tooth pulled.

    But by doing both we avoid worse pain in the future.

    _____

PRACTICE 6   Choose your favorite of the topic sentences you wrote in Practice 4 and make a plan for a paragraph. Arrange the points of contrast or comparison in the plan and number them in the order in which you wish to present them to the reader.

*For more work on this kind of comparison, see Chapter 15, "Revising for Language Awareness," Part D.

Journals: compare these two. Regard all of their similarities.

Writing Assignment 1

Study the two people in this photograph: the man and the baby he is holding. Then write a paragraph *contrasting* the two people. Begin by stating your overall impression of the differences between them. Then develop your paragraph with details that support your topic sentence—details of facial expression, posture, age, and so forth. Remember to conclude your paragraph; don't just stop abruptly.

Checklist: The Process of Writing a Contrast or Comparison Paragraph

Refer to this checklist of steps as you write a contrast or comparison paragraph of your own.

_✓_ 1. Narrow the topic in light of your audience and purpose.

_____ 2. Compose a topic sentence that clearly states that a contrast or a comparison will follow.

_____ 3. Freewrite or brainstorm for as many points of contrast or comparison as you can think of. (You may want to freewrite or brainstorm before you narrow the topic.)

_____ 4. Choose the points you will use, and drop any details that are not really part of the contrast or the comparison.

_____ 5. List parallel points of contrast or of comparison for both A and B.

_____ 6. Make a plan, numbering all the points of contrast or comparison in the order in which you will present them in the paragraph.

_____ 7. Write a draft of your contrast or comparison paragraph, using transitional expressions that stress either differences or similarities.

_____ 8. Revise as necessary, checking for support, unity, logic, and coherence.

_____ 9. Proofread for errors in grammar, punctuation, sentence structure, spelling, and mechanics.

Suggested Topics for Contrast or Comparison Paragraphs

1. Compare or contrast two attitudes toward money (the spendthrift and the miser), marriage (prefer being married and prefer being single), or ambition (aggressive go-getter and laid-back person)

2. Compare or contrast two ways of raising children: permissive and strict

3. Compare or contrast being a worker and being a student

4. Compare or contrast two bosses

5. Compare or contrast two magazines or newspapers that you read

6. Compare or contrast two high schools or colleges that you have attended (perhaps one in the United States and one in a different country)

7. Compare or contrast life in a big city and life in a small town

8. Compare or contrast two brands of products you have purchased or might purchase: TV sets, automobiles, microwaves, down coats

9. Compare or contrast two apartments or houses that you have lived in

10. Compare or contrast your parent and your spouse or partner

- Mom + girlfriend

PART B

The Comparison-Contrast Paragraph

Sometimes an assignment will call for you to write a paragraph that both compares and contrasts, that stresses both similarities and differences.

Here is a comparison-contrast paragraph:

> Although contemporary fans would find the game played by the Knickerbockers—the first organized baseball club—similar to modern baseball, they would also note some startling differences. As now, the four bases of the playing field were set in a diamond shape, ninety feet from one another. Nine players took the field. The object of the game was to score points by hitting a pitched ball and running around the bases. The teams changed sides after three outs. However, the earlier game was also different. The umpire sat at a table along the third base line instead of standing behind home plate. Unlike the modern game, the players wore no gloves. Rather than firing the ball over the plate at ninety miles an hour, the pitcher gently tossed it underhand to the batter. Since there were no balls and strikes, the batter could wait for the pitch he wanted. The game ended, not when nine innings were completed, but when one team scored twenty-one runs, which were called "aces."

■ How are the Knickerbockers' game and modern baseball similar?

Both have four bases ninety feet apart in a diamond shape, nine players, both

score points by runs, both have three outs.

■ How are these two versions of the game different? In Knickerbockers'

game, umpire sat at table on third base line, players wore no gloves, pitcher

gently tossed the ball, there were no balls and strikes, a team needed twenty-

one "aces" to win, and there were no innings. In modern game, umpire stands

at home plate, pitcher fires the ball, there are balls and strikes, the team with

the most runs wins, and game is composed of nine innings.

■ What transitional expressions in the paragraph emphasize similarities

and differences? ___although, as now, however, unlike, rather than, not when,__

__but when__

Before composing this comparison-contrast paragraph, the writer probably brainstormed or freewrote to gather ideas and then made a plan like this:

Topic Sentence: Although contemporary fans would find the game played by the Knickerbockers—the first organized baseball club—similar to modern baseball, they would also note some startling differences.

Comparisons	Knickerbockers	Modern Game
Point 1	four bases, ninety feet apart, in diamond shape	
Point 2	nine players	
Point 3	scoring points	
Point 4	three outs	
Contrasts		
Point 1	umpire sat at third base line	umpire at home plate
Point 2	no gloves	gloves
Point 3	pitcher gently tossed ball	pitcher fires ball at plate
Point 4	no balls and strikes	balls and strikes
Point 5	twenty-one "aces" to win, no innings	most runs to win, nine innings

■ A plan such as this makes it easier for the writer to organize a great deal of material.

■ The writer begins by listing all the points of comparison—how the Knickerbockers' game and modern baseball are similar. Then the writer lists all the points of contrast—how they are different.

PRACTICE 7   Here is a somewhat longer comparison and contrast (two paragraphs). Read it carefully and answer the questions.

No meal eaten in the Middle East ends without coffee or tea, but coffee takes precedence most of the time. Coffee is a social beverage, offered to

shows
now
detail

guests by housewives and to customers by merchants; to refuse it borders upon insult. There are two distinct but similar ways of preparing it, Turkish and Arabic. Both are served black, in cups the size of a demitasse or smaller. And both are brewed by starting with green beans, roasting them to a chocolate brown color, pulverizing them at once, either with mortar and pestle or in a handsome cylindrical coffee mill of chased brass, and quickly steeping them in boiling water.

The Turkish version is made in a coffee pot that has a long handle to protect the fingers from the fire and a shape narrowing from the bottom to the open neck to intensify the foaming action as the coffee boils up. Water, sugar and coffee are stirred together to your taste; then, at the first bubbling surge, the pot is whisked from the fire. It is returned briefly one or two more times to build up the foamy head, which is poured into each cup in equal amounts, to be followed by the rest of the brew, grounds and all. The dregs soon settle to the bottom, and the rich, brown coffee that covers them is ready to be enjoyed, with more sugar if you like. The Arabs prepare coffee in a single boil; they almost never use sugar; they pour the liquid into a second pot, leaving the sediment in the first, and then add such heady spices as cloves or cardamon seeds.

—Foods of the World/Middle Eastern Cooking,
Time-Life Books, Inc.

1. What two things does this writer contrast and compare? The writer
   contrasts and compares the Turkish and the Arabic methods of preparing
   coffee.

2. What words indicate that both contrast *and* comparison will follow?
   distinct but similar

3. How are Arabic and Turkish coffee similar? Both are served black in
   small cups; both start with green beans that are roasted dark brown and then
   immediately ground and steeped in boiling water.

4. How are Arabic and Turkish coffee different? Turkish coffee is boiled
   several times and is served with sugar and the dregs in the cup. Arabic coffee
   is boiled once and served with spices rather than sugar and grounds.

5. On a separate sheet of paper, make a plan for these paragraphs.

Writing Assignment 2

On the next two pages are photos of two couples. Study closely the details of facial expression, gesture, clothing, and so forth. For a paragraph that both *compares and contrasts* the two couples, jot down possible similarities and differences. Ask yourself, "What is my impression of each pair? How do they seem to be getting along with each other? How are the couples alike and how are they different?" Then plan and write your paragraph.

If you prefer, write a paragraph comparing and contrasting the two women *or* the two men.

Working Through the Comparison-Contrast Paragraph

You can work through the comparison-contrast paragraph in the same way as you do a comparison or a contrast paragraph. Follow the steps in the earlier checklist, but make certain that your paragraph shows both similarities and differences.

pairs similar? compare them.

Suggested Topics for Comparison-Contrast Paragraphs

1. Compare and contrast two ways to prepare for an examination

2. Compare and contrast the requirements for two jobs or careers

3. Compare and contrast your life now with your life five years ago

4. Compare and contrast two films with different ratings

5. Compare and contrast two players of the same sport or of two different sports

6. Compare and contrast two attitudes toward a subject (sexual activity, marriage, careers, children, and so forth)

7. Compare and contrast learning from experience and learning from books

8. Compare and contrast living alone and living with your parents

9. Compare and contrast customs in two different cultures

10. Compare and contrast two popular television programs

11

Classification

To classify is to gather into types, kinds, or categories according to a single basis of division.

Mailroom personnel, for example, might separate incoming mail into four piles: orders, bills, payments, and inquiries. Once the mail has been divided in this manner—according to which department should receive each pile—it can be efficiently delivered.

The same information can be classified in more than one way. The Census Bureau collects a variety of data about the people living in the United States. One way to classify this data is by age group—the number of people under eighteen, between eighteen and fifty-five, and over fifty-five. Such information might be useful in developing programs for college-bound youth or for the elderly. Other ways of dividing the population are by geographic location, occupation, family size, level of education, and so on.

Whether you classify rocks by their origin for a science course or children by their stages of growth for a psychology course, you will be organizing large groups into smaller, more manageable units that can be explained to your reader.

Topic Sentence

Here is the topic sentence for a classification paragraph:

> Traditional musical instruments can be classified as stringed, wind, and percussion instruments according to how they produce sound.

- The writer begins a classification paragraph with a topic sentence that clearly states what group of people or things will be classified.

- What group of items will be classified? __traditional musical instruments__

- Into how many categories will they be divided? What are the categories?

three: stringed instruments, wind instruments, and percussion instruments

Paragraph and Plan

Here is the entire paragraph:

> Traditional musical instruments can be classified as stringed, wind, and percussion instruments according to how they produce sound. Stringed instruments produce music through the vibration of taut strings that are plucked, strummed, or bowed. The violin, the banjo, and the guitar are examples of stringed instruments. Wind instruments are sounded by wind, usually by the player's breath; this category includes the clarinet, the tuba, the trumpet, and so on. Rather than being bowed or blown, percussion instruments make sounds when they are struck. Obvious examples of percussion instruments are drums, gongs, and cymbals. Surprisingly, the piano is also considered a percussion instrument because, when the player touches a key, a small hammer inside the piano strikes a string.

- On what basis does the writer classify musical instruments?

how they produce sound

- What information does the writer provide about the first type, stringed instruments?

Stringed instruments produce sound through the plucking, strumming, or bowing

of a taut string.

- Giving occasional examples is also helpful in a classification. What examples does the writer give of a stringed instrument?

violin, banjo, guitar

- What information does the writer provide about the second type, wind instruments?

The sound of wind instruments is produced by wind, usually a player's breath.

■ What examples does the writer give of a wind instrument?

clarinet, tuba, trumpet

■ What information does the writer provide about the third type, percussion instruments?

Percussion instruments produce sound when they are struck.

■ What examples of percussion instruments does the writer provide?

drum, gong, cymbals, piano

Before composing the paragraph, the writer probably brainstormed or freewrote to gather ideas and then made a plan like this:

Topic sentence: Traditional musical instruments can be classified as stringed, wind, and percussion instruments according to how they produce sound.

Type 1:   Stringed instruments
—vibration of taut string
—plucked, strummed, bowed
—examples: violin, banjo, guitar

Type 2:   Wind instruments
—sounded by wind
—examples: clarinet, tuba, trumpet

Type 3:   Percussion instruments
—struck
—examples: drums, gongs, cymbals
—piano, surprisingly, is a percussion instrument

■ Note that the body of the paragraph discusses all three types of instruments mentioned in the topic sentence and does not add any new ones.

This classification paragraph sticks to a single method of classification: *how instruments produce sound.* If the paragraph had also discussed a fourth category—*instruments made of wood*—the initial basis of classification would fall apart because *instruments made of wood* have nothing to do with *how instruments produce sound.*

There is no set rule about which category to present first, second, or last in a classification paragraph. However, the paragraph should follow some kind of **logical sequence:** from the least to the most expensive category, from the largest to the smallest category, and so on.*†

Transitional Expressions

Transitional expressions in classification paragraphs stress divisions and categories:

Transitional Expressions for Classification

can be divided	the first type
can be classified	the second kind
can be categorized	the last category

PRACTICE 1   Read the following paragraph carefully and answer the questions.

Commercial wool is divided into three categories: new, reprocessed, and reused. Most clothing is made from new, 100 percent virgin fiber wool. Reprocessed wool is made by reclaiming previously spun yarn or woven or knitted fabric that has never been used. Reprocessed wool lacks strength and beauty because its fibers have been weakened considerably during operations that reduce the original goods to fibers that can be respun to make less expensive, lower quality fabric. Reused wool is regenerated from fabric or clothing previously used. Wool from this last category is rarely used in garments made in this country but often appears as an ingredient in inexpensive wool camping blankets.

—Joanne Mattera, "The Story of Cotton, Wool, and Silk," *East West Journal*

1. How many categories are there and what are they?

    There are three categories: new, reprocessed, and reused.

2. On what basis does the writer classify wool?

    The writer classifies wool according to whether and how much it has been

    used.

3. Make a plan of the paragraph on a separate sheet of paper.

*For more work on order, see Chapter 4, "Achieving Coherence," Part A.
†For a complete essay developed by classification, see "The Potato Scale," Chapter 18, Part G.

PRACTICE 2   Each group of things or persons below has been divided according to a single basis of classification. However, one item in each group does not belong—it does not fit that single basis of classification.

Read each group of items carefully; then circle the letter of the one item that does *not* belong. Next write the single basis of classification that includes the rest of the group.

Example | shirts
a. cotton
b. suede
(c.) short-sleeved
d. polyester

_material they are made of_____

1. Shoes
   a. flat heels
   b. 2-inch heels
   (c.) patent leather
   d. 3-inch heels

   height of heels_____

2. Beds
   a. double
   b. twin
   (c.) water
   d. king

   size_____

3. House guests
   (a.) relatives
   b. very neat people
   c. slobs
   d. moderately neat people

   neatness_____

4. Contact lenses
   (a.) soft
   b. green
   c. brown
   d. lavender

   color_____

5. Apartments
   a. two bedroom
   b. three bedroom
   (c.) penthouse
   d. studio apartment

   number of bedrooms_____

6. Dates
   (a.) very good looking
   b. sometimes pay
   c. always pay
   d. expect me to pay

   financial arrangements_____

7. Plants
   a. full sunlight
   b. shade
   (c.) sandy soil
   d. moderate light

   amount of light needed_____

8. Drivers
   a. drivers who obey the speed limit
   (b.) teen-age drivers
   c. speeders
   d. creepers

   how fast they drive_____

PRACTICE 3   Any group of persons, things, or ideas can be classified in more than one way. For instance, students in your class can be classified on the basis of height (short, average, tall) or on the basis of class participation (often participate, sometimes participate, never participate). Both of these groupings are valid classifications of the same group of people.

Think of two ways in which each of the following groups could be classified. **Answers will vary**.

Example	Group		Can Be Classified According to
	Bosses	(A)	how demanding they are
		(B)	how generous they are
	1. Members of my family	(A)	how old they are
		(B)	how emotional they are
	2. Vacations	(A)	where you take them
		(B)	when you take them
	3. Fans of a certain sport	(A)	how many games they attend
		(B)	how long they have been fans
	4. Hats	(A)	what they are made of
		(B)	how much they cost
	5. Magazines	(A)	whom they appeal to
		(B)	content

PRACTICE 4   Listed below are three groups of people or things. Decide on a single basis of classification for each group and the categories that would develop from your basis of classification. Finally, write a topic sentence for each of your classifications.

Example	Group	Basis of Classification	Categories
	Professors at Pell College	methods of instruction	1. lectures
			2. class discussions
			3. some of both

Topic sentence: Professors at Pell College can be classified according to their methods of instructions: those who lecture, those who encourage class discussion, and those who do both.

Group	Basis of Classification	Categories
1. Car owners	how clean they keep their cars	very neat
		moderately neat
		not neat at all
		_____

Topic sentence: Most car owners can be classified according to how clean they keep their vehicles: those whose cars are very neat, those whose cars are moderately neat, and those whose cars are not neat at all.

_____

Group	Basis of Classification	Categories
2. Summer jobs	how much time spent outdoors	all outdoor work
		all indoor work
		both indoor and outdoor work

Topic sentence: The summer jobs available in our town fall into three categories: jobs done outdoors, jobs done indoors, and jobs done both indoors and outdoors.

_____

Group	Basis of Classification	Categories
3. Ways of reacting to crisis	how much emotion shown	people who cry or yell
		people who talk calmly
		people who don't talk at all

Topic sentence: People react to crises in very different ways: by crying or yelling, by talking calmly, or by remaining completely silent.

_____

_____

PRACTICE 5   On a separate sheet of paper, make a plan for one of the classifications in Practice 4. Be sure that you have listed all the categories that naturally evolve from your basis of classification; remember, every person or thing in the larger group should fit into one of these categories. Then write a brief description of each of the categories in your classification, perhaps including an example of each.

Checklist: The Process of Writing a Classification Paragraph

Refer to this checklist of steps as you write a classification paragraph.

_____ 1. Narrow the topic in light of your audience and purpose. Think in terms of a group of people or things that can easily be classified into types or categories.

_____ 2. Decide on a single basis of classification. This basis will depend on what information you wish to give your audience.

_____ 3. Compose a topic sentence that clearly shows what you are dividing into categories or types. If you wish, your topic sentence can state the basis on which you are making the classification and the types that will be discussed in the paragraph.

_____ 4. List the categories into which the group is being classified. Be sure that your categories cover all the possibilities. Do not add any new categories that are not logically part of your original basis of classification.

_____ 5. Freewrite or brainstorm for information, details, and examples for each of the categories. (You may want to freewrite or brainstorm before you narrow the topic.)

_____ 6. Select the best details and examples and drop those that are not relevant to your classification.

_____ 7. Make a plan for your paragraph, numbering the categories in the order in which you will present them.

_____ 8. Write a draft of your classification paragraph, using transitional expressions wherever they might be helpful.

_____ 9. Revise as necessary, checking for support, unity, logic, and coherence.

_____ 10. Proofread for errors in grammar, punctuation, sentence structure, spelling, and mechanics.

Suggested Topics for Classification Paragraphs

1. Shoppers in a department store
2. Movie-goers
3. Types of friends
4. Students in a particular class
5. Problems facing college freshmen or someone new to a job
6. Women or men you date
7. Clothing in your closet
8. Players of a certain sport
9. College classes
10. Parents' ways of disciplining their children
11. Coworkers
12. Kinds of success
13. Soap operas
14. Kinds of marriages
15. Brands of athletic shoes, or some other product

12

Persuasion

what does persuade mean?

To persuade is to convince someone that a particular opinion or point of view is the correct one.

Any time you argue with a friend, you are each trying to persuade, to convince, the other that your opinion is the right one. Commercials on television are another form of persuasion as advertisers attempt to convince viewers that the product they sell—whether a deodorant, soft drink, or automobile—is the best one to purchase.

You will often have to persuade in writing. For instance, if you want a raise, you would have to write a persuasive letter to convince your employer that you deserve one. You would have to back up, or support, your request with proof, listing important projects you have completed, noting new responsibilities you have taken upon yourself, or showing how you have increased sales.

Once you learn how to persuade logically and rationally, you will be less likely to accept the false, misleading, and emotional arguments that you hear and read every day. Persuasion is vital in nearly all college courses and in most careers.

Topic Sentence

Here is the topic sentence of a persuasive paragraph:

Read

> Passengers should refuse to ride in any vehicle driven by someone who has been drinking.

✓ ▪ The writer begins a persuasive paragraph by stating clearly what he or she is arguing for or against. What will this persuasive paragraph argue against?

This paragraph will argue against riding with a driver who has been drinking.

- Words like *should*, *ought*, and *must* (and the negatives *should not*, *ought not*, and *must not*) are especially effective in the topic sentence of a persuasive paragraph.

Paragraph and Plan

Here is the entire paragraph:

Read aloud

> Passengers should refuse to ride in any vehicle driven by someone who has been drinking. First and most important, such a refusal could save lives. The National Council on Alcoholism reports that drunk driving causes 25,000 deaths and 50 percent of all traffic accidents each year. Not only the drivers but the passengers who agree to travel with them are responsible. Second, riders might tell themselves that some people drive well even after a few drinks, but this is just not true. Dr. Burton Belloc of the local Alcoholism Treatment Center explains that even one drink can lengthen the reflex time and weaken the judgment needed for safe driving. Other riders might feel foolish to ruin a social occasion or inconvenience themselves or others by speaking up, but risking their lives is even more foolish. Finally, by refusing to ride with a drinker, one passenger could influence other passengers or the driver. Marie Furillo is an example. When three friends who had obviously been drinking offered her a ride home from school recently, she refused, despite the driver's teasing. Hearing Marie's refusal, two of her friends got out of the car. Until the laws are changed and a vast re-education takes place, the bloodshed on American highways will probably continue. But there is one thing people can do: They can refuse to risk their lives for the sake of a party.

- The first reason in the argument **predicts the consequence.** If passengers refuse to ride with drinkers, what will the consequence be?

  Lives could be saved.

What facts support?

- The writer also supports this reason with **facts.** What are the facts?

  Drunk driving causes 25,000 deaths and 50 percent of all traffic accidents each

  year.

Think what might the opposite pt Be?

- The second reason in the argument is really an **answer to the opposition.** That is, the writer anticipates the critics. What point is the writer answering?

  The writer is answering the point that some people drive well even after having

  a few drinks.

- The writer supports this reason by **referring to an authority.** That is, the writer gives the opinion of someone who can provide unbiased and valuable information about the subject. Who is the authority and what does this person say?

  Dr. Burton Belloc of the Alcoholism Treatment Center notes that even one drink

  affects a driver's reflexes.

- The third reason in the argument is that "risking your life is foolish." This reason is really another **answer to the opposition.** What point is the writer answering?

  The writer is answering the point that people hesitate to be "party poopers."

- The final reason in the argument is that "one passenger could influence others." What **example** does the writer supply to back up this reason?

  Marie Furillo refused a ride home from school because the driver had been

  drinking. Her refusal influenced the two passengers to get out of the car.

- Persuasive paragraphs can begin either with the most important reason and then continue with less important ones, or they can begin with the least important reasons, saving the most important for last.* This paragraph begins with what the author considers *most* important. How can you tell?

  The writer states that the first point is the most important.

Before composing this persuasive paragraph, the writer probably brainstormed or freewrote to gather ideas and then made a plan like this:

Topic sentence: Passengers should refuse to ride in any vehicle driven by someone who has been drinking.

Reason 1:   Refusal could save lives (**predicting a consequence**)
—statistics on deaths and accidents (**facts**)
—passengers are equally responsible

Reason 2:   Riders might say some drinkers drive well; not true (**answering the opposition**)
—Dr. Belloc's explanation (**referring to authority**)

Reason 3:   Others might feel foolish speaking up, but risking lives is more foolish (**answering the opposition**)

*For work on order of climax, see Chapter 4, "Achieving Coherence," Part A.

Reason 4: One rider might influence other passengers —Marie Furillo **(example)**

Conclusion: Bloodshed will probably continue, but people can refuse to risk their lives.

- Note how each reason clearly supports the topic sentence.

Transitional Expressions

The following transitional expressions are helpful in persuasive paragraphs:

Transitional Expressions for Persuasion

Give Reasons	***Answer the Opposition***	***Draw Conclusions***
first (second, third)	of course	therefore
another, next	some may say	thus
last, finally	nevertheless	hence
because, since, for	on the other hand	consequently
	although	

Methods of Persuasion

The drinking-and-driving example showed the basic kinds of support used in persuasive paragraphs: **facts, referring to an authority, examples, predicting the consequences,** and **answering the opposition.** Although you will rarely use all of them in one paragraph, you should be familiar with them all. Here are some more details:

Topic: present facts about pollution

1. Facts: Facts are simply statements of *what is.* They should appeal to the reader's mind, not just to the emotions. The source of your facts should be clear to the reader. If you wish to prove that children's eyesight should be checked every year by a doctor, you might look for supporting facts in appropriate books and magazines, or you might ask your eye doctor for information. Your paper might say, "Many people suffer serious visual impairment later in life because they received insufficient or inadequate eye care when they were children, according to an article in *Better Vision.*"

Avoid the vague "everyone knows that" or "it is common knowledge" or "they all say." Such statements will make your reader justifiably suspicious of your "facts."

2. Referring to an authority: An **authority** is an expert, someone who can be relied on to give unbiased facts and information. If you wish to convince your readers that smoking is a dangerous habit, you might use one of the Surgeon General's warnings that appear on every pack of cigarettes: "Smoking causes lung cancer, heart disease, emphysema, and may complicate pregnancy." The Surgeon General is an excellent and knowledgeable authority whose opinion on medical matters is considered valid and unbiased.

Avoid appealing to "authorities" who are interesting or glamorous but who are not experts. A basketball player certainly knows about sports, but probably knows little about cameras or pantyhose.

[margin note: Use knowledgeable people]

3. Examples: An **example** should clearly relate to the argument and should be typical enough to support it.* If you wish to convince your reader that high schools should provide more funds than they do for women's sports, you might say, "Jefferson High School, for instance, has received inquiries from sixty female students who would be willing to join a women's basketball or baseball team if the school could provide the uniforms, the space, and a coach."

Avoid examples that are not typical enough to support your general statement. That your friend was once bitten by a dog does not adequately prove that all dogs are dangerous pets.

[margin note: Use examples to support]

4. Predicting the consequence: Predicting the consequence helps the reader visualize what will occur if *something does or does not happen.* To convince your readers that a college education should be free to all qualified students, you might say, "If bright but economically deprived students cannot attend college because they cannot afford it, our society will be robbed of their talents."

Avoid exaggerating the consequence. For instance, telling the reader, "If you don't eat fresh fruit every day, you will never be truly healthy," exaggerates the consequences of not eating fresh fruit and makes the reader understandably suspicious.

[margin note: Say what will happen if we don't get in gear]

5. Answering the opposition: Answering possible critics shows that you are aware of the opposition's argument and are able to respond to it. If you wish to convince your readers that your candidate is the best on the ballot, you might say, "Some have criticized him for running a low-key campaign, but he feels that the issues and his stand on them should speak for themselves."

Avoid calling the opposition "fools" or "crooks." Attack their ideas, not them.

[margin note: use opposite view to acknowledge your awareness. Dispute it]

[margin note: Pollution is only bad in big cities, not in small towns — nowheres]

Considering the Audience

In addition to providing adequate proof for your argument, pay special attention to the **audience** as you write a persuasive paragraph. In general, we assume that our audience is much like us—reasonable and sensible people who wish to learn the truth. Often, however, a persuasive

*For more work on examples, see Chapter 5, "Illustration."

paper should be directed toward a particular audience. It is helpful to consider just *what kind of evidence* this audience would respond to. For instance, if you were attempting to convince parents to volunteer their time to establish a local Scout troop, you might explain to them the various ways in which their children would benefit from the troop. In other words, show these parents how the troop is important to *them.* You might also say that you realize how much time they already spend on family matters and how little spare time they have. By doing so, you let them know that you understand their resistance to the argument and that you are sympathetic to their doubts. When you take your audience into consideration, you will make your persuasive paragraph more convincing.*†

PRACTICE 1   Read the following persuasive paragraph carefully and answer the questions.

The Comtrex Corporation should provide day care for the children of its employees. First of all, Comtrex workers need such a program. According to the personnel director, about 850 employees with small children have spouses who also work outside the home; for these workers, day care is a constant problem. Second, the company would undoubtedly benefit from on-site day care since workers could concentrate more fully on their jobs, secure in the knowledge that their children were nearby and well cared for. Finally, although some critics may consider it charity, a program that benefits both employees and management makes good sense.

1. What is this paragraph arguing for or against? _The paragraph argues_ _for on-site day care at the Comtrex Corporation._

2. Which reason is supported by *facts?* _Comtrex workers need a day care_ _program._

    What are these facts? _About 850 employees with small children have_ _spouses who also work outside the home. Day care is a constant problem for_ _them._

    Where did the writer get them? _The writer consulted the personnel_ _director._

*For more work on audience, see Chapter 1, "Exploring the Writing Process," Part B.
†For a complete essay developed by persuasion, see "Keeping Older Workers on the Job," Chapter 18, Part H.

3. Which reason *answers the opposition?* <u>The third reason answers the</u>
<u>opposition.</u>

4. List the transitional expressions in this paragraph. <u>first of all, second,</u>
<u>finally, although</u>

PRACTICE 2   Read the following carefully and answer the questions.

Automatic sprinkler systems should be installed in all public and commercial buildings. First and foremost, sprinklers save lives. As Captain Hornak of the Department of Fire Prevention of Springfield City has noted, "A sprinkler system remains our first defense against a small blaze turning into a major conflagration. Two people needlessly lost their lives at the Springfield City Library fire last year because that sixty-year-old building did not have a sprinkler system." In addition, sprinklers can save property. Fire causes billions of dollars of damage every year to shopping centers, hotels, and office buildings. Sprinklers slow down the rapid spread of small fires, thereby limiting property damage. In states that have enacted stricter sprinkler system requirements—Florida, Hawaii, and Alaska, for instance—the amount of property damage caused by fire has declined. As a related benefit, sprinkler systems allow insurance companies to lower fire insurance rates. These savings can be passed on to consumers in the form of lower prices at department stores, hotels, and other commercial establishments.

1. What is this paragraph arguing for or against? <u>The paragraph argues</u>
<u>for the installation of sprinkler systems in all public and commercial buildings.</u>

2. Which reason appeals to an authority for support? <u>The first reason</u>
<u>appeals to authority.</u>

Who is the authority? <u>The authority is Captain Hornak of the Department</u>
<u>of Fire Prevention.</u>

3. Which reason uses examples for support? <u>The second reason uses</u>
<u>examples.</u>

What are the examples? <u>The examples are states that have legislated</u>
<u>sprinker requirements.</u>

4. Which reason predicts the consequences? <u>The third reason predicts the</u>
<u>consequences.</u>

5. How has the writer ordered the reasons in this paragraph, from most to least important or from least to most important? How do you know?

The order is from most to least important; the writer says that the first reason

is also foremost.

PRACTICE 3   So far you have learned five basic methods of persuasion: **facts, referring to an authority, examples, predicting the consequence,** and **answering the opposition.** Ten topic sentences for persuasive paragraphs follow. Write one reason in support of each topic sentence, using the method of persuasion indicated. Answers will vary.

Facts

1. A stop sign should be placed at the busy intersection of Hoover and Palm streets.

Reason: _In the last three months there have been fifteen accidents at this_

intersection.

2. People should not get married until they are at least twenty-five years old.

Reason: _Statistics show that 75 percent of couples who marry before that age_

eventually divorce.

Referring to an Authority

(If you cannot think of an authority offhand, name the kind of person who would be an authority on the subject.)

3. These new Sluggo bats will definitely raise your batting average.

Reason: _According to coach Bill Bartlett of the Madison High School baseball_

team, the design and weighting of these bats allow for a better swing—by any

batter.

4. Most people should get at least a half-hour of vigorous exercise every day.

   Reason: Dr. Pamela Lu of the Fitness Research Corporation notes that regular

   exercise can prevent heart attacks and other life-threatening afflictions.

   _____

   _____

Examples

5. Commercials shown during children's television programs can have a negative impact on young viewers.

   Reason: My daughter wants me to buy her every toy and every brand of junk

   food advertised on her favorite show.

   _____

   _____

6. High schools must provide young people with adequate sex education because ignorance can be harmful.

   Reason: In our high school, for example, seven young women dropped out last

   year to have babies.

   _____

   _____

Predicting the Consequence

7. The military draft should (should not) be brought back.

   Reason: Reinstatement of the draft would disrupt many lives.

   _____

   _____

   _____

8. The federal government should (should not) prohibit the sale of handguns through the mail.

   Reason: Without such a prohibition, anyone, no matter how unstable, could

   obtain a handgun.

   _____

   _____

Answering the Opposition

(State the opposition's point of view and then refute it.)

9. This college should (should not) drop its required-attendance policy.

    Reason: _Although some might argue that students would quickly stop going_

    to class, most students would make responsible decisions to attend classes

    and to get an education.

    _____

10. Teenagers should (should not) be required to get their parents' permission before being allowed to have an abortion.

    Reason: _Although some teenagers may make mature and informed decisions,_

    not all teenagers are able to make such important decisions by themselves.

    _____

    _____

PRACTICE 4   Each of the following sentences tells what you are trying to convince someone to do. Beneath each sentence are four reasons that attempt to convince the reader that he or she should take this particular course of action. Circle the letter of the reason that seems *irrelevant, illogical,* or *untrue.*

1. If you wanted to convince someone to do holiday shopping earlier, you might say that
   a. shopping earlier saves time.
   b. more gifts will be in stock.
   c. stores will not be overly crowded.
   d. Stevie Wonder shops early.

2. If you wanted to convince someone to buy a particular brand of cereal, you might say that
   a. it is inexpensive.
   b. it contains vitamins and minerals.
   c. it comes in an attractive box.
   d. it makes a hearty breakfast.

3. If you wanted to convince someone to move to your town, you might say that
   a. two new companies have made jobs available.
   b. by moving to this town, he or she will become the happiest person in the world.
   c. there is a wide selection of housing.
   d. the area is lovely and still unpolluted.

4. If you wanted to convince someone to vote for a particular candidate, you might say that
   a. she has always kept her promises to the voters.
   b. she has lived in the district for thirty years.
   c. she has substantial knowledge of the issues.
   d. she dresses very fashionably.

5. If you wanted to convince someone to learn to read and speak a foreign language, you might say that
   a. knowledge of a foreign language can be helpful in the business world.
   b. he or she may want to travel in the country where the language is spoken.
   c. Julio Iglesias sings in two languages.
   d. being able to read great literature in the original is a rewarding experience.

6. If you wanted to convince someone to quit smoking, you might say that
   a. smoking is a major cause of lung cancer.
   b. smoking stains teeth and softens gums.
   c. ashtrays are often hard to find.
   d. this bad habit has become increasingly expensive.

PRACTICE 5   As you write persuasive paragraphs, make sure that your reasons can withstand close examination. Here are some examples of *invalid* arguments. Read them carefully. Decide which method of persuasion is being used and explain why you think the argument is invalid. Refer to the list on pages 144–145.

1. Men make terrible drivers. That one just cut right in front of me without looking.

   Method of persuasion: _example_

   Invalid because: _The example of one careless male driver isn't enough to_

   support a general statement about all male drivers.

2. Many people have become vegetarians during the past ten or fifteen years, but such people are stupid.

   Method of persuasion: _answering the opposition_

   Invalid because: _The writer attacks the opposition rather than countering_

   the benefits of vegetarianism.   ↳ HOW now/why

3. Candy does not really harm children's teeth. Tests made by scientists at the Gooey Candy Company have proved that candy does not cause tooth decay.

Method of persuasion: referring to an authority

Invalid because: The scientists are employed by a candy company and may
therefore be biased.

4. Stealing pens and pads from the office is perfectly all right. Everyone does it.

   Method of persuasion: example

   Invalid because: Saying "everyone does it" is vague and does not justify
   stealing.

5. We don't want _____ in our neighborhood. We had a
   _____ family once, and they made a lot of noise.

   Method of persuasion: example

   Invalid because: Generalizations about an entire ethnic, religious, etc.,
   group based on one family's behavior are not convincing.

6. If our city doesn't build more playgrounds, a crime wave will destroy our homes and businesses.

   Method of persuasion: predicting the consequence

   Invalid because: This argument exaggerates the consequences.

7. Studying has nothing to do with grades. My brother never studies and still gets As all the time.

   Method of persuasion: example

   Invalid because: One person's experience doesn't adequately support such
   a sweeping statement.

8. Women bosses work their employees too hard. I had one once, and she never let me rest for a moment.

   Method of persuasion: example

   Invalid because: A single example cannot justify this broad statement.

9. The Big Deal Supermarket has the lowest prices in town. This must be true because the manager said on the radio last week, "We have the lowest prices in town."

Method of persuasion: referring to an authority

Invalid because: The "authority" cited was advertising the store, not

stating research findings.

10. If little girls are allowed to play with cars and trucks, they will grow up wanting to be men.

Method of persuasion: predicting the consequence

Invalid because: The writer cannot support such a sweeping prediction with

facts.

Writing Assignment

To help you take a stand for a persuasive paragraph of your own, try the following exercises on notebook paper:

1. List five things you would like to see changed at your college.

2. List five things you would like to see changed in your home *or* at your job.

3. List five things that annoy you or make you angry. What can be done about them?

4. Imagine yourself giving a speech on national television. What message would you like to convey?

From your lists, pick one topic you would like to write a persuasive paragraph about and write the topic sentence here:

Sample answer: The college library should be open all day on Sundays.

Now make a plan for a paragraph on a separate sheet of paper. Use at least two of the five methods of persuasion. Arrange your reasons in some logical order.

Checklist: The Process of Writing a Persuasive Paragraph

Refer to this checklist of steps as you write a persuasive paragraph of your own.

_____ 1. Narrow the topic in light of your audience and purpose. Of what do you wish to convince your reader?

_____ 2. Compose a topic sentence that clearly states your position for or against. Use *should, ought, must,* or their negatives.

_____ 3. Freewrite or brainstorm for all the reasons you can think of. (You may want to freewrite or brainstorm before you narrow the topic.)

_____ 4. Select the best three or four reasons and drop those that do not relate to your topic sentence.

_____ 5. If you use *facts,* be sure that they are accurate and that the source of your facts is clear. If you use an *example,* be sure that it is a valid one and adequately supports your argument. If you *refer to an authority,* be sure that he or she is really an authority and *not biased.* If one of your reasons *predicts the consequence,* be sure that the consequence flows logically from your statement. If one of your reasons is an *answer to the opposition,* be sure to state the opposition's point of view fairly and refute it adequately.

_____ 6. Make a plan for the paragraph, numbering the reasons in the order in which you will present them.

_____ 7. Write a draft of your persuasive paragraph, using transitional expressions wherever they might be helpful.

_____ 8. Revise as necessary, checking for support, unity, logic, and coherence.

_____ 9. Proofread for errors in grammar, punctuation, sentence structure, spelling, and mechanics.

[handwritten margin note: take care w/ transitions because many are still writing w/ the idea that the reader follows the logic in your head as though it were on the paper...]

Suggested Topics for Persuasive Paragraphs

A list of possible topic sentences for persuasive paragraphs follows. Pick one statement and decide whether you agree or disagree with it. Modify the topic sentence accordingly. Then write a persuasive paragraph that supports your view, explaining and illustrating from your own experience, your observations of others, or your reading.

1. College (or high school) sports place too much emphasis on winning.

2. Husbands of wives who work outside the home should share equally *Lori/Mike* in all housework.

3. Sterile needles should be provided to all addicts in order to stop the spread of AIDS.

4. English should be the official language of the United States.

5. People over sixty-five should be forced to retire to make room for the younger generation.

6. _____ (public speaking, wilderness survival, swimming, or whatever) should be a required course at this college.

7. Popular music today is more (or less) exciting than it was ten years ago.

8. Occasional arguments are good for friendship.

9. Parents should pay for the damage caused by their delinquent children.

10. Money is the key to happiness.

11. _____ is the most _____ (violent, educational, racist, ridiculous) program on TV.

12. Condom machines should be permitted on campus.

13. Single people should not be allowed to adopt children.

14. A woman's career can break up her marriage.

15. Colleges should require computer literacy courses.

16. People should laugh more because laughter heals.

17. Students should be allowed to attend any college course as frequently or infrequently as they like.

18. To respect all beliefs, including those of nonbelievers, prayers should not be allowed in public schools.

19. People convicted of drunk driving should lose their licenses for one year.

20. _____ company should provide _____ for its employees.

Adolescents convicted of murder should get the death penalty

Unit 4
Improving Your Writing

13

Revising for Consistency and Parallelism

PART A Consistent Tense
PART B Consistent Number and Person
PART C Parallelism
PART D Consistent Quotations

All good writing is **consistent.** That is, each sentence and paragraph in the final draft should move along smoothly without confusing shifts in **tense, number,** or **person.** In addition, good writing uses **parallel structure** to balance two or more similar words, phrases, or clauses.

Although you should be aware of consistency and parallelism as you write the first draft of your paragraph or essay, you might find it easier to **revise** for them—that is, to write your first draft and then, as you read it again later, check and rewrite for consistency and parallelism.

PART A

Consistent Tense

Consistency of tense means using the same verb tense whenever possible throughout a sentence or an entire paragraph. Do not shift from one verb tense to another—for example, from present to past or from past to present—unless you really mean to indicate different times.

1. Inconsistent tense:	We *stroll* down Bourbon Street as the jazz bands *began* to play.
2. Consistent tense:	We *strolled* down Bourbon Street as the jazz bands *began* to play.
3. Consistent tense:	We *stroll* down Bourbon Street as the jazz bands *begin* to play.

[handwritten margin notes: "What's wrong?" and "Both parts of sentence must be the same"]

158

- Sentence 1 begins in the present tense with the verb *stroll* but then slips into past tense with the verb *began.* The tenses are inconsistent since both actions (strolling and beginning) occur at the same time.

- Sentence 2 is consistent. Both verbs, *strolled* and *began*, are now in the past tense.

- Sentence 3 is also consistent, using the present tense forms of both verbs, *stroll* and *begin.* The present tense here gives a feeling of immediacy, as if the action is happening now.*

Of course, you should use different verb tenses in a sentence or paragraph if they convey the meaning that you wish to convey:

But be sure you see this:

> 4. Last fall I *took* English 02; now I *am taking* English 13.

- The verbs in this sentence accurately show the time relationship between the two classroom experiences.†

PRACTICE 1   Read the following sentences carefully for meaning. Then correct any inconsistencies of tense by changing the verbs that do not accurately show the time of events.

Example   I took a deep breath and opened the door; there stands a well-dressed man with a large box.

Consistent: I took a deep breath and opened the door; there ~~stands~~ **stood** a well-dressed man with a large box.

or

Consistent: I ~~took~~ **take** a deep breath and ~~opened~~ **open** the door; there stands a well-dressed man with a large box.

1. Two seconds before the buzzer sounded, Michael Jordan sank a basket from midcourt, and the crowd ~~goes~~ **went** wild.

gregg ✓ 2. Nestle introduced instant coffee in 1938; it ~~takes~~ **took** eight years to develop this product.

Victor ✓ 3. We ~~expand~~ **expanded** our sales budget, doubled our research, and soon saw positive results.

*For more work in spotting verbs, see Chapter 21, "The Simple Sentence," Part C.
†For more work work on particular verb tenses and forms, see Chapters 24, 25, and 26.

4. For twenty years, Dr. Dulfano observed animal behavior and ~~seeks~~ *sought* clues to explain the increasing violence among human beings.

Sally ✓ 5. I <u>knew</u> how this ~~work~~ *worked*.

6. I was driving south on Interstate 90 when a truck ~~approaches~~ *approached* with its bright lights on.

Juanita ✓ 7. Two brown horses ~~graze~~ *grazed* quietly in the field as the sun rose and the mist disappeared.

8. Lollie had a big grin on her face as she ~~walks~~ *walked* over and kicked the Coke machine.

Cathy ✓ 9. Maynard ~~stormed~~ *storms* down the hallway, <u>goes</u> right into the boss's office and shouts, "I want curtains in my office!"

10. The nurses quietly paced the halls, making sure their patients ~~rest~~ *rested* comfortably.

PRACTICE 2   Inconsistencies of tense are most likely to occur within paragraphs and longer pieces of writing. Therefore, it is important to revise your writing for tense consistency. Read this paragraph for meaning. Then revise, correcting inconsistencies of tense by changing incorrect verbs.

Many people know that the abacus is an ancient invention the Chinese still use for arithmetic. Many don't know, however, that the abacus is also used today in many other countries, including the Soviet Union. For instance, in a Soviet restaurant, a customer often ~~received~~ *receives* an abacus instead of a bill. The abacus ~~showed~~ *shows* the cost of the meal. At the border, workers figure out money exchanges with an abacus. They quickly ~~converted~~ *convert* foreign money into the corresponding amount of Soviet currency without the help of modern computers or fancy calculators. The simple, handy abacus does all the work.

PRACTICE 3   The following paragraph is written in the present tense. Rewrite it in consistent past tense.*

The tension builds as I get into my car. I sit down and go through the motions of changing the gears, practicing for the race. I look ahead at the long stretch of road equivalent to a quarter of a mile. My opponent enters his car, looks at me with a smirk on his face, and gives me the thumbs-down signal. I pay no attention to his teasing but wipe my hands on my shirt. I flex my fingers and grip the wheel. The race is about to begin.

The tension built as I got into my car. I sat down and went through the motions of

changing the gears, practicing for the race. I looked ahead at the long stretch of

road equivalent to a quarter of a mile. My opponent entered his car, looked at me

with a smirk on his face, and gave me the thumbs-down signal. I paid no attention

to his teasing but wiped my hands on my shirt. I flexed my fingers and gripped the

wheel. The race was about to begin.

PRACTICE 4   The following paragraph is written in the past tense. Rewrite it in consistent present tense; make sure all verbs agree with their subjects.†

The sculptor built the creation from a block that weighed more than 300 pounds. Using a hammer and chisel, he shaped and hewed the solid mass. After a few hours, a nose appeared, a leg kicked out, and a prehistoric tail trailed behind. In just a few days, the sculptor shaped a magnificent dragon that watched over the snowy city and sparkled magically at night. Under the streetlights, the statue shone like crystal—even though it was made only of ice.

The sculptor builds the creation from a block that weighs more than 300 pounds.

Using a hammer and chisel, he shapes and hews the solid mass. After a few

hours, a nose appears, a leg kicks out, and a prehistoric tail trails behind. In just a

few days, the sculptor shapes a magnificent dragon that watches over the snowy

city and sparkles magically at night. Under the streetlights, the statue shines like

crystal—even though it is made only of ice.

*For more work on the past tense, see Chapter 25, "Past Tense."
†For work on agreement, see Chapter 24, "Present Tense (Agreement)."

PRACTICE 5 Longer pieces of writing often use both the past tense and the present tense. However, switching from one tense to the other requires care. Read the following essay carefully and note when a switch from one tense to another is logically necessary. Then revise verbs as needed.

A Quick History of Chocolate

Most of us now take solid chocolate—especially candy bars—so much for granted that we find it hard to imagine a time when chocolate didn't exist. However, this delicious food ~~becomes~~ [became] an eating favorite only about one hundred and fifty years ago.

The ancient peoples of Central America began cultivating cacao beans almost three thousand years ago. A cold drink made from the beans ~~is~~ [was] served to Hernando Cortez, the Spanish conqueror, when he ~~arrives~~ [arrived] at the Aztec court of Montezuma in 1519. The Spanish took the beverage home to their king. He ~~likes~~ [liked] it so much that he kept the formula a secret. For the next one hundred years, hot chocolate was the private drink of the Spanish nobility. Slowly, it ~~makes~~ [made] its way into the fashionable courts of France, England, and Austria. In 1657, a Frenchman living in London opened a shop where blocks for making the beverage ~~are~~ [were] sold at a high price. Soon chocolate houses appeared in cities throughout Europe. Wealthy clients met in them, sipped chocolate, conducted business, and ~~gossip~~ [gossiped].

During the 1800s, chocolate became a chewable food. The breakthrough ~~comes~~ [came] in 1828, when cocoa butter was extracted from the bean. Twenty years later, an English firm mixed the butter with chocolate liquor, which ~~results~~ [resulted] in the first solid chocolate. Milton Hershey's first candy bar ~~come~~ [came] on the scene in 1894, and Tootsie Rolls hit the market two years later. The popularity of chocolate bars ~~soar~~ [soared] during World War I when they ~~are~~ [were] given to soldiers for fast energy. M & Ms gave the industry another boost during World War II; soldiers needed candy that wouldn't melt in their hands.

On the average, Americans today eat ten pounds of hard chocolate a year. Their number one choice is Snickers, which ~~sold~~ *sells* more than a billion bars every year. However, Americans consume far less chocolate than many Western Europeans. The average Dutch person ~~gobbled~~ *gobbles* up more than fifteen pounds a year, while the Swiss ~~packed~~ *packs* away almost twenty pounds. Chocolate is obviously an international favorite.

PART B

Consistent Number and Person

Nearly as important as verb tense consistency is consistency of **number** and **person.**

Consistency of Number

Consistency of number means avoiding confusing shifts from singular to plural or from plural to singular within a sentence or paragraph. Choose *either* singular *or* plural; then be *consistent.*

What is wrong? →

1. Inconsistent number:	*The wise jogger* chooses *their* running shoes with care.
2. Consistent number:	*The wise jogger* chooses *his* (or *her*) running shoes with care.
3. Consistent number:	*Wise joggers* choose *their* running shoes with care.

- Since the subject of sentence 1, *the wise jogger*, is singular, use of the plural pronoun *their* is *inconsistent.*

- Sentence 2 is *consistent.* The singular pronoun *his* (or *her*) now clearly refers to the singular *jogger.*

- In sentence 3, the plural number is used *consistently. Their* clearly refers to the plural *joggers.*

If you begin a paragraph discussing *the small businessman,* continue to refer to *him* in the **third person singular** throughout the paragraph:

> *The small businessman* . . . . *He* . . . .
> . . . . The law may not protect
> *him* . . . . Therefore, *he* . . . .

Do not confuse the reader by shifting unnecessarily to *they* or *you.*

PRACTICE 6 Correct any inconsistencies of **number** in the following sentences.* Also make necessary changes in verb agreement.

Example | A singer must protect ~~their~~ voice.
                                 his or her

1. An individual's self-esteem can affect ~~their~~ performance.
   his or her

Chris ✓ 2. Jorge gave up diet sodas only last November, but already he hates the taste of ~~it.~~
   them.

3. The sales figures encouraged us, but we feared that ~~it wasn't~~ accurate.
   they weren't

4. The defendant who wishes to do so may ask a higher court to overturn ~~their~~ conviction.
   his or her

5. Dreams fascinate me; ~~it is~~ like another world.
   they are

6. If ~~a person doesn't~~ know how to love themselves, they will not be able to love others.
   people don't

7. Oxford University boasts of the great number of ancient manuscripts ~~they own.~~
   it owns

Erica ✓ 8. Always buy fruit and vegetables when ~~it is~~ in season.
   they are

9. The average American takes ~~their~~ freedom for granted.
   his or her

10. ~~Women have~~ more opportunities than ever before. She is freer to go to school, get a job, and choose the kind of life she wants.
    A woman has

---

*For more practice in agreement of pronouns and antecedents, see Chapter 28, "Pronouns," Part B.

I am a cripple. I choose this word to name me. I choose from among several possibilities, the most common of which are "handicapped" or "disabled." I made the choice a number of years ago, unaware of my motives for doing so. People—crippled or not—wince at the world "cripple," as they do not at "handicapped" or "disabled." Perhaps I want them to wince. I want them to see me as a tough customer, one to whom the fates/gods/viruses have not been kind, but who can face the truth of her existence squarely. As a cripple, I swagger.

"Cripple" seems to me a clean word, straightforward and precise. As a lover of words, I like the accuracy with which it describes my condition: I have lost the full use of my limbs. "Disabled," by contrast, suggests any incapacity, physical or mental. And I certainly don't like "handicapped," which implies that I have deliberately been put at a disadvantage, by whom I can't imagine, in order to equalize chances in the great race of life. These words seem to me to be moving away from my condition, to be widening the gap between word and reality. Most remote is the recently coined euphemism[1] "differently abled," which strikes me as pure verbal garbage designed, by its ability to describe anyone, to describe no one.

I haven't always been crippled, a fact for which I am grateful. To be whole of limb is, I know from experience, infinitely more pleasant and useful than to be crippled; and if that knowledge leaves me open to bitterness at my loss, the physical soundness I once enjoyed (though I did not enjoy it half enough) is well worth the occasional stab of regret.

When I was 28 I started to trip and drop things. What at first seemed my natural clumsiness soon became too pronounced to shrug off. I consulted a neurologist, who told me that I had a brain tumor. About a year and a half later I developed a blurred spot in one eye. I had, at last, the episodes requisite for a diagnosis: multiple sclerosis. I have never been sorry for the doctor's initial misdiagnosis, however. For almost a week, until the negative results of the tests were in, I thought that I was going to die right away. Every day for the past nearly 10 years, then, has been a kind of gift. I accept all gifts.

Multiple sclerosis is a chronic degenerative disease of the central nervous system; during its course, which is unpredictable and uncontrollable, one may lose vision, hearing, speech, and ability to walk, control of bladder and/or bowels, strength in any or all extremities, sensitivity to touch, vibration, and/or pain, potency, coordination of movements—the list of possibilities is lengthy and, yes, horrifying. One may also lose one's sense of humor. That's the easiest to lose and the hardest to survive without.

In the past 10 years, I have sustained some of these losses; my disease has been slowly progressive. My left leg is now so weak that I walk with the aid of a brace and a cane. I no longer have much use of my left hand. Now my right side is weakening as well. Overall, though, I've been lucky so far; the terrain left me has been ample enough to continue many activities that absorb me: writing, teaching, raising children and plants and snakes, reading, speaking publicly about MS and depression, even playing bridge with people honorable enough to let me scatter cards without sneaking a peek.

Consistency of Person

Consistency of person—closely related to consistency of number—means using the same *person,* or indefinite pronoun, throughout a sentence or paragraph whenever possible.

First person is the most personal and informal in written work: (singular) *I,* (plural) *we*

Second person speaks directly to the reader: (singular and plural) *you*

Third person is the most formal and most frequently used in college writing: (singular) *he, she, it, one, a person, an individual, a student,* and so on; (plural) *they, people, individuals, students,* and so on

---

Avoid confusing shifts from one person to another. Choose one, then be *consistent.* When using a noun in a general way—*a person, the individual, the parent*—be careful not to slip into the second person, *you,* but continue to use the third person, *he* or *she.*

look at →

4. Inconsistent person:	A *player* collects $200 when *you* pass "Go."	
5. Consistent person:	A *player* collects $200 when *he* or *she* passes "Go."	
6. Consistent person:	*You* collect $200 when *you* pass "Go."	

- In sentence 4, the person shifts unnecessarily from the third person, *a player,* to the second person, *you.* The result is confusing.

- Sentence 5 maintains consistent third person. *He or she* now clearly refers to the third person subject, *a player.*

- Sentence 6 is also consistent, using the second person, *you,* throughout.

Of course, inconsistencies of person and number often occur together, as shown on the next page.

what's wrong?

7. Inconsistent person and number:	Whether *one* enjoys or resents commercials, *we* are bombarded with them every hour of the day.
8. Consistent person and number:	Whether *we* enjoy or resent commercials, *we* are bombarded with them every hour of the day.
9. Consistent person and number:	Whether *one* enjoys or resents commercials, *he* (or *she*, or *one*) is bombarded with them every hour of the day.

look at →

look at →

- Sentence 7 shifts from the third person singular, *one*, to the first person plural, *we*.

- Sentence 8 uses the first person plural consistently.

- Sentence 9 uses the third person singular consistently.

PRACTICE 7   Correct the shifts in **person** in these sentences. If necessary, change the verbs to make them agree with any new subjects.

Example   One should eliminate saturated fats from ~~your~~ *one's* diet.

1. A voter should listen to the candidates carefully before ~~they~~ *he or she* ~~vote~~ *votes*.

2. One problem facing students on this campus is that ~~a person~~ *they* ~~doesn't~~ *don't* know when the library will be open and when it will be closed.

3. Sooner or later, most smokers realize that ~~you~~ *they* can't just quit when ~~you~~ *they* want to.

4. I have reached a time in my life when what others expect is less important than what ~~one~~ *I* really ~~wants~~ *want* to do.

5. Members of the orchestra should meet after the concert and bring ~~your~~ *their* instruments and music.

6. The wise parent knows that she is asking for trouble if ~~you let~~ *she lets* a small child watch violent television shows.

7. The student who participates in this program will spend six weeks in
   He or she
   Spain and Morocco. ~~You~~ will study the art and architecture firsthand,

   working closely with an instructor.
                                                                he or she dresses
8. You shouldn't judge a person by how ~~they dress~~.
                                                     you need
9. If you have been working that hard, ~~one needs~~ a vacation.

10. People who visit the Caribbean for the first time are struck by the

    lushness of the landscape. The sheer size of the flowers and fruit
                              them
    amazes ~~you~~.

PRACTICE 8   The following paragraph consistently uses the third person singular—*the salesperson, he or she,* and so on. For practice in revising for consistency, rewrite the paragraph in **consistent third person plural.** Begin by changing *the salesperson* to *salespeople* or *salesclerks.* Then change verbs, nouns, or pronouns as necessary.

The salesperson is crucial to a customer's satisfaction or dissatisfaction with a particular store. In reality, the salesperson acts as the store's representative or ambassador; often he or she is the only contact a customer has with the store. Thousands of dollars may be spent in advertising to woo customers and build a favorable image, only to have this lost by the uncaring salesclerk.

—Robert F. Hartley, *Retailing: Challenge and Opportunity*

Salespeople are crucial to a customer's satisfaction or dissatisfaction with a

particular store. In reality, salespeople act as the store's representatives or

ambassadors; often they are the only contacts a customer has with the store.

Thousands of dollars may be spent in advertising to woo customers and build a

favorable image, only to have this lost by uncaring salesclerks.

PRACTICE 9   Revise the following essay for inconsistencies of person and number. Correct any confusing shifts (changing words if necessary) to make the writing clear and *consistent* throughout.

Immortality in Wax

"Madame Tussaud's. Come and find out who's in. And who's out." That's what English radios advertise to lure visitors to a most unusual show—a display of the rich and famous in the form of lifelike wax statues. Nearly 2.5 million line up each year to rub shoulders with the images of today's and yesterday's celebrities. ~~You~~ **They** make Madame Tussaud's the most popular paid tourist attraction in England.

Visitors are treated to some of Madame Tussaud's original handiwork, as well as to other figures that have been added over the past two hundred years. All told, tourists can see more than three hundred eerily lifelike statues. In the Grand Hall, ~~one~~ **they** can view British royalty standing with other leaders from history. The Chamber of Horrors introduces ~~you~~ **them** to the most infamous criminals of all time. They can walk through a street of Victorian London where scary special effects make ~~you~~ **them** feel as though ~~you~~ **they** are being stalked by Jack the Ripper. The Conservatory houses entertainers, such as the Beatles and Michael Jackson.

Each month, a committee decides who should be added or taken out of the collection. A celebrity is chosen for ~~your~~ **his or her** fame, recognizability, and publicity potential. ~~You are~~ **He or she is** invited to sit for moldings, each costing about sixteen thousand dollars. The celebrity usually poses for pictures with ~~their~~ **his or her** finished statue for the press. Then, the figure is put on display. Archbishop Tutu is there, as are Dudley Moore, Pablo Picasso, and Roger Rabbit. Even Queen Elizabeth regularly has her likeness updated for viewing at Madame Tussaud's.

PART C

Parallelism

Parallelism, or **parallel structure,** is an effective way to add smoothness and power to your writing. **Parallelism** is a balance of two or more similar words, phrases, or clauses.

Compare the two versions of each of these sentences:

Read aloud

---

1. She likes dancing, swimming, and to jog.
2. She likes *dancing, swimming,* and *jogging.*

3. The cable runs across the roof; the north wall is where it runs down.
4. The cable runs *across the roof* and *down the north wall.*

5. He admires people with strong convictions and who think for themselves.
6. He admires people *who have strong convictions* and *who think for themselves.*

- Sentences 2, 4, and 6 use **parallelism** to express parallel ideas.

- In sentence 2, *dancing, swimming,* and *jogging* are parallel; all three are the *-ing* forms of verbs, used here as nouns.

- In sentence 4, *across the roof* and *down the north wall* are parallel prepositional phrases, each consisting of a preposition and its object.

- In sentence 6, *who have strong convictions* and *who think for themselves* are parallel clauses beginning with the word *who.*

- Sometimes two entire sentences can be parallel:

In a democracy we are all equal before the law. In a dictatorship we are all equal before the police.

—Millor Fernandes

- In what ways are these two sentences parallel? __Both use the same__

    format: "In a _____ we are all equal before the _____."

Certain special constructions require parallel structure:

> 7. The fruit is *both* tasty *and* fresh.
>
> 8. He *either* loves you *or* hates you.
>
> 9. Yvette *not only* plays golf *but also* swims like a pro.
>
> 10. I would *rather* sing in the chorus *than* perform a solo.

Each of these constructions has two parts:

both . . . and

(n)either . . . (n)or

not only . . . but also

rather . . . than

The words, phrases, or clauses following each part must be parallel:

tasty . . . fresh

loves you . . . hates you

plays golf . . . swims like a pro

sing in the chorus . . . perform a solo

PRACTICE 10   Rewrite each of the following sentences using parallel structure to accent parallel ideas.

Example | The summer in Louisiana is very hot and has high humidity.

The summer in Louisiana is very hot and humid.

Ray ✓ 1. Teresa is a gifted woman—a chemist, does the carpentry, and she can cook.

Teresa is a gifted woman—a chemist, a carpenter, and a cook.

_____

2. The shape of the rock, how big it was, and its color reminded me of a small elephant.

The rock's shape, size, and color reminded me of a small elephant.

_____

3. Chia, my dog, is overweight and moves clumsily.

Chia, my dog, is overweight and clumsy.

4. Your job consists of arranging the books, cataloguing new arrivals, and the pamphlets have to be alphabetized.

Your job consists of arranging the books, cataloguing new arrivals, and

alphabetizing the pamphlets.

Vincent ✓5. A thin film of frost coated the trees. The hedges and shrubs had it also.

A thin film of frost coated the trees, the hedges, and the shrubs.

6. He is an affectionate husband, a thoughtful son, and kind to his kids.

He is an affectionate husband, a thoughtful son, and a kind father.

7. Marvin was happy to win the bowling tournament and he also felt surprised.

Marvin was happy and surprised to win the bowling tournament.

Antonette 8. He is a poet of great talent and who is insightful.

He is a poet of great talent and insight.

9. Dr. Tien is the kindest physician I know; she has the most concern of any physician I know.

Dr. Tien is the kindest and most concerned physician I know.

Victor ✓ 10. Joe would rather work on a farm than spending time in an office.

Joe would rather work on a farm than spend time in an office.

Teresa ✓11. Every afternoon in the mountains, it either rains or there is hail.

Every afternoon in the mountains, it either rains or hails.

12. "Sesame Street" teaches children nursery rhymes, songs, how to be courteous, and being kind.

"Sesame Street" teaches children nursery rhymes, songs, courtesy, and

kindness.

13. Alexis would rather give orders than taking them.

Alexis would rather give orders than take them.

14. His writing reveals not only intelligence but also it is humorous.

His writing reveals not only intelligence but also humor.

15. Last summer's vacation was exciting, restful, and it wasn't expensive.

Last summer's vacation was exciting, restful, and inexpensive.

PRACTICE 11   Write one sentence that is parallel to each sentence that follows, creating pairs of parallel sentences. Answers will vary.

Example   On Friday night, she dressed in silk and sipped champagne.

On Monday morning, she put on her jeans and crammed for a history test.

1. When he was twenty, he worked seven days a week in a fruit store.

When he was forty, he worked four days a week as the owner of a chain of

fruit stores.

2. The child in me wants to run away from problems.

The adult in me knows I must face them.

3. The home team charged enthusiastically onto the field.

The visiting team sat dejectedly in the dugout.

4. "Work hard and keep your mouth shut" is my mother's formula for success.

"Nothing ventured, nothing gained" is mine.
_____

_____

5. The men thought the movie was amusing.

The women thought it was insulting.
_____

_____

PRACTICE 12   Write five sentences of your own using **parallel structure.**

Sample answers:

1. The children played while the adults ate dinner.
_____

2. Can you rub your stomach while you pat your head?
_____

3. It took all day to cook the meal and fifteen minutes to eat it.
_____

4. Although I like hot days, I don't like humidity.
_____

5. Katrina can cut the cake and David can serve it.
_____

PRACTICE 13   The following paragraph contains both correct and faulty parallel structures. Revise the faulty parallelism.

When most people think of Walden Pond, they imagine the writer

meditating

Henry David Thoreau planting a garden, meditate in the silent woods,

, small

and living alone for years in a simple cabin that was small. This roman-

tic view of life at Walden Pond persists although Thoreau spent only

two years there. While Thoreau's life at Walden Pond was quiet and

simple

there was simplicity in it, he entertained many groups of his friends. In

and conventions

addition, committees ∧ met at Walden, ~~and conventions also had meetings~~
                                        ∧ *wore*
~~there~~. Thoreau "lived off the land" but ~~wearing~~ store-bought clothes and

store-bought

ate ∧ food ~~bought in a store~~. However, Thoreau's famous experiment

                                                                what
taught him many valuable lessons about what is essential and ~~that which~~

is not essential in life.

PRACTICE 14   The following essay contains both correct and faulty parallel structures.
Revise the faulty parallelism.

Nellie Bly

As a writer for the *New York World* in the 1880s, Nellie Bly was one

                                                                    courage
of the leading journalists of her time. With determination and ~~coura-~~

~~geously~~, she pioneered what we now call the "media event." Nellie's most

                                            and daring
renowned exploit was her famous trip ~~that was daring~~ around the world.

Nellie bet her publisher that she could beat the fictional record set by

Phileas Fogg in Jules Verne's novel *Around the World in Eighty Days*.

Moreover, her telegraphed reports of the trip would boost newspaper

                                                            traveled
sales. Nellie left Jersey City on November 14, 1889, and ~~to travel~~ first to

England, France, and ~~the land of~~ Italy. From there, she journeyed over

the Mediterranean Sea and the Indian Ocean to Ceylon. After stops in

Singapore, Hong Kong, and ~~also in~~ Tokyo, she set sail for San Francisco.

During this leg of the journey, she almost lost her bet. First, low winds

                                                    struck
delayed the sailing; then powerful storms ~~were striking~~ at sea. Adopting

the motto "We'll Win or Die for Nellie Bly," the crew managed to get the

                                        , fast
ship to America. An easy cross-country train trip ~~that was fast~~ returned

Nellie Bly to New York on January 25, 1890. Her trip had lasted 72 days,

6 hours, and ~~there were~~ 11 minutes.

Nellie arrived home a great hero and ~~to be~~ a national figure. Cheer-

ing crowds greeted her, songs were dedicated to her, toys were named after her, and ~~there were~~ parades ~~that~~ were organized in her honor. She

embarked on a national tour, making speeches about her travels and
fascinating
~~to fascinate~~ crowds with her tales. Nellie had shown the world that a
                      safely
gutsy American woman could travel the world alone, quickly and ~~with~~

~~safety.~~

PART D

Consistent Quotations

There are two ways in which a writer can record the words of another person: **direct discourse** and **indirect discourse.**

 Direct discourse _records the speaker's exact words inside quotation marks._ Note the punctuation:*

> 1. "Follow me," the guard told us.
> 2. Phil said, "I've just returned from Oregon."

Indirect discourse _reports what was said without quotation marks but in the writer's words._ Note the punctuation:

> 3. The guard told us to follow him.
> 4. Phil said that he had just returned from Oregon.

In addition to different punctuation, shifting from direct to indirect or from indirect to direct discourse may require a different verb tense, as in the following:

> 5. "These math problems _are_ impossible," Dana complained.
> 6. Dana complained that the math problems _were_ impossible.

*For practice in punctuating direct discourse, see Chapter 33, "Mechanics," Part C.

■ The present tense *are* used in direct discourse must be changed to the past tense *were* in indirect discourse since the problems *were impossible* at the same time that Dana *complained.*

Pronouns may also change when writing shifts between direct and indirect discourse, as in the following:

> 7. Our waitress said, "*I'm* working to finance *my* education."
>
> 8. Our waitress said *she* was working to finance *her* education.

■ The first person pronoun *I* in direct discourse changes to the third person *she* in indirect discourse, and the first person *my* changes to the third person *her.*

Consistency of discourse means using *either* direct *or* indirect discourse within a particular sentence. Do not mix direct and indirect discourse within one sentence, or the inconsistency will confuse the reader:

what is wrong?

Shows how punctuation makes a huge difference

9. Inconsistent discourse:	Tom growled that he was leaving and don't try to stop me.
10. Consistent discourse: (direct)	Tom growled, "I am leaving. Don't try to stop me."
11. Consistent discourse: (indirect)	Tom growled that he was leaving and we should not try to stop him.

■ The discourse in sentence 9 is inconsistent and incorrect.

■ Notice the differences in punctuation, verb tense, and pronouns between sentences 10 and 11.

12. Inconsistent discourse:	They asked the cashier, "Is the movie over? If he could change a twenty-dollar bill."
13. Consistent discourse: (direct)	They asked the cashier, "Is the movie over? Can you change a twenty-dollar bill?"
14. Consistent discourse: (indirect)	They asked the cashier if the movie was over and if he could change a twenty-dollar bill.

- Sentence 12 is inconsistent and incorrect.

- In sentence 13, the two questions *they* asked are shown in direct discourse; therefore, a question mark follows each. Sentence 14, however, states that *they asked if....* Thus no question mark is needed.

PRACTICE 15   Convert each of the following sentences from consistent direct to consistent indirect discourse, making all needed changes in verbs, pronouns, and punctuation. You may change words as long as you do not change the meaning. **Answers may vary.**

Example   "Does that blue junk heap belong to you?" the officer asked.

The officer asked whether the blue junk heap belonged to me.

1. The tag states, "This watch is waterproof."

   The tag states that this watch is waterproof.

2. Hope asked us, "Do you have any construction paper left?"

   Hope asked if we had any construction paper left.

3. *"Kakistocracy,"* Professor Davis explained, "means government by the worst."

   Professor Davis explained that *kakistocracy* means government by the worst.

4. "Watch your bags," he cautioned the shoppers.

   He cautioned the shoppers to watch their bags.

5. "My mind accepts changes months before my emotions do," the psychologist told us.

   The psychologist told us that her mind accepts changes months before her

   emotions do.

PRACTICE 16   Convert each sentence below from consistent indirect to consistent direct discourse. Make all necessary changes in punctuation, verbs, and pronouns. **Answers may vary.**

Example   The interviewer asked if I had ever written factual reports.

The interviewer asked, "Have you ever written factual reports?"

Hermano → 1. Sharon asked the realtor if any old farmhouses were available.

_____ Sharon asked the realtor, ''Are any old farmhouses available?'' _____

_____

2. The book advised that a career in law enforcement is not for the squeamish.

_____ The book advised, ''A career in law enforcement is not for the squeamish.'' _____

_____

Write Danielle this on board correctly → 3. He said he preferred silent films.

_____ He said, ''I prefer silent films.'' _____

4. The president's press secretary announced that the new tax plan would soon be presented to the nation.

_____ The president's press secretary announced, ''The new tax plan will be _____

_____ presented to the nation soon.'' _____

Alfred → 5. My neighbor said he wished I would soundproof my room.

_____ My neighbor said, ''I wish you would soundproof your room.'' _____

PRACTICE 17   Correct the inconsistent discourse in each of the following sentences. Rewrite each in consistent indirect discourse or consistent direct discourse. Change the wording if necessary but preserve the meaning of the sentence. Punctuate correctly. Answers may vary.

Example | John asked did I know who won Saturday's game.

John asked, "Do you know who won Saturday's game?"   (direct discourse)

or

John asked me if I knew who won Saturday's game.   (indirect discourse)

1. The speaker read a passage from *Animal Farm* and asked did we care to comment?

_____ The speaker read a passage from *Animal Farm* and asked, ''Does anyone care _____

_____ to comment?'' [or] . . . if anyone cared to comment. _____

2. Toni said that "she would drive if we needed extra cars."

_____ Toni said that she would drive if we needed extra cars. [or] Toni said, ''I'll drive _____

_____ if we need extra cars.'' _____

3. Don't be alarmed by the noise, they told us, that the boiler was being repaired.

"Don't be alarmed by the noise," they told us. "The boiler is being repaired."

[or] They told us that we shouldn't be alarmed by the noise, for the boiler was

being repaired.

4. He said we could sit on the antique chairs but please don't touch the cut glass bowls.

He said that we could sit on the antique chairs but not to touch the cut glass

bowls. [or] He said, "You can sit on the antique chairs, but please don't touch

the cut glass bowls."

5. The poet Kahlil Gibran says, I have learned silence from the talkative, tolerance from the intolerant, and kindness from the unkind. And that he should not be ungrateful to those teachers.

The poet Kahlil Gibran says, "I have learned silence from the talkative,

tolerance from the intolerant, and kindness from the unkind. I should not be

ungrateful to those teachers." [or] The poet . . . said that he had learned . . .

unkind, and that he should not . . . teachers.

PRACTICE 18 Revise the following sentences for **consistency of discourse.** You may use both direct and indirect discourse in the paragraph, but use *either* one *or* the other within each sentence. Write the revised paragraph in the space provided.

Yogi Berra, catcher for the New York Yankees from 1946 to 1963, was almost as famous for his wit as he was for his playing. For instance, when a waitress asked him "if she should cut his pizza into four or eight slices," Yogi replied, "Better make it four. I don't think I can eat eight." Then there was the time that Yogi was asked about a popular restaurant, and he commented "that it's so crowded nobody goes there anymore." On Yogi Berra Day at Yankee Stadium, the former catcher graciously said that I wanted to thank everyone who made today necessary. When asked about a decline in attendance at Yankee games, Yogi offered the following mind-bender: If people don't want to come out to the park, nobody's gonna stop 'em. One day a woman fan told Yogi that he looked cool in spite of the sweltering heat. He returned the compliment by saying, "Thank you ma'am" that you don't look so hot yourself. A reporter asked Yogi "how he had liked school as a child." Closed was Berra's one-word answer.

Yogi Berra, catcher for the New York Yankees from 1946 to 1963, was almost as famous for his wit as he was for his playing. For instance, when a waitress asked him if she should cut his pizza into four or eight slices, Yogi replied, ''Better make it four. I don't think I can eat eight.'' Then there was the time that Yogi was asked about a popular restaurant, and he commented, ''It's so crowded nobody goes there anymore.'' On Yogi Berra Day at Yankee Stadium, the former catcher graciously said, ''I want to thank everyone who made today necessary.'' When asked about a decline in attendance at Yankee games, Yogi offered the following mind-bender: ''If people don't want to come out to the park, nobody's gonna stop 'em.'' One day a woman fan told Yogi that he looked cool in spite of the sweltering heat. He returned the compliment by saying, ''Thank you ma'am. You don't look so hot yourself.'' A reporter asked Yogi how he had liked school as a child. ''Closed,'' was Berra's one-word answer.

14

Revising for Sentence Variety

PART A   Mix Long and Short Sentences
PART B   Use a Question, Command, or Exclamation
PART C   Vary the Beginnings of Sentences
PART D   Vary Methods of Joining Ideas
PART E   Review and Practice

Good writers pay attention to **sentence variety.** They notice how sentences work together within a paragraph, and they seek a mix of different sentence lengths and types. Experienced writers have a variety of sentence patterns from which to choose. They try not to overuse one pattern.

This chapter will present several techniques for varying your sentences and paragraphs. Some of them you may already know and use, perhaps unconsciously. The purpose of this chapter is to make you more conscious of the **choices** available to you as a writer.

Remember, you achieve sentence variety by practicing, by systematically **revising** your papers and trying out new types of sentences or combinations of sentences.

PART A

Mix Long and Short Sentences

One of the basic ways to achieve sentence variety is to use both long and short sentences. Beginning writers tend to overuse short, simple sentences, which quickly become monotonous. Notice the length of the sentences in the following paragraph:

> (1) There is one positive result of the rising crime rate. (2) This has been the growth of neighborhood crime prevention programs. (3) These programs really work. (4) They teach citizens to patrol their neighborhoods. (5) They teach citizens to work with the police. (6) They have dramatically reduced crime in cities and towns across the country. (7) The idea is catching on.

The sentences in this paragraph are all nearly the same length, and the effect is choppy and almost childish. Now read this revised version, which contains a variety of sentence lengths.

> (1) One positive result of the rising crime rate has been the growth of neighborhood crime prevention programs. (2) These programs really work. (3) By teaching citizens to patrol their neighborhoods and to work with the police, they have dramatically reduced crime in cities and towns across the country. (4) The idea is catching on.

This paragraph is more effective because it mixes two short sentences, 2 and 4, and two longer sentences, 1 and 3. Although short sentences can be used effectively anywhere in a paragraph or essay, they can be especially useful as introductions or conclusions, like sentence 4 above. Note the powerful effect of short sentences used between longer ones in the paragraph that follows. Underline the short sentences.

> (1) I recall being told, when I first moved to Los Angeles and was living on an isolated beach, that the Indians would throw themselves into the sea when the bad wind blew. (2) I could see why. (3) The Pacific turned ominously glossy during a Santa Ana period, and one woke in the night troubled not only by the peacocks screaming in the olive trees but by the eerie absence of surf. (4) The heat was surreal. (5) The sky had a yellow cast, the kind of light sometimes called "earthquake weather." (6) My only neighbor would not come out of her house for days, and there were no lights at night, and her husband roamed the place with a machete. (7) One day he would tell me that he had heard a trespasser, the next a rattlesnake.
>
> —Joan Didion, *Slouching Towards Bethlehem*

PRACTICE 1   Revise and rewrite the following paragraph in a variety of sentence lengths. Recombine sentences in any way you wish. You may add connecting words or drop words, but do not alter the meaning of the paragraph. Answers will vary.

The park is alive with motion today. Joggers pound up and down the boardwalk. Old folks watch them from the benches. Couples row boats across the lake. The boats are green and wooden. Two teen-agers hurl a Frisbee back and forth. They yell and leap. A shaggy white dog dashes in from nowhere. He snatches the red disk in his mouth. He bounds away. The teen-agers run after him.

The park is alive with motion today. Joggers pound up and down on the boardwalk, and old folks watch them from the benches. Couples row green wooden boats across the lake. On the nearby grass, two teen-agers hurl a Frisbee back and forth, yelling and leaping. Suddenly, a shaggy white dog dashes in from nowhere, snatches the red disk in his mouth, and bounds away. Yelling and laughing, the teen-agers run after him.

PART B

Use a Question, Command, or Exclamation

The most commonly used sentence is the **declarative sentence,** which is a statement. However, an occasional carefully placed **question, command,** or **exclamation** is an effective way to achieve sentence variety.

The Question

> *Why did I become a cab driver?* First, I truly enjoy driving a car and exploring different parts of the city, the classy avenues and the hidden back streets. In addition, I like meeting all kinds of people, from bookmakers to governors, each with a unique story and many willing to talk to the back of my head. Of course, the pay isn't bad and the hours are flexible, but it's the places and the people that I love.

This paragraph begins with a question. The writer does not really expect the reader to answer it. Rather, it is a **rhetorical question,** one that will be answered by the writer in the course of the paragraph. A rhetorical question used as a topic sentence can provide a colorful change from the usual declarative sentences: *Is America really the best-fed nation in the world? What is courage? Why do more young people take drugs today than ever before?*

The Command and the Exclamation

> (1) Try to imagine using failure as a description of an animal's behavior. (2) Consider a dog barking for fifteen minutes, and someone saying, "He really isn't very good at barking, I'd give him a C." (3) How absurd! (4) It is impossible for an animal to fail because there is no provision for evaluating natural behavior. (5) Spiders construct webs, not successful or unsuccessful webs. (6) Cats hunt mice; if they aren't successful in one attempt, they simply go after another. (7) They don't lie there and whine, complaining about the one that got away, or have a nervous breakdown because they failed. (8) Natural behavior simply is! (9) So apply the same logic to your own behavior and rid yourself of the fear of failure.
>
> —Dr. Wayne W. Dyer, *Your Erroneous Zones*

The paragraph above begins and ends with **commands,** or **imperative sentences.** Sentences 1, 2, and 9 address the reader directly and have as their implied subject *you.* They tell the reader to do something: *(You) try to imagine . . . , (you) consider . . . , (you) apply. . . .* Commands are most frequently used in giving directions,* but they can be used occasionally, as in the paragraph above, for sentence variety.

Sentences 3 and 8 in the Dyer paragraph are **exclamations,** sentences that express strong emotion and end with an exclamation point. These should be used very sparingly. In fact some writers avoid them altogether, striving for words that convey strong emotion instead.

Be careful with the question, the command, and the exclamation as options in your writing. Try them out, but use them—especially the exclamation—sparingly.

Writing Assignment 1

On a separate piece of paper, write a paragraph that begins with a rhetorical question. Choose one of the questions below or compose your own. Be sure that the body of the paragraph really does answer the question.

1. How has college (or anything else) changed me?

2. Is marriage worth the risks?

3. Does rock music encourage the mistreatment of women?

*For more work on giving directions, see Chapter 8, "Process."

4. Is anything safe to eat these days?

5. Should people pamper their pets?

PART C

Vary the Beginnings of Sentences

Begin with an Adverb

Since the first word of many sentences is the subject, one way to achieve sentence variety is by occasionally starting a sentence with a word or words other than the subject.

For instance, you can begin with an **adverb:***

---

1. He *laboriously* dragged the large crate up the stairs.

2. *Laboriously*, he dragged the large crate up the stairs.

3. The contents of the beaker *suddenly* began to foam.

4. *Suddenly*, the contents of the beaker began to foam.

- In sentences 2 and 4, the adverbs *laboriously* and *suddenly* are shifted to the first position. Notice the difference in rhythm that this creates, as well as the slight change in meaning: Sentence 2 emphasizes *how* he dragged the crate—*laboriously*; sentence 4 emphasizes the *suddenness* of what happened.

- A comma usually follows an adverb that introduces a sentence; however, adverbs of time—*often, now, always*—do not always require a comma. As a general rule, use a comma if you want the reader to pause briefly.

PRACTICE 2 Rewrite the following sentences by shifting the adverbs to the beginning. Punctuate correctly. Answers will vary.

Example | He skillfully prepared the engine for the race.

Skillfully, he prepared the engine for the race.

√ 1. Two deer moved silently across the clearing.

Silently, two deer moved across the clearing.

*For more work on adverbs, see Chapter 30, "Adjectives and Adverbs."

✓ 2. The chief of the research division occasionally visits the lab.

  Occasionally, the chief of the research division visits the lab.

✓ 3. Proofread your writing always.

  Always proofread your writing.

4. Children of alcoholics often marry alcoholics.

  Often children of alcoholics marry alcoholics.

5. Jake foolishly lied to his supervisor.

  Foolishly, Jake lied to his supervisor.

PRACTICE 3   Begin each of the following sentences with an appropriate adverb. Punctuate correctly. Answers may vary.

in class

✓ 1. Cautiously,   the detective approached the ticking suitcase.

2. Enthusiastically,   Jennifer Capriati powered a forehand past her opponent.

3. Yesterday   she received her check for $25,000 from the state lottery.

4. Reluctantly,   he gave back the keys.

✓ 5. Slowly,   the submarine sank out of sight.

  Quickly – Can subs sink quickly?

PRACTICE 4   Write five sentences of your own that begin with adverbs. Use different adverbs from those in Practices 1 and 2; if you wish, use *graciously, absent-mindedly, cheerfully, furiously, sometimes.* Punctuate correctly. Sample answers:

1. Graciously, Rosa offered us use of her vacation home.

2. Absent-mindedly, he left the tickets at home.

3. Cheerfully, Jim whistled as he waxed the car.

4. Furiously, she slammed the door.

5. Sometimes I go for long walks on the beach.

Begin with a Prepositional Phrase

A **prepositional phrase** is a group of words containing a **preposition** and its **object** (a noun or pronoun). *To you, in the evening,* and *under the old bridge* are prepositional phrases.*

Preposition	Object
to	you
in	the evening
under	the old bridge

Here is a partial list of prepositions:

Common Prepositions

about	beneath	into	throughout
above	beside	near	to
across	between	of	toward
against	by	on	under
among	except	onto	up
at	for	out	upon
behind	from	over	with
below	in	through	without

For variety in your writing, begin an occasional sentence with a prepositional phrase:

5. Charles left the room *without a word.*

6. *Without a word,* Charles left the room.

7. A fat yellow cat lay sleeping *on the narrow sill.*

8. *On the narrow sill,* a fat yellow cat lay sleeping.

*For work on spotting prepositional phrases, see Chapter 21, "The Simple Sentence," Part B.

- In sentences 6 and 8, the prepositional phrases have been shifted to the beginning. Note the slight shift in emphasis that results. Sentence 6 stresses that Charles left the room *without a word*, and 8 stresses the location of the cat, *on the narrow sill.*

- Prepositional phrases that begin sentences are usually followed by commas. However, short prepositional phrases need not be.

Prepositional phrases are not always movable; rely on the meaning of the sentence to determine whether or not they are movable:

> 9. The dress *in the picture* is the one I want.
>
> 10. Joelle bought a bottle *of white wine for dinner.*

- *In the picture* in sentence 9 is a part of the subject and cannot be moved. *In the picture the dress is the one I want* makes no sense.

- Sentence 10 has two prepositional phrases. Which one *cannot* be moved to the beginning of the sentence? Why?

    Of white wine cannot be moved because it describes the word *bottle* and should

    therefore follow it.

PRACTICE 5 Underline the prepositional phrases in each sentence. Some sentences contain more than one prepositional phrase. Rewrite each sentence by shifting a prepositional phrase to the beginning. Punctuate correctly.

Example | A large owl with gray feathers watched us from the oak tree.

From the oak tree, a large owl with gray feathers watched us.

in class

✓ 1. The coffee maker turned itself on at seven o'clock sharp.

At seven o'clock sharp, the coffee maker turned itself on.

✓ 2. A growling Doberman paced behind the chain link fence.

Behind the chain link fence, a growling Doberman paced.

3. My cousins ran the Fruit of the Month Club from this office.

From this office, my cousins ran the Fruit of the Month Club.

4. They have sold nothing except athletic shoes for years.

   For years, they have sold nothing except athletic shoes.

   _____

   _____

5. A group of men played checkers and drank iced tea beside the small shop.

   Beside the small shop, a group of men played checkers and drank iced tea.

   _____

   _____

PRACTICE 6 Begin each of the following sentences with a different prepositional phrase. Refer to the list and be creative. Punctuate correctly. Answers will vary.

1. From the à la carte menu,_____ we ordered potato skins, salad, and beer.

2. At the far table,_____ a woman in horn-rimmed glasses sat and wrote.

3. After work,_____ everyone congratulated Jim on his promotion.

4. In the museum,_____ one can see beaded moccasins, carved masks, and pipes.

5. Over our heads,_____ three helium-filled balloons drifted.

PRACTICE 7 Write five sentences of your own that begin with prepositional phrases. Use these phrases if you wish: *in the dentist's office, between them, at my wedding, under that stack of books, behind his friendly smile.* Punctuate correctly.

1. In the dentist's office, the patients waited nervously.

2. Between them, they own ten homes.

3. At my wedding, we had a live orchestra.

4. Under that stack of books, you'll find the grocery list.

5. Behind his friendly smile, he is a dishonest salesman.

PART D

Vary Methods of Joining Ideas*

Join Ideas with a Compound Predicate

A sentence with a **compound predicate** contains more than one verb, but the subject is *not* repeated before the second verb. Such a sentence is really composed of two simple sentences with the same subject:

1. The nurse entered.

2. The nurse quickly closed the door.

3. The nurse *entered* and quickly *closed* the door.

- *The nurse* is the subject of sentence 1 and *entered* is the verb; *the nurse* is also the subject of sentence 2 and *closed* is the verb.

- When these sentences are combined with a compound predicate in sentence 3, *the nurse* is the subject of both *entered* and *closed* but is not repeated before the second verb.

- No comma is necessary when the conjunctions *and, but, or,* and *yet* join the verbs in a compound predicate.

A compound predicate is useful in combining short, choppy sentences:

4. He serves elaborate meals.

5. He never uses a recipe.

6. He serves elaborate meals yet never uses a recipe.

7. Aviators rarely get nosebleeds.

8. They often suffer from backaches.

9. Aviators rarely get nosebleeds but often suffer from backaches.

- Sentences 4 and 5 are joined by *yet;* no comma precedes *yet.*

- Sentences 7 and 8 are joined by *but;* no comma precedes *but.*

*For work on joining ideas with coordination and subordination, see Chapter 22, "Coordination and Subordination."

PRACTICE 8   Combine each pair of short sentences into one sentence with a compound predicate. Use *and, but, or,* and *yet.* Punctuate correctly.

Answers will vary.

Example   Toby smeared peanut butter on a thick slice of white bread.

He devoured the treat in thirty seconds.

Toby smeared peanut butter on a thick slice of white bread and devoured the treat

in thirty seconds.

1. Americans eat more than 800 million pounds of peanut butter.

   They spend more than $1 billion on the product each year.

   Americans eat more than 800 million pounds of peanut butter and spend more

   than $1 billion on the product each year.

2. Peanut butter was first concocted in the 1890s.

   It did not become the food we know for thirty years.

   Peanut butter was first concocted in the 1890s but did not become the food we

   know for thirty years.

3. George Washington Carver did not discover peanut butter.

   He published many recipes for pastes much like it.

   George Washington Carver did not discover peanut butter yet published many

   recipes for pastes much like it.

4. The average American becomes a peanut butter lover in childhood.

   He or she loses enthusiasm for it later on.

   The average American becomes a peanut butter lover in childhood but loses

   enthusiasm for it later on.

5. Older adults regain their passion for peanut butter.

   They consume great quantities of the delicious stuff.

   Older adults regain their passion for peanut butter and consume great

   quantities of the delicious stuff.

PRACTICE 9   Complete the following compound predicates. *Do not repeat* the subjects.
Answers will vary.

1. Three Korean writers visited the campus and <u>met with aspiring</u>

<u>novelists</u>.

2. The singer breathed heavily into the microphone but <u>didn't sing a</u>

<u>note</u>.

3. Do your share of the housework or <u>move to a hotel</u>

_____.

4. The newspaper printed the story yet <u>didn't check the facts first</u>

_____.

5. Three men burst into the back room and <u>threw confetti on the surprised</u>

<u>card-players</u>.

PRACTICE 10   Write five sentences with compound predicates. Be careful to punctuate
correctly. Sample answers:

1. <u>Tonight I plan to study for my exam and start writing my paper.</u>

2. <u>Many people like to cook but do not like to clean up.</u>

3. <u>We could see a movie or go out to dinner.</u>

4. <u>Mike loves to sail yet cannot swim.</u>

5. <u>Renée can drive a car but has never parallel parked.</u>

Join Ideas with an *-ing* Modifier

An excellent way to achieve sentence variety is by occasionally combining
two sentences with an *-ing* modifier.

10. He peered through the microscope.

11. He discovered a squiggly creature.

12. *Peering through the microscope,* he discovered a squiggly
creature.

- Sentence 10 has been converted to an *-ing* modifier by changing the verb *peered* to *peering* and dropping the subject *he. Peering through the microscope* now introduces the main clause, *he discovered a squiggly creature.*

- A comma sets off the *-ing* modifier from the word it refers to, *he.* To avoid confusion, the word referred to must immediately follow the *-ing* modifier.

An *-ing* modifier indicates that two actions are occurring at the same time. The main idea of the sentence should be contained in the main clause, not in the *-ing* modifier. In the preceding example, the discovery of the creature is the main idea, not the fact that someone peered through a microscope.

Be careful: misplaced *-ing* modifiers can result in confusing sentences: *He discovered a squiggly creature peering through the microscope.* (Is the creature looking through the microscope?)

Convert sentence 13 into an *-ing* modifier and write it in the blank:

---

13. We drove down Tompkins Road.

14. We were surprised by the number of "for sale" signs.

15. __Driving down Tompkins Road_____, we were surprised by the number of "for sale" signs.

- The new *-ing* modifier is followed directly by the word to which it refers, *we.*

PRACTICE 11   Combine the following pairs of sentences by converting the first sentence into an *-ing* modifier. Make sure the subject of the main clause directly follows the *-ing* modifier. Punctuate correctly.

Example | Janet searched for her silk tunic.

She completely emptied the closet.

Searching for her silk tunic, Janet completely emptied the closet.

1. She installed the air conditioner.

   She saved herself $50 in labor.

   Installing the air conditioner, she saved herself $50 in labor.

2. The surgeons raced against time.

   The surgeons performed a liver transplant on the child.

   Racing against time, the surgeons performed a liver transplant on the child.

3. They conducted a survey of Jackson Heights residents.

   They found that most opposed construction of the airport.

   Conducting a survey of Jackson Heights residents, they found that most

   opposed construction of the airport.

4. Three flares spiraled upward from the little boat.

   They exploded against the night sky.

   Spiraling up from the little boat, three flares exploded against the night sky.

5. Virgil danced in the Pennsylvania Ballet.

   Virgil learned discipline and self-control.

   Dancing in the Pennsylvania Ballet, Virgil learned discipline and self-control.

6. The hen squawked loudly.

   The hen fluttered out of our path.

   Squawking loudly, the hen fluttered out of our path.

7. The engineer made a routine check of the blueprints.

   He discovered a flaw in the design.

   Making a routine check of the blueprints, the engineer discovered a flaw in the

   design.

8. Dr. Jackson opened commencement exercises with a humorous story.

   He put everyone at ease.

   Opening commencement exercises with a humorous story, Dr. Jackson put

   everyone at ease.

PRACTICE 12   Add either an introductory *-ing* modifier *or* a main clause to each sentence. Make sure that each *-ing* modifier refers clearly to the subject of the main clause.   Sample answers:

Examples   Reading a book a week _____ , Jeff increased his vocabulary.

Exercising every day, I lost five pounds _____ .

1. Finally finishing her report _____ , she felt a sense of accomplishment.

2. Growing up in Hollywood, he was not dazzled by movie stars. _____

3. Making a tremendous effort _____ , the swimmer broke the world record.

4. Interviewing his relatives, Jason collected many family stories. _____

5. Moving slowly on its long chain _____ , the wrecking ball swung through the air and smashed into the brick wall.

PRACTICE 13   Write five sentences of your own that begin with *-ing* modifiers. Make sure that the subject of the sentence follows the modifier and be careful of the punctuation.   Answers will vary.

1. Giving myself a pep talk, I sat down to study Japanese.

2. Crossing the street for the first time, the child carefully looked both ways.

3. Practicing with her roommate's manual, Ellen finally learned to use Word Perfect.

4. Rummaging through his drawers, Joe found a stack of unpaid bills.

5. Jogging the last mile, Ben got so tired that he had to stop.

Join Ideas with a Past Participial Modifier

Some sentences can be joined with a **past participial modifier.** A sentence that contains a *to be* verb and a **past participle*** can be changed into a past participial modifier:

> 16. Judith *is alarmed* by the increase in meat prices.
>
> 17. Judith has become a vegetarian.
>
> 18. *Alarmed by the increase in meat prices*, Judith has become a vegetarian.

- Sentence 16 has been made into a past participial modifier by dropping the helping verb *is* and the subject *Judith.* The past participle *alarmed* now introduces the new sentence.

- A comma sets off the past participial modifier from the word it modifies, *Judith.* To avoid confusion, the word referred to must directly follow the modifier.

Be careful: misplaced past participial modifiers can result in confusing sentences: *Packed in dry ice, Steve brought us some ice cream.* (Is Steve packed in dry ice?)

Sometimes two or more past participles can be used to introduce a sentence:

> 19. The term paper was *revised* and *rewritten.*
>
> 20. It received an A.
>
> 21. *Revised and rewritten*, the term paper received an A.

- The past participles *revised* and *rewritten* become a modifier that introduces sentence 21. What word(s) do they refer to?

  the term paper

PRACTICE 14   Combine each pair of sentences into one sentence that begins with a past participial modifier. Convert the sentence containing a form of *to be* plus

---

*For more work on past participles, see Chapter 26, "The Past Participle."

a **past participle** into a past participial modifier that introduces the new sentence.

Example | Duffy was surprised by the interruption.

He lost his train of thought.

Surprised by the interruption, Duffy lost his train of thought.

 1. My mother was married at the age of sixteen.

My mother never finished high school.

Married at the age of sixteen, my mother never finished high school.

2. The 2:30 flight was delayed by an electrical storm.

It arrived in Lexington three hours late.

Delayed by an electrical storm, the 2:30 flight arrived in Lexington three hours

late.

3. Pam was embarrassed by the reporter's questions.

She left the room.

Embarrassed by the reporter's questions, Pam left the room.

4. This engine is rebuilt and road-tested.

It runs perfectly.

Rebuilt and road-tested, this engine runs perfectly.

5. The Nineteenth Amendment was ratified in 1920.

It gave women the right to vote.

Ratified in 1920, the Nineteenth Amendment gave women the right to vote.

6. The manuscript is very hard to read.

It is written in longhand.

Written in longhand, the manuscript is very hard to read.

7. Dr. Bentley will address the premed students.

He has been recognized for his contributions in the field of immunology.

<u>Recognized for his contributions in the field of immunology, Dr. Bentley will</u>

<u>address the premed students.</u>

8. Mrs. Witherspoon was exhausted by night classes.

She declined the chance to work overtime.

<u>Exhausted by night classes, Mrs. Witherspoon declined the chance to work</u>

<u>overtime.</u>

PRACTICE 15 Complete each sentence by filling in *either* the past participial modifier *or* the main clause. Remember, the past participial modifier must clearly refer to the subject of the main clause.

Example Wrapped in blue paper and tied with string, <u>the gift arrived</u>.

<u>Chosen to represent the team</u>, Phil proudly accepted the trophy.

1. Made of gold and set with precious stones, <u>the snuff box was a wonder to behold</u>.

2. Overwhelmed by the response to her ad in *The Star*, <u>Mabel limited the number of people she would interview to ten</u>.

3. <u>Pursued by police in three states</u>, Tom left no forwarding address.

4. <u>Laden with parcels from a shopping trip</u>, we found a huge basket of fresh fruit on the steps.

5. Astonished by the scene before her, <u>Consuela reached for the telephone and dialed 911</u>.

PRACTICE 16   Write five sentences of your own that begin with past participial modifiers. If you wish, use participles from this list:

thrilled	moved	seen	honored
shocked	dressed	hidden	bent
awakened	lost	stuffed	examined
annoyed	found	pinched	rewired

Make sure that the subject of the sentence clearly follows the modifier. Sample answers:

1. _Awakened by the fire alarm, the hotel guests rushed outside._

2. _Annoyed by Louise's failure to keep appointments, I decided to stop calling her._

3. _Dressed in her ballet costume, the little girl performed for her parents._

4. _Lost for several hours, the hikers were cold and tired when they were rescued._

5. _Hidden in the back of the closet, my favorite shoes were lost for weeks._

Join Ideas with an Appositive

A fine way to add variety to your writing is to combine two choppy sentences with an appositive. An **appositive** is a word or group of words that renames or describes a noun or pronoun:

> 22. Carlos is the new wrestling champion.
>
> 23. He is a native of Argentina.
>
> 24. Carlos, *a native of Argentina*, is the new wrestling champion.

- *A native of Argentina* in sentence 24 is an appositive. It renames the noun *Carlos*.

- An appositive must be placed either directly *after* the word it refers to, as in sentence 24, or directly *before* it, as follows:

> 25. *A native of Argentina*, Carlos is the new wrestling champion.

- Note that an appositive is set off by commas.

Appositives can add versatility to your writing because they can be placed at the beginning, in the middle, or at the end of a sentence. When you join two ideas with an appositive, place the idea you wish to stress in the main clause and make the less important idea the appositive:

> 26. Naomi wants to become a fashion model.
>
> 27. She is the daughter of an actress.
>
> 28. *The daughter of an actress*, Naomi wants to become a fashion model.
>
> 29. FACT made headlines for the first time in 1986.
>
> 30. FACT is now a powerful consumer group.
>
> 31. FACT, *now a powerful consumer group*, made headlines for the first time in 1986.
>
> 32. Watch out for Smithers.
>
> 33. He is a dangerous man.
>
> 34. Watch out for Smithers, *a dangerous man*.

Using an appositive to combine sentences eliminates unimportant words and creates longer, more fact-filled sentences.

PRACTICE 17   Combine the following pairs of sentences by making the *second sentence* an appositive. Punctuate correctly.

These appositives should occur at the *beginning* of the sentences.

Example   My uncle taught me to use water colors.

He is a well-known artist.

A well-known artist, my uncle taught me to use water colors.

1. Don made baked fish with coconut for the party.

   He is a fine cook.

   A fine cook, Don made baked fish with coconut for the party.

   _____

2. Acupuncture is becoming more popular in the U.S.

   It is an ancient Chinese healing system.

   An ancient Chinese healing system, acupuncture is becoming more popular in

   the U.S.

   _____

3. The Cromwell Hotel was built in 1806.

   It is an elegant example of Mexican architecture.

   An elegant example of Mexican architecture, the Cromwell Hotel was built in

   1806.

   These appositives should occur in the *middle* of the sentences. Punctuate correctly.

Example   His black literature course is always popular with students.

   It is an introductory survey.

   His black literature course, an introductory survey, is always popular with

   students.

4. The Korean ping-pong champion won ten games in a row.

   She is a small and wiry athlete.

   The Korean ping-pong champion, a small and wiry athlete, won ten games in a

   row.

5. The pituitary is located below the brain.

   It is the body's master gland.

   The pituitary, the body's master gland, is located below the brain.

   _____

6. The elevator shudders violently and begins to rise.

It is an ancient box of wood and hope.

The elevator, an ancient box of wood and hope, shudders violently and begins

to rise.

These appositives should occur at the *end* of the sentences. Punctuate correctly.

Example   I hate fried asparagus.

It is a vile dish.

I hate fried asparagus, a vile dish.

7. Jennifer flaunted her new camera.

It was a Nikon with a telephoto lens.

Jennifer flaunted her new camera, a Nikon with a telephoto lens.

8. At the intersection stood a hitchhiker.

He was a young man dressed in a tuxedo.

At the intersection stood a hitchhiker, a young man dressed in a tuxedo.

9. We met for pancakes at the Cosmic Cafe.

It was a greasy diner on the corner of 10th and Vine.

We met for pancakes at the Cosmic Cafe, a greasy diner on the corner of 10th

and Vine.

PRACTICE 18   Write six sentences using appositives. In two sentences, place the appositive at the beginning; in two sentences, place the appositive in the middle; and in two sentences, place it at the end.
Sample answers:

1.   _An avid sailor, my brother-in-law dreams of owning a thirty-foot sailboat._

2. _____A state champion, that runner is supposed to win the marathon._____

_____

3. _____We serve vichyssoise, a cold potato soup, on hot summer days._____

_____

4. _____We stayed in Grantham, a small town in New Hampshire, for our vacation._____

_____

5. _____You can buy camping gear in Cherry Hill, the next town over._____

_____

6. _____The tall woman standing on the dock is Isabel, my mother's neighbor._____

_____

Join Ideas with a Relative Clause

Relative clauses can add sophistication to your writing. A **relative clause** begins with *who, which,* or *that* and describes a noun or pronoun. It can join two simple sentences in a longer, more complex sentence:

---

35. Jack just won a scholarship from the Arts Council.

36. He makes wire sculpture.

37. Jack, *who makes wire sculpture,* just won a scholarship from the Arts Council.

- In sentence 37, *who makes wire sculpture* is a relative clause, created by replacing the subject *he* of sentence 36 with the relative pronoun *who.*

- *Who* now introduces the subordinate relative clause and connects it to the rest of the sentence. Note that *who* directly follows the word it refers to, *Jack.*

The idea that the writer wishes to stress is placed in the main clause, and the subordinate idea is placed in the relative clause. Study the combinations in sentences 38–40 and 41–43 on the next page.

38. Carrots grow in cool climates.

39. They are high in vitamin A.

40. Carrots, *which* are high in vitamin A, grow in cool climates.

41. He finally submitted the term paper.

42. It was due six months ago.

43. He finally submitted the term paper *that* was due six months ago.

- In sentence 40, *which are high in vitamin A* is a relative clause, created by replacing *they* with *which.* What word in sentence 40 does *which* refer to?

  carrots

- What is the relative clause in sentence 43?

  that was due six months ago

- What word does *that* refer to?

  term paper

Punctuating relative clauses can be tricky; therefore, you will have to be careful:*

44. Claude, *who grew up in Haiti,* speaks fluent French.

- *Who grew up in Haiti* is set off by commas because it adds information about Claude that is not essential to the meaning of the sentence. In other words, the sentence would make sense without it: *Claude speaks fluent French.*

- *Who grew up in Haiti* is called a **nonrestrictive clause.** It does not restrict or provide vital information about the word it modifies.

45. People *who chew gum in theaters* annoy me.

*For more practice in punctuating relative clauses, see Chapter 32, "The Comma," Part D.

- *Who chew gum in theaters* is not set off by commas because it is vital to the meaning of the sentence. Without it, the sentence would read, *People annoy me;* yet the point of the sentence is that people *who chew gum in theaters* annoy me, not all people.

- *Who chew gum in theaters* is called a **restrictive clause** because it restricts the meaning of the word it refers to, *people.*

Note that *which* usually begins a nonrestrictive clause and *that* usually begins a restrictive clause.

PRACTICE 19   Combine each pair of sentences by changing the second sentence into a relative clause introduced by *who, which,* or *that.* Remember, *who* refers to persons, *that* refers to persons or things, and *which* refers to things.

These sentences require **nonrestrictive relative clauses.** Punctuate correctly.

Example   My cousin will spend the summer hiking in the Rockies.

She lives in Indiana.

My cousin, who lives in Indiana, will spend the summer hiking in the Rockies.

_____

1. Scrabble has greatly increased my vocabulary.

    It is my favorite game.

    Scrabble, which is my favorite game, has greatly increased my vocabulary.

    _____

2. Contestants on game shows often make fools of themselves.

    They may travel thousands of miles to play.

    Contestants on game shows, who may travel thousands of miles to play, often

    make fools of themselves.

3. Arabic is a difficult language to learn.

    It has a complicated verb system.

    Arabic, which has a complicated verb system, is a difficult language to learn.

    _____

The next sentences require **restrictive relative clauses.** Punctuate correctly.

Example | He described an attitude.

I have experienced it.

He described an attitude that I have experienced.

_____

4. The house is for sale.

I was born in it.

The house that I was born in is for sale.

_____

_____

5. My boss likes reports.

They are clear and to the point.

My boss likes reports that are clear and to the point.

_____

_____

6. People know how intelligent birds are.

They have owned a bird.

People who have owned a bird know how intelligent birds are.

_____

_____

PRACTICE 20 Combine each pair of sentences by changing one into a relative clause introduced by _who, which,_ or _that._ Remember, _who_ refers to persons, _that_ refers to persons or things, and _which_ refers to things.

Be careful of the punctuation. (Hint: _Which_ clauses are usually set off by commas and _that_ clauses are usually not.)

1. Her grandfather has joined the Gray Panthers.

He is seventy-seven years old.

Her grandfather, who is seventy-seven years old, has joined the Gray Panthers.

_____

_____

2. The Xerox machine earned millions for Chester Carlson.

It had been rejected by RCA, IBM, and G.E.

The Xerox machine, which earned millions for Chester Carlson, had been

rejected by RCA, IBM, and G.E.

_____

3. You just dropped an antique pitcher.

   It is worth two thousand dollars.

   You just dropped an antique pitcher that is worth two thousand dollars.

4. Parenthood has taught me acceptance, forgiveness, and love.

   It used to terrify me.

   Parenthood, which used to terrify me, has taught me acceptance, forgiveness,

   and love.

5. James Fenimore Cooper was expelled from college.

   He later became a famous American novelist.

   James Fenimore Cooper, who was expelled from college, later became a

   famous American novelist.

6. The verb *to hector* means "to bully someone."

   It derives from a character in Greek literature.

   The verb *to hector,* which derives from a character in Greek literature, means

   "to bully someone."

PRACTICE 21   Write six sentences with relative clauses. Make three relative clauses restrictive and three nonrestrictive. Be careful of the punctuation.

Sample answers:

1. Anyone who is over eighteen is eligible to win.

2. The health club that is on the corner used to be a warehouse.

3. Please return immediately any library books that are overdue.

4. Robin's birthday cake, which I baked this morning, is in the kitchen.

5. My bank, which is the oldest in the city, offers free checking.

_____

6. I'm leaving to pick up my term paper, which is at the copier's.

_____

PART E

Review and Practice

Before practicing some of the techniques of sentence variety discussed in this chapter, review them briefly:

go over in class

✱ 1. Mix long and short sentences.

✱ 2. Add an occasional question, command, or exclamation.

3. Begin with an adverb: *Unfortunately*, the outfielder dropped the fly ball.

4. Begin with a prepositional phrase: *With great style*, the pitcher delivered a curve.

5. Join ideas with a compound predicate: The fans *roared and banged* their seats.

6. Mix coordination and subordination.*

alter sentence structures for variety

Coordination	The fans hissed, *but* the umpire paid no attention.
	The fans hissed; the umpire paid no attention.
	The fans hissed; *however*, the umpire paid no attention.

| Subordination | The umpire paid no attention *although* the fans hissed. |
| | *Although* the fans hissed, the umpire paid no attention. |

7. Join ideas with an *-ing* modifier: *Diving chin first onto the grass*, Johnson caught the ball.

8. Join ideas with a past participial modifier: *Frustrated by the call*, the batter kicked dirt onto home plate.

9. Join ideas with an appositive: Beer, *the cause of much rowdiness*, should not be sold at games.

10. Join ideas with a relative clause: Box seats, *which are hard to get for important games*, are frequently bought up by corporations.

*For more work, see Chapter 22, "Coordination and Subordination."

Of course, the secret of achieving sentence variety is practice. Choose one, two, or three of these techniques to focus on and try them out in your writing. Revise your paragraphs and essays with an eye to sentence variety.

PRACTICE 22   Revise and then rewrite this essay, aiming for sentence variety. Vary the length and pattern of the sentences. Vary the beginnings of some sentences. Join two sentences in any way you wish, adding appropriate connecting words or dropping unnecessary words. Punctuate correctly.
Answers will vary.

Little Richard, the King of Rock 'n' Roll

With "A-Wop-Bop-A-Loo-Bop-A-Lop-Bam-Boom," Little Richard hit the American music scene on September 14, 1955. It has never been the same since. He had almost insane energy. He wore flamboyant clothes. He defined the rebellious behavior. This rebellious behavior was at the heart of rock 'n' roll.

Richard Wayne Penniman was born on December 5, 1932, in Macon, Georgia. He was the third of thirteen children. He and his siblings sang gospel music. They were called the Penniman Singers. Richard was a wild and independent child. He left home at fourteen. During his teens, he traveled throughout Georgia with musical shows of all kinds. These included "Dr. Hudson's Medicine Show" and the "Tidy Jolly Steppers." He appeared in "Sugarfoot Sam from Alabam." Here he played "Princess Lavonne" and wore a dress. He sang with B. Brown and his orchestra. He was called "Little Richard" for the first time.

By 1955, Richard had developed his own musical style. It combined gospel with rhythm and blues. At its center was a wild scream of pure joy. He had developed a stage style as well. It combined outrageous costumes, a mile-high pompadour, thick mascara, manic piano-playing, and uninhibited hip-swinging. "Tutti Frutti" made him an overnight sensation. Over the next two years, he produced one hit after another. Fans will never forget such classics as "Long Tall Sally," "Slippin' and Slidin'," "Rip It Up," "Lucille," and "Good Golly Miss Molly."

Richard had a five-year lull. He resurfaced in 1962. He became a cult figure for the next thirteen years. He was called "The Prince of Clowns" and "The King of Rock 'n' Roll." His behavior on and off the stage became more and more outrageous. In one show, he would dress as Queen Elizabeth. In the next show, he would dress as the pope. He once wore a suit covered with small mirrors. It prevented him from sitting in a car. His followers treated him royally. He was seated on a throne and crowned with jewels. He was carried into restaurants like a king.

Between 1957 and 1962, and then again in 1975, Little Richard had a spiritual awakening. The demon of rock 'n' roll dropped alcohol, drugs, and sexual promiscuity. He took on a devout lifestyle. He became an evangelist. He went to work for a Bible company. During these times, he returned to singing the gospel music of his youth.

Little Richard, the King of Rock 'n' Roll

With "A-Wop-Bop-A-Loo-Bop-A-Lop-Bam-Boom," Little Richard hit the American music scene on September 14, 1955. It has never been the same since. With his almost insane energy and flamboyant clothes, he defined the rebellious behavior that was at the heart of rock 'n' roll.

Richard Wayne Penniman was born on December 5, 1932, in Macon, Georgia. The third of thirteen children, he and his siblings sang gospel music. They were called the Penniman Singers. Richard was a wild and independent child who left home at fourteen. During his teens, he traveled throughout Georgia with musical shows of all kinds. These included "Dr. Hudson's Medicine Show" and the "Tidy Jolly Steppers." Playing "Princess Lavonne" and wearing a dress, he appeared in "Sugarfoot Sam from Alabam." When he sang with B. Brown and his orchestra, he was called "Little Richard" for the first time.

By 1955, Richard had developed his own musical style that combined gospel with rhythm and blues. At its center was a wild scream of pure joy. He had developed a stage style as well; it combined outrageous costumes, a mile-high pompadour, thick mascara, manic piano-playing, and uninhibited hip-swinging. "Tutti Frutti" made him an overnight sensation; then, over the next two years, he produced one hit after another. Fans will never forget such classics as "Long Tall Sally," "Slippin' and Slidin'," "Rip It Up," "Lucille," and "Good Golly Miss Molly."

After a five-year lull, Richard resurfaced in 1962. As a cult figure for the next thirteen years, he was called "The Prince of Clowns" and "The King of Rock 'n' Roll." His behavior on and off the stage became more and more outrageous. In one show, he would dress as Queen Elizabeth; in the next show, he would dress as the pope. He once wore a suit covered with small mirrors that prevented him from sitting in a car. His followers treated him royally. Seated on a throne and crowned with jewels, he was carried into restaurants.

Between 1957 and 1962, and then again in 1975, Little Richard had a

spiritual awakening. The demon of rock 'n' roll dropped alcohol, drugs, and sexual

promiscuity. He took on a devout lifestyle and became an evangelist, working for a

Bible company. During these times, he returned to singing the gospel music of his

youth.

Writing Assignment 2

Study this photograph of lightning striking; then write a paragraph describing it. What mood or feeling does the photograph convey to you? In your topic sentence, state this mood or feeling. Then describe the scene, choosing details that help create this mood.

Next, revise your paragraph, paying special attention to sentence variety. Aim for a variety of sentence lengths and types.

15

Revising for
Language Awareness

PART A Exact Language: Avoiding Vagueness
PART B Concise Language: Avoiding Wordiness
PART C Fresh Language: Avoiding Triteness
PART D Figurative Language: Similes and Metaphors

Although it is important to write grammatically correct English, good writing is more than just correct writing. Good writing has life, excitement, and power. It captures the attention of the reader and compels him or her to read further.

The purpose of this chapter is to increase your awareness of the power of words and your skill at making them work for you. The secret of powerful writing is **revision.** *Do not settle* for the first words that come to you, but go back over what you have written, replacing dull or confusing language with language that is exact, concise, fresh, and possibly figurative.

PART A

Exact Language: Avoiding Vagueness

Good writers express their ideas as *exactly* as possible, choosing *specific, concrete,* and *vivid* words and phrases. They do not settle for vague terms and confusing generalities.

Which sentence in each of the following pairs gives the more *exact* information? That is, which uses specific and precise language? What words in these sentences make them sharper and more vivid?

Look at:

> 1. A car went around the corner.
>
> 2. A battered blue Stanza careened around the corner.
>
> 3. Janet quickly ate the main course.
>
> 4. Janet devoured the plate of ribs in two and a half minutes.
>
> 5. The president did things that caused problems.
>
> 6. The president's military spending increased the budget deficit.

- Sentences 2, 4, and 6 contain language that is *exact*.

- Sentence 2 is more exact than sentence 1 because *battered blue Stanza* gives more specific information than the general term *car*. The verb *careened* describes precisely how the car went around the corner, fast and recklessly.

- What specific words does sentence 4 substitute for the more general words *ate*, *main course*, and *quickly* in sentence 3?

- <u>devoured</u> , <u>plate of ribs</u> , and

  <u>two and a half minutes</u>

  Why are these terms more exact than those in sentence 3?

  They tell exactly how Janet ate, what she ate, and how quickly she ate it.

- What words in sentence 6 make it more exact and clearer than sentence 5?

  military spending; increased the budget deficit

Concrete and detailed writing is usually exciting as well and makes us want to read on. Sportswriters know this:

> Fishing aboard George's 27-foot Silverton, the Craps 2–6, they rolled a seven when a 1039 pound mako slid into their chum slick of dried calves' blood and inhaled a herring bait. "She jumped 35 feet out of the water when we first hooked her," said George, his knuckles battered and bleeding after his titanic battle with the fish.
>
> —Paul Pucciarelli, "Record Mako Caught at Montauk" *The New York Post*

Now compare a similar account written in general and inexact language:

> Fishing on someone's boat, they got lucky when a big shark came by and took the bait. "She went way out of the water when we first caught her," said one guy, his hands in bad shape after his big fight with the fish.

You do not need a large vocabulary to write exactly and well, but you do need to work at finding the right words to fit each sentence. Cross out vague or dull words and phrases and replace them with more exact terms. When you are tempted to write *I feel good*, ask yourself exactly what *good* means in that sentence: *relaxed? proud? thin? in love?* When people walk by, do they *flounce, stride, lurch, wiggle,* or *sneak?* When they speak to you, do people *stammer, announce, babble, murmur,* or *coo?* Question yourself as you revise; then choose the right words to fit that particular sentence.

PRACTICE 1   Lively verbs are a great asset to any writer. The following sentences contain four overused general verbs—*to walk, to see, to eat,* and *to be.* In each case, replace the general verb in parentheses with a more exact verb *chosen to fit the context of the sentence.* Use a different verb in every sentence. Consult a dictionary or thesaurus* if you wish. Answers will vary.

Examples   In no particular hurry, we ___strolled___ (walked) through the botanical gardens.

Jane ___remains___ (is) at her desk and watches the clock.

1. With guns drawn, three police officers ___crept___ (walked) toward the door of the warehouse.

2. After four days without food and water, the man ___crawled___ *dragged* (walked) onward through the desert.

3. The four-year-old ___teetered___ (walked) onto the patio in her mother's high-heeled shoes.

4. A furious customer ___strode___ (walked) into the manager's office.

5. Two people who ___witnessed___ *saw* (saw) the accident must testify in court.

6. We crouched for hours in the underbrush just to ___spy___ (see) a rare white fox.

*A thesaurus is a book of *synonyms*—words that have the same or similar meanings.

7. Three green rowboats were __spotted__ (seen) off the coast this morning.

8. For two years, the zoologist __studied__ (saw) the behavior of bears in the wild.

9. There was the cat, delicately __munching__ (eating) my fern!

10. Senator Gorman astounded the guests by loudly __slurping__ (eating) his soup.

11. All through the movie, she __crunched__ (ate) hard candies in the back row.

12. Within seconds, Dick had bought two tacos from a street vendor and __downed__ (eaten) them both.

13. During rush hour, the temperature hit 98 degrees, and dozens of cars __stalled__ (were) on the highway.

14. A young man __lies__ (is) on a stretcher in the emergency room.

15. Workers who __sit__ (are) at desks all day should make special efforts to exercise.

16. Professor Nuzzo __paced__ (was) in front of the blackboard, excited about this new solution to the math problem.

PRACTICE 2   The sentences that follow contain vague and inexact language. Write at least one specific and vivid revision for each sentence. Use vivid verbs and adjectives whenever possible. Answers will vary.

Examples | A dog lies down in the shade.

A mangy collie flops down in the shade of a parked car.

My head hurts.

My head throbs.

I have shooting pains in the left side of my head.

1. Everything about the man looked mean.

Even the angle of the shifty-eyed stranger's hat looked mean.

✓ 2. I feel good today for several reasons.

I feel giddy today because it's Saturday, it's springtime, and I'm in love.

_____

✓ 3. A woman in unusual clothes went down the street.

A six-foot tall woman in flowing African robes strode regally down the street.

_____

4. The sunlight made the yard look pretty.

The streaming sunlight painted every corner of the yard in technicolor.

_____

5. What the company did bothered the townspeople.

The company's dumping practices enraged the townspeople.

_____

✓ 6. The pediatrician's waiting room was crowded.

The pediatrician's waiting room overflowed with whining children and

impatient parents.

7. As soon as he gets home from work, he hears the voice of his pet asking for dinner.

The minute he walks in the door from work, his ears are assailed by Rover's

piteous yelps begging for dinner.

✓ 8. The noises of construction filled the street.

A cacophony of jackhammers, diesel engines, and rumbling dump trucks rose

from the construction site.

9. When I was sick, you were helpful.

When I had the flu for a week, you brought me chicken soup every day.

_____

10. This college does things that make the students feel bad.

The inadequate security in the college's dormitories worries and angers the

students.

PRACTICE 3   A word that works effectively in one sentence might not work in another sentence. In searching for the right word, always consider the **context** of the sentence into which the word must fit. Read each of the following sentences for meaning. Then circle the word in parentheses that *most exactly fits* the context of the sentence.

Example | The alchemist cautiously (threw, (dripped) held) the liquid mercury onto copper in order to make it look like gold.

1. Alchemy, an early form of chemistry, was a (course, way, (science)) that flourished from ancient times until around 1700.

2. It was based on the (knowledge, (belief) fact) that a metal could be converted into another ore.

3. Alchemists considered gold the ((perfect) nicest, shiniest) metal.

4. Therefore, their goal was to ((transform) redo, make) base metals, like lead, into gold.

5. They searched ((eagerly) high and low, lots) for the "philosopher's stone," the formula that would make this change possible.

6. All "philosopher's stones" consisted of sulphur and mercury; the trick was to discover the proper way to ((combine) destroy, mix up) the two.

7. Over time, alchemy incorporated various ((aspects) things, stuff) of astrology and magic.

8. For example, certain metals were (the same as, (equated with) sort of like) specific heavenly bodies—gold with the sun or silver with the moon.

9. One famous alchemist proudly (said, muttered, (boasted)) that he could magically transform winter into summer.

10. Many alchemists went to work for greedy princes and kings, who always (liked, (lusted for) thought about) more gold.

11. It was dangerous work though; more than one alchemist was (done away with, (executed) knocked off) because he could not produce gold.

12. In their search for gold, however, some alchemists (foolishly, hopefully, (accidentally)) made valid scientific discoveries that led to the development of modern chemistry.

PRACTICE 4   The following paragraph is the beginning of a horror story. Revise the paragraph, making it as exact and exciting as possible. Then finish the story yourself; be careful to avoid vague language.

What an experience! The weather was bad and I was all alone in this old place. Suddenly, this ugly thing came after me. As I hurried to get away, I looked up and saw someone who did not look very nice coming at me. He was big, weirdly dressed, and had stuff all over him. I went around a corner and headed for what looked like a bridge over a river. On the way, I went by an interesting-looking tree. All around it were odd little beings who seemed to want to get me. By now I was running toward the bridge. When I got there, I saw it was not a bridge at all, but something else. I looked back and saw the whole group catching up. As I stepped onto the _____

_____

_____

_____

_____

_____

_____

_____

PART B

Concise Language: Avoiding Wordiness

Concise writing comes quickly to the point. It avoids **wordiness**—unnecessary and repetitious words that add nothing to the meaning.

Which sentence in each of the following pairs is more *concise?* That is, which does *not* contain unnecessary words?

1. Because of the fact that the watch was inexpensive in price, he bought it.

2. Because the watch was inexpensive, he bought it.

3. In my opinion I think that the financial aid system at Ellensville Junior College is in need of reform.

4. The financial aid system at Ellensville Junior College needs reform.

5. On October 10, in the fall of 1990, we learned the true facts about the robbery.

6. On October 10, 1990, we learned the facts about the robbery.

- Sentences 2, 4, and 6 are *concise* whereas sentences 1, 3, and 5 are *wordy*.

- In sentence 1, *because of the fact that* is really a *wordy* way of saying *because*. *In price* simply repeats information already given by the word *inexpensive*.

- The writer of sentence 3 undercuts the point with the wordy apology of *in my opinion I think*. As a general rule, leave out such qualifiers and simply state the opinion; but if you do use them, use either *in my opinion* or *I think*, not both! Sentence 4 replaces *is in need of* with one direct verb, *needs*.

- *In the fall of* in sentence 5 is *redundant;* it repeats information already given by what word?

  October
  _____

- Why is the word *true* also eliminated in version 6?

  Facts are always true.
  _____

Concise writing avoids wordiness, unnecessary repetition, and padding. Of course, conciseness *does not mean* writing short, bare sentences but simply cutting out all deadwood and never using fifteen words when ten will do.

PRACTICE 5   The following sentences are *wordy*. Make them more *concise* by crossing out or replacing unnecessary words or by combining two sentences into one concise sentence. Rewrite each new sentence on the lines beneath, capitalizing and punctuating correctly.

Examples   The U.S. Census uncovers many interesting facts that have a lot of truth to them.

  The U.S. Census uncovers many interesting facts.
  _____

  _____

In the year 1810, Philadelphia was called the cigar capital of the United States. The reason why was because the census reported that the city produced 16 million cigars each year.

  In 1810, Philadelphia was called the cigar capital of the United States because the
  _____

  census reported that the city produced 16 million cigars each year.
  _____

1. The Constitution requires and says that the federal government of the United States must take a national census every ten years.

  The Constitution requires the federal government to take a national census
  _____

  every ten years.
  _____

✓ 2. At first, the original function of the census was to ensure fair taxation and representation.

The original function of the census was to ensure fair taxation and

representation.

3. Since the first count in 1790, the census has become controversial. There are at least two main reasons why it has become controversial.

Since the first count in 1790, the census has become controversial for at least

two main reasons.

✓ 4. One reason why is because there are always some people who aren't included.

One reason is that some people aren't included.

_____

✓ 5. In the 1990 census, for example, many homeless people with no place to live were not counted.

In the 1990 census, for example, many homeless people were not counted.

_____

6. Another reason is due to the fact that many people think the census is too personal.

Another reason is that many people think the census is too personal.

_____

✓ 7. Many citizens were angry in 1800 when the census first began asking women the question of what their age was.

Many citizens were angry in 1800 when the census began asking women

their age.

8. People were also offended when they were asked to tell the answer to another question. The question was whether they had indoor or outdoor toilets.

People were also offended when they were asked whether they had indoor or

outdoor toilets.

9. In my opinion, I think that even in this day and age of today certain information should be private.

I think that even today certain information should be private.

_____

10. Despite controversy, the U.S. census still continues to serve beneficial functions that are for the good of our country.

Despite controversy, the census serves beneficial functions for our country.

_____

PRACTICE 6   Rewrite this essay *concisely*, cutting out all unnecessary words. Reword or combine sentences if you wish, but do not alter the meaning.
Answers may vary.

Dr. Alice Hamilton, Medical Pioneer

At the age of forty ~~years old~~, Dr. Alice Hamilton became a pioneer in ~~the field of~~ industrial medicine. In 1910, the governor of Illinois appointed her to investigate rumors that ~~people who were doing the work~~ **workers** in Chicago's paint factories were dying from lead poisoning. The result of her investigation was the first state law ~~that was passed~~ to protect workers.

The following year, the U.S. Department of Labor hired ~~this woman,~~ Dr. Hamilton, to study industrial illness throughout the country ~~of the United States~~. In the next decade, she researched ~~and studied~~ many occupational diseases, including tuberculosis among quarry workers and silicosis—clogged lungs—among sandblasters. To gather information, Dr. Hamilton went to the workplace—deep in mines, quarries, and underwater tunnels. She also spoke to the workers in their homes ~~where they lived~~.

With great zeal, Dr. Hamilton spread her message about poor health conditions on the job. ~~What happened with her reports is that they~~ **Her reports** led to new safety regulations, workmen's compensation insurance, and improved working conditions in many industries. She wrote many popular articles and spoke to groups of interested citizens. In ~~the year of~~ 1919, she became the first woman to ~~hold courses and~~ teach at Harvard University. Her textbook ~~which she wrote~~, *Industrial Poisons in the U.S.,* became the standard book on the subject. By the time she died in 1970—

she was 101—she had done much to improve the plight of many working

                                              She
people. ~~The reason why she~~ is remembered today ~~is~~ because she cared at

a time when many others seemed not to care at all.

PART C

Fresh Language: Avoiding Triteness

Fresh writing uses original and lively words. It avoids **clichés,** those
tired and trite expressions that have lost their power from overuse.

Which sentence in each pair that follows contains fewer expressions
that you have heard or read many times before?

Look at:

> 1. Some people can relate to the hustle and bustle of city life.
>
> 2. Some people thrive on the energy and motion of city life.
>
> 3. This book is worth its weight in gold to the car owner.
>
> 4. This book can save the car owner hundreds of dollars a year in
>   repairs.

■ You probably found that sentences 2 and 4 contained fresher language.
What words and phrases in sentences 1 and 3 have you heard or seen
before, in conversation, on TV, or in magazines and newspapers? List
them:

can relate to; the hustle and bustle; worth its weight in gold

Clichés and trite expressions like the following have become so familiar that they have almost no impact on the reader. Avoid them. Say what
you mean in your own words:

Cliché: She is pretty as a picture.

Fresh: Her amber eyes and wild red hair are striking.

Or occasionally, play with a cliché and turn it into fresh language:

Cliché: ... as American as apple pie.

Fresh: . . . as American as a Big Mac.

Cliché: The grass is always greener on the other side of the fence.

Fresh: "The grass is always greener over the septic tank."
            —Irma Bombeck

The following is a partial list of trite expressions to avoid. Add to it any others that you overuse in your writing.

Look at:

Trite Expressions

at a loss for words	last but not least
at this point in time	like there's no tomorrow
better late than never	living hand to mouth
cold cruel world	one in a million
cool, hot	out of this world
cry your eyes out	red as a rose
easier said than done	sad but true
free as a bird	tried and true
green with envy	under the weather
I can relate to that	where he/she is coming from
in this day and age	work like a dog

PRACTICE 7   Cross out clichés and trite expressions in the following sentences and replace them with fresh and exact language of your own.
Answers may vary.

1. In 1929, toy dealer Edwin S. Lowe came across people ~~having more~~ *enjoying* ~~fun than a barrel of monkeys~~ *themselves* while playing a game at a carnival in rural Georgia.

2. A leader called out each ~~and every~~ number, and the players used beans to cover the matching numbers on their cards.

3. The winners yelled "beano" ~~at the top of their lungs~~ when they had filled in a row of numbers.

4. According to the carnival owner, a stranger had brought the game

   from Europe, so ~~it went without saying that~~ no one owned the game.

   Immediately   *potential of the game*
5. ~~Quick as a wink~~, Lowe saw the ~~game was a winner~~.

   shrewd
6. As soon as he returned home, the businessman~~, who was as sharp as~~

   ~~a tack,~~ began testing beano out on friends.

   an excited
7. One night, instead of "beano," a guest ~~who was beside himself with~~

   ~~excitement~~ shouted out "bingo."

   phenomenally
8. Lowe went on to market the game as Bingo, and it sold ~~like crazy~~.

9. Soon many nonprofit organizations were holding bingo tournaments
   an effective
   as ~~a tried and true~~ method of raising funds.

10. Because Lowe had produced only twenty-four different cards, too
    winning
    many people were ~~cleaning up~~.

    a huge sum
11. Therefore, Lowe paid a mathematics professor ~~an awesome amount~~

    to develop six thousand cards, each with a different combination of

    numbers.

12. By 1934, hundreds of thousands of Americans were playing bingo
    enthusiastically
    ~~like there was no tomorrow~~.

PART D

Figurative Language: Similes and Metaphors

One way to add sparkle and exactness to your writing is to use an occasional simile or metaphor. A **simile** is a comparison of two things using the word *like* or *as:*

> "He was *as ugly as* a wart."   —Anne Sexton
>
> "The frozen twigs of the huge tulip poplar next to the hill clack in the cold *like* tinsnips."   —Annie Dillard

A **metaphor** is a similar comparison without the word *like* or *as:*

> "My soul is a dark forest."   —D. H. Lawrence
>
> Love is a virus.

- The power of similes and metaphors comes partly from the surprise of comparing two apparently unlike things. A well-chosen simile or metaphor can convey a lot of information in very few words.

- To compare a person to a wart, as Sexton does, lets us know quickly just how ugly that person is. And to say that *twigs clack like tinsnips* describes the sound so precisely that we can almost hear it.

- What do you think D. H. Lawrence means by his metaphor? In what ways is a person's soul like a *dark forest?*

  It is a tangle of emotions containing scary, unexplored areas.

- The statement *love is a virus* tells us something about the writer's attitude toward love. What is it? In what ways is love like a virus?

  The writer thinks that love is contagious; love is a kind of sickness with

  predictable symptoms.

Similes and metaphors should not be overused; however, once in a while, they can be a delightful addition to a paper that is also exact, concise, and fresh.

PRACTICE 8   The author of the following paragraph contrasts a fat priest and his thin parishioners. He uses at least one simile and two metaphors in his description. Underline the simile and circle the metaphors.

He was a large, juicy man, soft and sappy as a melon, and this sweet roundness made him appear spoiled and self-indulgent, especially when contrasted with the small, spare, sticklike peons* who comprised his parish.... Everything about them, the peons, was withered and bone-dry. Everything about him was full and fleshy and wet. They were mummies. He was a whale, beached upon the desert sands, draped in black to mourn his predicament.

—Bill Porterfield, *Texas Rhapsody*

*Peons: farm workers or laborers of Latin America.

[handwritten in margin: Look at pairs. Try writing a description paragraph.]

PRACTICE 9   Think of several similes to complete each sentence that follows. Be creative! Then underline your favorite simile, the one that best completes each sentence. Answers may vary.

Example | My English class is like an orchestra.
the Everglades.
a drive-in movie.
a vegetable garden.

1. Job hunting is like _____

a game of chess.

rock climbing.

a plunge into cold water.

2. Writing well is like _____

riding down the freeway.

sailing in a stiff wind.

reaching the top of a mountain.

3. My room looks like _____

yesterday's leftovers.

a shipwreck.

a supernova.

4. Marriage is like _____

spending all your money.

a kaleidoscope.

completing a puzzle.

PRACTICE 10   Think of several metaphors to complete each sentence that follows. Jot down three or four ideas, and then underline the metaphor that best completes each sentence. Answers may vary.

Example | Love is a blood transfusion.
a sunrise.
a broken record.
a roller coaster ride.

1. Television is _____

a bottle of sedatives.

an open door.

a seducer.

2. My car is _____

a two-eyed monster.

a goldfish bowl.

another child.

3. Registration is _____

a battlefield.

a snakepit.

a lesson in patience.

4. Courage is _____

a taut rope.

a tight fist.

a searchlight.

Writing Assignments

1. Good writing can be done on almost any subject if the writer approaches the subject with openness and with "new eyes." Take a piece of fruit or a vegetable—a lemon, a green pepper, a cherry tomato. Examine it as if for the first time. Feel its texture and parts, smell it, weigh it in your palm.

Now capture your experience of the fruit or vegetable in words. First jot down words and ideas, or freewrite, aiming for the most *exact* description possible. Don't settle for the first words you think of. Keep writing. Then go back over what you have written, underlining the most exact and powerful writing. Compose a topic sentence and draft a paragraph that conveys your unique experience of the fruit or vegetable.

2. In the paragraph that follows, Annie Dillard describes a "small" event in such rich, exact detail that it becomes amazing and intriguing to the reader as well. Read her paragraph, underlining language that strikes you as especially *exact and fresh.* Can you spot the two **similes?** Notice her forceful and varied verbs.

One night a moth flew into the candle, was caught, burnt dry, and held. I must have been staring at the candle, or maybe I looked up when a shadow crossed my page; at any rate, I saw it all. A golden female moth, a biggish one with a two-inch wingspan, flapped into the fire, dropped her abdomen into the wet wax, stuck, flamed, frazzled and fried in a second. Her moving wings ignited like tissue paper, enlarging the circle of light in the clearing and creating out of the darkness the sudden blue sleeves of my sweater, the green leaves of jewelweed by my side, the ragged red trunk of a pine. At once the light contracted again and the moth's wings vanished in a fine, foul smoke. At the same time her six legs clawed, curled, blackened, and ceased, disappearing utterly. And her head jerked in spasms, making a spattering of noise; her antennae crisped and burned away and her heaving mouth parts crackled like pistol fire. When it was all over, her head was, so far as I could determine, gone, gone the long way of her wings and legs. Had she been new, or old? Had she mated and laid her eggs, had she done her work? All that was left was the glowing horn shell of her abdomen and thorax—a fraying, partially collapsed gold tube jammed upright in the candle's round pool.

—Annie Dillard, *Holy the Firm*

Write a paragraph in which you also describe a brief but interesting event that caught your attention. As you freewrite or brainstorm, try to capture the most precise and minute details of what happened. Revise the paragraph, making the language as *exact, concise,* and *fresh* as you can.

3. The photo on p. 229 shows a sculpture by the artist Magritte. Look closely at the figure Magritte has created, noting the birdcage where the

chest should be, the positions of the two birds, and other details. Then write a two-paragraph composition discussing this sculpture. First, describe the sculpture very exactly, pointing out important details. Then discuss what you think Magritte is trying to say by creating such a figure.

As you revise, make your writing as exact, concise, and fresh as possible so that a reader who has not seen Magritte's sculpture can visualize and experience it as you have.

16

Putting Your Revision Skills to Work

In Unit 2 of this book, you learned to **revise** basic paragraphs—to rethink and rewrite them with such questions as the following in mind:

Can a reader understand and follow my ideas?

Is my topic sentence clear?

Have I fully supported my topic sentence with details and facts?

Does my paragraph have unity? That is, does every sentence relate to the main idea?

Does my paragraph have coherence? That is, does it follow a logical order and guide the reader from point to point?

Of course, the more writing techniques you learn, the more options you have as you revise. Unit 4 has moved beyond the basics to matters of style: consistency and parallelism, sentence variety, and clear, exact language. This chapter will guide you again through the revision process, adding questions like the following to your list:

Are my verb tenses and pronouns consistent?

Have I used parallel structure to highlight parallel ideas?

Have I varied the length and type of my sentences?

Is my language exact, concise, and fresh?

Many writers first revise and rewrite with questions like these in mind. They do *not* worry about grammar and minor errors at this stage. Then in a separate, final process, they proofread* for spelling and grammatical errors.

Here are two sample paragraphs by students, showing the first draft, the revisions made by the student, and the revised draft of each. Each revision has been numbered and explained to give you a clear idea of the thinking process involved.

*For practice proofreading for particular errors, see individual chapters in Unit 6.

Writing Sample 1

First Draft

I like to give my best performance. I must relax completely before a show. I often know ahead of time what choreography I will use and what I'll sing, so I can concentrate on relaxing completely. I usually do this by reading, etc. I always know my parts perfectly. Occasionally I look through the curtain to watch the people come in. This can make you feel faint, but I reassure myself and say I know everything will be okay.

Revisions

① **In order**

~~I like~~ to give my best performance⌒I must relax completely before a

② **and vocals**   **Add 6 here**
show. I often know ahead of time what choreography⌃I will use, and ~~what~~

③ **during that long, last hour before curtain,**   ④
I'll sing; so⌃I can concentrate on relaxing⌒~~completely.~~ I usually do this by

⑤ **an action-packed mystery, but sometimes I** ⌃ **joke with the**
   other performers or just walk around backstage.   ⑦ **peek**
reading⌃~~etc.~~ (I always know my parts perfectly,) Occasionally I ~~look~~

                                    ⑥
                        audience file   ⑧ **me**
through the curtain to watch the ~~people come~~ in. This can make ~~you~~ feel

                        ⑨ **"Vickie," I say, "the minute you're out there**
                            singing to the people, everything will be okay."
faint, but I reassure myself. ~~and say I know everything will be okay.~~

Reasons for Revisions

1. Combine two short sentences. (sentence variety)

2. Make *choreography* and *vocals* parallel and omit unnecessary words. (parallelism)

3. Make time order clear: First discuss what I've done during the days before the performance, and then discuss the hour before performance. (time order)

4. Drop *completely*, which repeats the word used in the first sentence. (avoid wordiness)

5. This is important! Drop *etc.*, add more details, and give examples. (add examples)

6. This idea belongs earlier in the paragraph—with what I've done during the days before the performance. (order)

7. Use more specific and interesting language in this sentence. (exact language)

8. Use the first person singular pronouns *I* and *me* consistently throughout the paragraph. (consistent person)

9. Dull—use a direct quotation, the actual words I say to myself. (exact language, sentence variety)

Revised Draft

In order to give my best performance, I must relax completely before a show. I often know ahead of time what choreography and vocals I will use, and I always know my parts perfectly, so during that long, last hour before curtain, I can concentrate on relaxing. I usually do this by reading an action-packed mystery, but sometimes I joke with the other performers or just walk around backstage. Occasionally I peek through the curtain to watch the audience file in. This can make me feel faint, but I reassure myself. "Vickie," I say, "the minute you're out there singing to the people, everything will be okay."

—Victoria DeWindt (Student)

Writing Sample 2

First Draft

My grandparents' house contained whole rooms that my parents' house did not (pantry, a parlor, a den where Grandpa kept his loot). The furniture and things always fascinated me. Best of all was the lake behind the house. Grandpa said that Evergreen Lake had grown old just like Grandma and him, that the game fish are gone and only a few bluegills remained. But one day he let me fish. No one thought I'd catch anything, but I caught a foot-long goldfish! Grandpa said it was a goddam carp, but it was a goldfish to me and I nearly fainted with ecstasy.

Revisions

① Visiting my grandparents at Evergreen Lake
   was always an exotic adventure.

② Their cavernous ③
~~My grandparents'~~ house contained whole rooms that my parents'

④ –a pantry,   with a big black grand piano, and
house did not (~~pantry,~~ a parlor⌃ a den where Grandpa kept his loot).
⑤ The rooms were furnished with musty deer heads,
hand-painted candlesticks, and velvet drapes.
~~The furniture and things always fascinated me.~~ Best of all was the lake

behind the house. Grandpa said that Evergreen Lake had grown old just

⑥ were
like Grandma and him, that the game fish ~~are~~ gone and only a few blue-

⑦ Add new section below*
gills remained. ~~But one day he let me fish. No one thought I'd catch any-~~

~~thing, but I caught a foot-long goldfish. Grandpa said it was a goddam~~

B
~~carp,~~ but it was a goldfish to me and I nearly fainted with ecstasy.   ⑧

> *Add: But one day he rigged up a pole for me and tossed my line into the water. I sat motionless for several hours, waiting for a miracle. Suddenly I felt a tug on my line. I screeched and yanked upward. By the time Grandpa arrived on the dock, there on the surface lazily moving its fins was the biggest goldfish I had ever seen, nearly a foot long! Grandpa reached down with the net and scooped the huge orange fish out of the water. "Bring down the pail," he shouted. "It's a goddam carp."

Reasons for Revisions

1. No topic sentence; add one. (topic sentence)

2. Now *grandparents* repeats the first sentence; use *their*. (pronoun substitution)

3. Add a good descriptive word to give the feeling of the house. (exact language)

4. Expand this; add more details. (details, exact language)

5. More details and examples needed for support! Try to capture the "exotic" feeling of the house. (details, exact language)

6. Verb shifts to present tense; use past tense consistently. (consistent tense)

7. This section is weak. Tell the story of the goldfish; try to create the sense of adventure this had for me as a kid. Quote Grandpa? (details, exact language, direct quotation)

8. Revised paragraph is getting long. Consider breaking into two paragraphs, one on the house and one on the lake.

Revised Draft

Visiting my grandparents at Evergreen Lake was always an exotic adventure. Their cavernous house contained whole rooms that my parents' house did not—a pantry, a parlor with a big black grand piano, and a den where Grandpa kept his loot. The rooms were furnished with musty deer heads, hand-painted candlesticks, and velvet drapes.

Best of all was the lake behind the house. Grandpa said that Evergreen Lake had grown old just like Grandma and him, that the game fish were gone and only a few bluegills remained. But one day he rigged up a pole for me and tossed my line into the water. I sat motionless for several hours, waiting for a miracle. Suddenly I felt a tug on my line. I screeched and yanked upward. By the time Grandpa arrived on the dock, there on the surface lazily moving its fins was the biggest goldfish I had ever seen, nearly a foot long! Grandpa reached down with the net and scooped the huge orange fish out of the water. "Bring down the pail," he shouted. "It's a goddam carp." But it was a goldfish to me, and I nearly fainted with ecstasy.

PRACTICE   Because revising, like writing, is a personal process, the best practice is to revise your own paragraphs and essays. Nevertheless, we include below a first draft that needs revision.

Revise this essay *as if you had written it.* Use and build on the good parts, but rewrite unclear or awkward sentences, drop unnecessary words, add details, perhaps reorder parts. Especially, ask yourself these questions: Are my verb tenses and pronouns consistent? Have I used parallel structure? Have I varied the length and type of my sentences? Is my language exact, concise, and fresh? Then write the revised draft on the lines below. Students' drafts will vary.

Breaking the Yo-Yo Syndrome

For years, I was a yo-yo dieter. I bounced from fad diets to eating binges when I ate a lot. This leaves you tired and with depression. Along the way, though, I have learned a few things. As a result, I personally will never go on a weight-loss diet again for the rest of my life.

I have learned that all weight-loss diets are short-term. I lose about ten pounds. I wind up gaining more weight than I originally lost. I get sick and tired of the restricted diet. On one diet, I ate six grapefruits and ten hard-boiled eggs a day. After two weeks, I never want to see another grapefruit or egg again. I also ended up craving all the foods I am not supposed to eat. Nutritionists say that the craving occurs because of the reason that weight-loss diets are nutritionally unbalanced. The body needs fat, and if the dieter takes in too little fat, you are constantly hungry. Moreover, in the short-term, all one loses is water; you cannot lose body fat—the real factor in weight loss—unless you reduce regularly and at a steady rate over a long period of time.

The main reason why I will not diet again is because diets are unhealthy even in the short term. For instance, many low-carbohydrate diets have appeared over the years. Some are high in fat, and accumulating fat through meat, eggs, and the eating of cheese can raise blood levels of cholesterol and led to artery and heart disease. Other diets are too high in protein and can cause kidney ailments, and other things can go wrong with your body too. Most diets also leave you deficient in essential vitamins and minerals that are necessary to health, such as calcium and iron.

In place of weight-loss dieting, I now follow a long-range plan. It is sensible, exciting, and improved my health. I eat three well-balanced meals, exercise daily, and meeting regularly with my support group for weight control. I am much happier and don't weigh as much.

For years, I was a yo-yo dieter, bouncing from fad diets to eating binges that left me tired and depressed. Along the way, though, I have learned a few things. As a result, I will never go on a weight-loss diet again.

I have learned that all weight-loss diets are short-term. First, I lose about ten pounds; then, I wind up gaining more weight than I originally lost. I get bored on the restricted diet. On one diet, I ate six grapefruits and ten hard-boiled eggs a day. After two weeks, I never wanted to see another grapefruit or egg again. I also ended up craving all the foods I was not supposed to eat. Nutritionists say that the craving occurs because weight-loss diets are nutritionally unbalanced. The body needs fat, and if you take in too little fat, you are constantly hungry. Moreover, in the short-term, all you lose is water; you cannot lose body fat—the real factor in weight loss—unless you reduce steadily over a long period of time.

I will not diet again because diets are unhealthy even in the short term. For instance, many low-carbohydrate diets have appeared over the years. Some are high in fat, and accumulating fat through meat, eggs, and cheese can raise blood levels of cholesterol and lead to artery and heart disease. Other diets are too high in protein and can cause kidney ailments and other disorders. Most diets also leave you deficient in essential vitamins and minerals, such as calcium and iron.

In place of weight-loss dieting, I now follow a long-range plan that is sensible, exciting, and healthful. I eat three well-balanced meals, exercise daily, and meet regularly with my support group for weight control. I am much happier and thinner.

Unit 5
Writing the Essay

17

The Process of Writing an Essay

PART A   Looking at the Essay
PART B   Writing the Thesis Statement
PART C   Gathering Ideas for the Body
PART D   Ordering and Linking Paragraphs in the Essay
PART E   Writing and Revising Short Essays

Although writing effective paragraphs will help you complete short-answer exams and do brief writing assignments, much of the time—in college and in the business world—you will be required to write essays and reports several paragraphs long. Essays are longer and contain more ideas than the single paragraphs you have practiced so far, but they require many of the same skills that paragraphs do.

This chapter will help you apply the skills of paragraph writing to the writing of short essays. It will guide you from a look at the essay and its parts through the planning and writing of essays.

Looking at the Essay

The **essay** is a group of paragraphs about one subject. In many ways, an essay is like a paragraph in extended, fuller form. Just as the paragraph has a topic sentence, body, and conclusion, so too the essay has an introduction, body, and conclusion.

The **introduction*** begins the essay and prepares the reader for what will follow. The introduction contains the **thesis statement,** which sets forth the main idea of the entire essay.

The **body** of the essay, like the body of a paragraph, is the longest part. Every paragraph in the body of the essay must support and explain the thesis statement.

*For more work on introductions, see Chapter 19, "The Introduction, the Conclusion, and the Title."

The **conclusion*** signals the end of the essay and leaves the reader with a final thought.

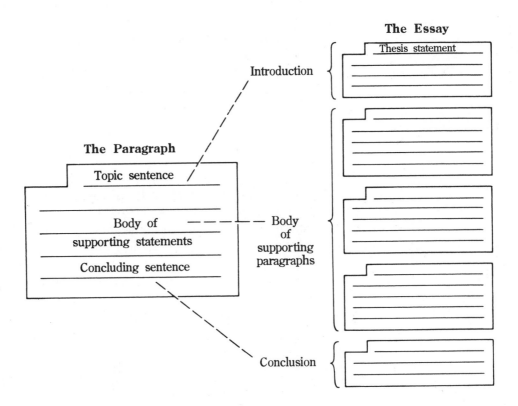

Here is a student essay:

Making a Difference

The Community Service Office at Westlake College offers placement opportunities for students who wish to do volunteer work. For a number of reasons, students who have the time should consider volunteering to help out their neighbors in the community.

Most important, volunteers can do much to improve the quality of life in Westlake. A sophomore named Annie Blakely, for instance, volunteered with a crew of other students to spruce up the run-down Stevenson Park. Because budget cuts had reduced the number of caretakers, some of its gardens had become overgrown. Supervised by the Parks Department, the crew cleared weeds, trimmed bushes, and planted several colorful flowerbeds. They also painted the park benches a bright red, a welcome change from their former drab and faded grey. For six Saturday afternoons, Annie and the other volunteers worked their magic. Thanks to them, the park is certainly prettier and more inviting than it had been.

*For more work on conclusions, see Chapter 19, "The Introduction, the Conclusion, and the Title."

While helping out, volunteers can also develop a deeper understanding and appreciation of others. Last year Bob Hairston worked for a few hours each week at the Westlake Home for the Aged. He began with many preconceptions about the elderly; however, his work with them convinced him how wrong he had been. For example, he assumed that the residents, because they lived in the home, had lost contact with the rest of the world. While playing chess or chatting with them, he realized that they avidly watched the news on TV, read newspapers, and were well-informed about local, national, and world affairs. Also a surprise to Bob, their opinions were often similar to his own. These seventy-year-olds were not as "old-fashioned" as he had thought. Bob Hairston, the person, owes his respect for the elderly and his open-mindedness to Bob Hairston, the volunteer.

Finally, volunteers can often learn new skills. Margo Rosa, a whiz in mathematics, volunteered to tutor Sandy Lewin, a junior high school student struggling with her math homework. Aspiring to become a teacher, Margo hoped this assignment would give her a head start on her future career. At first, she had trouble understanding why Sandy found fractions so confusing or decimals so difficult. Soon, however, Margo saw where and why Sandy got stuck and thought of creative ways to help. She also increased her patience, a necessary trait for any good teacher. By the end of the semester, when Sandy's grades had improved, Rosa was certain that she would become a first-rate teacher.

Community service not only benefits the community but also rewards the volunteer. Signing up can make a big difference in many lives.

- The last sentence in the introduction (the first paragraph) of this essay is the *thesis statement*. Just as the topic sentence sets forth the main idea of a paragraph, so the thesis statement sets forth the main idea of the entire essay. This means that the thesis statement *must be general enough to include every topic sentence in the body*:

1. INTRODUCTION and
   Thesis statement: For a number of reasons, students who have the time should consider volunteering to help out their neighbors in the community.

2. Topic sentence: Most important, volunteers can do much to improve the quality of life in Westlake.

3. Topic sentence: While helping out, volunteers can also develop a deeper understanding and appreciation of others.

4. Topic sentence: Finally, volunteers can often learn new skills.

5. CONCLUSION

- Note that *every topic sentence supports the thesis statement*. Every paragraph in the body discusses one *reason* for students to consider volunteering. Each paragraph also provides an *example* to back up that reason.

PRACTICE 1   Read this student essay carefully and then answer the questions.

Bottle Watching

(1) Every time I see a beer bottle, I feel grateful. This reaction has nothing to do with beer. The sight reminds me of the year I spent inspecting bottles at a brewery. <u>That was the most boring and painful job I've ever had, but it motivated me to change my life.</u>

(2) My job consisted of sitting on a stool and watching empty bottles pass by. A glaring light behind the conveyor belt helped me to spot cracked bottles or bottles with something extra—a dead grasshopper, for example, or a mouse foot. I was supposed to grab such bottles with my hooked cane and break them before they went into the washer. For eight or nine hours a day that was all I did. I got dizzy and sore in the eyes. I longed to fall asleep. I prayed that the conveyor would break down so the bottles would stop.

(3) After a while, to put some excitement into the job, I began inventing little games. I would count the number of minutes that passed before a broken bottle would come by, and I would compete against my own past record. Or I would see how many broken bottles I could spot in one minute. Once, I organized a contest for all the bottle watchers with a prize for the best dead insect or animal found in a bottle—anything to break the monotony of the job.

(4) After six months at the brewery, I began to think hard about my goals for the future. Did I want to spend the rest of my life looking in beer bottles? I realized that I wanted a job I could believe in. I wanted to use my mind for better things than planning contests for bleary-eyed bottle watchers. I knew I had to hand in my hook and go back to school.

(5) Today I feel grateful to that terrible job because it motivated me to attend college.

—Pat Barnum (Student)

1. Underline the **thesis statement** in the essay above.

2. What is the topic sentence of paragraph 2? <u>My job consisted of sitting</u>

   <u>on a stool and watching empty bottles pass by.</u>

   What is the topic sentence of paragraph 3? <u>After a while, to put</u>

   <u>some excitement into the job, I began inventing little games.</u>

   What is the topic of paragraph 4? <u>After six months at the brewery, I</u>

   <u>began to think hard about my goals for the future.</u>

3. Does every paragraph in the body support the thesis statement?

_____yes_____

4. Does the thesis statement include the main idea of every paragraph in the body? __yes_____

PART B

Writing the Thesis Statement

The steps in the essay-writing process are the same as those in the paragraph-writing process: **narrow the topic, write the thesis statement, develop ideas for the body,** and **organize them.** However, in essay writing, planning on paper and prewriting are especially important because an essay is longer than a paragraph and more difficult to organize.

Narrowing the Topic

The essay writer usually starts with a broad subject and then narrows it to a manageable size. An essay is longer than a paragraph and gives the writer more room to develop ideas; nevertheless, the best essays, like the best paragraphs, are often quite specific. For example, if you are assigned a three-hundred-word essay entitled "A Trip You Won't Forget," a description of your recent trip to Florida would be too broad a subject. You would need to *narrow* the topic to just one aspect of the trip. Many writers list possible narrowed subjects on paper:

1. huge job of packing was more tiring than the trip
2. how to pack for a trip with the children without exhausting yourself
3. Disney World, more fun for adults than for children
4. our afternoon of deep-sea fishing: highlight of the trip
5. terrible weather upset many of my sightseeing plans

Any one of these topics is narrow enough and specific enough to be the subject of a short essay. If you had written this list, you would now consider each narrowed topic and perhaps freewrite or brainstorm possible ways to support it. Keeping your audience and purpose in mind may also help you narrow your topic. Your audience here might be a friend or more likely your instructor and classmates; your purpose might be to inform (by giving tips about packing) or to entertain (by narrating a funny or a dramatic incident). Having considered your topic, audience, and purpose, you would then choose the topic that you could best develop into a good essay.

If you have difficulty with this step, reread Chapter 2, "Gathering Ideas."

Writing the Thesis Statement

The thesis statement—like the topic sentence in a paragraph—further focuses the subject because it must clearly state, in sentence form, the writer's **central point:** the main idea or opinion that the rest of the essay will support and discuss.

The thesis statement should be as **specific** as possible. By writing a specific thesis statement, you focus on your subject and give yourself and your reader a clearer idea of what will follow in the body of the essay.

There are many ways to make a vague thesis statement more specific. As a general rule, replace vague words with more exact words* and replace vague ideas with more complete information:

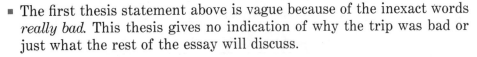

Vague thesis statement:	My recent trip to Florida was really bad.
Revised thesis statement:	My recent trip to Florida was disappointing because the weather upset my sightseeing plans.

- The first thesis statement above is vague because of the inexact words *really bad.* This thesis gives no indication of why the trip was bad or just what the rest of the essay will discuss.

- The second thesis statement is more specific. The words *really bad* are replaced by the more exact word *disappointing.* In addition, the writer has added more complete information about why the trip was disappointing. From this thesis statement, it is clear that the essay will discuss the ways in which the weather upset the writer's plans.

It is sometimes possible to make a thesis statement more specific by stating the natural divisions of the subject. Done thoughtfully, this approach can set up an outline for the entire essay:

Vague thesis statement:	The movie *Southern Smoke* seemed phony.
Revised thesis statement:	The costumes, the dialogue, and the plot of the movie *Southern Smoke* all seemed phony.

*For more practice in choosing exact language, see Chapter 15, "Revising for Language Awareness," Part A.

- The first thesis statement above gives little specific direction to the writer or the reader.

- The second thesis statement, however, actually sets up a plan for the whole essay. The writer has divided the subject into three parts—the costumes, the dialogue, and the plot—and he or she will probably devote one paragraph to discussing the "phoniness" of each one. This writer probably first "thought on paper" to get ideas.

PRACTICE 2   Revise each vague thesis statement, making it more specific. Remember, a specific thesis statement should give the reader a clear idea of what the essay will discuss. Answers will vary.

Example | Watching TV has its good points.

Watching news and public affairs programs on TV can make one a more informed
and responsible citizen.

1. The library at this college is bad.

    Our college library has short hours, cranky librarians, and few books.

2. Some workers should not be allowed to strike.

    Firefighters, members of the police force, trash collectors, and teachers should
    not be allowed to strike.

3. There are many nice people in my family.

    My aunt and uncle, who once traveled the world as circus acrobats, are the
    most unusual members of my family.

4. Marriage is a good idea.

    Marriage is a commitment that two people make to grow and to help each
    other grow.

5. I work at a great place.

    I work as a researcher for a company that plans and builds exhibits for science
    museums.

6. Professors should teach better.

    Professors should organize difficult material more carefully.

7. You can learn a lot by observing children.

You can learn a lot about children's developing social sense by observing three-

year-olds at play.

8. Sketching caricatures is a great hobby.

Sketching caricatures relaxes me, brings out my creativity, and allows me to

earn extra money.

PRACTICE 3   Eight possible topics for short essays follow. Pick three that interest you and **narrow** the topic to just one aspect that you would like to write about. Then, keeping in mind your audience and purpose, compose a specific thesis statement for each of three essays. Answers will vary.

a time you surprised yourself	why sports fans get violent
ways to start (or stop) an argument	something that angers you at work
unusual relatives	staying healthy
a neighborhood problem	falling in (or out) of love

1. Subject: ___insufficient penalties for violent sports fans___

    Thesis statement: ___Sports fans get violent—and then continue to get___

    violent—because the penalties for their violence are insufficient.

2. Subject: ___employees' suggestions and complaints ignored at work___

    Thesis statement: ___People who work at a job for any length of time develop___

    ways of improving the job, but at my company, workers' suggestions and

    complaints are completely ignored.

3. Subject: ___falling in love as a time of discovery___

    Thesis statement: ___Falling in love is a time of great discovery—finding out___

    about the loved one's past, hopes, likes, and dislikes—and finding out new

    things about oneself.

PART C

Gathering Ideas for the Body

The thesis statement sets forth the main idea of the entire essay, but it is the **body** of the essay that must fully support and discuss that thesis statement. In composing the thesis statement, the writer should already have given some thought to what the body will contain. Now he or she should make a **plan** that includes the following:

1. Two to four main ideas to support the thesis statement

2. Two to four topic sentences stating these ideas

3. A plan for each paragraph in the body (developed in any of the ways explained earlier in this book)

4. A logical order in which to present these paragraphs

Different writers create such plans in different ways. Some writers brainstorm or freewrite ideas and then find paragraph groups. Others first write topic sentences and then plan paragraphs.

   1. **Brainstorm ideas and then find paragraph groups.** Having written the thesis statement, some writers brainstorm—they jot down any ideas that develop the thesis statement, including main ideas, specific details, and examples, all jumbled together. Only after creating a long list do they go back over it, drop any ideas that do not support the thesis statement, and then look for "paragraph groups."
   Suppose, for instance, that you have written this thesis statement: *Although people often react to stress in harmful ways, there are many positive ways to handle stress.* By brainstorming and then dropping ideas that do not relate, you would eventually produce a list like this:

   work out

   dig weeds or rake leaves

   call a friend

   talking out problems relieves stress

   jogging

   many sports ease tension

   go to the beach

   take a walk

   taking breaks, long or short, relieves stress

   talk to a shrink if the problem is really bad

   escape into a hobby—photography, bird watching

go to a movie

talk to a counselor at the college

talk to a minister, priest, rabbi, etc.

many people harm themselves trying to relieve stress

they overeat or smoke

drinking too much, other addictions

do vigorous household chores—scrub a floor, beat the rugs, pound pillows

doing something physical relieves stress

some diseases are caused by stress

take a nap

some people blow up to help tension, but this hurts their relationships

Now read over the list, looking for groups of ideas that could become paragraphs. Some ideas might become topic sentences; others might be used to support a topic sentence. How many possible paragraphs can you find in this list?

_____four_____

PRACTICE 4   From the list, make a **plan** for an essay that supports the thesis statement *Although people often react to stress in harmful ways, there are many positive ways to handle stress.*

Plan four paragraphs for the body of the essay. Find four paragraph groups in the list and determine the main idea of each paragraph; then write a topic sentence stating this main idea.

Now make a plan by arranging the topic sentences in an order that makes sense. Under each topic sentence, list supporting examples of details. **Answers will vary.**

1. INTRODUCTION and
Thesis statement: Although people often react to stress in harmful ways, there are many positive ways to handle stress.

2. Topic sentence: ____**Many people actually harm themselves trying to relieve**____

____**stress.**_____

(examples) ____**overeat; smoke; drink too much; get stress-induced diseases;**____

____**blow up at others**_____

3. Topic sentence: For some people, doing something physical is a positive way
   to relieve stress.

   (examples) walk; jog; work out; vigorous household chores; dig weeds or rake
   leaves

4. Topic sentence: Taking breaks, long or short, is another positive way to
   relieve stress.

   (examples) take a nap; escape into a hobby; go to a movie, to the beach

5. Topic sentence: Discussing one's problems can relieve stress and sometimes
   resolve the cause of it.

   (examples) call a friend; talk to a minister, etc.; talk to a counselor at the
   college; talk to a shrink if necessary

6. CONCLUSION: Stress is a fact of life and we all react to it whether we
   know it or not. We should incorporate these positive responses into our lives so
   that we can live more happily and more productively.

- Does every topic sentence support the thesis statement?
- Have you arranged the paragraphs in a logical order?

   2. **Write topic sentences and then plan paragraphs.** Sometimes a
writer can compose topic sentences directly from the thesis statement
without extensive jotting first. This is especially true if the thesis statement itself shows how the body will be divided or organized. Such a thesis
statement makes the work of planning paragraphs easy because the
writer has already broken down the subject into supporting ideas or
parts:

Thesis statement:	Because of the student cafeteria's many problems, the college should hire a new administrator to see that it is properly managed in the future.

*outlining
technique*

■ This thesis statement contains two main ideas: (1) that the cafeteria has many problems and (2) that a new administrator should be hired. The first idea states the problem and the second offers a solution.

From this thesis statement, a writer could logically plan a two-paragraph body, with one paragraph explaining each idea in detail. He or she might compose two topic sentences as follows:

Thesis statement:	Because of the student cafeteria's many problems, the college should hire a new administrator to see that it is properly managed in the future.
Topic sentence:	Foremost among the cafeteria's problems are the unappetizing food, the slow service, and the high prices.
Topic sentence:	A new administrator could do much to improve these terrible conditions.

These topic sentences might need to be revised later, but they will serve as guides while the writer further develops each paragraph.

The writer might develop the first paragraph in the body by giving **examples*** of the unappetizing foods, the slow service, and the high prices.

He or she could develop the second paragraph through **process,†** by describing the **steps** that the new administrator could take to solve the cafeteria's problems. The completed essay **plan** might look like this:

1. INTRODUCTION and
   Thesis statement: Because of the student cafeteria's many problems, the college should hire a new administrator to see that it is properly managed in the future.

2. Topic sentence: Foremost among the cafeteria's problems are the unappetizing food, the slow service, and the high prices.

   Problem 1: Food is unappetizing

   —sandwiches with tough meat, stale bread
   —salads with wilted lettuce, tasteless tomatoes
   —hot meals often either overcooked or undercooked

---

*For more work on developing paragraphs with examples, see Chapter 5, "Illustration."
†For more work on developing paragraphs by process, see Chapter 8, "Process."

Problem 2: Service is slow

—students wait 30 minutes for sandwiches
—students wait 15 minutes for just a cup of coffee
—have to gulp meals to get to class on time

Problem 3: Prices too high

—sandwiches overpriced
—coffee or tea costs eighty-five cents

3. Topic sentence: A new administrator could do much to improve these terrible conditions.

Step 1. Set minimum quality standards

—personally oversee purchase of healthful food
—set and enforce rules about how long food can be left out
—set cooking times for hot meals

Step 2. Reorganize service lines

—study which lines are busiest at different times of the day
—shift cooks and cashiers to those lines
—create a separate beverage line

Step 3. Lower prices

—better food and faster service would attract more student customers
—cafeteria could then lower prices

4. CONCLUSION

Note that the order of paragraphs logically follows the order in the thesis statement, discussing first the problem and then the solution.

The writer now has a clear plan from which to write the first draft of the essay.

PRACTICE 5   Write from two to four topic sentences to support *three* of the thesis statements that follow. (First you may wish to brainstorm or freewrite on scratch paper.) Make sure that every topic sentence really supports the thesis statement and that every one could be developed into a good paragraph. Then arrange your topic sentences in a **plan** in the space provided. Answers will vary.

Example | Before you buy a VCR, do these three things.

Topic sentence: __Decide how much you can spend, and determine your price__

__range.__

Topic sentence: __Examine the models that are within your price range.__

_____

Topic sentence: __Shop around; do not assume that all electronics stores are__

__created equal.__

1. I vividly recall the sights, smells, and tastes of the baking table at the county fair.

   Topic sentence: __Everywhere was a smorgasbord of homemade cakes, pies,__

   __cookies, and bread.__

   Topic sentence: __The enticing fragrances of yeast, spices, fruit, and__

   __chocolate were heavy in the air.__

   Topic sentence: __Some of the bakers proudly offered samples of their freshly__

   __baked wares.__

   Topic sentence: _____

   _____

2. Living alone has both advantages and disadvantages.

   Topic sentence: __When you live alone, you can make spur-of-the-moment__

   __decisions about what you want to do.__

   Topic sentence: __Living by yourself, you can keep your apartment as neat or__

   __as sloppy as you like.__

   Topic sentence: __Living alone allows you to eat whatever and whenever you__

   __want.__

   Topic sentence: __Living alone, however, makes you especially vulnerable to__

   __crime.__

3. Doing well at a job interview requires careful planning.

   Topic sentence: First, learn as much as possible about the company where you are interviewing.

   Topic sentence: Try to anticipate the kinds of questions the interviewer might ask.

   Topic sentence: Choose appropriate clothing to wear at the interview.

   Topic sentence: _____

   Topic sentence: Get a good night's sleep and practice relaxation techniques.

4. Jewelry making is a fascinating and profitable hobby.

   Topic sentence: Jewelry making provides an outlet for creative energies.

   Topic sentence: One can always work on new designs and experiment with new materials.

   Topic sentence: There is a large and growing market for handmade jewelry.

   Topic sentence: _____

5. My three children have individual techniques for avoiding housework.

   Topic sentence: Bob always remembers that he needs to go somewhere important.

   Topic sentence: Zena remembers that she has to do her homework.

   Topic sentence: Bill says he will help but procrastinates until someone else does his work for him.

   Topic sentence: _____

PRACTICE 6   Choose *one* thesis statement that you wrote for Practice 3, and develop the plan for an essay of your own. Your plan should include your thesis sentence, two to four topic sentences, plus supporting details, examples, and so forth. Brainstorm or freewrite every time you need ideas; rewrite the thesis and topic sentences until they are sharp and clear.

PART D

Ordering and Linking Paragraphs in the Essay

An essay, like a paragraph, should have **coherence.** That is, the paragraphs in an essay should be arranged in a clear, logical order and should follow one another like links in a chain.

Ordering Paragraphs

It is important that the paragraphs in your plan, and later in your essay, follow a **logical order.** The rule for writers is this: Use your common sense and plan ahead. *Do not* leave the order of your paragraphs to chance.

The types of order often used in single paragraphs—**time order, space order,** and **order of climax***—can sometimes be used to arrange paragraphs within an essay. Essays about subjects that can be broken into stages or steps, with each step discussed in one paragraph, should be arranged according to *time. Space order* is used occasionally in descriptive essays. A writer who wishes to save the most important or convincing paragraph for last would use *order of climax.* Or he or she might wish to reverse this order and put the most important paragraph first.

Very often, however, the writer simply arranges paragraphs in whatever order makes sense in the particular essay. Suppose, for example, that you have written the thesis statement *Laura and Janet have much in common,* and you plan three paragraphs with these topic sentences:

They have the same taste in clothes.

They have similar career goals.

People tell them that they look alike.

Since taste in clothes and looks are both *physical* similarities, it would be logical to arrange these two paragraphs one after the other. Furthermore, it makes sense to begin rather than end the essay with a physical

---

*For more work on time order, space order, and order of climax, see Chapter 4, "Achieving Coherence," Part A.

description so that the reader can visualize the two women while reading more about them. A logical order of paragraphs, then, would be the
following:

1. INTRODUCTION and
   Thesis statement: Laura and Janet have much in common.

2. Topic sentence: People tell them that they look alike.

3. Topic sentence: They have the same taste in clothes.

4. Topic sentence: They have similar career goals.

5. CONCLUSION

   Finally, if your thesis statement is divided into two, three, or four
parts, the paragraphs in the body should follow the order in the thesis;
otherwise the reader will be confused. Assume, for instance, that you are
planning three paragraphs to develop the thesis statement *My first flight
on a 747 was frightening, exciting, and educational.*

   Paragraph 2 should discuss __its frightening aspects_____

   Paragraph 3 should discuss __its exciting aspects_____

   Paragraph 4 should discuss __its educational aspects_____

PRACTICE 7   Plans for three essays follow, each containing a thesis statement and several topic sentences in scrambled order. Number the topic sentences in
each group according to an *order that makes sense.* Be prepared to explain
your choices.

*# in class
In group as whole*

1. Thesis statement: The new computer is fast, versatile, and small.

   Topic sentences: __3__ The compact size of this computer sets it
                                apart.

                                __1__ The computer produces information in a
                                matter of seconds.

                                __2__ It can be programmed in a number of use-
                                ful ways.

2. Thesis statement: The history of European contact with the
                                Karaja Indians of Brazil is one of violence and
                                exploitation.

   Topic sentences: __2__ The Karaja, exposed to European dis-
                                eases during the nineteenth century, were
                                reduced in numbers by 90 percent!

___1___ During the eighteenth century, the *bandeirantes* led attacks on Karaja villages to get slaves.

___3___ Since the turn of the twentieth century, Brazilian pioneers have increasingly used Indian territory as grazing land.

3. Thesis statement: Although "convenience" foods offer short-term ease to the modern cook, they may result in long-term health hazards.

Topic sentences: ___3___ The health hazards these foods pose, when used consistently, may be serious.

___1___ By "convenience" foods, I refer to canned, frozen, and boxed dinners.

___2___ For the busy cook, convenience foods offer several advantages.

PRACTICE 8   Now, go over the essay plan that you developed in Practice 6 and decide which paragraphs should come first, which second, and so forth. Does time order, space order, or order of climax seem appropriate to your subject? Number your paragraphs accordingly.

Linking Paragraphs

Just as the sentences within a paragraph should flow smoothly, the paragraphs within an essay should be clearly **linked** one to the next. As you write your essay, do not make illogical jumps from one paragraph to another. Instead, guide your reader. Link the first sentence of each new paragraph to the thesis statement or to the paragraph before. Here are four ways to link paragraphs:

1. Repeat key words or ideas from the thesis statement.
2. Refer to words or ideas from the preceding paragraph.
3. Use transitional expressions.
4. Use transitional sentences.

quiz + write answers on board

   1. Repeat key words or ideas from the thesis statement.* The topic sentences in the essay plan on the next page repeat key words from the thesis statement.

*For more work on repetition of key words, see Chapter 4, "Achieving Coherence," Part B. See also "Synonyms and Substitutions" in the same section.

> Thesis statement: Many films show the glamour but not the pain of street life.
>
> Topic sentence: These films portray drug dealers and pimps as glamorous and exciting.
>
> Topic sentence: These movies do not show the pain of wasted lives.

- In the first topic sentence, the words *these films* and *glamorous* repeat, in slightly altered form, words from the thesis statement.

- What words in the second topic sentence repeat key words from the thesis statement?

  these movies; pain; lives

2. Refer to words or ideas from the preceding paragraph. Link the first sentence of a new paragraph to the paragraph before, especially by referring to words or ideas near the end of the paragraph. Note how one writer links two paragraphs in the following passage from her essay on sky diving:

> (1) I wanted all of it: the rising of a tiny plane with the door off, the earth rushing away, the plunge, the slap of the wind, my hands on the back straps, the huge curve of white silk above me, the drift through the space we call sky.
>
> (2) It looked pale green that morning I fell into it, not the baby blue I expected. I must have been crying; my cheeks were wet. Only the thumps of a wild heart made noise; I did not know how to keep it quiet.
>
> —Gloria Emerson, "Take the Plunge"

- Emerson twice uses the word *it* in the first sentence of paragraph (2). What word (or words) located at the end of the paragraph (1) does *it* refer to?

  the space we call sky

3. Use transitional expressions.* Transitional expressions—words like *for example*, *therefore*, and *later on*—are used within a paragraph to show the relationship between sentences. Transitional expressions can also be used within an essay to show the relationships between paragraphs:

> (1) The house where I grew up was worn out and run-down. The yard was mostly mud, rock hard for nine months of the year but wet and swampy for the other three. Our nearest neighbors were 40 miles away, so it got pretty lonely. Inside, the house was shabby. The living room furniture was covered in stiff, nubby material that had lost its color over the years and become a dirty brown. Upstairs in my bedroom, the wooden floor sagged a little further west every year.
>
> (2) *Nevertheless*, I love the place for what it taught me. There I learned to thrive in solitude. During the hours I spent alone, when school was over and the chores were done, I learned to play the guitar and sing. Wandering in the fields around the house or poking under stones in the creek bed, I grew to love the natural world. Most of all, I learned to see and to appreciate small wonders.

- The first paragraph above describes some of the negative details about the writer's early home. The second paragraph *contrasts* the writer's attitude, which is positive. The transitional expression *nevertheless* eases the reader from one paragraph to the next by pointing out the exact relationship between the paragraphs.

- Transitional expressions can also highlight the *order* in which paragraphs are arranged.† Three paragraphs arranged in time order might begin: *First . . . , Next . . . , Finally. . . .* Three paragraphs arranged in order of climax might begin: *First . . . , More important . . . , Most important. . . .* Use transitional expressions alone or together with other linking devices.

4. Use transitional sentences. From time to time, you may need to write an entire sentence of transition to link one paragraph to the next, as shown in the passage on page 258.

---

*For a complete list of transitional expressions, see Chapter 4, "Achieving Coherence," Part B. See also the chapters in Unit 3 for ways to use transitional expressions in each paragraph and essay pattern.

†For more work on transitional expressions of time, space, and climax, see Chapter 4, "Achieving Coherence," Part A.

> (1) With his restaurant forced to close because of a new highway, Sanders took five frozen frying-chickens, a special cooker, and some flour and spices, and attempted to interest restaurant managers in his method of high temperature cooking. Acceptance was slow. He gave franchises away; he leased cookers; he supplied at cost paper, napkins, and buckets with his picture and the Kentucky Fried Chicken name.
>
> (2) *After three years he finally made some headway.* Then the idea caught on. In eight years he had sold over 500 franchises. Receiving 5 cents for each chicken sold by these restaurants, he made over $2.3 million. In 1962, then seventy-two years of age, he expanded the business to include take-home sales. In 1964 he sold the entire business for $2 million. By 1968 sales were over $250 million and there were over 1,500 outlets. His age when all this began? Sixty-five years.
>
> —Robert F. Hartley, *Retailing: Challenge and Opportunity*

- In the first paragraph above, Sanders is a struggling businessman. In the second paragraph, he makes it big. The topic sentence of paragraph 2 is the second sentence: *Then the idea caught on.*

- The first sentence of paragraph 2 is actually a **sentence of transition** that eases the reader from failure to success. (Note that it includes a transitional expression of time, *after three years.*)

Use all four methods of linking paragraphs as you write your essays.

PRACTICE 9 Read the essay that follows, noting the paragraph-to-paragraph *links*. Then answer the questions.

Banking in Computer Wonderland

(1) Although computer banking is clearly here to stay, I for one wish it were not. Now I know that a computer counts much faster than some human with a pencil, and that it frees up the bank personnel to spend more time with the customers, and that it gives me money on the weekends. I am a reasonable woman. These arguments should convince me.

(2) However, it is not admiration for technology I feel as I stick my plastic card into the slot and push my secret code number (my shirt size plus my shoe size with a three in between for good luck). "Hello," say the lighted green dots, brainlessly reporting the time right down to the second. "How can I assist you?" Conversing with a machine gives me the creeps. Soon, I imagine, it will be calling me "Susan" and noticing my

*Read r
work out
#1, 2, 3
in small
groups.*

outfit. Worse, if someone steals my plastic card, will I spend my life in prison?

(3) *This fear* is firmly based on past experience. "Sorry," the green dots told me recently. "I am unable to give you cash at this time. Your current balance is minus $10,303.00." Isn't that strange, I thought; the computer is making a mistake. Only later did I learn that computers never make mistakes. Therefore, I was told, I *must* have overdrawn my account by $10,303.00. It took four hours of my time and a year off my life to fix up that minor error.

(4) The bank employees are little help *in situations like this.* First of all, they have to spend a lot of time protecting the reputation of the computer, reminding the customers that it never makes mistakes. Second, they are allowed to tell me only what the computer tells them, and often, the computer isn't talking. I demand an explanation. I am told that the information is "in the computer" and cannot be reached for comment. "In the computer," I have learned, is much worse than "lost under the porch" or "fallen down the drain in the bathtub." There is nothing to be done. "But that's crazy," I shout and am coolly informed that it is I who am irrational.

(5) In spite of all this, I feel sorry for the bank personnel. It must be pretty depressing to be bested by a computer all day long, then yelled at besides. It is my theory that bank employees begin to feel ashamed that they are only human and that they *do* make mistakes. After a while, some of them start to pretend that they, too, are error-proof. A story will illustrate. I know a young woman whose computerized bank statement reported one day that she had $24,132.00 in her checking account, instead of $132.00. A moral person, she brought this bonanza to the attention of a bank officer. He insisted that, since the computer doesn't make mistakes, it had to be true. Perhaps she had forgotten having made the deposit. "Do you mean to tell me I could withdraw this money right now and it would all belong to me?" she asked. "Of course," he said. And that is what she did. Rather than give up his faith in computers or take the rap, he gave away $24,000.

(6) Meanwhile, my bank becomes more and more computerized. White modular hoods with digital screens swivel on the counter tops. The surveillance equipment is computerized; the doors and windows are computerized. The vault boasts a computerized lock, and along the walls gleam computerized banking terminals. And what of the people in this computer wonderland? From one side of the bank to the other, the tellers and officers, freed up to spend more time with people, are fighting with the customers about all the computer's mistakes.

1. What transitional expressions does this writer use to link paragraphs? (Find at least three.)

however; in spite of all this; meanwhile

2. How does the writer link paragraphs 2 and 3?

The first sentence of paragraph 3 refers to a fear expressed in paragraph 2.

_____

3. How does the writer link paragraphs 3 and 4?

The first sentence of paragraph 4 refers to "situations like this"; the

"situation" is described in paragraph 3.

PART E

Writing and Revising Short Essays

Writing the First Draft

Make sure you have a clear plan from which to write your first draft. This plan should include your thesis statement, two to four topic sentences that support it, details and facts to develop each paragraph, and a logical order. Write on every other line to leave room for later corrections, including all your ideas and paragraphs in the order you have chosen to present them. Explain your ideas fully, but avoid getting stuck on a particular word or sentence. When you have finished the draft, set it aside, if possible, for several hours or several days.

PRACTICE 10   Write a first draft of the essay you have been working on in Practices 6 and 8.

Revising

Revising an essay involves the same principles as revising a paragraph.* Read your first draft slowly and carefully to yourself—aloud if possible. Imagine you are a reader who has never seen the paper before. As you read, underline trouble spots, draw arrows, and write in the margins, if necessary, to straighten out problems.

Here are some questions to keep in mind as you revise:

✳ 1. Is my thesis statement clear?

✳ 2. Does the body of the essay fully support my thesis statement?

✳ 3. Does the essay have unity; does every paragraph relate to the thesis statement?

*For more work on revising, see Chapter 3, "The Process of Writing Paragraphs," Part F, and Chapter 16, "Putting Your Revision Skills to Work."

4. Does the essay have coherence; do the paragraphs follow a logical order?

5. Are my topic sentences clear?

6. Does each paragraph provide good details, well-chosen examples, and so on?

7. Is the language exact, concise, and fresh?

8. Are my sentences varied in length and type?

9. Does the essay conclude, not just leave off?

What does a peer reviewer do?

If possible, ask a "peer reviewer"—a trusted classmate or friend—to read your paper and give you feedback. Of course, this person should not rewrite or correct the essay but should simply tell you what parts are clear and what parts are confusing.

To guide your peer reviewer, you might ask him or her to answer these questions in writing:

1. What do you like about this piece of writing?

2. What seems to be the main point?

3. What parts could be improved (meaning not clear, supporting points missing, order mixed up, writing not lively, and so forth)? Please be specific.

4. What one change would most improve this essay?

Proofreading and Writing the Final Draft

Next, carefully **proofread** the draft for grammar and spelling. Check especially for those errors you often make: verb errors, comma splices, and so forth.* If you are unsure about the spelling of a word, check a dictionary.

Finally, recopy your essay. Type or write neatly on 8½-by-11-inch paper, using one side only. When you finish, proofread the final copy.

The following sample essay by a student shows his first draft, the revisions he made, and the revised draft. Each revision has been numbered and explained to give you a clear idea of the thinking process involved.

First Draft

Portrait of a Bike Fanatic

(1) I first realized how serious Diane was when I joined her on a long trip one Sunday afternoon. Her bike looked new, so I asked her if it was.

*For practice proofreading for individual errors, see chapters in Unit 6.

When she told me she had bought it three years ago, I asked her how she kept it looking so good. She showed me how she took good care of it.

(2) Diane had just about every kind of equipment I've ever seen. She put on her white crash helmet and attached a tiny rearview mirror on it—the kind the dentist uses to check out the backs of your teeth. She put a warning light on her left leg. She carried a whole bag full of tools. When I looked into it, I couldn't believe how much stuff was in there (wrenches, inner tubes, etc.)—tools to meet every emergency. I was tempted to see if it had a false bottom.

(3) I had no idea she was such a bike nut. We rode thirty miles and I was exhausted. Her equipment was something else, but useful because she had a flat and was able to fix it, saving our trip.

(4) She doesn't look like a bike fanatic, just a normal person. You'd never guess that her bike has more than 10,000 miles on it.

(5) As we rode, Diane told me about her travels throughout the Northeast (Cape Cod, Vermont, Penn., New York). Riding to work saved her money, kept her in shape. Her goal for the next summer was a cross-country tour over the Rockies!

(6) Our trip was no big deal to her but to me it was something. I might consider biking to work because it keeps you in shape. But basically I'm lazy. I drive a car or take the bus. I do like to walk though.

Revisions

Portrait of a Bike Fanatic

① Add intro and thesis   ② about bicycling

I first realized how serious Diane was ∧ when I

③ thirty-mile

joined her on a ~~long~~ trip one Sunday afternoon. Her

bike looked new, so I asked her if it was. When she

told me she had bought it years ago, I asked her

④ Describe in detail

how she kept it looking so good. ~~She showed me~~

~~how she took good care of it.~~

Diane had just about every kind of equipment

⑤ For example,

I've ever seen. ∧ She put on her white crash helmet

and attached a tiny rearview mirror on it—the kind

⑥ examine

the dentist uses to ~~check out~~ the backs of your

⑦ strapped   to   , just below the knee

teeth. She ∧ put a warning light on her left leg ∧

(handwritten in margin:) groups day 2 of ch 17 — in class — what's wrong with . . .

⑧ Mention trip location

She carried a whole bag full of tools. When I looked into it, I couldn't believe how much stuff was in there (wrenches, inner tubes, etc.)—tools to meet every emergency. I was tempted to see if it had a false bottom.

⑨ New ¶ on tools, flat tire

⑩ ~~I had no idea she was such a bike nut. We rode thirty miles and I was exhausted.~~ Her equipment was something else, but useful because she had a flat and was able to fix it, saving our trip.

⑪ Combine into one ¶ on tools

⑫ Move to intro.?

She doesn't look like a bike fanatic, just a normal person. You'd never guess that her bike has more than 10,000 miles on it.

⑬ Describe in detail. Make interesting!

As we rode, Diane told me about her travels throughout the Northeast (Cape Cod, Vermont, Penn., New York). Riding to work saved her money, kept her in shape. Her goal for the next summer was a cross-country tour over the Rockies!

⑭ Better conclusion needed

Our trip was no big deal to her but to me it was something. ~~I might consider biking to work because it keeps you in shape. But basically I'm lazy. I drive a car or take the bus. I do like to walk though.~~

⑮ Drop. Irrelevant

Reasons for Revisions

1. No thesis statement. Add catchy introduction. (introduction and thesis statement)

2. Add *bicycling*. What she is serious *about* is not clear. (exact language)

3. Tell *how* long! (exact language)

4. Expand this; more details needed. (support, exact language)

5. Add transition. (transitional expressions)

6. Wrong tone for college essay. (exact language)

7. Find more active verb; be more specific. (exact language)

8. Conclude paragraph; stress time order. (order)

9. This section is weak. Add one paragraph on tools. Tell story of flat tire? (paragraphs, support)

10. Drop! Repeats thesis. Not really a paragraph. (unity, paragraphs)

11. Put this in tools paragraph. Order is mixed up. (order)

12. Put this in introduction? (order)

13. Add details; make this interesting! (support, exact language)

14. Write a better conclusion. (conclusion)

15. Drop! Essay is about Diane and biking, not my bad exercise habits. (unity)

Final Draft

Portrait of a Bike Fanatic

(1) You'd never guess that the powder blue ten-speed Raleigh had more than 10,000 miles on it. And you'd never guess that the tiny woman with the swept-back hair and the suntanned forearms had ridden those miles over the last two years, making trips through eleven states. But Diane is a bicycle fanatic.

(2) I first realized how serious Diane was about bicycling when I joined her on a thirty-mile trip one Sunday afternoon. Her bike looked new, so I asked her if it was. When she told me she had bought it three years ago, I asked her how she kept it looking so good. From her saddlebag she took the soft cloth that she wiped the bike down with after every long ride and the plastic drop cloth that she put over it every time she parked it outdoors overnight.

(3) Diane had just about every kind of bike equipment I've ever seen. For example, she put on her white crash helmet and attached a tiny rearview mirror to it—the kind the dentist uses to examine the backs of your teeth. She strapped a warning light to her left leg, just below the knee. Then we set off on our trip, starting at Walden Pond in Concord and planning to go to the Wayside Inn in Sudbury and back again before the sun set.

(4) We were still in Concord when Diane signaled me to stop. "I think I have a flat," she said. I cursed under my breath. I was sure that would mean the end of our trip; we'd have to walk her bike back to the car and she'd have to take it to the shop the next day. But she reached into her

saddlebag again, and out came a wrench and a new tube. Before I knew it, she took the rear wheel off the bike, installed the new tube, and put the wheel back on. I began to wonder what else was in that saddlebag. When I asked, she showed me two sets of wrenches, another spare inner tube, two brake pads, a can of lubricating oil, two screwdrivers, a roll of reflective tape, extra bulbs for her headlight and taillight, and an extra chain. She had so much in the bag, I was tempted to see if it had a false bottom. Diane is one of those bicyclists who have tools to meet any emergency and know how to use them.

(5) As we rode along, Diane told me about her travels throughout the Northeast. She had taken her bike on summer vacations on Cape Cod and fall foliage tours in Vermont. She had ridden all over Pennsylvania and upstate New York, covering as much as seventy miles in a single day. She also rode to and from work every day, which she said saved money, kept her in shape, and helped her start each day feeling good. Her goal for the next summer, she said, was a cross-country tour. "All the way?" I asked. "What about the Rockies?" I know," she said. "What a challenge!"

(6) Our trip took a little less than three hours, but I'm sure Diane was slowing down to let me keep up with her. When we got back to the parked car, I was breathing hard and had worked up quite a sweat. Diane was already there waiting for me, looking as if she did this every day—which she does. For Diane, riding a bike is as easy and natural as walking is for most people. Look out, Rockies.

PRACTICE 11   Now, carefully read over the first draft of your essay from Practice 10 and **revise** it, referring to the checklist of questions. Take your time and write the best essay you can. Once you are satisfied, **proofread** your essay for grammar and spelling errors. Neatly write the final draft.

Writing Assignments

The assignments that follow will give you practice in writing short essays. In each, concentrate on writing a clear thesis statement and a full, well-organized body. Because introductions and conclusions are not discussed until Chapter 19, you may wish to begin your essay with the thesis statement and conclude as simply as possible.

Before you write, make a **plan** that includes:

what does your writing plan include?

- a clear thesis statement

- two to four topic sentences that support the thesis statement

- details, facts, and examples to develop each paragraph

- a logical order of paragraphs

- clean thesis
- supporting topic sentences
- details, examples
- order

1. Many people assume that aging is a negative process. Set out to prove the opposite. Discuss some of the positive aspects of growing older, some of the benefits: physical, emotional, financial, spiritual. What changes in self-knowledge and self-confidence go along with aging? Do relationships with others change for the better? Choose one main idea to write about. Consider using examples from your experience to back up your thesis statement.

2. Do you feel that certain television programs show stereotypical women, blacks, Hispanics, or members of any other group instead of believable people? Examine and discuss just one such program and one group of people. What situations, words, and actions by the TV characters are stereotypical, not real? Focus your subject, make a plan, and write a well-organized essay.

   You might wish to construct a thesis statement divided in this way: On the television program _____(name show)_____, _____(name group)_____ are often portrayed as being _____(name stereotype)_____.

3. Interview a classmate (or, if you do this assignment at home, someone with an unusual skill). As you talk to the person, look for a thesis: ask questions, take notes. What stands out about the person? Is there an overall impression or idea that can structure your essay? Use your descriptive powers. Notice the person's looks, clothes, typical expressions, and gestures. Later, formulate a thesis statement about the person, organize your ideas, and write.

4. Give advice to the weary job hunter. Describe the most creative job-hunting strategies you have ever tried or heard about. Support your thesis statement with examples, or consider using time order to show a successful job-hunting day in the life of the expert, you.

5. For better or worse, sex education begins at home—whether or not parents speak about the subject, whether parents' words reinforce or contradict the message of their own behavior. How do you think a parent should handle this responsibility? Be as specific as possible, including details from your own and your friends' experiences to make your point.

6. Have you ever had a close call with death? Describe the experience and its effect, if any, on your attitudes and actions since. If it has had little or no effect on you, try to explain why. Be sure to unify your essay with a clear thesis statement.

7. One marriage out of every two in America now ends in divorce. Think about this fact, its causes and implications. Are people less loyal? More free? Is marriage changing, or should it change? Are you or do you plan to be married in spite of the odds? Why? Focus on one aspect of the subject that you can discuss fully in a short essay.

Checklist: The Process of Writing an Essay

_____ 1. Narrow the topic in light of your audience and purpose. Be sure you can discuss this topic fully in a short essay.

_____ 2. Write a clear thesis statement. If you have trouble, freewrite or brainstorm first; then narrow the topic and write the thesis statement.

_____ 3. Freewrite or brainstorm, gathering facts, details, and examples to support your thesis statement.

_____ 4. Choose from two to four main ideas to support the thesis statement.

_____ 5. Write a topic sentence that expresses each main idea.

_____ 6. Decide on a logical order in which to present the paragraphs.

_____ 7. Plan the body of each paragraph, using all you have learned about paragraph development in Unit 2 of this book.

_____ 8. Write the first draft of your essay.

_____ 9. Revise as necessary, checking your essay for support, unity, and coherence. Refer to the list of revision questions on pages 260–261.

_____ 10. Proofread carefully for grammar, punctuation, sentence structure, spelling, and mechanics.

Suggested Topics for Essays

1. My Community's Worst Problem (propose a solution)

2. The Phone Call I Hated to Make

3. The Best (or Worst) Teacher I Ever Had

4. Portrait of a Special (or Unusual) Person

5. Parenting: Basic Rules for Raising Children

6. The Career for Which I Am Best Suited

7. How to Resolve a Disagreement with a Close Friend

8. Self-Discipline

9. Family Ties

10. What My Future Holds

11. Someone Who Changed My Life (tell how he or she changed it)

12. What This College Needs

13. Crime Does (Does Not) Pay

14. How to Get a Raise

15. Changing Bad Habits

16. What I Never Told Anyone

17. A Moving Film (Magazine, Program)

18. Portrait of a (Sports, Neatness, Homework, or other) Fanatic

19. How to Shop on a Budget

20. Should Courts Require a One-Year "Cooling Off" Period before a Divorce?

18

Types of Essays

PART A   The Illustration Essay
PART B   The Narrative Essay
PART C   The Descriptive Essay
PART D   The Process Essay
PART E   The Definition Essay
PART F   The Comparison or Contrast Essay
PART G   The Classification Essay
PART H   The Persuasive Essay

Because an essay is like an expanded paragraph, the methods for developing a paragraph that you learned in Unit 3—illustration, process, and so forth—can also be used to develop an entire essay. The rest of this chapter will show you how.

PART A

The Illustration Essay

The **illustration** essay is one of the most frequently used in college writing and in business. For papers and exams in history, psychology, health, English, and other subjects, you will often be asked to develop a main point with examples. In a letter of job application, you might wish to give examples of achievements that demonstrate your special skills.

Here is an illustration essay:

Acting to Save Mother Earth

(1) Every day we hear more bad news about our planet. Reports tell us that wildlife and forests are disappearing at an alarming rate. Newscasts give the latest word on how quickly earth is losing its protective shield and warming up. Newspapers lament the pollution of our air, water, and soil. What can we do in the face of such widespread gloom?

In fact, we do not have to feel helpless. We can each learn practical ways to better our environment.

(2) For example, saving and recycling newspapers has a number of positive results. First, recycling newspaper saves trees. The average American consumes about 120 pounds of newsprint a year—enough to use up one tree. That means close to 250 million trees each year are destroyed for paper in this country alone. If we recycled only one-tenth of our newspaper, we would save 25 million trees a year. Second, making new paper from old paper uses up much less energy than making paper from trees. Finally, this process also reduces the air pollution of paper-making by 95 percent.

(3) Another earth-saving habit is "precycling" waste. This means buying food and other products packaged only in materials that will decay naturally or that can be recycled. The idea is to prevent unrecyclable materials from even entering the home. For instance, 60 of the 190 pounds of plastic—especially styrofoam—each American uses a year are thrown out as soon as packages are opened. Be kind to your planet by buying eggs, fast food, and other products in cardboard instead of styrofoam cartons. Buy beverages in glass or aluminum containers instead of plastic ones. Buy in bulk to reduce the amount of packaging; you will save money too. Finally, when you can, buy products whose packaging shows the "recycled" logo. Materials that have been recycled once can be recycled again.

(4) Wise management of hazardous household wastes is yet another way of taking action for the planet. Hazardous wastes include paint, old car batteries, oven and drain cleaners, mothballs, floor and furniture polish, pesticides, and even toilet bowl cleaners. First of all, we should store hazardous materials properly by keeping them in their original containers, making sure they are clearly labeled, and keeping them in a cool, dry place that is out of the reach of children. Second, we can reduce our use of these products by buying only what we need and by sharing anything that might be left over. Third, we should take great care in disposing of hazardous wastes. Certain wastes such as old car batteries and motor oil can be refined and reused, and in some cities they can be turned in for special burning. However, local authorities have to be contacted because disposal practices vary so much from place to place.

(5) These personal actions may not *seem* important. At the very least, though, they can relieve some of the helplessness we all feel when faced with threats of global disaster. If carried out on a larger scale by millions of individuals, they could greatly improve our environment and lives.

- The **thesis statement** of an illustration essay states the writer's central point—a general statement that the rest of the essay will develop with examples.

- Which sentence in the introductory paragraph is the thesis statement?

  We can each learn practical ways to better our environment.

- How many examples does the writer use to develop the thesis statement? What are they?

  three; recycling newspaper, precycling waste, and managing hazardous

  household wastes

- Underline the topic sentence of each supporting paragraph.

- The thesis statement and topic sentences setting forth the three examples create a **plan** for this essay. The writer no doubt made such a plan before she wrote the first draft.

Before writing an illustration essay, you may wish to reread Chapter 5, "Illustration." As you pick a topic and plan your illustration essay, make sure your thesis statement can be richly developed by examples. Then brainstorm or freewrite, jotting down as many possible examples as you can think of; choose the best two or three examples. If you devote one paragraph to each example, each topic sentence should introduce the example to be developed. As you revise, make sure you have fully discussed each example, including all necessary details and facts.

PRACTICE 1   Choose a topic from the following list or one that you or your instructor has chosen. Write an illustration essay, referring to the essay checklist at the end of Chapter 17.

Suggested Topics: The Illustration Essay

1. Strange ways in which people get ready to write

2. TV programs that present the elderly (or another group) in a positive or negative light

3. Single parents: how they manage

4. Odd places to get married or have parties

5. People who have overcome handicaps, poverty, prejudice, and so on

6. Professors with unusual but effective teaching techniques

PART B

The Narrative Essay

The narrative essay is used frequently in college writing. For instance, in a history course you might be assigned a paper on the major battles of World War I or be given an essay examination on the story of women's struggle to gain the right to vote. An English teacher may ask you to write a composition in which you retell a meaningful incident or personal experience. In all of these instances, your ability to organize facts and details in clear chronological or time order—to tell a story well—will be a crucial factor in the success of your paper.

Here is a narrative essay:

Maya Lin's Vietnam War Memorial

(1) The Vietnam War, which lasted from 1965 until 1975, was the longest war in United States history. It was also the most controversial, leaving a deep wound in the nation's conscience. The creation of the Vietnam War Memorial—despite disagreements about its design—helped this wound to heal.

(2) In 1980, when the call went out for designs for a Vietnam War Memorial, no one could have predicted that as many as 14,000 entries would be submitted. The rules were clear. The memorial had to be contemplative, harmonize with its surroundings, list the names of those dead or missing and—most important—make no political statement about the war. When the judges, all well-known architects and sculptors, met in April 1981, they unanimously chose entry number 1026. The winner was Maya Lin, a twenty-one-year-old Asian-American architecture student who, ironically, was too young to have had any direct experience of the war.

(3) Lin envisioned shiny black granite slabs embedded in a long V-shaped trench, with one end pointing toward the Lincoln Memorial and the other toward the Washington Monument. She defined the trench as a cut in the earth, "an initial violence that in time would heal." Names would be carved into the granite in the order of the dates on which the soldiers had died or disappeared. Lin felt that finding a name on the memorial with the help of a directory would be like finding a body on a battlefield.

(4) Although her design satisfied all the contest criteria and was the judges' clear favorite, it aroused much controversy. Some critics called it a "black gash of shame and sorrow," labeling it unpatriotic, unheroic, and morbid. They were upset that the memorial contained no flags, no statues of soldiers, and no inscription other than the names. Privately, some complained that Lin was too young to win the contest—and that she was female besides. She fought back. She claimed that a flag would make the green area around the memorial look like a golf course and that a traditional statue on her modern structure would be like a mustache drawn on someone else's portrait. At last, a compromise was reached: A flag and a statue were added to the memorial, and the critics withdrew their complaints. On Veteran's Day, November 11, 1982, the Vietnam War Memorial was finally dedicated.

(5) Since then, the memorial has become the most popular site in Washington, D.C. Some visit to see the monument and pay tribute to those who died in the war. Others come to locate and touch the names of loved ones. As they stand before the wall, they also learn the names of those who served and died with their relatives and friends. When the rain falls, all the names seem to disappear. Visitors often leave memorials of

their own—flowers, notes to the departed, bits of old uniforms. A place of national mourning and of love, Maya Lin's monument has helped to heal the wounds of the Vietnam War.

- The **thesis statement** of a narrative essay gives the point of the essay.
- What is the thesis statement of the essay?

  The creation of the Vietnam War Memorial—despite disagreements about its

  design—helped this wound to heal.

- Paragraphs 2, 4, and 5 of this essay tell in chronological order the incidents of the narrative.
- What are the incidents?

  the call for designs, the judges' decision, the controversy, the dedication, the

  healing result

- What is the main idea of paragraph 3?

  a description of Maya Lin's design

- Paragraph 1 provides background information that helps the reader understand the narrative.
- What background material is given in this paragraph?

  The Vietnam War was the longest and most controversial war in U.S. history.

Before writing a narrative essay, you may wish to reread Chapter 6, "Narration." Make sure that your thesis statement clearly states the point of your narrative. Organize all the incidents and details in chronological or time order, in general beginning with the earliest event and ending with the latest. Be sure to supply any necessary background information. As you plan your essay, pay careful attention to paragraphing; if your narrative consists of just a few major incidents, you may wish to devote one paragraph to each one. Use transitional expressions that indicate time order to help your reader follow the narrative easily.

PRACTICE 2   Choose a topic from the following list or one that you or your instructor has chosen. Write a narrative essay, referring to the essay checklist at the end of Chapter 17.

Suggested Topics: The Narrative Essay

1. A family event that changed your view of yourself

2. An incident in which you or someone you know "saved the day"

3. Your "man or woman of the year" and what he or she did to merit that award

4. A successful struggle to achieve something by you or someone you admire

5. A real-life incident you have witnessed

6. A plot line for a movie or TV show you would like to produce

The Descriptive Essay

Although paragraphs of **description** are more common than whole essays, you will sometimes need to write a descriptive essay. In science labs, you may need to describe accurately cells under a microscope or a certain kind of rock. In business, you might have to describe a product or piece of equipment. Travel writers frequently use description, and personal letters often call on your descriptive powers.

Here is a descriptive essay:

Disney's Perfect World

(1) Disney World in Orlando, Florida, is America's best-known, busiest, and most profitable tourist attraction. Of all its wonders, Magic Kingdom draws the most visitors. Tourists can step into the past, ride a sleek spaceship into the future, or dance with a mouse. Magic Kingdom certainly delivers the fantasy it promises. However, for me, its most fantastic aspect is that everything seems so perfect—or almost everything.

(2) Every building, object, and decoration is sparkling clean. Take Main Street, for example, Disney's recreation of small-town America in 1900. Visitors walking from Town Square toward Cinderella's Castle cannot help but notice the gleaming paint on every well-kept building. Right down to their gold signs and gingerbread moldings, such shops as the Emporium and the House of Magic are freshly painted several times a year. Every window, streetlamp, and display is free of smudges. In fact, white-suited maintenance workers rush to pick up any litter, including droppings left by the horses that pull the shiny trolley cars along Main Street. Each night, all of Main Street is hosed down and scrubbed.

(3) The people of Magic Kingdom are equally flawless. As a marching band drums in the distance, cartoon characters like Goofy and Snow White stop mingling with the tourists and begin to usher them to the sides of Main Street for a parade. This parade differs from any other you have seen, however. Here no one is drunk, sloppy, or unusual; no band member trips on a shoelace or toots a wrong note. Dressed in spotless uniforms, the fit, attractive band members hold their instruments at the perfect angle. The shapely twirlers always catch their batons. All strut

in unison, only to reappear like clockwork in an hour. At nighttime parades, spectacular fireworks are electronically detonated in sync with the announcer's pleasant, perfectly modulated voice.

(4) Only the all-too-human visitors, thousands of us who come to gape and marvel, bring reality into this paradise. We grumble and fidget in endless lines, then jam into attractions like the Haunted Mansion in Liberty Square and the Space Mountain roller coaster in Tomorrowland. We dribble chili on our shirts, cut ahead of each other, shout at our crying children, and glare suspiciously if a stranger jostles our pocketbook. I watched one couple dressed in cute Mickey Mouse hats plop themselves down at the end of an empty row at the Hall of Presidents show, then hiss obscenities at everyone who was forced to climb over them. Of course, we visitors are not all young or beautiful either. I am a case in point, a balding, hefty gent who neither dresses nor carries himself very well.

(5) At Disney World, it occurred to me that I like imperfection. As the lights dimmed right on cue for yet another precision performance, I noted a mist of dandruff on the shoulders of the woman in front of me, and I felt fine.

—Angus Fletcher (Student)

- The **thesis statement** of a descriptive essay says what will be described and sometimes gives an overall impression of it.

- Which sentence in the introductory paragraph is the thesis statement?

  However, for me, its most fantastic aspect is that everything seems so

  perfect—or almost everything.

- Each paragraph in the body of this essay describes one scene or aspect of the topic. How many scenes or aspects are described and what are they?

  three; clean buildings and streets, flawless employees, less-than-perfect visitors

- What kind of **order** does the writer follow in organizing paragraph 2?

  space order: overall views of buildings, specific buildings and details, the street

  itself

- Note that the thesis statement and topic sentences make a **plan** for the whole essay.

Before writing an essay of description, you may wish to reread Chapter 7, "Description." Make sure that your thesis statement clearly sets forth the precise subject your essay will describe. Use your senses—sight, smell, hearing, taste, and touch—as you jot down ideas for the body. As you plan, pay special attention to organizing details and observations;

this is what we've looking for ✱

space order is often the best way to organize a description. As you revise, pay special attention to the richness and exactness of your language and details; these are what make good descriptions come alive.

PRACTICE 3   Choose a topic from the following list or one that you or your instructor has chosen. Write an essay of description, referring to the essay checklist at the end of Chapter 17.

Suggested Topics: The Descriptive Essay

1. Life in the twenty-first century

2. Your neighborhood or hometown

3. A person or animal you have closely observed

4. A place you know from your travels or from reading

5. An appliance or machine

6. A health club, park, or other place where people pursue fitness

PART D

The Process Essay

The **process** essay is frequently used in college and business. In psychology, for example, you might describe the stages of personality development. In history, you might explain the process of electing a president or how a battle was won or lost, while in business, you might set forth the steps of an advertising campaign. In science labs, you will often have to record the stages of an experiment.

Here is a process essay:

How to Prepare for a Final Exam

1) problem
2) why had to solve
3) what he did

(1) At the end of my first semester at college, I postponed thinking about final examinations, desperately crammed the night before, drank enough coffee to keep the city of Cincinnati awake, and then got C's and D's. I have since realized that the students who got As on their finals weren't just lucky; they knew how to *prepare*. There are many different ways to prepare for a final examination, and each individual must perfect his or her own style, but over the years, I have developed a method that works for me.

step 1

(2) First, when your professor announces the date, time, and place of the final—usually at least two weeks before—ask questions and take careful notes on the answers. What chapters will be covered? What kinds of questions will the test contain? What materials and topics are most

important? The information you gather will help you study more effectively.

(3) Next, survey all the textbook chapters the test will cover, using a highlighter or colored pen to mark important ideas and sections to be studied later. Many textbooks emphasize key ideas with boldface titles or headlines; others are written so that key ideas appear in the topic sentences at the beginning of each paragraph. Pay attention to these guides as you read.

(4) Third, survey your class notes in the same fashion, marking important ideas. If your notes are messy or disorganized, you might want to rewrite them for easy reference later.

(5) Fourth, decide approximately how many hours you will need to study. Get a calendar and clearly mark off the hours each week that you will devote to in-depth studying. If possible, set aside specific times: Thursday from 1 to 2 pm, Friday from 6 to 8 pm, and so on. If you have trouble committing yourself, schedule study time with a friend; but pick someone as serious as you are about getting good grades.

(6) Fifth, begin studying systematically, choosing a quiet place free from distractions in which to work—the library, a dorm room, whatever helps you concentrate. One of my friends can only study in his attic, another, in her car. As you review the textbook and your notes, ask yourself questions based on your reading. From class discussions, try to spot the professor's priorities and to guess what questions might appear on the exam. Be creative; one friend of mine puts important study material on cassette tapes, which he plays walking to and from school.

(7) Finally, at least three days before the exam, start reviewing. At the least opportunity, refer to your notes, even if you are not prepared to digest all the material. Use the moments when you are drinking your orange juice or riding the bus; just looking at the material can promote learning. By the night before the exam, you should know everything you want to know—and allow for a good night's sleep!

(8) By following these simple procedures, you may find, as I do, that you are the most prepared person in the exam room, confident that you studied thoroughly enough to do well on the exam.

—Mark Reyes (Student)

- The **thesis statement** in a process essay tells the reader what process the rest of the essay will describe.

- What is the thesis statement in this essay?

  There are many different ways to prepare for a final examination, and each

  individual must perfect his or her own style, but over the years, I have developed

  a method that works for me.

- What process will be described?

  preparing for a test

■ How many steps make up this process and what are they?

six; ask questions about the test, survey the chapters to be tested, survey class

notes, plan studying times, begin studying systematically, review material

■ What kind of order does the writer use to organize his essay?

chronological order

Before writing a process essay, you may wish to reread Chapter 8, "Process." The thesis statement should clearly set forth the process you intend to describe. As you plan your essay, make sure you jot down all the necessary steps or stages and put them in logical order. As you revise, make sure you have fully and clearly explained each step so that a reader who may not be familiar with the subject matter can follow easily. Clear language and logical organization are the keys to good process writing. Pay special attention to paragraphing; if the process consists of just three or four steps, you may wish to devote one paragraph to each step. If the steps are short or numerous, you will probably wish to combine two or three steps in each paragraph.

you need
1) clear language
2) logical organization

PRACTICE 4   Choose a topic from the list below or one that you or your instructor has chosen. Write a process essay, referring to the essay checklist at the end of Chapter 17.

groups of 2:
you are going on
a trip to Hawaii
describe the whole
process of getting there

Suggested Topics: The Process Essay

1. How someone became a success

2. How to find something in the library

3. How to plan a great party

4. How to toilet train your child (or teach your child some task or skill)

5. How to get an *A*

6. How to prepare for a backpacking trip, vacation, and so on

PART E

The Definition Essay

Although paragraphs of **definition** are more common in college writing than essays are, you may at some time have to write a definition essay. In a computer course, for example, you might be called on to define *disk* *operating system.* In psychology, you might need to define the *Oedipus complex*, or in biology, the term *DNA.*

Here is a definition essay:

Winning

(1) The dictionary defines winning as "achieving victory over others in a competition, receiving a prize or reward for achievement." Yet some of the most meaningful wins of my life were victories over no other person, and I can remember winning when there was no prize for performance. To me, winning means overcoming obstacles.

(2) My first experience of winning occurred in elementary school gym. Nearly every day, after the preparatory pushups and squat-thrusts, we had to run relays. Although I had asthma as a child, I won many races. My chest would burn terribly for a few minutes, but it was worth it to feel so proud—not because I'd beaten others or won a prize, but because I'd overcome a handicap. (By the way, I "outgrew" my asthma by age eleven.)

(3) In high school, I had another experience of winning. Although I loved reading about biology, I could not bring myself to dissect a frog in lab. I hated the smell of the dead animals, and the idea of cutting them open disgusted me. Every time I tried, my hands would shake and my stomach would turn. Worst of all, my biology teacher reacted to my futile attempts with contempt. After an upsetting couple of weeks, I decided to get hold of myself. I realized that I was overreacting. "The animals are already dead," I told myself. With determination, I swept into my next lab period, walked up to the table, and with one swift stroke, slit open a frog. After that, I excelled in biology. I had won again.

(4) I consider the fact that I am now attending college winning. To get here, I had to surmount many obstacles, both outside and inside myself. College costs money, and I don't have much of it. College takes time, and I don't have much of that either with a little son to care for. But I overcame these obstacles and a bigger one still—lack of confidence in myself. I had to keep saying, "I won't give up." And here I am, winning!

(5) These examples should clarify what winning means to me. I don't trust anything that comes too easily. In fact, I expect the road to be rocky, and I appreciate a win more if I have to work, sacrifice, and overcome. This is a positive drive for me, the very spirit of winning.

—Audrey Holmes (Student)

- The **thesis statement** of a definition essay tells the reader what term will be defined and usually defines it as well.

- Which sentence in the introductory paragraph is the thesis statement?

  To me, winning means overcoming obstacles.

- What is the writer's definition of *winning?*

  Winning to this writer means overcoming obstacles.

- Underline the topic sentences of paragraphs 2, 3, and 4.

- How do paragraphs 2, 3, and 4 develop the thesis statement?

  They give examples of how the writer overcame obstacles in her life.

- What order does the writer follow in paragraphs 2, 3, and 4?

  time order

Before writing a definition essay, you may wish to reread Chapter 9, "Definition." Choose a word or term that truly interests you, one about which you have something to say. Decide what type of definition you will use and write the thesis statement, which should state and define your term. Then brainstorm ideas to explain your definition. Consider using two or three examples to develop the term—the way the writer does in the preceding essay—devoting one paragraph to each example. As you revise, make sure your writing is very clear, so the reader knows exactly what you mean.

PRACTICE 5   Choose a topic from the following list or one that you or your instructor has chosen. Write a definition essay, referring to the essay checklist at the end of Chapter 17.

Suggested Topics: The Definition Essay

1. A responsible (or irresponsible) person
2. A good student (or a good teacher)
3. Loyalty
4. A term you know from sports, science, art, psychology, or some other field
5. Success
6. A happy marriage (or good relationship)

PART F

The Comparison or Contrast Essay

Essays of **comparison** or **contrast** are frequently called for in college courses. In an English or drama class, you might be asked to contrast two of Shakespeare's villains—perhaps Iago and Claudius. In psychology, you might have to contrast the training of the clinical psychologist and that of the psychiatrist, or in history, to compare ancient Greek and Roman religions.

Does the following essay compare or contrast?

Two Childhoods

(1) When I was young, my mother told me stories about her childhood. I loved her tales and still think of them. It was intriguing to hear about life thirty years before mine began. What fascinated me most, however, were the differences between her youth and mine.

(2) My mother grew up in the country. She spent most of her young years on a farm in South Carolina, surrounded by animals, orchards, cane fields, and agricultural machinery. By the time she was six, she was a walking agricultural textbook. Hers was a simple, serene, and comfortable life within a close-knit, neighborly environment. My mother's days were filled with swimming in nearby rivers and lakes, climbing and falling off trees, scooter-riding down country lanes, playing marbles with siblings and friends, bird watching and mending of wings, and building fences and tree houses.

(3) My childhood, on the other hand, was spent in New York City, without animals, scenic surroundings, or close-knit neighbors. Mine was a lifestyle of fast activity crammed into a tight schedule. Nature was replaced by shops and businesses, trees by tall buildings. My knowledge was not based on the simple things at hand, but on expensive toys, the latest clothes, and the newest sneakers. Compared to my mother's country existence, my city childhood seems humdrum—a constant series of trips to the park or movies, visits to the grocery store or shopping center, picnics at the amusement park or beach, and a few birthday parties thrown in.

(4) Just as our lifestyles differed, so too did our personalities. Relatives say that my mother was a loving, caring child who was always willing to help. She was praised for being clever and vibrant, levelheaded and respectful to others. My mother was strong-willed and spoke her mind when she saw fit, but she placed few demands on her parents for toys or fancy clothes. Somehow her environment, which had instilled in her an appreciation of nature and living things, was enough.

(5) I, on the other hand, was considered a bit too extroverted, selfish, and stubborn. I reveled in being petulant, pigheaded, demanding, and unstable. Although I could be loving, I cleverly used this trait to my advantage in an attempt to manipulate my parents and get the beautiful

toys and clothes I wanted. After all, these gave me all the aesthetic appreciation I needed. In fact, I was a brazenfaced brat.

(6) Looking back, I think it would have been nice as a child to have fallen off a few trees or driven a scooter at maniacal speeds or even milked a cow or crushed some coffee beans in a mortar. Yes, that would have been nice. It really would have been.

—Cheryl Parris (Student)

- The **thesis statement** of a comparison or contrast essay tells what two persons or things will be compared or contrasted.

- What is the thesis statement of this essay?

  What fascinated me most, however, were the differences between her youth

  and mine.

- Will this essay compare or contrast the two people? What words in the thesis indicate this?

  contrast; differences

- Does the writer discuss all points about A and then all points about B, or skip back and forth from A to B?

  skips back and forth from A to B

- Note that the thesis statement and topic sentences make a **plan** for this essay.

Before you plan your essay, you may wish to reread Chapter 10, "Comparison and Contrast." Bear in mind, as you choose a subject, that the most interesting essays usually compare two things that are different or contrast two things that are similar. Otherwise, you run the risk of saying the obvious ("Cats and dogs are two different animals.").

Here are a few tips to keep in mind as you write your thesis statement: Don't just say that A and B are similar or different; instead, say *in what way* A and B are similar or different, as the writer does above. You may wish to use this form for a contrast thesis: *Although A and B have this similarity, they are different in these ways*. And for a comparison: *Although A and B are unlike in this way, they are similar in these ways.*

As you plan the body of your essay, you might wish to make a chart of all your points of comparison or contrast. In any case, if you discuss the food, service, price, and atmosphere of Restaurant A, you must discuss the food, service, price, and atmosphere of Restaurant B as well.

In your essay, you can first discuss A (one paragraph), then discuss B (one paragraph), or you can skip back and forth between A and B (one paragraph on point one, A and B, one paragraph on point two, A and B, and one paragraph on point three, A and B). Refer to the charts in Chapter 10, pages 117–118.

PRACTICE 6   Choose a topic from the list below or one that you or your instructor has chosen. Write either a comparison or a contrast essay, referring to the essay checklist at the end of Chapter 17.

Suggested Topics: The Comparison or Contrast Essay

1. Two athletes, entertainers, philosophers, political figures, and so forth

2. Two restaurants

3. Your mother's or father's childhood and your own

4. Challenging classes and mediocre classes

5. Two types of engines, computers, and so forth

6. A current and a past love interest

PART G

The Classification Essay

The **classification** essay is useful in college and business. In music, for example, you might have to classify Mozart's compositions according to the musical periods of his life. A retail business might classify items in stock according to popularity—how frequently they must be reordered.

While the classification essay is usually serious, the pattern can make a good humorous essay, as this essay shows:

The Potato Scale

(1) Television has become the great American pastime. Nearly every household has a TV, which means that people are spending time watching it, unless, of course, they bought it to serve as a plant stand. Television viewers can be grouped in many ways—by the type of shows they watch (but there is no accounting for taste) or by hours per week of watching (but that seems unfair since a working, twelve-hour-a-week viewer could conceivably become a fifty-hour-a-week viewer if he or she were out of a job). So I have developed the Potato Scale. The four major categories of the Potato Scale rank TV viewers on a combination of leisure time spent watching, intensity of watching, and the desire to watch versus the desire to engage in other activities.

(2) First, we have the True Couch Potatoes. They are diehard viewers who, when home, will be found in front of their televisions. They no longer eat in the dining room, and if you visit them, the television stays on. The *TV Guide* is their Bible. They will plan other activities and chores around their viewing time, always hoping to accomplish these tasks in front of the tube. If a presidential address is on every channel but one, and they dislike the president, they will tune in that one channel, be it

Bugs Bunny or Polynesian barge cooking. These potatoes would never consider turning off the box.

(3) The second group are the Pseudo Couch Potatoes. These are scheduled potatoes. They have outside interests and actually eat at the table, but for a certain period of time (let's say from 7 to 11 in the evening), they will take on the characteristics of True Couch Potatoes. Another difference between True and Pseudo Potatoes deserves note. The True Potato must be forced by someone else to shut off the television and do something different; however, if the Pseudo Potato has flipped through all the channels and found only garbage, he or she still has the capacity to think of other things to do.

(4) Third, we have the Selective Potatoes. These more discriminating potatoes enjoy many activities, and TV is just one of them. They might have a few shows they enjoy watching regularly, but missing one episode is not a world-class crisis. After all, the show will be on next week. They don't live by the *TV Guide*, but use it to check for interesting specials. If they find themselves staring at an awful movie or show, they will gladly, and without a second thought, turn it off.

(5) The fourth group consists of Last Resort Potatoes. These people actually prefer reading, going to the theatre, playing pickup basketball, walking in the woods, and many other activities to watching television. Only after they have exhausted all other possibilities or are dog-tired or shivering with the flu, will they click on the tube. These potatoes are either excessively choosy or almost indifferent to what's on, hoping it will bore them to sleep.

(6) These are the principal categories of the Potato Scale. What type of potato are you?

—Helen Petruzzelli (Student)

- The **thesis statement** in a classification essay tells the reader what group will be classified and on what basis.

- This entire essay **classifies** people on the basis of their television viewing habits. Which sentence is the thesis statement?

  The four major cateogries of the Potato Scale rank TV viewers . . . to engage in

  other activities.

- Into how many categories are TV viewers divided?

  four

- Each paragraph in the body of the essay discusses one of four categories, which the writer names. What are they?

  1: True Couch Potatoes

  2: Pseudo Couch Potatoes

3: _____Selective Potatoes_____

4: _____Last Resort Potatoes_____

- The thesis statement and the topic sentences setting forth the four categories create a **plan** for the essay. The writer no doubt made the plan before she wrote the first draft.

- Can you see the logic in the writer's *order* of paragraphs? That is, why does she present True Couch Potatoes first, Pseudo Potatoes second, Selective Potatoes third, and Last Resort Potatoes last?

  She moves from people who watch TV the most to those who watch it the least.

  _____

Before writing your classification essay, you may wish to reread Chapter 11, "Classification." Choose a topic that lends itself to classification. Your thesis statement should state clearly the group you will classify and your basis of classification. As you plan, make sure that all your categories (three or four is a good number) reflect that basis of classification. Discuss one category per paragraph, including enough examples, details, and facts so that the reader completely understands your ideas.

PRACTICE 7   Choose a topic from the following list or one that you or your instructor has chosen. Write a classification essay, referring to the essay checklist at the end of Chapter 17.

Suggested Topics: The Classification Essay

1. Members of your family

2. Cars, computers, or some other machines

3. Couples in a restaurant

4. People studying in the library

5. Houseplants

6. Teaching styles of college professors

PART H

The Persuasive Essay

Persuasive essays are perhaps the essay type most frequently called for in college and business. That is, you will often be asked to take a stand on an issue—legalized abortion, capital punishment, whether a company should invest in on-site child care—and then try to convince others to agree with you. Examination questions asking you to "agree or disagree" are really asking you to take a stand and make a persuasive case for that stand—for example, "World War II was basically a continuation of World War I. Agree or disagree." You are asked to muster factual evidence to support your stand.

Here is a persuasive essay:

Keeping Older Workers on the Job

(1) Sixty-five is the traditional age for workers to retire in the United States. Conventional wisdom says that they have fulfilled their work obligations and should now leave job openings for those on the way up the career ladder, including young people just starting out. However, for many reasons, today's companies should look for ways to keep their older employees instead of forcing people to retire at age sixty-five.

Consequence →

Facts →

(2) First and most important, if companies do not retain their older workers, they may run out of workers altogether. Census figures tell us that America is growing older. In 1982, one American in five was over fifty-five; by the year 2020, one American in *three* will be over fifty-five. Right now, there are more Americans over sixty-five than teenagers, and the pool of new workers between sixteen and twenty-four is shrinking rapidly. Shortages of new workers have already occurred in such vital fields as nursing and teaching. The growing number of older workers will fill all kinds of service positions—from security guards, limousine drivers, and hotel clerks to media advisors, political lobbyists, and insurance-claims adjustors.

Answers points opposition has : old workers cost too much

(3) Next, some people claim that older workers cost too much, but often just the opposite is true. According to Mike Bradford, a corporate agent for Metropolitan Insurance Company, while older workers may command higher wages, they miss fewer work days than younger workers and file fewer medical insurance claims. Bradford adds that it costs a company less to insure a sixty-year-old employee with one or no dependents than to insure a thirty-five-year-old employee with a spouse and two children. Furthermore, older workers often cost less than younger ones because they are more productive. A study done in Great Britain in 1985 found that sixty-year-olds were more productive than twenty-year-olds in many kinds of work.

(4) Finally, many large and small companies that keep and even recruit older employees report good results. For example, Macy's, the famous New York department store, has never practiced mandatory retirement and values its older workers. McDonald's now actively recruits from senior citizens clubs for its special "McMasters" training program, offering a choice of days, hours, and jobs to trainees. Travelers Insurance, a large firm in Connecticut, has created a number of attractive work options for its older employees. A final example is Health-Wise, a small publishing house, half of whose employees are over fifty-five. All these companies are profiting from the sound judgment, personal skills, and accumulated experience of older employees.

(5) As our population changes and grows, more companies will have to change too. Although younger employees might not appreciate the competition, smart employers will keep their older workers on the job.

- The **thesis statement** in a persuasive essay clearly states the issue to be discussed and the writer's position on it.

✓ - What is the thesis statement?

Today's companies should look for ways to keep their older employees instead of

forcing people to retire at age sixty-five.

✓ - How many reasons does the writer give to back up the thesis statement?

three   First, Next, Finally

- Notice that the writer presents one reason per paragraph.

✓ - Which reason *predicts the consequence?*

the first one

✓ - The writer also supports this reason with facts. What facts are given, and what is the source of these facts?

the number of Americans who were over fifty-five in 1982 and the number who

will be in 2020; the U.S. Census Bureau

- Which reason is supported by referring to an *authority?*

the second one

- Who is that authority?

Mike Bradford, a corporate agent for Metropolitan Insurance Company

- What reason is supported by *examples?*

the third one

✗ - Which reason is really an *answer to the opposition?*

reason 2   argues contrary to belief that older
workers cost too much.

- Note that the thesis statement and topic sentences make up a **plan** for the whole essay.

Before writing an essay of persuasion, reread Chapter 12, "Persuasion." Make sure your thesis statement takes a clear stand. Devote one paragraph to each reason, developing each paragraph fully with facts and discussion. Try to use some of the methods of persuasion discussed in Chapter 12. Revise for clarity and support; remember, ample factual support is the key to successful persuasion.

PRACTICE 8   Choose a topic from the list below or one that you or your instructor has chosen. Write a persuasive essay, referring to the essay checklist at the end of Chapter 17.

Suggested Topics: The Persuasive Essay

1. A college education is (not) worth the time and money.
2. Sexually explicit magazines should (not) be sold at newsstands.
3. Only minority police should patrol minority neighborhoods.
4. Gay couples should (not) be allowed to adopt children.
5. The United States should (not) have sent troops to Iraq in 1990.
6. Suicides of teen-agers should (not) be reported in national media.

give 2 reasons why yes
      "   "   "   no

19

The Introduction, the Conclusion, and the Title

PART A The Introduction
PART B The Conclusion
PART C The Title

The Introduction

An **introduction** has two functions in a composition. First, it contains the **thesis statement** and, therefore, tells the reader what central idea will be developed in the rest of the paper. Since the reader should be able to spot the thesis sentence easily, it should be given a prominent place— for example, the first or the last sentence in the introduction. Second, the introduction has to interest the reader enough so that he or she will want to continue reading the paper.

Sometimes the process of writing the essay will help clarify your ideas about how best to introduce it. So once you have completed your essay, you may wish to revise and rewrite the introduction, making sure that it clearly introduces the essay's main idea.

There is no best way to introduce a composition, but you should certainly avoid beginning your work with "I'm going to discuss" or "this theme is about." You needn't tell the reader you are about to begin; just begin!

Below are seven basic methods for beginning your composition effectively. In each example, the thesis statement is italicized.

1. Begin with a single-sentence thesis statement. A single-sentence thesis statement can be effective because it quickly and forcefully states the main idea of the essay:

> *Final examinations should be abolished.*

■ Note how quickly and clearly a one-sentence thesis statement can inform the reader what will follow in the rest of the essay.

2. Begin with a general idea and then narrow to a specific thesis statement. The general idea gives the reader background information or sets the scene. Then the topic narrows to one specific idea—the thesis statement. The effect is like a funnel, from wide to narrow.

> Few Americans stay put for a lifetime. We move from town to city to suburb, from high school to college in a different state, from a job in one region to a better job elsewhere, from the home where we raise our children to the home where we plan to live in retirement. *With each move we are forever making new friends, who become part of our new life at that time.*
>
> —Margaret Mead and Rhoda Metraux, "On Friendship," in *A Way of Seeing*

■ What general idea precedes the thesis statement and then leads the reader to focus on the specific main point of the essay?

Americans move often.

3. Begin with an illustration. An illustration in the introduction of an essay makes the thesis statement more concrete and vivid:

> All last week, fourth-grade teacher Jennifer McKee became a student again. For six hours a day, she sat in front of a donated machine, trying to understand instructions, asking questions, and making mistakes. *Jennifer is just one of thousands of teachers around the country who are learning to use computers.*

■ What example does the writer provide to make the thesis statement more concrete?

Jennifer McKee, a teacher, is learning to use a computer.

4. Begin with a surprising fact or idea. A surprising fact or idea arouses the reader's curiosity about how you will support this initial startling statement.

> *Millions of law-abiding Americans are physically addicted to caffeine—and most of them don't even know it.* Caffeine is a powerful central nervous system stimulant with substantial addiction potential. When deprived of their caffeine, addicts experience often severe withdrawal symptoms, which may include: a throbbing headache, disorientation, constipation, nausea, sluggishness, depression, and irritability. As with other addictive drugs, heavy users develop a tolerance and require higher doses to obtain the expected effect.
>
> —Tom Ferguson and Joe Graedon, "Caffeine," *Medical Self-Care*

- Why are the facts in this introduction likely to startle or surprise the reader?

  So many people drink caffeine-containing beverages that they think caffeine is

  harmless.

5. Begin with a contradiction. In this type of introduction, your thesis statement contradicts what many or most people believe. In other words, your essay will contrast your opinion with the widely held view.

> Most people believe that stress has a negative effect on their lives. Under severe stress, most cannot function effectively—or at all. Pressured by tight deadlines, heavy workloads, or competitive situations, they may suffer from such problems as anxiety, sleeplessness, or ulcers. Yet stress is not necessarily bad. *Contrary to popular opinion, people can learn to turn stress into a valuable asset in the classroom and the workplace.*

- What is the widely held view?

  Stress has a negative effect on people's lives.

- How does the writer contradict this idea?

  The writer says that people can learn to turn stress into an asset.

- What will the rest of the essay discuss?

  The rest of the essay will discuss how stress can be turned into an asset.

---

6. Begin with a direct quotation. A direct quotation is likely to catch your reader's attention and to show that you have explored what others have to say about the subject. You can then proceed to agree or to disagree with the direct quotation.

> "I get a little weary of hearing broken homes being blamed for the 96.3 percent of American youth's difficulties," observed Jim Brown. He has a point. Many of my friends grew up in broken homes, being raised by only one parent. Yet they are doing fine now. Some are teachers, some are salespeople, and some are just raising families of their own. *In fact, I'm the product of a broken home, but I too was able to overcome this supposed disadvantage.*

- Does the author agree or disagree with the statement by Jim Brown?

  The author agrees.

Of course, definitions, comparisons, or any of the other kinds of devices you have already studied can also make good introductions. Just make sure that the reader knows exactly which sentence is your thesis statement.

Writing Assignment 1

Here are five statements. Pick three that you would like to write about and compose an introduction for each one. Use any of the methods for beginning compositions discussed above.

1. Sometimes, you should look before you leap.

2. Parents should not be financially responsible for the damage their children cause.

3. Noise is definitely a form of pollution.

4. Studying with someone else can pay off in better grades.

5. My college should offer a three-day course in "How to _____."

The Conclusion

A conclusion signals the end of the essay and leaves the reader with a final thought. As with the introduction, you may wish to revise and rewrite the conclusion once you have completed your essay. Be certain your conclusion flows logically from the body of the essay.

Like introductions, conclusions can take many forms, and the right one for your essay depends on how you wish to complete your paper—with what thought you wish to leave the reader. However, never conclude your paper with "as I said in the beginning," and try to avoid the overused "in conclusion" or "in summary." Don't end by saying you are going to end; just end!

Here are three ways to conclude an essay.

1. **End with a call to action.** The call to action says that, in view of the facts and ideas presented in the essay, the reader should *do something*.

> Finally, riding with others in a carpool is much more enjoyable and sociable than driving alone every day. When I was new at Tybold Incorporated, I joined a carpool. My travel companions have since become my closest business associates, best friends, and racquetball buddies. You have a choice! Call your local carpool number tonight and start reaping the benefits of shared transportation tomorrow.

■ What does the writer want the reader to do?

The writer wants the reader to join a carpool.

2. **End with a final point.** The final point can tie together all the other ideas in the essay; it provides the reader with the sense that the entire essay has been leading up to this one final point.

> What the reader would strive for, then, is a more *active* kind of listening. Whether you listen to Mozart or Duke Ellington, you can deepen your understanding of music only by being a more conscious and aware listener—not someone who is just listening, but someone who is listening *for* something.
>
> —Aaron Copland, *What to Listen for in Music*

■ What word in the first sentence of this conclusion tells the reader that Copland is about to *draw a conclusion* or *make a final point?*

then

3. End with a question. By ending with a question, you leave the reader with a final problem that you wish him or her to think about.

> Illness related to chemical dumping is increasing in Larkstown, yet only a handful of citizens have joined the campaign to clean up the chemical dump on the edge of town and to stop further dumping. Many people say that they don't want to get involved, but with their lives and their children's futures at stake, can they afford not to?

■ What problem does the writer's final question point to?

the problem of passivity: people not wanting to ''get involved''

Writing Assignment 2

Review two or three essays that you have written recently. Do the conclusions bring the essays to clear ends? Are they interesting? How could they be improved? Using one of the three strategies taught in this section, write a new conclusion for one of the essays.

PART C

The Title

If you are writing just one paragraph, chances are that you will not be required to give it a title, but if you are writing a multiparagraph theme, a title is definitely in order.

The title is centered on the page above the body of the theme and separated from it by several blank lines (about 1 inch of space):

Title

← about 1½″
← about 1″

If you are writing just one paragraph, chances are that you will not be required to give it a title, but if you are writing a multiparagraph theme, a title is definitely in order.

The title is centered on the page above the body of the theme and separated from it by several blank lines (about 1 inch of space).

- *Do not* put quotation marks around the title of your own paper.

- *Do not* underline the title of your own paper.

- Remember, unlike the topic sentence, the title is not part of the first paragraph; in fact, it is usually only four to five words long and is rarely an entire sentence.

A good title has two functions: to suggest the subject of the essay and to spark the reader's interest. Although the title is the first part of your essay the reader sees, the most effective titles are usually written *after* the essay has been completed.

To create a title, reread your essay, paying special attention to the **thesis statement** and the **conclusion**. Try to come up with a few words that express the main point of your paper.

Here are some basic kinds of titles.

1. The most common title used in college writing is the no-nonsense descriptive title. In writing such a title, stress key words and ideas developed in the essay:

The Search for Identity in *Native Son*

Advantages and Disadvantages of Buying on Credit

The Role of Chlorophyll in Photosynthesis

2. Two-part titles are also effective; write one or two words stating the general subject, then add several words that narrow the topic:

> Legal Gambling: Pro and Con
>
> The Greenhouse Effect: An Issue of the 90's
>
> Mother Teresa: A Life Lived for Others

3. Write the title as a rhetorical question. Then answer the question in your theme:

> What Can Be Done about Child Abuse?
>
> Should Students Rate Teachers?

4. Relate the title to the method of development used in the essay (see Unit 3 and Chapter 18):

Illustration:	Democracy in Action Three Roles I Play
Narration:	The Development of Rap Music
Description:	Portrait of a Farm Worker A Mountain Scene
Process:	How to Get Organized How to Wire a Lamp
Definition:	What It Means to Be Unemployed A Definition of Love
Comparison:	James Woods: The New Bogart Julian Lennon: In His Father's Footsteps
Contrast:	Pleasures and Problems of Owning a Home Montreal: City of Contrasts
Classification:	Three Types of Soap Operas
Persuasion:	Pornography Should Be Banned The Need for Discipline in Our Schools

Use this list the next time you title a paper.

Writing Assignment 3

Review two or three essays that you have written recently. Are the titles clear and interesting? Applying what you've learned in this chapter, write a better title for at least one paper.

20

The Essay Question

PART A   Budgeting Your Time
PART B   Reading and Understanding the Essay Question
PART C   Choosing the Correct Paragraph or Essay Pattern
PART D   Writing the Topic Sentence or the Thesis Statement

Throughout your college career, you will have to take essay examinations. In fact, you probably took a "placement" examination before you were enrolled in your first college English class. You may also be asked to take an "exit" examination when you complete this course to see whether you have mastered good writing skills. Clearly, it is important that you learn how to do your best on essay examinations.

To do well on an essay test, it is not enough to know the material. You must also be able to call forth what you know, organize it, and present it in writing—all under pressure in a limited time! Like it or not, how well you do on an essay test depends partly on how well you write.

An essay question requires the same skills that a student uses in writing a paragraph or essay, but many students, under the pressure of a test, forget or fail to apply what they know about good writing. This chapter should improve your ability to take essay tests. Many of the sample questions on the following pages are questions from real examinations.

Practice will pay off. Remember, an adept taker of essay tests is made, not born.

PART A

Budgeting Your Time

Since most essay examinations are timed, it is important that you learn how to **budget** your time effectively so that you can devote adequate time to each question *and* finish the test. The following five tips will help you budget your time well.

1. **Make sure you know exactly how long the examination lasts.** A one-hour examination may really be only fifty minutes; a two-hour examination may last only one hour and forty-five minutes.

2. **Note the point value of all questions and allot time accordingly to each question.** That is, allot the most time to questions that are worth the most points and less time to ones that are worth fewer.

3. **Decide on an order in which to answer the questions.** You do not have to begin with the first question on the examination and work, in order, to the last. Instead, you may start with the questions worth the most points. Some students prefer to begin with the questions they feel they can answer most easily, thereby guaranteeing points toward the final grade on the examination. Others combine the two methods. No matter which system you use, be sure to allot enough time to the questions that are worth the most points—whether you do them first or last.

4. **Time yourself.** As you begin a particular question, calculate when you must be finished with that question in order to complete the examination, and note that time in the margin. As you write, check the clock every five minutes so that you remain on schedule.

5. **Finally, do not count on having enough time to recopy your essay.** Skip lines and write carefully so that the instructor can easily read your writing as well as any neat corrections you might make.

PRACTICE 1   Imagine that you are about to take the two-hour history test shown in the following two boxes. Read the test carefully, noting the point value of each question, and then answer the questions that follow the examination. Answers may vary.

Part I   Answer both questions. 15 points each.

  1. Do you think that the Versailles Peace Treaty was a "harsh" one? Be specific.

  2. List the basic principles of Karl Marx. Analyze them in terms of Marx's claim that they are scientific.

Part II   Answer two of the following questions. 25 points each.

  3. Describe the origins of, the philosophies behind, and the chief policies of either Communist Russia or Fascist Italy. Be specific.

  4. What were the causes of the attempted overthrow of Gorbachev in 1991? Why did it fail?

  5. European history of the nineteenth and twentieth centuries has been increasingly related to that of the rest of the world. Why? How? With what consequences for Europe?

Part III Briefly identify ten of the following. 2 points each.

a. John Locke
b. Franco-Prussian War
c. Stalingrad
d. Cavour
e. Manchuria, 1931
f. Entente Cordiale
g. Existentialism

h. Jacobins
i. The Opium Wars
j. Social Darwinism
k. The Reform Bill of 1832
l. The most interesting reading you have done this term (from the course list)

1. Which part would you do first and why? _I would do Part II first because it is worth the most points (50)._

How much time would you allot to the questions in this part and why? _I would allot approximately half of my time because it is half of the exam._

2. Which part would you do second and why? _I would do Part I second because it is worth 30 points._

How much time would you allot to the questions in this part and why? _I would allot about half my remaining time because this part is about one-fourth of the exam._

3. What part would you do last and why? _I would do Part III last because it is worth the least number of points (20). Also, I would get some credit for each item that I answer correctly; if I run out of time, my score would be hurt less on this kind of question than on an essay question._

How much time would you allot to the questions in this part and why? _I would allot most of my remaining time, answering all of the questions I could. I'd save some time to review my other answers._

PART B

Reading and Understanding the Essay Question

Before you begin writing, carefully examine each question to decide exactly what your purpose is, that is, what the instructor expects you to do.

> *Question:*   Using either Communist China or Nazi Germany as a model, (a) describe the characteristics of a totalitarian state, and (b) explain how such a state was created.

- This question contains three sets of instructions.

- First, you must use "either Communist China or Nazi Germany as a model." That is, you must **choose** *one or the other* as a model.

- Second, you must **describe** and, third, you must **explain.**

- Your answer should consist of two written parts, a **description** and an **explanation.**

It is often helpful to underline the important words, as shown in the box above, to make sure you understand the entire question and have noted all its parts.

> *The student must:*   (1) *choose* to write about *either* Communist China or Nazi Germany, not both; (2) *describe* the totalitarian state; (3) *explain* how such a state was created.

PRACTICE 2   Read each essay question and underline key words. Then, on the lines beneath the question, describe in your own words exactly what the question requires: (1) What directions does the student have to follow? (2) How many parts will the answer contain?

Example | What were the causes of the Cold War? What were its chief episodes? Why has there not been a "hot" war?

Student must: __(1) tell what caused the Cold War (two or more causes), (2)__

mention main events of Cold War, (3) give reasons why we haven't had a full-scale

war. The essay will have three parts: causes, main events, and reasons.

1. State Newton's First Law and give examples from your own experience.

   Student must: (1) write out Newton's First Law and (2) give examples of the law from his or her own experience. The essay will have two parts: the law and examples.

2. Choose one of the following terms. Define it, give an example of it, and then show how it affects *your* life: (a) freedom of speech, (b) justice for all, (c) equal opportunity.

   Student must: (1) define one term: freedom of speech, justice for all, or equal opportunity and (2) show how it affects his or her life. The essay will have two parts: a definition and effects.

3. Shiism and Sunni are the two great branches of Islam. Discuss the religious beliefs and the politics of each branch.

   Student must: (1) discuss the religious beliefs and the politics of Shiism and (2) discuss the religious beliefs and the politics of Sunni. The essay will have two parts: Shiism and Sunni.

4. Name and explain four types of savings institutions. What are three factors that influence one's choice of a savings institution?

   Student must: (1) identify and describe four types of savings institutions and (2) name three factors influencing one's choice of a savings institution. The essay will have two parts: types and factors.

5. Steroids: the athlete's "unfair advantage." Discuss.

   Student must: (1) explain what advantage steroids offer to athletes and (2) explain why the advantage is considered unfair. The essay will have two parts: explanation of advantage and explanation of why advantage is unfair.

6. Since the 1970s, increasing numbers of women have received under-graduate and graduate degrees in business. Discuss this change, sug-gesting reasons and consequences.

   Student must: (1) describe the rise in women getting business degrees, (2) suggest reasons, and (3) suggest consequences. The essay will have three parts: description, reasons, and consequences.

7. Define the Monroe Doctrine of the early nineteenth century and weigh the arguments for and against it.

   Student must: (1) define the Monroe Doctrine, (2) evaluate the arguments for it, and (3) evaluate the arguments against it. The essay will have three parts: definition, arguments for, and arguments against.

8. The sixteenth century is known for the Renaissance, the Reformation, and the Commercial Revolution. Discuss each event, showing why it was important to the history of Western civilization.

   Student must: discuss the historical importance of (1) the Renaissance, (2) the Reformation, and (3) the Commercial Revolution. The essay will have three parts: the Renaissance, the Reformation, and the Commercial Revolution.

9. Erik Erikson has theorized that adult actions toward children may produce either (a) trust or mistrust, (b) autonomy or self-doubt, (c) initiative or guilt. Choose one of the pairs above and give examples of the kinds of adult behavior that might create these responses in a child.

   Student must: (1) choose one pair of terms, (2) give examples of adult behavior that might create trust (autonomy, initiative) in a child, and (3) give examples of adult behavior that might create mistrust (self-doubt, guilt) in a child. The essay will have two parts: behavior creating positive traits and behavior creating negative traits.

10. Simon Bolivar may not have been as great a <u>hero</u> as he was portrayed. <u>Agree</u> or <u>disagree</u>.

Student must: <u>(1) state the "heroic" traits that Bolivar was portrayed as</u>

<u>having and (2) give reasons supporting or contradicting that portrayal. The</u>

<u>essay will have two parts: an explanation of Bolivar's "heroic" traits and the</u>

<u>supporting or opposing evidence.</u>

PART C

Choosing the Correct Paragraph or Essay Pattern

Throughout this book, you have learned how to write various types of paragraphs and compositions. Many examinations will require you simply to **illustrate, define, compare,** and so forth. How well you answer the question may depend partly on how well you understand these terms.

1. *Illustrate* "behavior modification."
2. *Define* "continental drift."
3. *Compare* Agee and Nin as diarists.

■ The key words in these questions are *illustrate, define,* and *compare*—**instruction words** that tell you what you are supposed to do and what form your answer should take.

Here is a review list of some common instruction words used in college examinations:

1. **Classify:**   Gather into categories, types, or kinds according to a single basis of division (see Chapter 11).

2. **Compare:**   Point out similarities (see Chapter 10). Instructors often use *compare* to mean point out both *similarities* and *differences.*

3. **Contrast:**   Point out differences (see Chapter 10).

4. **Define:**   State clearly and exactly the meaning of a word or term (see Chapter 9). You may be required to write a single-sentence definition or a full paragraph. Instructors may use *identify* as a synonym for *define* when they want a short definition.

5. **Discuss:**   Often an instructor uses these terms to mean (analyze, "thoughtfully examine a subject, approaching it decribe, or from different angles." These terms allow the explain) writer more freedom of approach than many of the others.

6. **Evaluate:**   Weigh the pros and cons, advantages and disadvantages (see Chapters 10 and 12).

7. **Identify:**   Give a capsule who-what-when-where-why answer. Sometimes *identify* is a synonym for *define.*

8. **Illustrate:**   Give one or more examples (see Chapter 5).

9. **Narrate:**   Follow the development of something through (trace) time, event by event (see Chapters 6 and 8).

10. **Summarize:**   Write the substance of a longer work in condensed form.

PRACTICE 3   You should have no trouble deciding what kind of paragraph or composition to use if the question uses one of the terms just defined—*contrast, trace, classify,* and so on. However, questions are often worded in such a way that you have to discover what kind of paragraph or essay is required. What kind of paragraph or essay is required by each of the following questions?

Example   What is *schizophrenia?* Write a paragraph to: define

1. In one concise paragraph, give   summarize
   the main ideas of Simone de
   Beauvoir's famous book *The
   Second Sex.*

2. What is the difference   contrast
   between debit and credit?

3. Follow the development of   narrate
   Miles Davis's musical style.

4. How do jet- and propeller-   contrast
   driven planes differ?

5. Who or what is each of the following: the Gang of Four, Ho Chi Minh, Tiananmen Square.

identify *or* define

6. Explain the causes of the American Civil War.

discuss

7. Explain what is meant by *inertia.*

define

8. Take a stand for or against legalizing drugs in this country. Give reasons to support your stand.

evaluate

9. Give two instances of the way in which demand in one industry affects demand in another industry.

illustrate

10. Divide into groups the different kinds of television programs that are aired on a typical day.

classify

PART D

Writing the Topic Sentence or the Thesis Statement

A good way to ensure that your answer truly addresses itself to the question is to compose a topic sentence or thesis statement that contains the key words of the question.

Question: How do savings banks and commercial banks differ?

- The key words in this question are *savings banks, commercial banks,* and *differ.*
- What kind of paragraph or essay would be appropriate for this question?

a paragraph or essay of contrast

> *Topic Sentence* or *Thesis Statement of Answer:* Savings banks and commercial banks differ in three basic ways.

- The answer repeats the key words of the question: *savings banks, commercial banks,* and *differ.*

PRACTICE 4   Here are eight examination questions. Write a topic sentence or thesis statement for each question by using the question as part of the answer. Even though you may not know anything about the subjects, you should be able to formulate a topic sentence or thesis statement based on the question. Answers may vary.

1. Do you think the Dawes Allotment Act was fair to Native Americans?

    Topic sentence or thesis statement: ___The Dawes Allotment Act was unfair

    ___(fair) to Native Americans, for several reasons.___

    _____

2. Contrast high school requirements in Jamaica with those in the United States.

    Topic sentence or thesis statement: ___High school requirements in Jamaica

    ___are more demanding than those in the United States.___

    _____

3. What steps can a busy person take to reduce the destructive impact of stress in his or her life?

    Topic sentence or thesis statement: ___A busy person can take several steps

    ___to help reduce the destructive impact of stress in his or her life.___

    _____

4. Gay couples should be allowed to adopt children. Agree or disagree with this statement.

    Topic sentence or thesis statement: ___Gay couples definitely should (should

    ___not) be allowed to adopt children.___

    _____

5. Assume that you manage a small shop that sells men's apparel. What activities would you undertake to promote the sale of sportswear?

Topic sentence or thesis statement: ___As manager of a small shop that sells

men's apparel, I would do three things to promote the sale of sportswear.___

_____

6. The U.S. government should cover the medical costs of AIDS. Agree or disagree with this statement.

   Topic sentence or thesis statement: ___The U.S. government should cover___

   ___(not cover) the medical costs of AIDS.___

   _____

7. The state should subsidize students in medical school because the country needs more doctors. Agree or disagree with this statement.

   Topic sentence or thesis statement: ___The state should (should not)___

   ___subsidize students in medical school.___

   _____

8. Does religion play a more vital role in people's lives today than it did in your parents' generation?

   Topic sentence or thesis statement: ___Religion plays a more (less) vital role___

   ___in people's lives today than it did in my parents' generation.___

   _____

PRACTICE 5
Review

This practice asks you to apply what you've learned in this chapter as you answer an essay question by following the steps listed.

1. Here is a question that might appear on a history examination. Read the question carefully, underlining important words:

   Several events in the year 1963 confirmed Martin Luther King, Jr., as the most important leader in the struggle for civil rights for blacks. Name at least three of these events, and tell how they demonstrated King's effectiveness and advanced his cause.

2. Decide how many parts the answer should contain.

   ___Each of three parts would name an event from 1963 and explain how it___

   ___demonstrated King's effectiveness and advanced his cause.___

3. Choose the paragraph or essay pattern that would best develop an answer to the question.

illustration

4. Write a topic sentence that repeats the key words of the question. Use the information provided in step 5. Answers may vary.

The nonviolent direct action in Birmingham, Alabama, the publication of "Letter

from Birmingham Jail," and the march on Washington in August of 1963 all

confirmed Martin Luther King, Jr., as the most important leader in the struggle

for black civil rights.

5. Quickly jot down ideas on scrap paper. Select the ideas you wish to use in your answer and drop those that are irrelevant or repetitious. Here are some facts and ideas you may find helpful. Use this information to write a topic sentence (step 4) and cross out any information you do not need for your answer.

- August '63: Marches on Washington with 250,000 people to demand passage of a civil rights law ("I have a dream" speech).
- Important—meets with President Kennedy immediately after march on Washington; Kennedy enthusiastic.
- December '64: Wins Nobel Prize for Peace.
- April '68: Assassinated in Memphis, Tenn.
- November '63: Kennedy assassinated in Dallas.
- April–May '63: Leads nonviolent direct action in Birmingham, Ala., to fight segregation in public places. Boycotts, marches, police with attack dogs and fire hoses. King arrested.
- April '63: Writes "Letter from Birmingham Jail," explaining why he & his followers disobey unjust laws, why they act now. ("Freedom is never voluntarily given by the oppressor; it must be demanded by the oppressed.") Published in several magazines, and more than 1 million copies circulated in churches.
- May '63: Leads children's marches in Birmingham. Some police refuse orders to turn fire hoses on crowds of black children.
- May '63: Birmingham merchants agree to desegregate stores, hire some blacks.
- June '63: After Birmingham, at MLK's urging, Kennedy submits civil rights bill to Congress. (Passed June '64.)
- June '63: Medgar Evers assassinated in Mississippi.

6. Decide on a logical order in which to present your ideas, numbering the ideas on your list. Using the information in step 5, create a plan of the information you wish to present, in the order you wish to present it. Answers will vary.

7. Using your numbered list of facts and ideas, write the clearest and best answer you can on a separate sheet of paper.

8. Now proofread your answer, correcting any grammatical errors or misspelled words.

Checklist: The Process of Writing the Essay Question

_____ 1. Survey the test and budget your time.

_____ 2. Read each question carefully, underlining important words.

_____ 3. Determine how many parts the answer should contain.

_____ 4. Considering your audience (usually the teacher) and purpose, choose the paragraph or essay pattern that would best answer the question.

_____ 5. Write a topic sentence or thesis statement that repeats the key words of the question.

_____ 6. Quickly freewrite or brainstorm ideas on scrap paper, and arrange them in a logical order.

_____ 7. Write your paragraph or essay neatly, skipping lines so you will have enough room to make corrections.

_____ 8. Revise your paper and proofread it carefully, making corrections above the lines.

Unit 6

Reviewing the Basics

21

The Simple Sentence

PART A   Defining and Spotting Subjects
PART B   Spotting Prepositional Phrases
PART C   Defining and Spotting Verbs

PART A

Defining and Spotting Subjects

Every sentence must contain two basic elements: a **subject** and a **verb.**

A subject is the *who* or *what* word that performs the action or the *who* or *what* word about which a statement is made:

---

1. Three *hunters* tramped through the woods.

2. The blue *truck* belongs to Ralph.

- In sentence 1, *hunters*, the *who* word, performs the action—"tramped through the woods."

- In sentence 2, *truck* is the *what* word about which a statement is made—"belongs to Ralph."

- Some sentences have more than one subject, joined by *and:*

---

3. Her *aunt and uncle* love country music.

- In sentence 3, *aunt and uncle*, the *who* words, perform the action—they "love country music."

- *Aunt and uncle* is called a **compound subject.**

Sometimes an *-ing* word can be the subject of a sentence:

> 4. *Reading* strains my eyes.

■ *Reading* is the *what* word that performs the action—"strains my eyes."

PRACTICE 1   Circle the subjects in these sentences.

1. Do (you) know the origin and customs of Kwanzaa?

2. This African-American (holiday) celebrates black heritage and lasts for seven days—from December 26 through January 1.

3. (Maulana Karenga) introduced Kwanzaa to America in 1966.

4. In Swahili, (Kwanzaa) means "first fruits of the harvest."

5. During the holiday, (families) share simple meals of foods from the Caribbean, Africa, South America, and the American South.

6. Specific (foods) have special meaning.

7. For instance, certain (fruits and vegetables) represent the products of group effort.

8. Another important (symbol) is corn, which stands for children.

9. At each dinner, (celebrants) light a black, red, or green candle and discuss one of the seven principles of Kwanzaa.

10. These seven (principles) are unity, self-determination, collective work and responsibility, cooperative economics, purpose, creativity, and faith.

PART B

Spotting Prepositional Phrases

One group of words that may confuse you as you look for subjects is the prepositional phrase. A **prepositional phrase** contains a **preposition** (a word like *at, in, of, from,* and so forth) and its **object.**

Preposition	Object
at	the beach
on	time
of	the students

The object of a preposition *cannot be* the subject of a sentence. Therefore, spotting and crossing out the prepositional phrases will help you find the subject.

---

1. The sweaters in the window look handmade.

2. The sweaters ~~in the window~~ look handmade.

3. ~~On Tuesday,~~ a carton ~~of oranges~~ was left ~~on the porch.~~

- In sentence 1, you might have trouble finding the subject. But once the prepositional phrase is crossed out in sentence 2, the subject, *sweaters*, is easy to spot.

- In sentence 3, once the prepositional phrases are crossed out, the subject, *carton*, is easy to spot.

Here are some common prepositions that you should know:

Common Prepositions

about	before	in	through
above	behind	into	to
across	between	like	toward
after	by	near	under
along	during	of	until
among	for	on	up
at	from	over	with

PRACTICE 2   Cross out the prepositional phrases in each sentence. Then circle the subject of the sentence.

1. ~~From 6 A.M. until 10 A.M.,~~ (Angel) works out.

2. Local (buses) ~~for Newark~~ leave every hour.

3. (Three) ~~of my friends~~ take singing lessons.

4. That (man) ~~between Ralph and Cynthia~~ is the famous actor Hank the Hunk.

5. ~~Near the door,~~ a (pile) ~~of laundry~~ sits ~~in a basket.~~

6. Toward evening, the (houses) across the river disappear in the thick fog.

7. Before class, (Helena and (I) meet for coffee.

8. In one corner of the lab, (beakers) of colored liquid bubbled and boiled.

PART C

Defining and Spotting Verbs

Action Verbs

In order to be complete, every sentence must contain a **verb.** One kind of verb, called an **action verb,** expresses the action that the subject is performing:

1. The star quarterback *fumbled.*

2. The carpenters *worked* all day, but the bricklayers *went* home early.

- In sentence 1, the action verb is *fumbled.*

- In sentence 2, the action verbs are *worked* and *went.**

Linking Verbs

Another kind of verb, called a **linking verb,** links the subject to words that describe or identify it:

3. Don *is* a fine mathematician.

4. This fabric *feels* rough and scratchy.

- In sentence 3, the verb *is* links the subject *Don* with the noun *mathematician.*

- In sentence 4, the verb *feels* links the subject *fabric* with the adjectives *rough* and *scratchy.*

*For work on compound predicates, see Chapter 14, "Revising for Sentence Variety," Part D.

Here are some common linking verbs:

Common Linking Verbs

appear	feel
be (am, is, are, was, were, has been, have been, had been . . .)	look
become	seem

Verbs of More Than One Word—Helping Verbs

So far you have dealt with verbs of only one word—*fumbled, worked, is, feels,* and so on. But many verbs consist of more than one word:

5. He *should have taken* the train home.

6. *Are* Tanya and Joe *practicing* the piano?

7. The lounge *was painted* last week.

- In sentence 5, *taken* is the main verb; *should* and *have* are the **helping verbs.**

- In sentence 6, *practicing* is the main verb; *are* is the helping verb.

- In sentence 7, *painted* is the main verb; *was* is the helping verb.*

PRACTICE 3   Underline the verbs in these sentences.

1. Daphne blushed.

2. This sheepskin coat looks warm.

3. You should have seen Karen at her first golf lesson.

4. Is he a magician?

5. Professor Avery was humming the latest Randy Travis hit.

6. Shall we visit Dime Box, Texas?

7. The costumes for the play will be delivered tonight.

*For more work on verbs in the passive voice, see Chapter 26, "The Past Participle," Part E.

8. The carrot seeds <u>have</u> finally <u>sprouted</u>.

9. Al and Leon <u>are writing</u> a script for a documentary about jazz.

10. At midnight my roommate <u>closed</u> his books, but I <u>studied</u> until 2 A.M.

PRACTICE 4   Circle the subjects and underline the verbs in the following sentences. First, cross out any prepositional phrases.

1. <u>Do</u> (you) <u>think</u> ~~of baseball~~ as America's oldest team sport?

2. ~~In fact,~~ (lacrosse) <u>takes</u> that honor.

3. (Native Americans) <u>were playing</u> the sport long ~~before the arrival of Europeans.~~

4. ~~In order to score,~~ one (team) <u>must throw</u> a ball ~~into the opposing team's goal.~~

5. The (goal) <u>is</u> ferociously <u>guarded</u> ~~by a goalie.~~

6. Each (player) <u>uses</u> a curved racket ~~with a mesh basket at its end.~~

7. Algonquin (tribes) ~~in the valley of the St. Lawrence River~~ <u>invented</u> the game.

8. The (Hurons and Iroquois) soon <u>learned</u> this demanding sport.

9. ~~By 1500,~~ the rough and tumble (game) <u>was played</u> ~~by dozens of tribes in Canada and the United States.~~

10. Sometimes (matches) <u>could require</u> hundreds ~~of players~~ and <u>might last</u> ~~for days.~~

11. (Playing) lacrosse <u>trained</u> young warriors ~~for battle.~~

12. ~~With this in mind,~~ the (Cherokees) <u>named</u> lacrosse "little brother ~~of war."~~

13. However, (tribes) often <u>settled</u> their differences peaceably ~~with a lacrosse match.~~

14. French (missionaries) <u>saw</u> a resemblance ~~between the racket and a bishop's cross.~~

15. (They) <u>changed</u> the name ~~of the game from *boggotaway*,~~ the native word, ~~to *lacrosse*,~~ a French word ~~for *cross*.~~

22

Coordination and Subordination

PART A   Coordination
PART B   Subordination
PART C   Semicolons
PART D   Conjunctive Adverbs
PART E   Review

PART A

Coordination

A **clause** is a group of words that contains a subject and a verb. If a clause can stand alone as a complete idea, it is an **independent clause** and can be written as a **simple sentence.***

Here are two independent clauses written as simple sentences:

> 1. The dog barked all night.
>
> 2. The neighbors didn't complain.

You can join two clauses together by placing a comma and a **coordinating conjunction** between them:

> 3. The dog barked all night, *but* the neighbors didn't complain.
>
> 4. Let's go to the beach today, *for* it is too hot to do anything else.

---

*For more work on simple sentences, see Chapter 21, "The Simple Sentence."

- The coordinating conjunctions *but* and *for* join together two clauses.
- Note that *a comma precedes each coordinating conjunction.*

Here is a list of the most common coordinating conjunctions:

> ### Coordinating Conjunctions
> | | | | |
> |------|------|------|------|
> | and | for | or | yet |
> | but | nor | so | |

Be sure to choose the coordinating conjunction that best expresses the *relationship* between the two clauses in a sentence:

> 5. It was late, *so* I decided to take a bus home.
>
> 6. It was late, *yet* I decided to take a bus home.

- The *so* in sentence 5 means that the lateness of the hour caused me to take the bus. (The trains don't run after midnight.)
- The *yet* in sentence 6 means that despite the late hour I still decided to take a bus home. (I knew I might have to wait two hours at the bus stop.)
- Note that a comma precedes the coordinating conjunction.

PRACTICE 1   Read the following sentences for meaning. Then fill in the coordinating conjunction that *best* expresses the relationship between the two clauses. Don't forget to add the comma.

1. Diners still dot the highways of the United States ___, but/yet___ they are not as popular as they once were.

2. In 1872, Walter Scott of Providence, Rhode Island, decided to make prepared and cooked food easier to buy ___, so___ he started selling sandwiches and pies from a large horse-drawn wagon.

3. Customers flocked to this first "diner" ___, for___ the food was delicious, plentiful, and inexpensive.

4. Many did not like standing outside to eat ___, so___ another businessman, Sam Jones, redecorated the wagon and invited customers inside to dine.

5. In order to widen the appeal of their diners, some owners installed stained-glass windows __, and__ other proprietors added elegant decorations.

6. In the 1920s, narrow booths began to replace stools __, and__ diners were fixed permanently on the ground.

7. Stainless steel, efficient-looking diners were everywhere by the 1940s __, but/yet__ even this style gave way to the fancy colonial and Mediterranean designs of the 1960s.

8. Diners are not as common as they were twenty years ago __, nor__ can they compete with fast food take-out chains like McDonald's and Wendy's.

9. Nonetheless, customers do have a choice; they can stand in line and wait for a quick hamburger __, or__ they can sit and be waited on in a diner.

10. Most choose fast food __, but/yet__ the more leisurely diner still has its charm.

PRACTICE 2   Combine these simple sentences with a coordinating conjunction. Punctuate correctly.

1. My daughter wants to be a mechanic. She spends every spare minute at the garage.

   My daughter wants to be a mechanic, so she spends every spare minute at the garage.

2. Ron dared not look over the edge. Heights made him dizzy.

   Ron dared not look over the edge, for heights made him dizzy.

3. Tasha's living room is attractive. Her guests always gather in the kitchen.

   Tasha's living room is attractive, but her guests always gather in the kitchen.

4. Meet me by the bicycle rack. Meet me at Lulu's Nut Shop.

   Meet me by the bicycle rack, or meet me at Lulu's Nut Shop.

5. In 1969, the first manned spaceship landed on the moon. Most Americans felt proud.

In 1969, the first manned spaceship landed on the moon, and most Americans

felt proud.

Subordination

Two clauses can also be joined with a **subordinating conjunction.** The clause following a subordinating conjunction is called a **subordinate** or **dependent clause** because it depends on the independent clause to complete its meaning:

1. We will light the candles *when Flora arrives.*

- *When Flora arrives* is a subordinate or dependent clause introduced by the subordinating conjunction *when.*

- By itself, *when Flora arrives* is incomplete; it depends on the independent clause to complete its meaning.*

Note that sentence 1 can also be written this way:

2. *When Flora arrives,* we will light the candles.

- The meaning of sentences 1 and 2 is the same, but the punctuation is different.

- In sentence 1, because the subordinate clause *follows* the independent clause, *no comma* is needed.

- In sentence 2, however, because the subordinate clause *begins* the sentence, it is followed by a *comma.*

*For more work on incomplete sentences, or fragments, see Chapter 23, "Avoiding Sentence Errors," Part B.

Here is a partial list of subordinating conjunctions:

Subordinating Conjunctions			
after	because	since	when(ever)
although	before	unless	whereas
as (if)	if	until	while

Be sure to choose the subordinating conjunction that *best expresses the relationship* between the two clauses in a sentence:

> 3. This course was excellent *because* Professor Green taught it.
>
> 4. This course was excellent *although* Professor Green taught it.

- Sentence 3 says that the course was excellent *because* Professor Green, a great teacher, gave it.

- Sentence 4 says that the course was excellent *despite the fact that* Professor Green, apparently a bad teacher, gave it.

PRACTICE 3   Read the following sentences for meaning. Then fill in the subordinating conjunction that *best* expresses the relationship between the two clauses.

1. We could see very clearly last night ___because___ the moon was so bright.

2. Violet read *Sports Illustrated* ___while___ Daisy walked in the woods.

3. ___Whenever___ it is cold outside, our new wood-burning Franklin stove keeps us warm.

4. The students buzzed with interest ___when___ Professor Hargrave announced that classes would be held at the zoo.

5. ___Until___ the college hires more faculty, classes will continue to be overcrowded.

PRACTICE 4   Punctuate the following sentences by adding a comma where necessary. Put a *C* after any correct sentences.

1. Carmen worked on her art project until the studio closed for the night. c

2. Whenever Hank and Reggie get together ‸ they argue about computers.

3. I admire Thomas Edison because he dedicated his life to useful inventions. c

4. Since you are very good at mathematics ‸ why don't you work as a tutor in the mathematics laboratory?

5. Although few people realize it ‸ the planet Pluto was discovered only about sixty years ago.

PRACTICE 5   Combine each pair of ideas below by using a subordinating conjunction. Write each combination twice, once with the subordinating conjunction at the beginning of the sentence and once with the subordinating conjunction in the middle of the sentence. Punctuate correctly.

Example   We stayed on the beach.

The sun went down.

We stayed on the beach until the sun went down.

Until the sun went down, we stayed on the beach.

1. The wilderness inspires him.
2. He hopes to settle in northern Ontario.

He hopes to settle in northern Ontario because the wilderness inspires him.

Because the wilderness inspires him, he hopes to settle in northern Ontario.

_____

_____

3. Hilda breaks out in a rash.
4. Ragweed blooms in the back yard.

Hilda breaks out in a rash whenever ragweed blooms in the back yard.

Whenever ragweed blooms in the back yard, Hilda breaks out in a rash.

_____

_____

5. I knew you were coming.

6. I would have vacuumed the guest room.

If I knew you were coming, I would have vacuumed the guest room.

I would have vacuumed the guest room if I knew you were coming.

7. This typewriter has a memory.

8. It can recall and correct a whole line of type.

This typewriter can recall and correct a whole line of type because it has a memory.

Because this typewriter has a memory, it can recall and correct a whole line of type.

9. The bird watchers were just about to go home.

10. A rose-breasted grosbeak flew into view.

A rose-breasted grosbeak flew into view when the bird watchers were just about to go home.

When the bird watchers were just about to go home, a rose-breasted grosbeak flew into view.

11. Few soap operas remain on the radio.

12. Daytime television is filled with them.

Daytime television is filled with soap operas although few of them remain on the radio.

Although few soap operas remain on the radio, daytime television is filled with them.

13. The snow stopped.

14. People with sleds and toboggans headed for White Knuckle Hill.

People with sleds and toboggans headed for White Knuckle Hill when the snow stopped.

When the snow stopped, people with sleds and toboggans headed for White Knuckle Hill.

15. The chimney spewed black smoke and soot.

16. Nobody complained to the local environmental agency.

Nobody complained to the local environmental agency although the chimney

spewed black smoke and soot.

Although the chimney spewed black smoke and soot, nobody complained to

the local environmental agency.

PART C

Semicolons

You can join two independent clauses by placing a **semicolon** between them. The semicolon takes the place of a conjunction:

> 1. She hopes to receive good grades this semester; her scholarship depends on her maintaining a 3.5 index.
>
> 2. Tony is a careless driver; he has had three minor accidents this year alone.

- Each of the sentences above could also be made into two *separate sentences* by replacing the semicolon with a period.

- Note that the first word after a semicolon is *not* capitalized.

PRACTICE 6   Combine each pair of independent clauses by placing a semicolon between them.

1. A warm rain began to fall the children took off their shoes.

2. The senator appeared ill at ease at the news conference he seemed afraid of saying the wrong thing.

3. The new seed catalogue, a fifteen-hundred-page volume, was misplaced the volume weighed ten pounds.

4. On Thursday evening, Stuart decided to take a trip to the Rocky Mountains ; on Friday morning, he packed his bags and left.

5. In the early 1960s, the Beatles burst on the rock scene ; rock music has never been the same.

6. Ron Jackson has been promoted ; he is an effective manager.

7. This stream is full of trout ; every spring men and women with waders and fly rods arrive on its banks.

8. Not a single store was open at that hour ; not a soul walked the streets.

PRACTICE 7   Each independent clause that follows is the first half of a sentence. Add a semicolon and a second independent clause. Make sure your second thought is also independent and can stand alone. Answers will vary.

1. The engineers worked on the design all night ___; by 10:00 A.M. they were satisfied.

2. Toby rented a VCR on Thursday ___; by Friday evening she had watched all of Charlie Chaplin's movies.

3. The police officer lobbed tear gas through the warehouse window ___; soon three gunmen ran out, their hands up and their eyes streaming.

4. Faulkner's stories often depict life in the South ___; he himself came from an old Mississippi family.

5. His mud-covered boots looked like antiques ___; he must have had them twenty years or longer.

6. During the Great Depression, millions of workers were unemployed ___; men selling apples on street corners were a common sight.

7. The moon floated in the dark blue sky ___; not a cloud obscured it from view.

8. Employees objected to the drug tests ___; they felt the tests invaded their privacy.

PART D

Conjunctive Adverbs

A **conjunctive adverb** placed after the semicolon can help clarify the relationship between two clauses:

> 1. I like the sound of that stereo; *however*, the price is too high.
>
> 2. They have not seen that film; *moreover*, they have not been to a theater for three years.

- Note that a comma follows the conjunctive adverb.

Here is a partial list of conjunctive adverbs.

Conjunctive Adverbs		
consequently	in fact	nevertheless
furthermore	indeed	then
however	moreover	therefore

PRACTICE 8   Punctuate each sentence correctly by adding a semicolon, a comma, or both, where necessary. Put a *C* after any correct sentences.

1. I hate to wash my car windows; nevel-theless, it's a job that must be done.

2. Sonia doesn't know how to play chess; however, she would like to learn.

3. Dean Fader is very funny; in fact, he could be a professional comedian.

4. Crystal-ball gazing fascinates Kate; therefore, she is always searching for books on the subject.

5. I like this painting; the soft tones of peach and blue remind me of tropical sunsets. C

6. The faculty approved of the new trimester system; furthermore, the students liked it too. c

7. Bill has a cassette recorder plugged into his ear all day ^; consequently ^, he misses a lot in class lectures.

8. We toured the darkroom ^; then we watched the models pose for the photographer.

PRACTICE 9　Combine each pair of independent clauses by placing a semicolon and a conjunctive adverb between them. Punctuate correctly.
Answers may vary.

1. The lake is quite long ^; however, we rowed from one end of it to the other.

2. The plastics factory agreed to stop polluting the water ^; consequently, the towns-people applauded the factory's cooperation.

3. Mr. Farrington loves bluegrass music ^; furthermore, he plays with a local bluegrass band every Saturday night.

4. Jay, a tall boy, has poor eyesight ^; therefore, he was turned down for the basket-ball team.

5. Yesterday, hikers from the Nature-Walkers' Club couldn't handle that trail ^; in fact, they managed to get only as far as the foot of Mt. Lookout.

6. By midnight Tien had finished tuning his engine ^; therefore, he still had enough time for a short nap before the race.

7. An arthroscope helps doctors examine the inside of an injured knee ^; consequently, the use of this instrument can prevent unnecessary surgery.

8. Dolphins are protected by international laws ^; however, thousands of dolphins die each year in the nets of tuna fishermen.

PART E

Review

In this chapter, you have combined simple sentences by means of a **coordinating conjunction**, a **subordinating conjunction**, a **semicolon**, and

a **semicolon** and **conjunctive adverb.** Here is a review chart
tence patterns discussed in this chapter.*

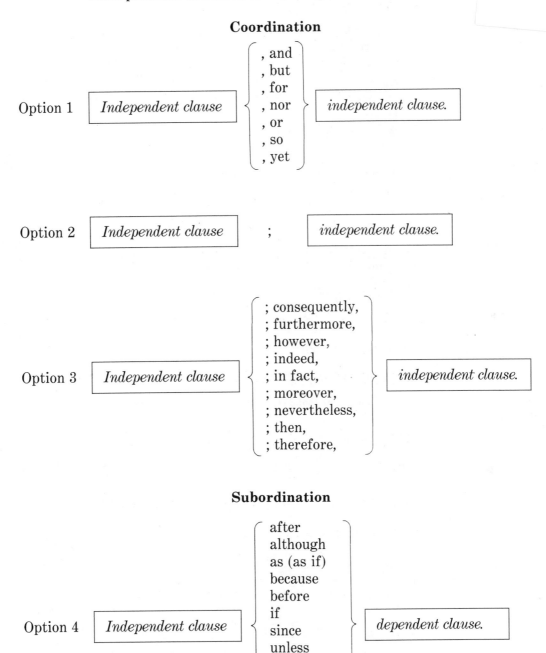

Coordination

Option 1

| Independent clause | { , and / , but / , for / , nor / , or / , so / , yet } | independent clause. |

Option 2

| Independent clause | ; | independent clause. |

Option 3

| Independent clause | { ; consequently, / ; furthermore, / ; however, / ; indeed, / ; in fact, / ; moreover, / ; nevertheless, / ; then, / ; therefore, } | independent clause. |

Subordination

Option 4

| Independent clause | { after / although / as (as if) / because / before / if / since / unless / until / when(ever) / whereas / while } | dependent clause. |

*For more ways to combine sentences, see Chapter 14, "Revising for Sentence Variety,"
Part D.

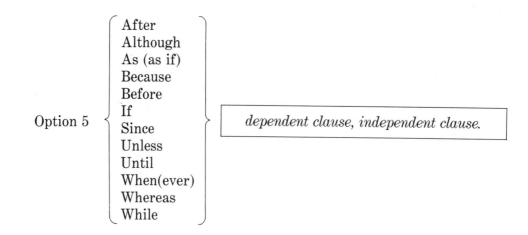

Option 5 { After / Although / As (as if) / Because / Before / If / Since / Unless / Until / When(ever) / Whereas / While } | *dependent clause, independent clause.* |

PRACTICE 10   Read each pair of simple sentences to determine the relationship between them. Then join each pair in three different ways, using the conjunctions or conjunctive adverbs in parentheses at the left. Punctuate correctly. Answers will vary.

Example | The typewriter ribbon is old.

The print looks very light.

(for) __The print looks very light, for the typewriter ribbon is old.__

(because) __Because the typewriter ribbon is old, the print looks very light.__

(therefore) __The typewriter ribbon is old; therefore, the print looks very light.__

1. This rug costs a great deal.

   It is hand-loomed.

   (for) __This rug costs a great deal, for it is hand-loomed.__

   _____

   (because) __Because this rug is hand-loomed, it costs a great deal.__

   _____

   (therefore) __This rug is hand-loomed; therefore, it costs a great deal.__

   _____

2. Soviet basketball coaches recruit players years in advance of the Olympic games.

   They have experienced Olympic teams.

(since) _Since Soviet basketball coaches recruit players years in advance of the Olympic games, they have experienced Olympic teams._

(because) _Soviet basketball coaches have experienced Olympic teams because they recruit players years in advance of the Olympic games._

(consequently) _Soviet basketball coaches recruit players years in advance of the Olympic games; consequently, they have experienced Olympic teams._

3. The fishermen trolled in the bay for hours.

   They caught nothing.

   (but) _The fishermen trolled in the bay for hours, but they caught nothing._

   (although) _Although the fishermen trolled in the bay for hours, they caught nothing._

   (however) _The fishermen trolled in the bay for hours; however, they caught nothing._

4. Don is an expert mechanic.

   He intends to open a service center.

   (and) _Don is an expert mechanic, and he intends to open a service center._

   (since) _Since Don is an expert mechanic, he intends to open a service center._

   (furthermore) _Don is an expert mechanic; furthermore, he intends to open a service center._

5. We haven't heard from her.

   We haven't given up hope.

   (but) _We haven't heard from her, but we haven't given up hope._

(although) _Although we haven't heard from her, we haven't given up hope._

_____

(nevertheless) _We haven't heard from her; nevertheless, we haven't given_

up hope.
_____

PRACTICE 11   In your writing, aim for variety by mixing coordination, subordination, and simple sentences.* Rewrite the following paragraphs to eliminate monotonous simple sentences. First, read the paragraph to determine the relationships between ideas; then choose the conjunctions that best express these relationships. Punctuate correctly. Answers will vary.

Paragraph a: Difficult situations sometimes bring out the best in people. A blizzard struck our city last week. I huddled on a corner, shivering and grumbling. The bus arrived. It was crowded and cold on board. The mood was cheery, almost partylike. The driver was a kind and patient man. His pleasantness seemed to spread to the passengers. He allowed them to alight at unscheduled stops. They didn't have to walk a block or two out of their way. People were fighting the wind on their way to the bus stop. He would wait for them. The passengers were very grateful. One woman bowed to the bus driver. She got off. She exclaimed not simply, "Thank you" or "Have a good evening," but "Have a good life!"

_____Difficult situations sometimes bring out the best in people. As a blizzard struck_

our city last week, I huddled on a corner, shivering and grumbling. When the bus

arrived, it was crowded and cold on board. Nevertheless, the mood was cheery,

almost partylike. The driver was a kind and patient man, and his pleasantness

seemed to spread to the passengers. He allowed them to alight at unscheduled

stops, so they didn't have to walk a block or two out of their way. If people were

fighting the wind on their way to the bus stop, he would wait for them. The

passengers were very grateful; one woman bowed to the bus driver. As she got

off, she exclaimed not simply, "Thank you" or "Have a good evening," but "Have

a good life!"

_____

_____

_____

*For more work on sentence variety, see Chapter 14, "Revising for Sentence Variety."

Paragraph b: A great star blazed in the sky. Paiea was born in Hawaii in 1758. Seers had foretold that this son of a chieftain would defeat his enemies and govern a united Hawaii. A jealous former ruler ordered the baby killed. Sympathetic courtiers hid the noble infant in a cave. There he was renamed Kamehameha. This name means "The Lonely One" or "The One Set Apart." In time, it was safe for young Kamehameha to leave the cave. He was very strong and agile. He excelled in war games. James Cook, an English sea captain, landed in Hawaii in 1778. Kamehameha had already become the most important chieftain. He gained even more power by conquering one independent island after another. With the help of English sailors, he successfully invaded Maui. Eventually, the rest of the Hawaiian islands came under his control. By 1810, this shrewd and powerful king ruled a united country. A lover of his native culture, he continued many ancient traditions of his homeland. He also borrowed many ideas from the Europeans. The prophecies at his birth had come true. He had defeated his enemies and become the sole ruler of a united Hawaii.

A great star blazed in the sky when Paiea was born in Hawaii in 1758. Seers had foretold that this son of a chieftain would defeat his enemies and govern a united Hawaii. A jealous former ruler ordered the baby killed, but sympathetic courtiers hid the noble infant in a cave. There he was renamed Kamehameha, meaning "The Lonely One" or "The One Set Apart." In time, it was safe for young Kamehameha to leave the cave. Because he was very strong and agile, he excelled in war games. When James Cook, an English sea captain, landed in Hawaii in 1778, Kamehameha had already become the most important chieftain. He gained even more power by conquering one independent island after another. With the help of English sailors, he successfully invaded Maui, and eventually the rest of the Hawaiian islands came under his control. By 1810, this shrewd and powerful king ruled a united country. A lover of his native culture, he continued many ancient traditions of his homeland; however, he also borrowed many ideas from the Europeans. The prophecies at his birth had come true, for he had defeated his enemies and become the sole ruler of a united Hawaii.

23

Avoiding
Sentence Errors

PART A Avoiding Run-Ons and Comma Splices
PART B Avoiding Fragments

Avoiding Run-Ons and Comma Splices

Be careful to avoid **run-ons** and **comma splices.**

A **run-on sentence** incorrectly runs together two independent clauses without a conjunction or punctuation. This error confuses the reader, who cannot tell where one thought stops and the next begins:

---

1. Run-on: My neighbor Mr. Hoffman is seventy-five years old he plays tennis every Saturday afternoon.

A **comma splice** incorrectly joins two independent clauses with a comma but no conjunction:

---

2. Comma splice: My neighbor Mr. Hoffman is seventy-five years old, he plays tennis every Saturday afternoon.

The run-on and the comma splice can be corrected in five ways:

Use two separate sentences.	My neighbor Mr. Hoffman is seventy-five years old. He plays tennis every Saturday afternoon.
Use a coordinating conjunction. (See Chapter 22, Part A.)	My neighbor Mr. Hoffman is seventy-five years old, but he plays tennis every Saturday afternoon.
Use a subordinating conjunction. (See Chapter 22, Part B.)	Although my neighbor Mr. Hoffman is seventy-five years old, he plays tennis every Saturday afternoon.
Use a semicolon. (See Chapter 22, Part C.)	My neighbor Mr. Hoffman is seventy-five years old; he plays tennis every Saturday afternoon.
Use a semicolon and a conjunctive adverb. (See Chapter 22, Part D.)	My neighbor Mr. Hoffman is seventy-five years old; however, he plays tennis every Saturday afternoon.

PRACTICE 1   Some of these sentences contain run-ons or comma splices; others are correct. Put a *C* next to the correct sentences. Revise the run-ons and comma splices in any way you choose. Be careful of punctuation.
Answers may vary.

1. Ms. Jones took the Concorde to Paris the flight lasted just three hours.

    Revised: _Ms. Jones took the Concorde to Paris; the flight lasted just three_

    hours.

2. That bench was just painted don't sit there.

    Revised: _That bench was just painted; don't sit there._

3. Ken started wearing a toupee, everyone complimented him on how young he looked.

Revised: When Ken started wearing a toupee, everyone complimented him on how young he looked.

4. Most successful people don't fear failure, they know that mistakes are good teachers.

Revised: Most successful people don't fear failure because they know that mistakes are good teachers.

5. Our dormitory bought a Canon copier for the library, many students use it.

Revised: Our dormitory bought a Canon copier for the library, and many students use it.

6. The movie will not begin for two hours let's window-shop.

Revised: The movie will not begin for two hours, so let's window-shop.

7. The hot-air balloon rose off the ground the crowd gasped.

Revised: When the hot-air balloon rose off the ground, the crowd gasped.

8. Solar energy may be the fuel of the future, and many home owners are beginning to use it.

Revised: C

9. When I first moved into this house, I never dreamed I would live here for fifteen years.

Revised: C

10. Students applying to the Fashion Institute of Technology must show creative talent only one student in six gets accepted.

Revised: Students applying to the Fashion Institute of Technology must show creative talent; in fact, only one student in six gets accepted.

PRACTICE 2 Proofread the following essay for run-ons and comma splices. Correct them in any way you choose, writing your revised essay on a separate sheet of paper. Be careful of the punctuation. Answers will vary.

Will K. Kellogg, Least Likely to Succeed

(1) *Although* Will Kellogg was an unlikely candidate for fame and fortune, he became one of America's great successes.

(2) The two Kellogg boys could not have been more different. (3) Will was a slow learner with few friends and interests. (4) His father pulled him from school at the age of thirteen*;* he made Will a traveling broom salesman for the family company. (5) Eight years older than Will, John Harvey Kellogg was the family genius. (6) He became a noted surgeon and head of an exclusive health resort. (7) He treated his patients with exercise and a strict vegetarian diet*; furthermore,* he wrote best-selling books about healthful living.

(8) In 1880, *when* Will was twenty years old, Dr. John hired him to work at the resort. (9) For the next twenty-five years, Will served as his brother's flunky. (10) According to rumor, he shaved Dr. John every day and shined his shoes. (11) *While* John bicycled to work, Will jogged alongside getting his daily work orders. (12) Dr. John was a wealthy man, *but* he never paid Will more than eighty-seven dollars a month.

(13) One of the special foods at the resort was pressed wheat. (14) The brothers boiled wheat dough*, and* then they pressed it through rollers into thin sheets. (15) One night, they left the boiled dough out. (16) When they pressed it, it turned into flakes instead of forming sheets. (17) Will suggested they toast the flakes. (18) Resort guests loved the new cereal, *and* former guests ordered it from their homes. (19) To meet the demand, the

brothers opened a mail-order business; however, the snobbish Dr. John refused to sell the flakes to grocery stores.

(20) In 1906, Will finally bought out John's share of the cereal patents. He struck out on his own. (21) Will turned out to be a business genius. (22) He invented advertising techniques that made his new product, Kellogg's Corn Flakes, a household word. (23) Will K. Kellogg quickly became one of the richest men in America.

(24) Sadly, the two brothers never reconciled. (25) In 1943, ninety-one-year-old Dr. John wrote Will an apology, but John died before the letter reached his younger brother.

PART B

Avoiding Fragments

Another error to avoid is the **sentence fragment.** A **sentence** must contain a subject and a verb and must be able to stand alone as a complete idea. A **sentence fragment,** therefore, can be defined in terms of what it lacks: either a subject or a verb, or both—it cannot stand alone as a complete idea.

Here are some common kinds of sentence fragments and ways to correct them:

Complete sentence:	1. Kirk decided to major in psychology.
Fragment:	2. Since human behavior has always fascinated him.

- Example 1 is a complete simple sentence.

- Example 2 is a fragment because it is a dependent clause beginning with the subordinating conjunction *since.* Furthermore, it is not a complete idea.

This fragment can be corrected in two ways:

> Corrected: 3. Kirk decided to major in psychology since human behavior has always fascinated him.
>
>   4. Kirk decided to major in psychology. Human behavior has always fascinated him.

- In sentence 3, the fragment is combined with the sentence before it.
- In sentence 4, the fragment is changed into a complete sentence.

> Fragment: 5. A fine pianist.
>
> Complete sentence: 6. Marsha won a scholarship to Juilliard.

- Example 5 is a fragment because it lacks a verb and is not a complete idea.
- Example 6 is a complete sentence.

This fragment can be corrected in two ways:

> Corrected: 7. A fine pianist, Marsha won a scholarship to Juilliard.
>
>   8. Marsha won a scholarship to Juilliard. She is a fine pianist.

- In sentence 7, the fragment is combined with the sentence after it.
- In sentence 8, the fragment is changed into a complete sentence by the addition of a verb *is* and a subject *she*.

> Complete sentence: 9. Daniel can always be seen on the track in the morning.
>
> Fragment: 10. Running a mile or two before breakfast.

- Example 9 is a complete sentence.

- Example 10 is a fragment because it lacks a subject and because an -*ing* verb cannot stand alone without a helping verb.*

This fragment can be corrected in two ways:

Corrected: 11. Daniel can always be seen on the track in the morning, running a mile or two before breakfast.

12. Daniel can always be seen on the track in the morning. He runs a mile or two before breakfast.

- In sentence 11, the fragment is combined with the sentence before it.

- In sentence 12, the fragment is changed into a complete sentence.

Complete sentence: 13. Luz is a chemistry teacher who never runs out of creative ideas.

Fragment: 14. Who has the ability to keep her classes involved throughout the lesson.

- Example 13 is a complete sentence.

- Example 14 is a fragment because it is a relative clause beginning with *who*.†

The fragment in example 14 can be corrected in two ways, as shown on the following page.

*For work on joining ideas with an -*ing* modifier, see Chapter 14, "Revising for Sentence Variety," Part D.
†For more work on relative clauses, see Chapter 14, "Revising for Sentence Variety," Part D, and Chapter 24, "Present Tense (Agreement)," Part G.

> Corrected: 15. Luz is a chemistry teacher who never runs out of creative ideas and who has the ability to keep her classes involved throughout the lesson.
>
> 16. Luz is a chemistry teacher who never runs out of creative ideas. She has the ability to keep her classes involved throughout the lesson.

- In sentence 15, the fragment is combined with the sentence before it.
- In sentence 16, the fragment is changed into a complete sentence.

> Complete sentence: 17. Laura has always wanted to become a travel agent.
>
> Fragment: 18. To tell people about exotic countries that they might visit.

- Example 17 is a complete sentence.
- Example 18 is a fragment because it lacks a subject and contains only the infinitive form of the verb—*to* plus the simple form of the verb *tell*.

This fragment can be corrected in two ways:

> Corrected: 19. Laura has always wanted to become a travel agent and to tell people about exotic countries that they might visit.
>
> 20. Laura has always wanted to become a travel agent. She would find it exciting to tell people about exotic countries that they might visit.

- In sentence 19, the fragment is combined with the sentence before it.
- In sentence 20, the fragment is changed into a complete sentence.

PRACTICE 3   Some of these examples are fragments; others are complete sentences. Put a *C* next to the complete sentences. Revise the fragments in any way you choose. Answers will vary.

Example | Leaping into the air.

Revised | _Leaping into the air, she shouted, "I won, I won!"_

1. Interviewing divorced people for her research project.

   Revised: _Interviewing divorced people for her research project, Anna made_
   some surprising discoveries.

2. Since we live near the Colorado River.

   Revised: _We're used to tourists since we live near the Colorado River._

3. Couldn't find the group's new album.

   Revised: _Abdul looked in every record shop in town, but he couldn't find the_
   group's new album.

4. A tall, thin man with bushy eyebrows.

   Revised: _Dad is a tall, thin man with bushy eyebrows._

5. To travel around the world.

   Revised: _The homebound youth longed to travel around the world._

6. Ten minutes after they won the Super Bowl.

   Revised: _Ten minutes after they won the Super Bowl, the players were_
   wildly spraying each other with champagne in the locker room.

7. She has patented three of her inventions.

   Revised: _C_

8. Frantically flipping through the pages of the dictionary.

   Revised: _Jed is in the library, frantically flipping through the pages of the_

   dictionary.

9. Someone who loves to take risks.

   Revised: _Harriet is someone who loves to take risks._

   _____

10. Although we studied hard for the German exam.

    Revised: _Although we studied hard for the German exam, we didn't get the_

    A's we had hoped for.

PRACTICE 4   Proofread this essay for fragments. Correct them in any way you choose, either adding the fragments to other sentences or making them into complete sentences. Write your revised essay on a separate piece of paper. Be careful of punctuation. Answers will vary.

The Regent Diamond

(1) Throughout its exciting history, (2) ~~The~~ the Regent Diamond has been one of the world's most desired jewels.

(3) In 1701, the 410-carat gem was discovered in an Indian mine by a slave, (4) ~~Who~~ who risked his life to smuggle it out. (5) Slashing his leg, (6) ~~He~~ he stuffed the huge diamond into the wound and headed for the seacoast. (7) A shifty sea captain offered to sail him to freedom for half the value of the jewel. (8) When at sea, the captain stole the stone, (9) ~~And~~ and threw the slave overboard. (10) He then sold the precious rock to a powerful diamond merchant.

(11) The merchant had difficulty unloading the diamond, (12) ~~Because~~ because it was so large and because it was stolen. (13) He finally sold it to Robert Pitt, a young Englishman, (14) ~~Who~~ who had come to India seeking his fortune. (15) By the time this shrewd adventurer returned home, (16) ~~The~~ the English had nicknamed him "Diamond" Pitt and christened the stone "the Pitt."

(17) Few people believed Pitt had come by the diamond honestly. (18) So he also had trouble selling it. (19) Pitt was terrified of being robbed and murdered. (20) Whenever he carried the stone, (21) He disguised himself and would not sleep in the same place for more than two nights. (22) If someone recognized him, (23) He would deny that he carried the stone with him. (24) It took years, (25) But he finally sold his diamond in 1717 for an enormous sum to the Duke of Orleans, (26) The Regent of France.

(27) Now called the Regent Diamond, (28) The fabulous stone was the most valuable French crown jewel. (29) In 1792 during the French Revolution, (30) It disappeared, only to be found in a ditch in the middle of Paris. (31) Upon becoming emperor, (32) Napoleon had the diamond set into the hilt of his ceremonial sword. (33) In 1887 when the last French monarchy fell and the jewel collection was auctioned, (34) The Regent Diamond was placed in the Louvre, the famous museum in Paris, (35) Where it still glitters today.

PRACTICE 5
Review

Proofread these two essays for run-ons, comma splices, and fragments. Correct the errors in any way you choose, writing the revised draft on a separate piece of paper. Answers will vary.

Words for the Wise

(1) Everyone knows that Scrabble is America's favorite word game. (2) It was invented by Alfred Butts, (3) An architect who wanted to create a word game that required both luck and skill. (4) In 1938, Butts produced a board with 225 squares and 100 tiles with letters on them. (5) Each letter was worth a certain number of points, depending on how easy it was to use that letter in a word.

(6) Butts made fifty Scrabble sets by hand, he gave them to his friends, (7) Who loved playing Scrabble. (8) Strangely enough, Butts could

not interest a manufacturer in the game. (9) A friend of his, James Brunot, asked Butts for permission to manufacture and sell the game. (10) However, Brunot also had little success (11) ~~Selling~~ [, selling] only a few sets a year. (12) Then suddenly, in 1953, Scrabble caught on [, and] a million sets were sold in that year.

(13) Butts and Brunot couldn't keep up with the demand, [so] they sold the rights to a game manufacturer. (14) The rest is history ~~today~~ [Today,] Scrabble is produced in half a dozen foreign languages[;] it is also used as a learning tool[.] (15) ~~To~~ [to] teach children spelling and vocabulary.

A Royal Refreshment

(1) The simple marmalade that many people spread on toast each morning has a long, distinguished history. (2) The preferred food of kings and queens[,] (3) ~~Marmalade~~ [marmalade was] the favorite food of Henry VIII, King of England. (4) Mary, Queen of Scots, believed that marmalade cured seasickness[, so] she ate some on her long Channel crossings. (5) The table at Queen Elizabeth I's court always included a serving of marmalade.

(6) Served for hundreds of years as a dessert[,] (7) ~~Marmalade~~ [marmalade] finally became a breakfast food in the 1700s. (8) Because it was an aid to digestion, people ate it for their first meal of the day[;] it tasted delicious on a cold morning. (9) No longer just a royal treat, it [became] very popular.

(10) There are many recipes for marmalade[,] (11) ~~Which~~ [which] is prepared all over the world. (12) British cooks use bitter Seville oranges from Spain[,] (13) ~~To~~ [to] make a thick jelly filled with shredded orange peel. (14) Some recipes call for quince,* [and] others use lemons or grapefruit. (15) Boiling these fruits and their peels[,] (16) ~~The~~ [the] chefs of many countries create their own special versions of marmalade.

*Quince: a fruit that resembles an apple.

24

Present Tense (Agreement)

PART A   Defining Subject-Verb Agreement
PART B   Three Troublesome Verbs in the Present Tense: *To Be, To Have, To Do*
PART C   Special Singular Constructions
PART D   Separation of Subject and Verb
PART E   Sentences Beginning with *There* and *Here*
PART F   Agreement in Questions
PART G   Agreement in Relative Clauses

PART A

Defining Subject-Verb Agreement

Subjects and verbs in the present tense must **agree** in number; that is, singular subjects take verbs with singular endings, and plural subjects take verbs with plural endings.

Verbs in the Present Tense — Sample Verb: To Leap			
Singular		**Plural**	
If the subject is	*the verb is*	*If the subject is*	*the verb is*
1st person: I	leap	we	leap
2nd person: you	leap	you	leap
3rd person: he she it	leaps	they	leap

- Use an *-s* or *-es* ending on the verb only when the subject is *he, she,* or *it* or the equivalent of *he, she,* or *it.*

346

The subjects and verbs in the following sentences agree:

> 1. He *bicycles* to the steel mills every morning.
>
> 2. They *bicycle* to the steel mills every morning.
>
> 3. This student *hopes* to go to social work school.
>
> 4. The planets *revolve* around the sun.

- In sentence 1, the singular subject, *he*, takes the singular form of the verb, *bicycles*. *Bicycles* agrees with *he*.

- In sentence 2, the plural subject, *they*, takes the plural form of the verb, *bicycle*. *Bicycle* agrees with *they*.

- In sentence 3, the subject, *student*, is equivalent to *he* or *she* and takes the singular form of the verb, *hopes*.

- In sentence 4, the subject, *planets*, is equivalent to *they* and takes the plural form of the verb, *revolve*.

Subjects joined by the conjunction *and* usually take a plural verb:

> 5. Kirk and Quincy attend a pottery class at the Y.

- The subject, *Kirk and Quincy*, is plural, the equivalent of *they*.

- *Attend* agrees with the plural subject.*

PRACTICE 1   Underline the subject and circle the correct present tense verb.

1. Many <u>Americans</u> (thinks, (think)) of Seattle, Washington, as the ideal city.

2. <u>They</u> (praises, (praise)) it for many reasons, including a relaxed lifestyle, cultural diversity, and spectacular natural scenery.

3. <u>Puget Sound and Lake Washington</u> (surrounds, (surround)) most of Seattle.

4. Beyond the water, <u>mountains</u> (looms, (loom)) on the horizon, Mount Rainier the tallest of all.

*For work on consistent verb tense, see Chapter 13, "Revising for Consistency and Parallelism," Part A.

5. Seattle Center, the site of the 1962 World's Fair, (symbolizes, symbolize) the city's energy.

6. The Space Needle tower (rises, rise) 605 feet above the center.

7. At its top, a revolving restaurant (treats, treat) diners to a stunning view.

8. To learn the city's history, visitors (explores, explore) such areas as the Water Front and Pioneer Square.

9. Seattle's East Asian community, the third largest in the country, (congregates, congregate) in the International District.

10. Splashing fountains and sculpture (lines, line) the streets and other public areas.

11. The city also (boasts, boast) an extensive park system, complete with an aquarium and zoo.

12. Running and hiking trails (lures, lure) athletes.

13. Some people (complains, complain) about the amount of rain that falls on Seattle.

14. However, thousands (flocks, flock) to this vibrant city each year to live and vacation.

15. Can you (blames, blame) them?

PART B

Three Troublesome Verbs in the Present Tense: *To Be, To Have, To Do*

Choosing the correct verb form of *to be, to have,* and *to do* can be tricky. Study these charts:

Reference Chart—*To Be*
Present Tense

Singular		*Plural*	
If the subject is	*the verb is*	*If the subject is*	*the verb is*
1st person: I	am	we	are
2nd person: you	are	you	are
3rd person: he she it	is	they	are

Reference Chart—*To Have*
Present Tense

Singular		**Plural**	
If the subject is	*the verb is*	*If the subject is*	*the verb is*
1st person: I	have	we	have
2nd person: you	have	you	have
3rd person: he she it	has	they	have

Reference Chart—*To Do*
Present Tense

Singular		**Plural**	
If the subject is	*the verb is*	*If the subject is*	*the verb is*
1st person: I	do	we	do
2nd person: you	do	you	do
3rd person: he she it	does	they	do

PRACTICE 2   Write the correct present tense form of the verb in the space at the right of the pronoun.

To be

I am
we are
he is
you are
it is
they are
she is

To have

we have
she has
he has
they have
I have
it has
you have

To do

it does
they do
she does
you do
he does
we do
I do

PRACTICE 3   Fill in the correct present tense form of the verb in parentheses.

1. She __has__ (to have) a habit of calling on people in the back row.

2. The old churchyard __is__ (to be) a wonderful place to think.

3. You always __do__ (to do) well in statistics.

4. To earn tuition money, Angel and she __are__ (to be) working as writing tutors.

5. Tyrone __has__ (to have) a large collection of Chinese jade.

6. __Does__ (to do) he always act so pleased with himself?

7. These felt-tip pens __are__ (to be) useful for highlighting important ideas in books and magazines.

8. This apartment __has__ (to have) a view of the river; those apartments __have__ (to have) views of Euclid Avenue.

9. Mr. Weston __is__ (to be) an excellent photographer; you __have__ (to have) to see his show at the museum.

10. The employment agency __has__ (to have) a number of jobs available in word processing and dental hygiene.

11. The ferret and the llama __are__ (to be) Mr. Caproni's pets.

12. The electric fans __are__ (to be) turning at full speed; unfortunately, the room __is__ (to be) still warm.

13. As soon as Leslie and Bob __are__ (to be) ready, we __have__ (to have) to get started.

14. The judges __have__ (to have) doubts about the suspect's chances of getting a fair trial, but it __does__ (to do) seem that the case will go to court anyway.

15. The Jeep and the tractor __are__ (to be) in decent condition, but the pickup truck __does__ (to do) need work.

PART C

Special Singular Constructions

Each of these constructions takes a **singular** verb:

> ### Special Singular Constructions
>
> either (of) . . .   each (of) . . .   every one (of) . . .
> neither (of) . . .   one (of) . . .   which one (of) . . .

> 1. *Neither* of the birds *has* feathers yet.
> 2. *Each* of the solutions *presents* difficulties.

- In sentence 1, *neither* means *neither one*. *Neither* is a singular subject and requires the singular verb *has*.

- In sentence 2, *each* means *each one*. *Each* is a singular subject and requires the singular verb *presents*.

However, an exception to this general rule is the case in which two subjects are joined by *(n)either . . . (n)or. . . .* Here, the verb agrees with the subject closer to it:

> 3. Neither the teacher nor the *pupils want* the semester shortened.
> 4. The graphs or the *map has* to be changed.

- In sentence 3, *pupils* is the subject closer to the verb. The subject *pupils* takes the verb *want*.

- In sentence 4, *map* is the subject closer to the verb. The subject *map* takes the verb *has*.

PRACTICE 4   Underline the subject and circle the correct verb in each sentence.

1. Each of these ferns ((needs,) need) special care.

2. One of the customers always (forget, (forgets)) his or her umbrella.

3. Which <u>one</u> of the flights ((goes,) go) nonstop to Dallas?

4. Every <u>one</u> of those bicycles ((has,) have) ten speeds.

5. Either you or <u>Doris</u> ((is,) are) correct.

6. <u>Either</u> of these computer diskettes (contain, (contains)) the information you need.

7. Do you really believe that <u>one</u> of these oysters ((holds,) hold) a pearl?

8. <u>Neither</u> of the twins ((resembles,) resemble) his parents.

9. <u>One</u> of the scientists ((is,) are) working on a cream to prevent baldness.

10. <u>Each</u> of these inventions ((has,) have) has a profound effect on the modern world.

PART D

Separation of Subject and Verb

Sometimes a phrase or clause separates the subject from the verb. First, look for the subject; then make sure that the verb agrees with the subject.

> 1. The economist's *ideas* on this matter *seem* well thought out.
>
> 2. *Radios* that were made in the 1930s *are* now collectors' items.

- In sentence 1, the *ideas* are well thought out. The prepositional phrase *on this matter* separates the subject *ideas* from the verb *seem*.*

- In sentence 2, *radios* are now collectors' items. The relative clause *that were made in the 1930s* separates the subject *radios* from the verb *are*.

PRACTICE 5   Read each sentence carefully for meaning. Cross out any phrase or clause that separates the subject from the verb. Underline the subject and circle the correct verb.

1. The <u>plums</u> ~~in that bowl~~ (tastes, (taste)) sweet.

2. The <u>instructions</u> ~~on the package~~ (is, (are)) in French and English.

3. Our new <u>campus</u>, ~~which has a swimming pool and tennis courts,~~ ((keeps,) keep) everyone happy.

*For more work on prepositional phrases, see Chapter 21, "The Simple Sentence," Part B.

4. The lamp shades ~~that are made of stained glass~~ (looks, (look)) beautiful at night.

5. All the CD players ~~on that shelf~~ (costs, (cost)) $99 each.

6. The book ~~you gave me~~ ((makes) make) me laugh out loud.

7. The man ~~with the dark sunglasses~~ ((looks) look) like a typical movie villain.

8. The two nurses ~~who check blood pressure~~ (enjoys, (enjoy)) chatting with the patients.

9. The function ~~of these metal racks~~ ((remains) remain) a mystery to me.

10. The green lizard ~~on the wall~~ ((hasn't) haven't) moved for hours.

PART E

Sentences Beginning with *There* and *Here*

In sentences that begin with **there** or **here,** the subject usually follows the verb:

> 1. There *seem* to be two *flies* in my soup.
>
> 2. Here *is* my *prediction* for the coming year.

- In sentence 1, the plural subject *flies* takes the plural verb *seem.*

- In sentence 2, the singular subject *prediction* takes the singular verb *is.*

You can often determine what the verb should be by reversing the word order: *two flies seem . . .* or *my prediction is. . . .*

PRACTICE 6 Underline the subject and circle the correct verb in each sentence.

1. There ((goes) go) Tom Cruise.

2. There (is, (are)) only a few seconds left in the game.

3. Here ((is) are) a terrific way to save money—make a budget and stick to it!

4. There (has, (have)) been too many robberies in the neighborhood lately.

5. Here (is, (are)) my reactions to your essay.

6. Here ((comes) come) Johnny, the television talk-show host.

7. There ((is) are) no direct route to Black Creek from here.

8. There (seems) seem) to be something wrong with the doorbell.

9. Here (is, (are)) the teapot and sugar bowl I've been looking for.

10. There (is, (are)) eight nuclear power plants in the state.

Agreement in Questions

In questions, the subject usually follows the verb:

1. What *is* the *secret* of your success?
2. Where *are* the *copies* of the review?

- In sentence 1, the subject *secret* takes the singular verb *is*.

- In sentence 2, the subject *copies* takes the plural verb *are*.

You can often determine what the verb should be by reversing the word order: *the secret of your success is . . .* or *the copies are. . . .*

PRACTICE 7   Underline the subject and circle the correct verb in each sentence.

1. How ((does), do) the combustion engine actually work?

2. Why (is, (are)) Robert and Charity starting a study group?

3. Where (is, (are)) the beach chairs?

4. ((Have), Has) the grades for the biology final been posted yet?

5. ((Are), Is) Dianne and Bill starting a mail-order business?

6. What ((seems), seem) to be the problem here?

7. Why (is, (are)) all his ties so ugly?

8. ((Is), Are) the mattress factory really going to close in June?

9. How (does, (do)) you feel about their replacing this orchard with a shopping mall?

10. Who (is, (are)) those people on the fire escape?

PART G

Agreement in Relative Clauses

A **relative clause** is a subordinate clause that begins with *who, which,* or *that.* The verb in the relative clause must agree with the antecedent of the *who, which,* or *that.**

---

1. People *who have a good sense of humor* make good neighbors.

2. Be careful of a scheme *that promises you a lot of money fast.*

- In sentence 1, the antecedent of *who* is *people. People* takes the verb *have.*

- In sentence 2, the antecedent of *that* is *scheme. Scheme* takes the verb *promises.*

PRACTICE 8   Underline the antecedent of the *who, which,* or *that.* Then circle the correct verb.

1. Most patients prefer <u>doctors</u> who (spends, spend) time talking with them.

2. The gnarled <u>oak</u> that (shades, shade) the garden is my favorite tree.

3. Laptop <u>computers</u>, which (has, have) become very popular recently, are still fairly expensive.

4. My <u>neighbor</u>, who (swims, swim) at least one hour a day, is seventy years old.

5. <u>Listing</u> things to do, which (saves, save) hours of wasted time, is a good time management technique.

6. Employers often appreciate <u>employees</u> who (asks, ask) intelligent questions.

7. This <u>air conditioner</u>, which now (costs, cost) eight hundred dollars, rarely breaks down.

8. Everyone admires her because she is <u>someone</u> who always (sees, see) the bright side of a bad situation.

*For more work on relative clauses, see Chapter 14, "Revising for Sentence Variety," Part D.

9. He is the man who ((creates,) create) inlaid furniture from walnut, cherry, and birch.

10. Foods that (contains, (contain)) artificial sweeteners may be hazardous to your health.

PRACTICE 9
Review

Proofread the following essay for verb agreement errors. Correct any errors by writing above the lines.

Chimp Smarts

(1) Chimpanzees sometimes seem uncannily human, especially in their use of tools and language. (2) Neither the gorilla nor the orangutan, both close relatives of the chimp, ~~exhibit~~ *exhibits* such behavior.

(3) Chimps ~~employs~~ *employ* a number of tools in their everyday lives. (4) They dine by inserting sticks into insect nests and then licking their utensils clean. (5) Each of these intelligent animals also ~~crack~~ *cracks* fruit and nuts with stones. (6) What's more, chimpanzees ~~creates~~ *create* their own tools. (7) They make their eating sticks by cleaning leaves from branches. (8) They even ~~attaches~~ *attach* small sticks together to make longer rods for getting at hard-to-reach insects. (9) Some of the other tools chimps make ~~is~~ *are* flywhisks, sponges of chewed bark, and leaf-rags to clean themselves with. (10) Scientists on safari ~~has~~ *have* observed infant chimps imitating their parents' use of these tools.

(11) Experiments indicate that chimpanzees probably also ~~understands~~ *understand* language though they lack the physical ability to speak. (12) There ~~are~~ *is* little doubt that they can comprehend individual words. (13) Using sign language and keyboards, more than one chimp in captivity speaks nearly two hundred words. (14) This vocabulary ~~include~~ *includes* nouns, verbs, and prepositions. (15) Hunger and affection ~~is~~ *are* needs that they have expressed by punching keyboard symbols. (16) Do chimps ~~has~~ *have* the

ability to string words into sentences? (17) Intriguingly, one chimp

named Lucy has shown that she ~~understand~~ ^understands^ the difference between such

statements as "Roger tickles Lucy" and "Lucy tickles Roger."

(18) Scientists still argue about just how much language a chimpanzee

truly ~~comprehend~~ ^comprehends^. (19) However, no one who ~~have~~ ^has^ watched them closely

~~doubt~~ ^doubts^ the intelligence of these remarkable beings.

25

Past Tense

PART A   Regular Verbs in the Past Tense
PART B   Irregular Verbs in the Past Tense
PART C   A Troublesome Verb in the Past Tense: *To Be*
PART D   Troublesome Pairs in the Past Tense: *Can/Could, Will/Would*

PART A

Regular Verbs in the Past Tense

Regular verbs in the past tense take an *-ed* or *-d* ending:

---

1. The captain *hoisted* the flag.

2. They *purchased* lawn furniture yesterday.

3. We *deposited* a quarter in the meter.

- *Hoisted*, *purchased*, and *deposited* are regular verbs in the past tense.
- Each verb ends in *-ed* or *-d*.

PRACTICE 1   Fill in the past tense of the regular verbs in parentheses.*

1. On December 28, 1958, more than 64,000 people _____packed_____ (pack) Yankee Stadium in New York City to witness one of the most exciting football games of all time.

*If you have questions about spelling, see Appendix 1, "Spelling," Parts C, D, and E.

2. The Baltimore Colts __battled__ (battle) the New York Giants for the National Football League Championship.

3. In the first quarter, the Giants __scored__ (score) a field goal; however, the Colts __earned__ (earn) two touchdowns during the second quarter.

4. At halftime, the scoreboard __flashed__ (flash) 14 to 3 in favor of the Colts.

5. Early in the third quarter, Frank Gifford, the Giants' halfback, __snatched__ (snatch) a 15-yard touchdown pass from quarterback Charlie Conerly.

6. Later in the quarter, Conerly __passed__ (pass) to left end Kyle Rote, who __dodged__ (dodge) down the field and then __fumbled__ (fumble) at the 25-yard line.

7. Alex Webster __recovered__ (recover) the ball, leading the Giants to another touchdown.

8. Going into the final quarter, the Colts __trailed__ (trail) 17 to 14, but Johnny Unitas, their quarterback, soon __changed__ (change) all that as he __maneuvered__ (maneuver) the team down the field.

9. The Colts __reached__ (reach) the Giants' 13-yard line with only eight seconds remaining in the game.

10. Steve Myrha __booted__ (boot) a perfect field goal and __tied__ (tie) the score, 17 to 17.

11. For the first time ever, a regular league game __extended__ (extend) into sudden-death overtime.

12. The Giants just __missed__ (miss) a first down by inches.

13. Then, the great Unitas __completed__ (complete) four of six passes, driving the Colts eighty yards in thirteen plays.

14. At the Giants' 1-yard line, Johnny Unitas __handed__ (hand) off the ball to "Horse" Ameche, who __plunged__ plunge across the goal line.

15. In 8 minutes, 15 seconds of overtime, the Colts __prevailed__ (prevail), winning the game 23 to 17.

PART B

Irregular Verbs in the Past Tense

Irregular verbs do not take an *-ed* or *-d* ending in the past but change internally:

---

1. I *wrote* that letter in ten minutes.

2. Although the orange cat *fell* from a high branch, she escaped unharmed.

3. The play *began* on time but ended fairly late.

- *Wrote* is the past tense of *write*.

- *Fell* is the past tense of *fall*.

- *Began* is the past tense of *begin*.

Here is a partial list of irregular verbs.

Reference Chart
Irregular Verbs in the Past Tense

Simple Form	Past Tense	Simple Form	Past Tense
be	was, were	draw	drew
become	became	drink	drank
begin	began	drive	drove
blow	blew	eat	ate
break	broke	fall	fell
bring	brought	feed	fed
build	built	feel	felt
✓ buy	bought	fight	fought
catch	caught	find	found
choose	chose	fly	flew
come	came	forbid	forbade
cut	cut	forget	forgot
deal	dealt	forgive	forgave
✓ dig	dug	freeze	froze
dive	dove (dived)	get	got
✓ do	did	give	gave

(continued)

Reference Chart
Irregular Verbs in the Past Tense
(continued)

Simple Form	Past Tense	Simple Form	Past Tense
✓ go	went	sell	sold
grow	grew	send	sent
✓ have	had	shake	shook
hear	heard	shine	shone (shined)
hide	hid	sing	sang
hold	held	sit	sat
hurt	hurt	sleep	slept
✓ keep	kept	speak	spoke
✓ know	knew	spend	spent
lay	laid	split	split
lead	led	spring	sprang
leave	left	stand	stood
let	let	steal	stole
lie	lay	stink	stank
lose	lost	swim	swam
make	made	take	took
mean	meant	teach	taught
meet	met	tear	tore
pay	paid	tell	told
quit	quit	think	thought
read	read	throw	threw
ride	rode	understand	understood
✓ rise	rose	wake	woke (waked)
run	ran	wear	wore
say	said	win	won
see	saw	write	wrote
seek	sought		

PRACTICE 2   Fill in the past tense of the regular and irregular verbs in parentheses. If you are not sure of the past tense, use the chart. Do not guess.

The Tragic Fate of Port Royal

(1) In its heyday, Port Royal ___had___ (have) a reputation as the most wicked city in the world. (2) Situated on a beautiful bay, the Jamaican port ___welcomed___ (welcome) English

pirates like Henry Morgan, who __preyed__ (prey) on Spanish galleons loaded with gold from Mexico and Peru. (3) Port Royal __bustled__ (bustle) with the immoral activities of the unsavory characters who __swaggered__ (swagger) down its crowded streets. (4) Suddenly, in three minutes on June 7, 1692, this thriving city __met__ (meet) its untimely end.

(5) At 11:40 a.m., the first of three earth tremors __shook__ (shake) the city. (6) Citizens __fled__ (flee) from their homes and __took__ (take) to the streets. (7) Before they __recovered__ (recover), a second, more powerful shock __knocked__ (knock) them to the ground. (8) As they __lay__ (lie) there, the worst tremor of all __toppled__ (topple) most of the town's buildings. (9) People __fell__ (fall) into gaping holes. (10) Later shocks actually __belched__ (belch) a few lucky ones back up. (11) As the quakes __hit__ (hit), water __withdrew__ (withdraw) from the harbor and then __tumbled__ (tumble) back to shore in monstrous waves, flooding half the city. (12) The harbor area __slid__ (slide) into the sea. (13) Ships either __capsized__ (capsize) or __ran__ (run) aground far into town. (14) Close to half the city's population __died__ (die) instantly.

(15) Some __thought__ (think) the city __deserved__ (deserve) its terrible fate. (16) Others __mourned__ (mourn) the town's bad luck. (17) Thirty years after the earthquake, a fierce hurricane __wiped__ (wipe) out the little that __remained__ (remain) of Port Royal. (18) For more than one hundred years, sailors __said__ (say) that complete houses, bright and perfect, still __stood__ (stand) beneath the sea.

PART C

A Troublesome Verb in the Past Tense: *To Be*

To be is the only verb that in the past tense has different forms for different persons. Be careful of subject-verb agreement:

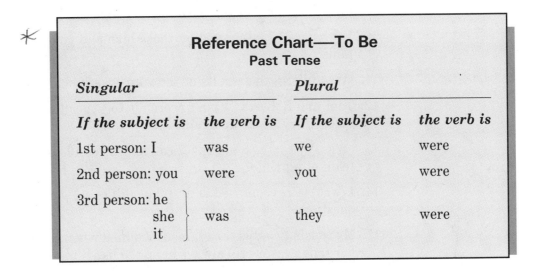

Reference Chart—To Be
Past Tense

Singular		*Plural*	
If the subject is	*the verb is*	*If the subject is*	*the verb is*
1st person: I	was	we	were
2nd person: you	were	you	were
3rd person: he she it	was	they	were

- Note that the form for the first-person singular and the third-person singular is the same—*was*.

Be especially careful of agreement when adding *not* to *was* or *were* to make a contraction:

was + not = wasn't

were + not = weren't

PRACTICE 3   Circle the correct form of the verb *to be* in the past tense. Do not guess. If you are not sure of the correct form, use the chart.

1. Edward (was, were) curious about how bees communicate.

2. These biology books (was, were) expensive, but I needed them for my research.

3. Camping and sports cars (was, were) his passions.

4. The play (was, were) well acted, but the staging and the choreography (was, were) weak.

5. Why (wasn't, weren't) you at the restaurant when I (was, were)?

6. Cynthia and Lou (was, were) partners in the music business.

7. How (was, were) the sweet potato fries? They (wasn't, weren't) good the last time we (was, were) here.

8. We (was, were) where the action (was, were).

9. (Wasn't, Weren't) you born in Sweden?

10. I (was, were) fascinated by those blue and gold tropical fish in your tank.

11. (Was, Were) the results of the vote exactly what you had expected?

12. Tom and Roberta (wasn't, weren't) together for more than a month before they broke up again.

13. (Was, Were) the San Francisco 49ers of the 1980s the greatest football team of all time?

14. I (was, were) confused at first, but Bill (was, were) able to answer my questions.

15. My cousin (was, were) a famous violinist when she (was, were) a child; her fans (was, were) always happy to listen to her perform. Ah, those (was, were) the days!

PART D

Troublesome Pairs in the Past Tense: *Can/Could, Will/Would*

Use **could** as the past tense of **can**.

> 1. Maria is extraordinary because she *can* remember what happened to her when she was three years old.
>
> 2. When I was in high school, I *could* do two sit-ups in an hour.

- In sentence 1, *can* shows the action is in the present.
- In sentence 2, *could* shows the action occurred in the past.

PRACTICE 4 Fill in either the present tense *can* or the past tense *could*.

1. Tom is so talented that he ___can___ play most music on the piano by ear.

2. The economy ___can___ improve only when we reduce the deficit.

3. Last week we ___could___ not find fresh strawberries.

4. When we were in Spain last summer, we ___could___ see all of Madrid from our hotel balcony.

5. As a child, I ___could___ perform easily in public, but I ___can___ no longer do it.

6. Anything you ___can___ do, he ___can___ do better.

7. Nobody ___could___ find the guard after the robbery yesterday.

8. These days, Fred ___can___ usually predict the weather from the condition of his bunions.

Use **would** as the past tense of **will.**

> 3. Roberta says that she *will* arrive with her camera in ten minutes.
>
> 4. Roberta said that she *would* arrive with her camera in ten minutes.

- In sentence 3, *will* points to the future from the present.
- In sentence 4, *would* points to the future from the past.

PRACTICE 5   Fill in either the present tense *will* or the past tense *would.*

1. He hoped that he ___would___ succeed in his new career.

2. He hopes that he ___will___ succeed in his new career.

3. I said what I liked and didn't like about my friend's essay, but I ___would___ not rewrite it for her.

4. The guests promised that they ___would___ help clean up the messy kitchen.

5. The guests promise that they ___will___ help clean up the messy kitchen.

6. Robert thinks that he ___will___ enroll in a swimming course next semester.

7. The customer stood by the door, but she ___would___ not leave.

PRACTICE 6   Proofread the following essay for past tense errors. Then write the cor-
Review   rect past tense form above the line.

The Warrior Queen of Jhansi

(1) The British cursed her as a devil; the people of India revered her

almost as a god. (2) All agreed, however, that the Indian queen, Lakshmi
                    was
Bai, ~~were~~ a powerful and daring woman.

(3) Before the ruler of Jhansi died in 1853, he willed his land and title
                                              told
to his five-year-old son. (4) He ~~telled~~ his young wife, Lakshmi Bai, to rule
                          came
until their child ~~come~~ of age. (5) Despite the young queen's ability and
                                                              seized
popularity, the British declared the will illegal and ~~seize~~ the kingdom.

(6) Lakshmi Bai swallowed the insult and remained loyal to the British.

(7) However, throughout India, discontent against the British grew
                     broke   took
until rebellion ~~broken~~ out in 1857. (8) In Jhansi, rebels ~~taked~~ the British

fort and then massacred the British women and children living in the
                                   did
city. (9) Though the queen ~~do~~ not support this bloodshed, the British

held her responsible. (10) For a while in late 1857, in the absence of the
                                 got
British, the queen ~~gotten~~ her chance to rule. (11) Rising at 3:00 a.m., she
spent
~~spended~~ her days first attending to matters of state, then riding and

training with arms, and later meditating and praying.
                                                             made
(12) Finally, in early 1858, the British ~~maked~~ the queen an outlaw
       laid
and ~~lay~~ siege to Jhansi for more than two weeks. (13) The queen hero-
             fought
ically ~~fighted~~ for her city from a high tower where her people and the
             could
enemy ~~can~~ clearly see her. (14) As the city prepared for defeat, the queen,
                                     fled
an expert horsewoman, ~~fleed~~. (15) After riding for four days, she at last
                 joined
formally ~~join~~ the rebelling forces.
                 led
(16) The queen ~~lead~~ the defense at Gwalior, the last rebel stronghold.

(17) Leading her men in hand-to-hand combat, she wore trousers, a silk

blouse, and a red silk cap with a loose turban around it. (18) A pearl neck-

lace that ~~were~~ *was* one of the treasures of India ~~hang~~ *hung* around her neck. (19)

Mortally wounded in this battle, she immediately ~~become~~ *became* a beloved hero

of the Indian nationalist movement.

26

The Past Participle

PART A   Past Participles of Regular Verbs
PART B   Past Participles of Irregular Verbs
PART C   Using the Present Perfect Tense
PART D   Using the Past Perfect Tense
PART E   Using the Passive Voice (*To Be* and the Past Participle)
PART F   Using the Past Participle as an Adjective

PART A

Past Participles of Regular Verbs

The **past participle** is the form of the verb that can be combined with helping verbs like *have* and *has* to make verbs of more than one word:

Present Tense	Past Tense	Helping Verb plus Past Participle
1. They *skate.*	1. They *skated.*	1. They *have skated.*
2. Beth *dances.*	2. Beth *danced.*	2. Beth *has danced.*
3. Frank *worries.*	3. Frank *worried.*	3. Frank *has worried.*

- *Skated, danced,* and *worried* are all past participles of regular verbs.

- Note that both the *past tense* and the *past participle* of regular verbs end in *-ed* or *-d*.

PRACTICE 1   The first sentence of each pair that follows contains a regular verb in the past tense. Fill in *have* or *has* plus the past participle of the same verb to complete the second sentence.

1. Vance locked his keys in the car.

   Vance ___has___ ___locked_____ his keys in the car.

2. The carpenters gathered their tools from the littered floor.

   The carpenters ___have___ ___gathered_____ their tools from the littered floor.

3. Clearly, you planned the speech with care.

   Clearly, you ___have___ ___planned_____ the speech with care.

4. Twice, Dianne and Carol visited the Dominican Republic.

   Twice, Dianne and Carol ___have___ ___visited_____ the Dominican Republic.

5. Detectives discovered the love letters in the garage.

   Detectives ___have___ ___discovered_____ the love letters in the garage.

6. Mr. Yosufu carved this chess set out of wood.

   Mr. Yosufu ___has___ ___carved_____ this chess set out of wood.

7. My boss impressed everyone with her ability to read Chinese.

   My boss ___has___ ___impressed_____ everyone with her ability to read Chinese.

8. Illness interrupted his work on the film.

   Illness ___has___ ___interrupted_____ his work on the film.

9. The windshields reflected the glow of the streetlights.

   The windshields ___have___ ___reflected_____ the glow of the streetlights.

10. These three women studied with Madame Tebaldi.

    These three women ___have___ ___studied_____ with Madame Tebaldi.

PART B

Past Participles of Irregular Verbs

Most verbs that are irregular in the past tense are also irregular in the past participle, as shown in the box on the top of the next page.

Present Tense	Past Tense	Helping Verb plus Past Participle
1. We *sing*.	1. We *sang*.	1. We *have sung*.
2. Bill *writes*.	2. Bill *wrote*.	2. Bill *has written*.
3. I *think*.	3. I *thought*.	3. I *have thought*.

- Irregular verbs change from present to past to past participle in unusual ways.

- *Sung, written,* and *thought* are all past participles of irregular verbs.

- Note that the past tense and past participle of *think* are the same— *thought*.

Reference Chart
Irregular Verbs, Past and Past Participle

Simple Form	Past Tense	Past Participle
be	was, were	been
become	became	become
begin	began	begun
blow	blew	blown
break	broke	broken
bring	brought	brought
build	built	built
buy	bought	bought
catch	caught	caught
choose	chose	chosen
come	came	come
cut	cut	cut
dive	dove (dived)	dived
do	did	done
draw	drew	drawn
drink	drank	drunk
drive	drove	driven
eat	ate	eaten
fall	fell	fallen
feed	fed	fed
feel	felt	felt
fight	fought	fought
find	found	found

(continued)

Reference Chart
Irregular Verbs, Past and Past Participle
(continued)

Simple Form	Past Tense	Past Participle
fly	flew	flown
forget	forgot	forgotten
forgive	forgave	forgiven
freeze	froze	frozen
get	got	got (gotten)
give	gave	given
go	went	gone
grow	grew	grown
have	had	had
hear	heard	heard
hide	hid	hidden
hold	held	held
hurt	hurt	hurt
keep	kept	kept
know	knew	known
lay	laid	laid
lead	led	led
leave	left	left
let	let	let
lie	lay	lain
lose	lost	lost
make	made	made
meet	met	met
pay	paid	paid
quit	quit	quit
read	read	read
ride	rode	ridden
rise	rose	risen
run	ran	run
say	said	said
see	saw	seen
sell	sold	sold
send	sent	sent
shake	shook	shaken
shine	shone (shined)	shone (shined)
sing	sang	sung
sit	sat	sat
sleep	slept	slept
speak	spoke	spoken
spend	spent	spent
spring	sprang	sprung
stand	stood	stood

(continued)

Reference Chart
Irregular Verbs, Past and Past Participle
(continued)

Simple Form	Past Tense	Past Participle
steal	stole	stolen
stink	stank	stunk
swim	swam	swum
take	took	taken
teach	taught	taught
tear	tore	torn
tell	told	told
think	thought	thought
throw	threw	thrown
understand	understood	understood
wake	woke (waked)	woken (waked)
wear	wore	worn
win	won	won
write	wrote	written

PRACTICE 2   The first sentence of each pair that follows contains an irregular verb in the past tense. Fill in *have* or *has* plus the past participle of the same verb to complete the second sentence.

1. Sean took plenty of time buying the groceries.

    Sean ___has___ ___taken___ plenty of time buying the groceries.

2. We sent our latest song to a music publisher.

    We ___have___ ___sent___ our latest song to a music publisher.

3. My daughter hid her diary.

    My daughter ___has___ ___hidden___ her diary.

4. The jockey rode all day in the hot sun.

    The jockey ___has___ ___ridden___ all day in the hot sun.

5. Hershey, Pennsylvania, became a great tourist attraction.

    Hershey, Pennsylvania, ___has___ ___become___ a great tourist attraction.

6. The company's managers knew about these hazards for two years.

The company's managers ___have___ ___known___ about these hazards for two years.

7. Carrie floated down the river on an inner tube.

   Carrie ___has___ ___floated___ down the river on an inner tube.

8. At last, our team won the bowling tournament.

   At last, our team ___has___ ___won___ the bowling tournament.

9. Larry and Marsha broke their long silence.

   Larry and Marsha ___have___ ___broken___ their long silence.

10. This discussion was very helpful.

    This discussion ___has___ ___been___ very helpful.

PRACTICE 3 Complete each sentence by filling in *have* or *has* plus the past participle of the verb in parentheses. Some verbs are regular, some irregular.

1. Over the past decade, rap music ___has___ ___moved___ (move) beyond the streets where it began.

2. It ___has___ ___entered___ (enter) the mainstream of popular American music.

3. Groups like M.C. Hammer and Vanilla Ice ___have___ ___produced___ (produce) albums that ___have___ ___sold___ (sell) millions of copies.

4. Queen Latifah and others ___have___ ___helped___ (help) women find a voice in rap.

5. Rappers ___have___ ___filled___ (fill) concert halls and stadiums with thousands of screaming fans.

6. There are other indications that rap ___has___ ___captured___ (capture) the American imagination.

7. Corporations ___have___ ___found___ (find) that rap sells products from soda to jeans.

8. In addition, commercial rap messages ___have___ ___warned___ (warn) teens of the dangers of drugs and AIDS.

9. Even politicians ___have___ ___used___ (use) rap in their campaigns.

10. Without doubt, the sound of the energetically rhyming and dancing rapper _____has_____ _____become_____ (become) a common one in the 1990s.

Using the Present Perfect Tense

The **present perfect tense** is composed of the present tense of *to have* plus the past participle. The present perfect tense shows that an action has begun in the past and is continuing into the present.

1. Past tense:	Beatrice *taught* English for ten years.
2. Present perfect tense:	Beatrice *has taught* English for ten years.

- In sentence 1, Beatrice *taught* English in the past, but she no longer does so. Note the use of the simple past tense, *taught.*

- In sentence 2, Beatrice *has taught* for ten years and is still teaching English *now. Has taught* implies that the action is still continuing.

PRACTICE 4   Read these sentences carefully for meaning. Then circle the correct verb—either the **past tense** or the **present perfect tense.**

1. He (directed, has directed) traffic for many years now.

2. Emilio lifted the rug and (has swept, swept) the dust under it.

3. Kenneth (traveled, has traveled) throughout the Caribbean every summer for the past five years and plans to go again in June.

4. She (went, has gone) to the library last night.

5. The coffee maker gurgled so loudly that the noise (awakened, has awakened) me at 6 A.M.

6. For the past four years, I (enrolled, have enrolled) in summer school every summer.

7. We (talked, have talked) about the problem of your lateness for three days; it's time for you to do something about it.

8. While I was in Mexico, I (took, have taken) many photographs of Aztec ruins.

9. She ((won,) has won) that contest ten years ago.

10. The boxers (fought, (have fought)) for an hour, and they look very tired.

11. He ((applied,) has applied) to three colleges and attended the one with the best engineering department.

12. Raymond looked at the revised plans for his new house and ((decided,) has decided) he could not afford to build.

13. These useless tools ((have been,) were) here for quite a while, but no one wants to throw them out.

14. One of the most amusing incidents on my trip (has occurred, (occurred)) on May 5, 1987.

15. The coauthors (worked, (have worked)) together for eight years and are now planning a new book.

PART D

Using the Past Perfect Tense

The **past perfect tense** is composed of the past tense of *to have* plus the past participle. The past perfect tense shows that an action occurred further back in the past than another past action.

1. Past tense:	Rhonda *left* for the movies.
2. Past perfect tense:	Rhonda *had* already *left* for the movies by the time we *arrived.*

- In sentence 1, *left* is the simple past.

- In sentence 2, the past perfect *had left* shows that this action occurred even before another action in the past, *arrived.*

PRACTICE 5   Read these sentences carefully for meaning. Then circle the correct verb—either the **past tense** or the **past perfect tense.**

1. Tony came to the theater with a cane last week because he (sprained, (had sprained)) his ankle a month ago.

2. As Jay ((piled,) had piled) the apples into a pyramid, he thought, "I should become an architect."

3. Celia (finished, (had finished)) her gardening by the time I ((drove,) had driven) up in my new convertible.

4. Bonnie (operated, had operated) a drill press for years before she became a welder.

5. The man nervously (looked, had looked) at his watch and then walked a bit faster.

6. Last year Ming bought a compact disk player; he (wanted, had wanted) one for years.

7. Dr. Johnson told us that he (decided, had decided) to live in Morocco for a year.

8. I (worked, had worked) on that essay for a week before I handed it in.

9. The caller asked whether we (received, had received) our free toaster yet.

10. Dianne (completed, had completed) college before her younger brother was old enough for the first grade.

11. Last October he told us he (graduated, had graduated) the previous June.

12. As the curtain went down, everyone (rose, had risen) and applauded the African dance troupe.

13. Scott (closed, had closed) his books and went to the movies.

14. Brad missed the rehearsal on Saturday because no one (notified, had notified) him earlier in the week.

15. The prosecutor proved that the defendant was lying; until then I (believed, had believed) he was innocent.

PART E

Using the Passive Voice (*To Be* and the Past Participle)

The **passive voice** is composed of the past participle with some form of *to be* (*am, is, are, was, were, has been, have been,* or *had been*). In the passive voice, the subject does not act but is *acted upon.*

Compare the passive voice with the active voice in the following pairs of sentences:

1. Passive voice:	This newspaper *is written* by journalism students.
2. Active voice:	Journalism students *write* this newspaper.
3. Passive voice:	My garden *was devoured* by rabbits.
4. Active voice:	Rabbits *devoured* my garden.

- In sentence 1, the subject, *this newspaper*, is passive; it is acted upon. In sentence 2, the subject, *students*, is active; it performs the action.

- Note the difference between the passive verb *is written* and the active verb *write*.

- However, both verbs (*is written* and *write*) are in the *present tense*.

- The verbs in sentences 3 and 4 are both in the *past tense: was devoured* (passive) and *devoured* (active).

Use the passive voice sparingly. Write in the passive voice when you want to emphasize the receiver of the action rather than the doer.

PRACTICE 6   Fill in the correct **past participle** form of the verb in parentheses. If you are not sure, check the chart.

1. The barn was __built_____ (build) by friends of the family.

2. Who was __chosen_____ (choose) to represent us at the convention?

3. These ruby slippers were __given_____ (give) to me by my grandmother.

4. These jeans are __sold_____ (sell) in ten countries.

5. On their weekend camping trip, Sheila and Una were constantly

   __bitten_____ (bite) by mosquitoes and gnats.

6. It was __decided_____ (decide) that Bill would work the night shift.

7. The getaway car is always __driven_____ (drive) by a man in a gray fedora.

8. Her articles have been __published_____ (publish) in the *Texas Monthly*.

9. Harold was __seen_____ (see) sneaking out the back door.

10. A faint inscription is __etched_____ (etch) on the back of the old gold watch.

PRACTICE 7   Rewrite each sentence, changing the verb into the **passive** voice. Make all necessary verb and subject changes. Be sure to keep the sentence in the original tense.

Example | My father wore this silk hat.

This silk hat was worn by my father.

1. The goalie blocked the shot.

   The shot was blocked by the goalie.

2. The lifeguard taught us to swim.

   We were taught to swim by the lifeguard.

3. The usher warned the noisy group.

   The noisy group was warned by the usher.

4. Her rudeness hurt her reputation.

   Her reputation was hurt by her rudeness.

5. J. C. Penney imported these Oriental rugs.

   These Oriental rugs were imported by J. C. Penney.

6. Hooker Chemical dumped the poisons at Love Canal.

   The poisons were dumped at Love Canal by Hooker Chemical.

7. The conductor punched my ticket full of holes.

   My ticket was punched full of holes by the conductor.

8. The interviewer asked too many personal questions.

   Too many personal questions were asked by the interviewer.

PART F

Using the Past Participle as an Adjective

The **past participle** form of the verb can be used as an **adjective** after a linking verb:

> 1. The window is *broken*.

■ The adjective *broken* describes the subject *window*.

The **past participle** form of the verb can sometimes be used as an adjective before a noun or a pronoun.

> 2. This *fried* chicken tastes wonderful.

- The adjective *fried* describes the noun *chicken*.

PRACTICE 8   Use the past participle form of the verb in parentheses as an adjective in each sentence.

1. My __used__ (use) car was a great bargain at only $400.

2. The __hidden__ (hide) scrolls were discovered accidentally.

3. Bob is highly __qualified__ (qualify) to install a water heater.

4. The __air-conditioned__ (air-condition) room was making every-one sneeze.

5. A raise was granted to the __overworked__ (overwork) mainte-nance staff.

6. Two stylishly __dressed__ (dress) women gave make-up demonstrations.

7. It is a widely __known__ (know) fact that Laura is an avid hockey fan.

8. Were you __surprised__ (surprise) to see your picture on the cover of *Time Magazine?*

9. This car is carefully __designed__ (design) for comfort.

10. He feels __depressed__ (depress) on rainy days.

11. The newly __risen__ (rise) cinnamon bread smelled wonderful.

12. In the tiny office, Wilfred felt like a __forgotten__ (forget) man.

13. She knows the power of the __written__ (write) word.

14. I love that old shirt even though it is __torn__ (tear).

15. Happily, the __stolen__ (steal) wallet was returned to its owner.

16. My gym teacher seems __prejudiced_____ (prejudice) against short people.

17. Funny, you don't act like a __married_____ (marry) man.

18. Don't be __annoyed_____ (annoy) by my sloppiness; I can't help it.

19. The __embarrassed_____ (embarrass) child pulled her jacket over her head.

20. We ordered __tossed_____ (toss) salad, __broiled_____ (broil) chicken, __mashed_____ (mash) potatoes, and __baked_____ (bake) apples.

PRACTICE 9   Proofread the following paragraph for past participle errors. Correct
Review   the errors by writing above the lines.

The Community College:
An American Phenomenon

(1) Uniquely American, community colleges are publicly supported two-year institutions of higher education. (2) Almost from the time California introduced the first community college system in 1907, this type of two-year school has drawed *drawn* millions of students. (3) Growth has been especially rapid since World War II when thousands of returning soldiers were gived *given* funds for college. (4) Nearly one-half of all college students in the United States are now teached *taught* in more than 1,200 community colleges.

(5) Community colleges are ideal for marry *married* or employed people because they are conveniently located near home and the workplace. (6) To increase their appeal even more, they have began *begun* offering innovative programs, such as part-time study, evening and weekend sessions, televise *televised* classes, computer-assisted instruction, and work-study education. (7) Community colleges have traditionally provide *provided* three types of

programs. (8) They offer the first two years of traditional college work;

therefore, ~~advance~~ ^{advanced} students can then transfer to four-year colleges. (9)

Second, and equally popular, are their two-year associate degree pro-

grams. (10) These prepare students for careers in technical and other

vocational areas that require ~~specialize~~ ^{specialized} training. (11) Finally, commu-

nity colleges give uncredited courses in a variety of subjects that meet

the needs of ~~interest~~ ^{interested} adults and the community.

27

Nouns

PART A   Defining Singular and Plural
PART B   Signal Words: Singular and Plural
PART C   Signal Words with *Of*

Defining Singular and Plural

Nouns are words that refer to people, places, or things. They can be either singular or plural. **Singular** means one. **Plural** means more than one.

Singular	Plural
the glass	the glasses
a lamp	lamps
a lesson	the lessons

- As you can see, nouns usually add *-s* or *-es* to form the plural.

Some nouns form their plurals in other ways; here are a few examples:

Singular	Plural
child	children
crisis	crises
criterion	criteria
foot	feet
goose	geese

man	men
medium	media
memorandum	memoranda (memorandums)
phenomenon	phenomena
tooth	teeth
woman	women

These nouns ending in -*f* or -*fe* change endings to -*ves* in the plural:

Singular	Plural
half	halves
knife	knives
life	lives
scarf	scarves
shelf	shelves
wife	wives
wolf	wolves

Hyphenated nouns form plurals by adding -*s* or -*es* to the main word:

Singular	Plural
brother-in-law	brothers-in-law
inspector-general	inspectors-general
passer-by	passers-by

Others do not change at all to form the plural; here are a few examples:

Singular	Plural
deer	deer
fish	fish
moose	moose
sheep	sheep

If you are unsure about the plural of a noun, check a dictionary. For example, if you look up the noun *woman* in the dictionary, you will find an entry like this:

woman, women

The first word listed, *woman*, is the singular form of the noun; the second word, *women*, is the plural.

Some dictionaries list the plural form of a noun only if the plural is unusual. If no plural is listed, that noun probably adds -*s* or -*es*.* *Remember:* Do not add an -*s* to words that form plurals by changing an internal letter. For example, the plural of *man* is *men*, not *mens*; the plural of *woman* is *women*, not *womens*; the plural of *foot* is *feet*, not *feets*.

PRACTICE 1   Make these singular nouns plural.

1. man __men__
2. half __halves__ ✗
3. foot __feet__
4. son-in-law __sons-in-law__ ✗
5. moose __moose__
6. life __lives__
7. tooth __teeth__ ✗
8. medium __media__ ✗
9. woman __women__
10. crisis __crises__

11. passer-by __passers-by__
12. criterion __criteria__
13. shelf __shelves__ ✗
14. mouse __mice__
15. child __children__
16. father-in-law __fathers-in-law__
17. knife __knives__
18. deer __deer__
19. secretary __secretaries__ ✗
20. goose __geese__

PART B

Signal Words: Singular and Plural

A **signal word** tells you whether a singular or a plural noun usually follows.

*For more work on spelling plurals, see Appendix 1, "Spelling," Part G.

- These signal words tell you that a singular noun usually follows:

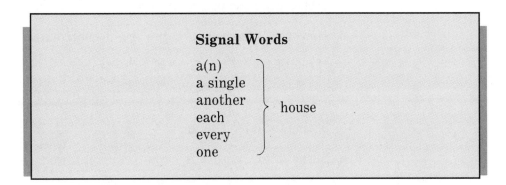

Signal Words

a(n)
a single
another   } house
each
every
one

- These signal words tell you that a plural noun usually follows:

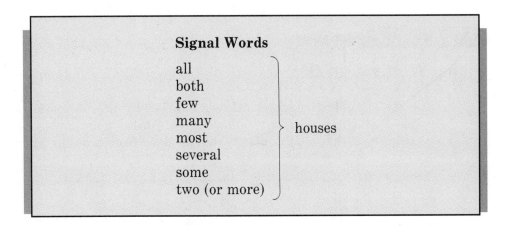

Signal Words

all
both
few
many   } houses
most
several
some
two (or more)

PRACTICE 2   Some of the following sentences contain incorrect singulars and plurals. Correct the errors. Put a *C* after correct sentences.

                      person
X 1. The brain of every ~~people~~ is divided into two parts: a left and a right

   side.

                     humans
  2. For all but a few ~~human~~, the left side of the brain specializes in verbal

   and logical thinking.

                 example
X 3. An everyday ~~examples~~ of primarily left-brain thinking is the ability

   to understand directions.

                       ways
X 4. Different in many important ~~way~~, the brain's right side processes visual and spatial information.

5. An example of primarily right-brain thinking is the ability to put together a jigsaw puzzle. **c**

6. However, each ~~sides~~ *side* of the brain contributes to the completion of every task.

7. The majority of right-handed individuals rely on the left side of their brains for language. **c**

✗ 8. Surprisingly, most left-handed ~~man~~ *men* and ~~woman~~ *women* depend on both sides of their brains for language.

PART C

Signal Words with *Of*

Many signal words are followed by *of . . .* or *of the. . . .* Usually, these signal words are followed by a **plural** noun (or a collective noun) because they really refer to one or more from a larger group.

one of the each of the	pictures is . . .
many of the a few of the lots of the	pictures are . . .

- *Be careful:* The signal words *one of the* . . . and *each of the* . . . are followed by a **plural** noun, but the verb is **singular** because only the signal word (*one* or *each*) is the real subject.*

> *One* of the coats *is* on sale.
>
> *Each* of the flowers *smells* sweet.

*For more work on this type of construction, see Chapter 24, "Present Tense (Agreement)," Part C.

PRACTICE 3 Fill in your own nouns in the following sentences. Use a different noun in each sentence. Answers will vary.

1. Since Jacob wrote each of his ____exams____ with care, the *A*'s came as no surprise.

2. You are one of the few ____people____ I know who can listen to the radio and watch television at the same time.

3. Naomi liked several of the new ____rock singers____ but remained faithful to her long-time favorites.

4. Many of the ____people____ on the beach carried picnic baskets.

5. Determined to win the Salesperson of the Year award, Clyde called on all of his ____clients____ two or three times a month.

6. One of my ____cars____ has a red racing stripe down the side.

7. Before spring, each of these old ____sheds____ will have to be demolished.

✗ 8. Although the weather bureau predicted rain, many of the ____students____ attended the rally anyway.

PRACTICE 4
Review

Proofread the following essay for errors in singular and plural nouns. Correct the errors above the lines.

Hot Off the Press

(1) Although it was certainly not the *New York Times* or the *Washington Post*, the first newspaper was a media not all that different from
                                    medium
today's tabloids.

✗ (2) In 59 B.C., the Roman government began to publish *Action Journal*, which carried many story of social events and political activities. (3)
                        stories
Roman men and woman could read about the births of childrens, as
            women   children
well as the marriages and deaths of other citizen. (4) The trials of
                                             citizens ✗
thiefs and other lawless persons—and their executions—were also
thieves
described. (5) In addition, this early newspaper reviewed the many spectacular show presented at the Colosseum.
         shows

(6) Several ~~century~~ *centuries* later, on another ~~continents~~ *continent*, the Chinese government began publishing a news sheet. ✗(7) Each government ~~officials~~ *official* could read about social and political occurrences, as well as about court intrigues and gossip. (8) Many ~~diplomat~~ *diplomats* also found out about natural ~~phenomenons~~ *phenomena*—like eclipses and meteors—which they believed were good or bad omens. (9) This court chronicle was the first printed newspaper. (10) It lasted for almost 1200 ~~year~~ *years* until the Chinese Empire fell in 1911.

(11) The main difference between both of these ~~newspaper~~ *newspapers* and today's American press is that they were state run and controlled. ✗(12) Roman and Chinese ~~inspector-generals~~ *inspectors-general* applied strict ~~criterions~~ *criteria* of censorship to every ~~articles~~ *article*. (13) In contrast, the modern press, freely written and circulated, was begun by Dutch merchants in the two ~~city~~ *cities* of Antwerp and Venice during the seventeenth century.

28

Pronouns

PART A   Defining Pronouns and Antecedents
PART B   Making Pronouns and Antecedents Agree
PART C   Referring to Antecedents Clearly
PART D   Special Problems of Case
PART E   Using Pronouns with -*Self* and -*Selves*

PART A

Defining Pronouns and Antecedents

Pronouns take the place of or refer to nouns, other pronouns, or phrases. The word that the pronoun refers to is called the **antecedent** of the pronoun.

What does "it" refer to?

> 1. *Clyde* ordered *baked chicken* because *it* is *his* favorite dish.
>
> 2. *Simone and Lee* painted *their* room.
>
> 3. *Doing heavy exercise on a hot day* can be dangerous since *it* can cause heart failure.

- In sentence 1, *it* refers to the antecedent *baked chicken*, and *his* refers to the antecedent *Clyde*.

- In sentence 2, *their* refers to the plural antecedent *Simone and Lee*.

- In sentence 3, *it* refers to the antecedent *doing heavy exercise on a hot day*. (This antecedent is a whole phrase.)

PRACTICE 1   In each sentence, a pronoun is circled. Write the pronoun first and then its antecedent as shown in the example.

Example	Have you ever wondered why we exchange rings in (our) wedding ceremonies?	our _____ we _____
	1. When a man buys a wedding ring, (he) follows an age-old tradition.	he _____ man _____
	2. Rich Egyptian grooms gave (their) brides gold rings five thousand years ago.	their _____ grooms _____
	3. To Egyptian couples, the ring represented eternal love; (it) was a circle without beginning or end.	it _____ ring _____
	4. By Roman times, gold rings had become more affordable, so ordinary people could also buy (them.)	them _____ rings _____
	5. Still, many a Roman youth had to scrimp to buy (his) bride a ring.	his _____ youth _____
	6. The first bride to slip a diamond ring on (her) finger lived in Venice about five hundred years ago.	her _____ bride _____
	7. The Venetians knew that setting a diamond in a ring was an excellent way of displaying (its) beauty.	its _____ diamond _____
	8. Nowadays, a man and a woman exchange rings to symbolize the equality of (their) relationship.	their _____ a man and a _____ woman _____

PART B

Making Pronouns and Antecedents Agree

A pronoun must *agree* with its antecedent in number and person.*

*For more work on pronoun agreement, see Chapter 13, "Revising for Consistency and Parallelism," Part B.

> 1. When *Tom* couldn't find *his* pen, *he* asked to borrow mine.
>
> 2. The three *sisters* wanted to start *their* own business.

Why is it "their"?

- In sentence 1, *Tom* is the antecedent of *his* and *he*. Since *Tom* is singular and masculine, the pronouns referring to Tom are also singular and masculine.

- In sentence 2, *sisters* is the antecedent of *their*. Since *sisters* is plural, the pronoun referring to sisters must also be plural.

As you can see from these examples, making pronouns agree with their antecedents is usually easy. However, three special cases can be tricky.

1. Indefinite Pronouns

anybody
anyone
everybody
everyone
nobody
no one
one
somebody
someone

Each of these words is **singular.** Any pronoun that refers to one of them must also be singular: *he, him, his, she,* or *her.*

> 3. *Anyone* can quit smoking if *he* or *she* wants to.
>
> 4. *Everybody* should do *his* or *her* best to keep the reception area uncluttered.

KNOW THIS: *

- *Anyone* and *everybody* require the singular pronouns *he, she, his,* and *her.*

In the past, writers used *he* or *him* to refer to both men and women. Now, however, many writers use *he or she, his or her,* or *him or her.* Of course, if *everyone* is a woman, use *she* or *her;* if *everyone* is a man, use *he* or *him.* For example:

Look at this:

> 5. Someone left her bracelet on the sofa.
>
> 6. Someone left his sport jacket in the cafeteria.

What's wrong with this?: Someone left their presents in the room.

PRACTICE 2   Fill in the correct pronoun and circle its antecedent. Make sure each pronoun agrees in number and person with its antecedent.

1. (Anyone) can become a good cook if _____ he or she _____ tries.

2. (Someone) dropped _____ her _____ lipstick behind the record cabinet.

3. (No one) in the mixed doubles let _____ his or her _____ guard down for a minute.

4. (Everybody) wants _____ his or her _____ career to be rewarding.

5. (Everyone) is entitled to _____ his or her _____ full pension.

6. (Mr. Hernow) will soon be here, so please get _____ his _____ contract ready.

7. (One) should wear a necktie that doesn't clash with _____ one's _____ suit.

8. The movie theater was so cold that (nobody) took off _____ his or her _____ coat.

2. Special Singular Antecedents

each (of) . . .
either (of) . . .
neither (of) . . .   } Each of these constructions is **singular.** Any pronoun that refers to one of them must also be singular.*
every one (of) . . .
one (of) . . .

---

7. *Neither* of the two men paid for *his* ticket to the wrestling match.

8. *Each* of the houses has *its* own special charm.

- The subject of sentence 7 is the singular *neither*, not *men;* therefore, the singular masculine pronoun *his* is required.

- The subject of sentence 8 is the singular *each*, not the plural *houses;* therefore, the singular pronoun *its* is required.

PRACTICE 3   Fill in the correct pronoun and circle its antecedent. Make sure each pronoun agrees in number and person with its antecedent.

---

*For more work on prepositional phrases, see Chapter 21, "The Simple Sentence," Part B.

✱ 1. ⟨Each⟩ of the men wanted to be ___his___ own boss.

✱ 2. ⟨One⟩ of the saleswomen left ___her___ sample case on the counter.

3. ⟨Every one⟩ of the colts has a white star on ___its___ forehead.

4. ⟨Neither⟩ of the actors knew ___his___ lines by heart.

5. ⟨Neither⟩ of the dentists had ___his or her___ office remodeled.

6. ⟨Each⟩ of these arguments has ___its___ flaws.

7. ⟨Every one⟩ of the houses has a swimming pool in ___its___ yard.

✱8. ⟨Either⟩ of these telephone answering machines will work very well if ___it___ is properly cared for.

3. Collective Nouns

Collective nouns represent a group of people but are usually considered **singular.** They usually take singular pronouns.

> 9. The *jury* reached *its* decision in three hours.
>
> 10. The debating *team* is well known for *its* fighting spirit.

- In sentence 9, *jury* is a collective noun. Although it has several members, the jury acts as a unit—as one. Therefore, the antecedent *jury* takes the singular pronouns *its*.

- In sentence 10, why does the collective noun *team* take the singular pronoun *its?*

Here is a partial list of collective nouns:

Be aware of these. ✱

Common Collective Nouns		
class	faculty	panel
college	flock	school
committee	government	society
company	group	team
family	jury	tribe

PRACTICE 4   Read each sentence carefully for meaning. Circle the antecedent and then fill in the correct pronoun.

1. A (family) should provide __its__ members with love and emotional support.

2. The (government) should reexamine __its__ domestic policy.

3. The (college) honored __its__ graduates with a reception.

4. The (company) has just begun to market a new pollution-free detergent that __it__ is proud of.

5. The (panel) will soon announce __its__ recommendations to the hospital.

✱ 6. The two (teams) gave __their__ fans a real show.

7. The (jury) deliberated for six days before reaching __its__ verdict.

✱ 8. After touring the Great Pyramid, the (class) headed back to Cairo in __its__ air-conditioned bus.

PART C

Referring to Antecedents Clearly

A pronoun must refer *clearly* to its antecedent. ✱Avoid vague, repetitious, or ambiguous pronoun reference.

1. Vague pronoun:	At the box office, *they* said that tickets were no longer available.
2. Revised: →	The cashier at the box office said . . .
	or
3. Revised: →	At the box office, I was told . . .

✱ ▪ In sentence 1, <u>who is *they?*</u> *They* does not clearly refer to an antecedent.

▪ In sentence 2, *they* is replaced by *the cashier.*

▪ In sentence 3, the problem is avoided by a change of language.*

*For more work on using exact language, see Chapter 15, "Revising for Language Awareness," Part A.

---

4. Repetitious pronoun: <u>In the article</u>, *it* says that Tyrone was a boxer.

5. Revised: ✱ ⎧ The article says that ...
              ⎪   *or*
6. Revised: ⎩ It says that ...

- In sentence 4, *it* merely repeats *article*, the antecedent preceding it.

- Use either the pronoun or its antecedent, but not both.

what's wrong w/ this →

---

7. Ambiguous pronoun: Mr. Tedesco told his son that *his* car had a flat tire.

8. Revised: Mr. Tedesco told his son that the younger man's car had a flat tire.

9. Revised: Mr. Tedesco told his son Paul that Paul's car had a flat tire.

- In sentence 7, *his* could refer either to Mr. Tedesco or to his son.

PRACTICE 5   Revise the following sentences, removing vague, repetitious, or ambiguous pronoun references. Make the pronoun references clear and specific. Answers may vary.

1. In this book it says that most ducks and geese travel between forty and sixty miles per hour.

   Revised: ___This book says that most ducks and geese travel between forty and___

   ___sixty miles per hour.___

2. On the radio they warned drivers that the Interstate Bridge was closed.

   Revised: ___The radio announcer warned drivers that the Interstate Bridge was___

   ___closed.___

3. Sandra told her friend that she shouldn't have turned down the promotion.

   Revised: ___Sandra told her friend Janet that Janet shouldn't have turned down___

   ___the promotion.___

Do evens

4. In North Carolina they raise tobacco.

   Revised: ___Tobacco is raised in North Carolina.___

   _____

5. The moving van struck a lamppost; luckily, no one was injured, but it was badly damaged.

   Revised: ___The moving van struck a lamppost; luckily, no one was injured, but___

   ___the lamppost was badly damaged.___

6. In this college, they require every entering student to take a hearing test.

   Revised: ___This college requries every entering student to take a hearing test.___

   _____

7. Professor Grazel told his parrot that he had to stop chewing telephone cords.

   Revised: ___Professor Grazel told his parrot that the bird had to stop chewing___

   ___telephone cords.___

8. Vandalism was so out of control at the local high school that they stole sinks and lighting fixtures.

   Revised: ___Vandalism was so out of control at the local high school that___

   ___vandals stole sinks and lighting fixtures.___

9. On the news, it said that the president hopes to spend more time with his family.

   Revised: ___The news anchor reported that the president hopes to spend more___

   ___time with his family.___

10. Mr. Highwater informed his cousin that his wholesale rug business was a success.

    Revised: ___Mr. Highwater informed his cousin Wes that Wes' wholesale rug___

    ___business was a success.___

11. The saleswoman at Wigged Out, she said I look like a rock star in this wig.

    Revised: ___The saleswoman at Wigged Out said that I look like a rock star in___

    ___this wig.___

12. I don't watch Sunday night wrestling because they show ten commercials an hour.

Revised: <u>I don't watch Sunday night wrestling because the station airs ten</u>

<u>commercials an hour.</u>

13. Keiko is an excellent singer, yet she has never taken a lesson in it.

Revised: <u>Keiko is an excellent singer, yet she has never taken a voice lesson.</u>

_____

14. Rosalie's mother said that she was glad that she had gone to night school.

Revised: <u>Rosalie's mother said that she was glad that Rosalie had gone to</u>

<u>night school.</u>

15. At my church, they run a soup kitchen for people who need a hot meal.

Revised: <u>My church runs a soup kitchen for people who need a hot meal.</u>

_____

PART D

Special Problems of Case

Personal pronouns take different forms depending on how they are used in a sentence. Pronouns can be **subjects, objects,** or **possessives.**
Pronouns used as **subjects** are in the **subjective case:**

noTe:
it's noT
"Him + me"

> 1. *He* and *I* go backpacking together.
> 2. The peaches were so ripe that *they* fell from the trees.

- *He, I,* and *they* are in the subjective case.

Pronouns that are **objects of verbs** or **prepositions** are in the **objective case.** Pronouns that are **subjects of infinitives** are also in the **objective case:**

> 3. A sudden downpour soaked *her.* (object of verb)
> 4. Please give this card to *him.* (object of preposition)
> 5. We want *them* to leave right now. (subject of infinitive)

- *Her, him,* and *them* are in the objective case.

Pronouns that **show ownership** are in the **possessive case:**

6. The carpenters left *their* tools on the windowsill.

7. This flower has lost *its* brilliant color.

- *Their* and *its* are in the possessive case.

Pronoun Case Chart

Singular	Subjective	Objective	Possessive
1st person	I	me	my (mine)
2nd person	you	you	your (yours)
	he	him	his (his)
	she	her	her (hers)
3rd person	it	it	its (its)
	who	whom	whose
	whoever	whomever	

Plural			
1st person	we	us	our (ours)
2nd person	you	you	your (yours)
3rd person	they	them	their (theirs)

Using the correct case is usually fairly simple, but three problems require special care.

1. Case in Compound Constructions

A **compound construction** consists of two nouns, two pronouns, or a noun and a pronoun joined by *and.* Make sure that both pronouns in a compound construction are in the correct case.

8. *Serge* and *I* went to the pool together.

9. Between *you* and *me*, this party is a bore.

- In sentence 8, *Serge* and *I* are subjects.

- In sentence 9, *you* and *me* are objects of the preposition *between.*

Never use *myself* as a substitute for either *I* or *me* in compound constructions.

PRACTICE 6 Determine the case required by each sentence and circle the correct pronoun.

1. (He, Him) and Harriet want to be police officers.

2. It was as if a barrier stood between my friend and (I, me).

3. He used the software and then returned it to Barbara and (I, me, myself).

4. The reporter's questions caught June and (we, us) off guard.

5. That price sounds fair to my brother and (I, me).
   omit + check

6. After work, Carl and (he, him) left for Bear Lake.

7. These charts helped (she, her) and (I, me) with our statistics homework.

8. Senator Grimley granted Diane and (she, her) an interview.
   omit + check

2. Case in Comparisons

Pronouns that complete **comparisons** may be in the **subjective, objective,** or **possessive** case:

---

10. His son is as stubborn as *he*. (subjective) *is*

11. The cutbacks will affect you more than *her*. (objective)

12. This essay is better organized than *mine*. (possessive)

To decide on the correct pronoun, simply complete the comparison mentally and then choose the pronoun that naturally follows:

see how to check →

---

13. She trusts him more than I ... (trust him).

14. She trusts him more than ... (she trusts) ... me.

■ Note that, in sentences 13 and 14, the case of the pronoun in the comparison can change the meaning of the entire sentence.

PRACTICE 7   Circle the correct pronoun.

1. Your hair is much shorter than (she, her, (hers)).

↗ 2. We tend to assume that others are more self-confident than ((we), us). *are...*

3. She is just as funny as ((he), him).

↗ 4. Is Hans as trustworthy as ((she) her)? *is...*

5. Although they were both air traffic controllers, he received a higher salary than ((she) her).

↗ 6. I am not as involved in this project as ((they) them). *are...*

7. Sometimes we become impatient with people who are not as quick to learn as ((we,) us).

8. Michael's route involved more overnight stops than (us, our, (ours)).

3. Use of *Who* (or *Whoever*) and *Whom* (or *Whomever*)

Who and **whoever** are the **subjective** case. **Whom** and **whomever** are the **objective** case.

> 15. *Who* is at the door?
>
> 16. For *whom* is that gift?
>
> 17. *Whom* is that gift for?

- In sentence 15, *who* is the subject.

- The same question is written two ways in sentences 16 and 17. In both, *whom* is the object of the preposition *for*.

- Sometimes, deciding on *who* or *whom* can be tricky:

he deserves it — subjective case

> 18. I will give the raise to *whoever* deserves it.
>
> 19. Give it to *whomever* you like.

- In sentence 18, *whoever* is the subject in the clause—*whoever deserves it.*

- In sentence 19, *whomever* is the object in the clause—*whomever you like.*

example: Voter registration drives attempt to enroll whoever is eligible to vote. He (not him) is eligible to vote.

*   If you have trouble deciding on *who* or *whom*, change the sentence to eliminate the problem.

> 20. I prefer working with people *whom* I don't know as friends.
> *or*
> I prefer working with people I don't know as friends.

PRACTICE 8   Circle the correct pronoun or rewrite the sentence to eliminate the problem.

1. (Who, Whom) will deliver the layouts to the pressroom?

   _____

2. To (who, whom) are you speaking?

   _____

3. (Who, Whom) prefers hiking to skiing?

   _____

4. For (who, whom) are those boxes piled in the corner?

   _____

5. She will marry (whoever, whomever) the astrologer decides upon.
   She will marry him — objective case

6. (Who, Whom) do you wish to invite to the open house?

   _____

7. At (who, whom) did the governor fling the cream pie?

   _____

8. I will hire (whoever, whomever) can use a computer and speak Korean.

   _____

example: The senior citizens can vote for whomever they wish. They can vote for him (not he).

PART E

Using Pronouns with -*Self* and -*Selves*

Pronouns with -*self* or -*selves* can be used in two ways—as reflexives or as intensives.

A reflexive pronoun indicates that someone did something to himself or herself:

> 1. My daughter Miriam felt very grown-up when she learned to dress *herself*.

- In sentence 1, Miriam did something to *herself*; she *dressed herself*. An intensive pronoun emphasizes the noun or pronoun it refers to:

> 2. Anthony *himself* was surprised at how relaxed he felt during the interview.

- In sentence 2, *himself* emphasizes that Anthony—much to his surprise—was not nervous at the interview.

The following chart will help you choose the correct reflexive or intensive pronoun.

	Antecedent	Reflexive or Intensive Pronoun
Singular	I	myself
	you	yourself
	he	himself
	she	herself
	it	itself
Plural	we	ourselves
	you	yourselves
	they	themselves

Note that in the plural *-self* is changed to *-selves*.

- *Be careful:* Do not use reflexives or intensives as substitutes for the subject of a sentence.

note this:

> Incorrect: Harry and *myself* will be there on time.
>
> Correct: Harry and *I* will be there on time.

PRACTICE 9   Fill in the correct reflexive or intensive pronoun. Be careful to make pronouns and antecedents agree.

1. Though he hates to cook, André __himself__ sautéed the mushrooms.

2. Tanya found __herself__ in a strange city with only the phone number of a cousin whom she had not seen for years.

3. Her computer automatically turns __itself__ on in the morning and off in the evening.

4. The librarian and I rearranged the children's section __ourselves__.

5. When it comes to horror films, I know that you consider __yourself__ an expert.

6. If they __themselves__ do not want to have the VCR repaired, why should we bother taking it to the shop?

7. After completing a term paper, I always buy __myself__ a little gift to celebrate.

8. Larry __himself__ was surprised at how quickly he was able to paint the shed.

PRACTICE 10 Review   Proofread the following paragraph for pronoun errors. Then write the correct pronoun above the line.

Mikimoto, the Pearl King

(1) Few businesspersons can boast a career as meteoric as ~~him~~ his, for Kokichi Mikimoto began as a noodle maker and became the king of the pearl industry.

(2) Born in 1858, Mikimoto was a dynamo even as a child. (3) The orphan made noodles at night and then sold ~~it~~ them, along with other products, throughout the day. (4) In his early twenties, he revived the pearl business in Toba, his home town. (5) ~~In Toba they had~~ fishermen ~~who~~ harvested pearls, but most made their money by selling the oysters for food. (6) Mikimoto urged fishermen to harvest oysters only for pearls. (7) Anyone who followed his advice risked losing ~~their~~ his or her livelihood because at that time oysters produced pearls only by chance.

(8) Mikimoto, he changed all that by discovering, over a grueling twelve years of trial and error, how to cultivate these white gems. (9) With his own hands, he bedded thousands of oysters under water, inserting foreign matter into each shell. (10) A few years later, he dove to examine each of the oysters hisself [himself] to see if they [it] had formed a pearl. (11) His wife complained that she lost her husband to an oyster; at one point, she even had to sell her best kimono to meet expenses. (12) Nevertheless, her [she] and Mikimoto stayed together. (13) In the end, Mikimoto's oysters made not only pearls but also the most valuable kind—perfectly round ones.

(14) Mikimoto's real genius, however, it lay in aggressive merchandising. (15) By 1900 he was selling pearls throughout Japan; fifteen years later, they [he] owned shops throughout the world. (16) He won legal battles in the United States and France to get his cultured pearls accepted as genuine, not artificial, gems. (17) He also knew how to generate publicity. (18) When fake pearls flooded the market during the 1930s, he bought quantities of it [them] and dramatically burned them. (19) At the height of his career, Mikimoto's twelve million oysters were producing 75 percent of the world's pearls. (20) His company had become the largest one of their [its] kind in the world. (21) Whomever [Whoever] wanted pearls probably had to go to Mikimoto.

(22) As he prospered, Mikimoto set up model communities for his workers; each of the communities provided housing and education for their [its] inhabitants. (23) At ninety, he was still juggling, a skill he learned as a youngster, for the amusement of his employees. (24) Up until he died in 1954 at the age of ninety-six, he had been actively in control of his pearl empire.

29

Prepositions

Prepositions are words like *about, at, behind, from, into, of, on,* and *with.*

Prepositions are often combined with other words to form fixed expressions. Determining the correct preposition in these expressions can sometimes be confusing. Below is a list of some troublesome expressions with prepositions. Consult a dictionary if you need help with others.*

Expressions with Prepositions

Expression	*Example*
according to	*According to* the directions, this flap fits here.
acquainted with	Tom became *acquainted with* his class-mates.
addicted to	He is *addicted to* soap operas.
afraid of	Tanya is *afraid of* flying.
agree on (a plan)	Can we *agree on* our next step?
agree to (another's proposal or to do something)	Roberta *agreed to* her secretary's request for a raise.
angry about or at (a thing)	Jake seemed *angry about* his meager bonus.
angry with (a person)	Sonia couldn't stay *angry with* Felipe.
apply for (a position)	By accident, the twins *applied for* the same job.
approve of	Do you *approve of* bilingual education?
argue about (an issue)	I hate *arguing about* money.
argue with (a person)	Edna *argues with* everyone about everything.

*For more work on prepositions, see Chapter 21, "The Simple Sentence," Part B.

capable of	Mario is *capable of* accomplishing anything he attempts.
complain about (a situation)	Patients *complained about* the long wait to see the dentist.
complain to (a person)	Knee-deep in snow, Jed vowed to *complain to* a maintenance person.
comply with	Each contestant must *comply with* contest regulations.
consist of	This article *consists of* nothing but false accusations and half-truths.
contrast with	The light blue shirt *contrasts* sharply *with* the dark brown tie.
convenient for	A 10:00 A.M. appointment will be *convenient for* Ms. Belgrade.
correspond with (write)	We *corresponded with* her for two months before we met.
deal with	Ron *deals* well *with* temporary setbacks.
depend on	Miriam can be *depended on* to say the embarrassing thing.
differ from (something)	A typewriter *differs from* a word processor.
differ with (a person)	Kathleen *differs with* you on the gun control issue.
different from	Children are often *different from* their parents.
displeased with	Mr. Withers was *displeased with* his doctor's advice to eat less fatty foods.
fond of	Ed is *fond of* his pet tarantula.
grateful for	Be *grateful for* good health and take steps to maintain it.
grateful to (someone)	The team was *grateful to* the coach for his inspiration and confidence.
identical with	Scott's ideas are often *identical with* mine.
inferior to	Saturday's performance was *inferior to* the one I saw last week.
in search of	I hate to go *in search of* change at the last moment before the toll.
interested in	Willa is *interested in* results, not excuses.
interfere with	That dripping faucet *interferes with* my concentration.

object to	Martin *objected to* the judge's comment.
protect against	This heavy wool scarf will *protect* your throat *against* the cold.
reason with	It's hard to *reason with* an angry person.
rely on	If Toni made that promise, you can *rely on* it.
reply to	He wrote twice, but the president did not *reply to* his letters.
responsible for	Kit is *responsible for* making two copies of each document.
sensitive to	Professor Godfried is *sensitive to* his students' concerns.
shocked at	We were *shocked at* the graphic violence in that PG-rated film.
similar to	Some poisonous mushrooms appear quite *similar to* the harmless kind.
specialize in	This disc jockey *specializes in* jazz of the 1920s and the 1930s.
succeed in	Oscar *succeeded in* painting the roof in under five hours.
superior to	It's clear that the remake is *superior to* the original.
take advantage of	Celia *took advantage of* the snow day to visit the science museum.
worry about	Never *worry about* more than one problem at a time.

PRACTICE Review Proofread this essay for preposition errors. Cross out the errors and write corrections above the lines.

Dr. Daniel Hale Williams, Pioneer Surgeon

(1) In a lifetime of many successes, Dr. Daniel Hale Williams' greatest achievement was to pioneer open-heart surgery.

(2) Young Williams, an African-American who grew up in the mid-1800s, knew poverty. (3) He relied ~~to~~ on his wits to get by, becoming, in turn, a shoemaker, musician, and barber. (4) At the age of twenty-two, he met

Dr. Henry Palmer, who soon saw he was capable ~~on~~ [of] becoming a physician. (5) Williams' medical education, the usual one at the time, consisted ~~in~~ [of] a two-year apprenticeship with Dr. Palmer, followed by three years at the Chicago Medical College where he specialized ~~on~~ [in] surgery.

(6) It was an exciting time in medicine, for surgeons had just started using antiseptics in order to protect patients ~~for~~ [against] infection. (7) "Dr. Dan," as he was now called, became an expert ~~on~~ [in] the new surgical techniques and a leader in Chicago's medical and African-American communities. (8) In 1891, he succeeded ~~with~~ [in] opening Provident Hospital, the first interracial hospital in the United States. (9) There, African-Americans were assured first-rate medical care; moreover, black interns and nurses received thorough professional training.

(10) It was to Provident Hospital that frightened friends brought James Cornish on the evening of July 9, 1893. (11) Near death, the young man had received a deep knife gash near his heart during a fight. (12) Sensitive to the dangerous situation, Dr. Williams decided to operate immediately. (13) According ~~with~~ [to] eyewitnesses, he first made a six-inch incision and removed Cornish's fifth rib. (14) Then, he repaired a torn artery and stitched up the punctured sac surrounding the heart. (15) Fifty-one days later, Cornish left the hospital, recovered and deeply grateful ~~for~~ [to] Dr. Williams ~~to~~ [for] his life. (16) The age of open-heart surgery had begun.

(17) Much lay ahead for Dr. Williams. (18) He was responsible ~~to~~ [for] reorganizing the Freedmen's Hospital at Howard University from 1894 to 1898; in 1913, he accepted an invitation from the American College of Surgeons and succeeded ~~on~~ [in] becoming its only African-American charter member. (18) The high point of his life, however, remained that night in 1893.

30

Adjectives and Adverbs

PART A   Defining and Using Adjectives and Adverbs
PART B   The Comparative and the Superlative
PART C   A Troublesome Pair: *Good/Well*

PART A

Defining and Using Adjectives and Adverbs

Adjectives and **adverbs** are two kinds of descriptive words. **Adjectives** describe or modify nouns or pronouns:

> 1. A *black* cat slept on the piano.
> 2. We felt *giddy*.

- *Black* describes the noun *cat*.

- *Giddy* describes the pronoun *we*.

Adverbs describe or modify verbs, adjectives, or other adverbs:

> 3. Joe dances *gracefully*.
> 4. Birgit is *extremely* tall.
> 5. He travels *very* rapidly on that skateboard.

- *Gracefully* describes the verb *dances*. How does Joe dance? He dances *gracefully*.

- *Extremely* describes the adjective *tall*. How tall is Birgit? She is *extremely* tall.

- *Very* describes the adverb *rapidly*, which describes the verb *travels*. How rapidly does he travel? He travels *very* rapidly.

409

Many adjectives can be changed into adverbs by adding an -*ly* ending. For example, *glad* becomes *gladly*, *hopeful* becomes *hopefully*, *awkward* becomes *awkwardly*.

Note the pairs on this list; they are easily confused:

Adjectives	Adverbs
awful	awfully
bad	badly
poor	poorly
quick	quickly
quiet	quietly
real	really
sure	surely

6. The fish tastes *bad*.

7. It was *badly* prepared.

- In sentence 6, the adjective *bad* describes the noun *fish*.

- In sentence 7, the adverb *badly* describes the verb *was prepared*.

PRACTICE 1   Circle the correct adjective or adverb in parentheses. Remember that adjectives modify nouns or pronouns; adverbs modify verbs, adjectives, or adverbs.

1. Have you ever seen (real, really) emeralds?

2. Professor Barnett always dresses (neat, neatly).

3. We will (glad, gladly) take you on a tour of the Crunchier Cracker factory.

4. Lee, a (high, highly) skilled electrician, rewired this entire house last year.

5. She made a (quick, quickly) stop at the photocopy machine.

6. It was (awful, awfully) cold today; the weather was terrible.

7. The fans from Cleveland (enthusiastic, enthusiastically) clapped for the Browns.

8. Are you (sure, surely) this bus stops in Dusty Gulch?

9. He (hasty, (hastily)) wrote the essay, leaving out several important ideas.

10. It was a funny joke, but the comedian told it (bad, (badly)).

11. Tina walked (careful, (carefully)) down the ((icy), icily) road.

12. Sam rides (poor, (poorly)), although he grew up around horses.

13. Sasha the crow is an ((unusual,) unusually) pet and a ((humorous,) humorously) companion.

14. The painting is not (actual, (actually)) a Picasso; in fact, it is a (real, (really)) bad imitation.

15. It is an (extreme, (extremely)) hot day, and I could (sure, (surely)) go for some ((real,) really) orange juice.

PART B

The Comparative and the Superlative

The **comparative** of an adjective or adverb compares two persons or things:

---

1. Ben is *more creative* than Robert.

2. Marcia runs *faster* than the coach.

- In sentence 1, Ben is being compared with Robert.

- In sentence 2, Marcia is being compared with the coach.

The **superlative** of an adjective or adverb compares three or more persons or things:

---

3. Sancho is the *tallest* of the three brothers.

4. Marion is the *most intelligent* student in the class.

- In sentence 3, Sancho is being compared to the other two brothers.

- In sentence 4, Marion is being compared to all the other students in the class.

Adjectives and adverbs of one syllable usually form the **comparative** by adding *-er*. They form the **superlative** by adding *-est*.

Adjective	Comparative	Superlative
fast	fast*er*	fast*est*
smart	smart*er*	smart*est*
tall	tall*er*	tall*est*

Adjectives and adverbs of more than one syllable usually form the **comparative** by using *more*. They form the **superlative** by using *most*.

Adjective	Comparative	Superlative
beautiful	*more* beautiful	*most* beautiful
brittle	*more* brittle	*most* brittle
serious	*more* serious	*most* serious

Note, however, that adjectives that end in *-y* (like happy, lazy, and sunny) change the *-y* to *-i* and add *-er* and *-est*.

Adjective	Comparative	Superlative
happy	happ*ier*	happ*iest*
lazy	laz*ier*	laz*iest*
sunny	sunn*ier*	sunn*iest*

PRACTICE 2   Write the comparative or the superlative form of the words in parentheses. Remember: Use the comparative to compare two items; use the superlative to compare more than two. Use *-er* or *-est* for one-syllable words; use *more* or *most* for words of more than one syllable.*

1. The ocean is _____colder_____ (cold) than we thought it would be.

*If you have questions about spelling, see Appendix 1, "Spelling," Part F.

2. Please read your lines again, ___more slowly___ (slowly) this time.

3. She is the ___youngest___ (young) actress in the company.

4. Which of these two roads is the ___shorter___ (short) route?

5. Which of these three highways is the ___shortest___ (short) route?

6. Dimitri is the ___busiest___ (busy) person I know.

7. You clipped the hedges ___more quickly___ (quickly) last time.

8. That red felt hat with feathers is the ___most outlandish___ (outlandish) one I've seen.

9. Today is ___warmer___ (warm) than yesterday, but Thursday was the ___warmest___ (warm) day of the month.

10. The gold and diamond watch you selected is the ___most expensive___ (expensive) one in the shop.

11. Each one of Woody's stories is ___funnier___ (funny) than the last.

12. That trip to Mexico was the ___most enjoyable___ (enjoyable) vacation our family has ever taken.

13. As a rule, mornings in Los Angeles are ___hazier___ (hazy) than afternoons.

14. Is Pete ___taller___ (tall) than Louie? Is Pete the ___tallest___ (tall) player on the team?

15. If you don't do these experiments _____ (carefully), you will blow up the chemistry lab.

16. This farmland is much ___rockier___ (rocky) than the farmland in Iowa.

17. Dissecting a worm is ___easier___ (easy) than I thought it would be.

18. Therese says that Physics 201 is the ___most challenging___ (challenging) course she has ever taken.

19. Tim's early experience proved __more valuable__ (valuable) than he once thought; growing up in an alcoholic home has made

him a __more understanding__ (understanding) drug counselor
than he might have been otherwise.

20. Mr. Wells is the __wisest__ (wise) and __most
experienced__ (experienced) leader in the community.

PART C

A Troublesome Pair: *Good/Well*

Adjective	Comparative	Superlative
good	better	best
bad	worse	worst
Adverb	**Comparative**	**Superlative**
well	better	best
badly	worse	worst

Be especially careful not to confuse the adjective **good** with the
adverb **well:**

1. Jessie is a *good* writer.
2. She writes *well.*

- *Good* is an **adjective** modifying *writer.*
- *Well* is an **adverb** modifying *writes.*

Note that *well* can be used as an adjective meaning *in good health.* For
example, *I feel well today.*

PRACTICE 3   Fill in either the adjective *good* or the adverb *well* in each blank.

1. How __well__ do you understand Chinese?

2. He is a __good__ tree surgeon who does his job __well__.

3. Cornbeef definitely goes ___well___ with cabbage.

4. He may not take phone messages very ___well___, but he is a
   ___good___ typist.

5. Alice is a ___good___ competitor; she performs ___well___
   under pressure.

✓PRACTICE 4   Fill in the correct comparative or superlative of the word in parentheses.

1. Gina likes rock climbing ___better___ (good) than fishing.

2. Jason is the ___worst___ (bad) designer in the company.

3. Of the two sisters, Lee is the ___better___ (good) marks-
   woman.

4. September is the ___best___ (good) month of the year for bird
   watching.

5. Your cold seems ___worse___ (bad) today than it was yesterday.

PRACTICE 5   Proofread the following essay for adjective and adverb errors. Correct
Review   errors by writing above the lines.

Julia Morgan, Architect

(1) Julia Morgan was one of San Francisco's ~~most~~ finest architects, as

well as the first woman licensed as an architect in California. (2) In 1902,

successfully
Morgan became the first woman to finish ~~successful~~ the program in

architecture at the School of Fine Arts in Paris. (3) Returning to San

Francisco, she opened her own office and hired and trained a very talented

eventually
staff that ~~eventual~~ grew to thirty-five full-time architects. (4) Her first

major commission was to reconstruct the Fairmont Hotel, one of the

best   badly
city's ~~bestest~~-known sites, which had been damaged ~~bad~~ in the 1906

earthquake. (5) Morgan earned her reputation by designing elegant

inexpensive
homes and public buildings out of ~~inexpensively~~ and available materials

really well
and by treating her clients ~~real good~~. (6) She went on to design more

than eight hundred residences, stores, churches, offices, and educational buildings, most of them in California.

(7) Her ~~bestest~~ **best** customer was William Randolph Hearst, one of the country's ~~most rich~~ **richest** newspaper publishers. (8) Morgan designed newspaper buildings and more than twenty pleasure palaces for Hearst in California and Mexico. (9) She maintained a private plane and pilot to keep her moving from project to project. (10) The ~~most big~~ **biggest** and ~~famousest~~ **most famous** of her undertakings was ~~sure~~ **surely** San Simeon. (11) Morgan worked on it ~~steady~~ **steadily** for twenty years. (12) She converted a large ranch overlooking the Pacific into a hilltop Mediterranean village composed of three of the ~~beautifullest~~ **most beautiful** guest houses in the world. (13) The ~~larger~~ **largest** of the three was designed to look like a cathedral and incorporated Hearst's fabulous art treasures from around the world. (14) The finished masterpiece had 144 rooms and was more larger than a football field. (15) San Simeon is now one of the most visited tourist attractions in California and seems to grow ~~popularer~~ **more popular** each year.

31

The Apostrophe

PART A   The Apostrophe for Contractions
PART B   The Apostrophe for Ownership
PART C   Special Uses of the Apostrophe

The Apostrophe for Contractions

Use the **apostrophe** in a **contraction** to show that letters have been omitted.

---

1. *I'll* buy that coat if it goes on sale.

2. At nine *o'clock* sharp, the store opens.

- *I'll*, a contraction, is a combination of *I* and *will*. *Wi* is omitted.
- The contraction *o'clock* is the shortened form of *of the clock*.

Be especially careful in writing contractions that contain pronouns:

Common Contractions

I + am = I'm	you + have = you've
I + have = I've	you + will or shall = you'll
I + will or shall = I'll	we + are = we're
he + will or shall = he'll	let + us = let's
she + is or has = she's	they + are = they're
it + is or has = it's	they + have = they've
you + are = you're	who + is or has = who's

PRACTICE 1   Proofread these sentences and supply any missing apostrophes in the contractions above the lines.

1. Bears havent been seen here in years.

2. Lets go for a dip in the lake.

3. Heres to success in your new career!

4. As soon as youre ready, Ill start the car.

5. Shell arrive at 1:30 A.M., and thats why theyre at the airport.

6. Whos been eating Fig Newtons in the physics lab?

7. Its eight oclock and time for my favorite TV show.

8. If hes home, theres no reason why we cant drop in unexpectedly.

9. Its raining so hard that shell have to swim home.

10. Whats in the leather satchel?

11. They have been studying ballet with a woman whos danced with the Bolshoi in Russia.

12. Theres no doubt that youre the best postal worker in the county.

13. As soon as were in Raleigh, lets call Uncle Charles.

14. Shes a cat lover, and hes allergic to fur.

15. We cant agree about anything, but dont worry; we will all have a wonderful time.

PART B

The Apostrophe for Ownership

Use the apostrophe to show ownership: add an *'s* if a noun or indefinite pronoun (like, someone, anybody, and so on) does not already end in *-s*:

> 1. I cannot find my *friend's* book bag.
>
> 2. *Everyone's* right to privacy should be respected.
>
> 3. *John and Julio's* apartment has velvet wallpaper.

- The *friend* owns the book bag.

- *Everyone* owns the right to privacy.

- Both John and Julio own one apartment. The apostrophe follows the compound *John and Julio.*

> Add only an apostrophe to show ownership if the word already ends in -s:

4. My *aunts' houses* are filled with antiques.

5. The *knights'* table was round.

6. *Mr. Jonas' company* manufactures sporting goods and uniforms.

- My *aunts* (at least two of them) own the houses.

- The *knights* (at least two) own the table.

- *Aunts* and *soldiers* already end in -s, so only an apostrophe is added.

- *Mr. Jonas* owns the company. *Mr. Jonas* already ends in -s, so only an apostrophe is added.

> Note that *possessive pronouns never take an apostrophe: his, hers, theirs, ours, yours, its:*

7. *His* car gets twenty miles to the gallon, but *hers* gets only ten.

8. That computer is *theirs; ours* is coming soon.

PRACTICE 2   Proofread the following sentences and add apostrophes where necessary to show ownership. In each case, ask yourself if the word already ends in -s. Put a *C* after any correct sentences.

1. Bills bed has a down comforter.

2. Martha and Davids house is a log cabin made entirely by hand.

3. Somebodys wedding ring was left on the sink.

4. During the eighteenth century, ladies dresses were heavy and uncomfortable.

5. Have you seen the childrens watercolor set?

√ 6. Mr. James fried chicken and rice dish was crispy and delicious.

7. The class loved reading about Ulysses travels.

8. The Surgeon Generals latest report was just released.

√ 9. Our citys water supply must be protected.

10. They found his ticket, but they cannot find hers. c

11. Every spring, my neighbors porch is completely covered with purple wisteria.

12. Jacks Health Club just opened at Locust and Broad.

13. Celias final, a brilliant study of pest control on tobacco farms, received a high grade.

14. The mens locker room is on the right; the womens is on the left.

15. Several ambassadors met to discuss the problem of world hunger. c

PART C

Special Uses of the Apostrophe

Use an apostrophe in certain expressions of time:

> 1. I desperately need a *week's* vacation.

■ Although the week does not own a vacation, it is a vacation of a week— *a week's vacation.*

Use an apostrophe to pluralize letters, numbers, and words that normally do not have plurals:

> 2. Be careful to cross your *t*'s.
>
> 3. Your *8*'s look like *F*'s.
>
> 4. Don't use so many *but*'s in your writing.

hours worth in a months time

Use an apostrophe to show omitted numbers:

---

5. The class of '72 held its annual reunion last week.

PRACTICE 3   Proofread these sentences and add an apostrophe wherever necessary.

1. Cross your *t*'s and dot your *i*'s.

2. I would love a *month*'s vacation on a dude ranch.

3. Too many *and*'s make this paragraph dull.

4. Those *9*'s look crooked.

5. You certainly put in a hard day's work!

PRACTICE 4
Review   Proofread the following paragraph for apostrophe errors. Correct the errors by adding apostrophes above the lines where needed and crossing out those that do not belong.

The True Story of Superman

(1) Sometimes, things just don't work out right. (2) That's how the creators of Superman felt for a long time.

(3) Superman's first home wasn't the planet Krypton, but Cleveland. (4) There in 1933, Superman was born. (5) Jerry Siegel's story, "Reign of Superman," accompanied by Joe Shuster's illustrations, appeared in the boys' own magazine, *Science Fiction*. (6) Later, the teen-agers continued to develop their idea. (7) Superman would come to earth from a distant planet to defend freedom and justice for ordinary people. (8) He would conceal his identity by living as an ordinary person himself. (9) Siegel and Shuster hoped their character's strength and morality would boost people's spirits during the Great Depression.

(10) At first, the creators weren't able to sell their concept; then, Action Comics' Henry Donnenfield bought it. (11) In June of 1938, the first

Superman comic hit the stands. (12) Superman's success was immediate and overwhelming. (13) Finally, Americans had a hero who wouldn't let them down! (14) Radio and TV shows, movie serials, feature films, and generations of superheros followed.

(15) While others made millions from their idea, Siegel and Shuster didn't profit from its success. (16) They produced Superman for Action Comics for a mere fifteen dollars a page until they were fired a few years later, when Joe Shusters eyes began to fail. (17) They sued, but they lost the case. (18) For a long time, both lived in poverty, but they continued to fight. (19) In 1975, Siegel and Shuster finally took their story to the press; the publicity won them lifelong pensions. (20) The two mens long struggle had ended with success.

32

The Comma

PART A   Commas for Items in a Series
PART B   Commas with Introductory Phrases, Transitional
Expressions, and Parentheticals
PART C   Commas for Appositives
PART D   Commas with Nonrestrictive and Restrictive Clauses
PART E   Commas for Dates and Addresses
PART F   Minor Uses of the Comma

PART A

Commas for Items in a Series

Use commas to separate the items in a series:*

1. You need *bolts, nuts,* and *screws.*

2. I will be happy to *read your poem, comment on it,* and *return it to you.*

3. *Mary paints pictures, Robert plays the trumpet,* but *Sam just sits and dreams.*

Do not use commas when all three items are joined by *and* or *or:*

4. I enjoy *biking* and *skating* and *swimming.*

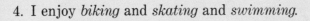

*For work on parallelism, see Chapter 13, "Revising for Consistency and Parallelism," Part C.

PRACTICE 1   Punctuate the following sentences.

1. At the banquet, Ed served a salad of juicy red tomatoes, crunchy green lettuce, and stringless snap beans.

2. As a nurse's aide, Reva learned to dispense medication, disinfect wounds, and take blood samples.

Hermano ✓ 3. Ali visited Santa Barbara, Concord, and Berkeley.

4. The woman of the 1990s often tries to be a wife, a mother, and a career woman.

Erica 5. The police found TV sets, blenders, and blow dryers stacked to the ceiling in the abandoned house.

6. I spent my ski vacation waiting in lift lines, sliding out of control on the ice, and hobbling around with my leg in a cast.

7. Don't eat strange mushrooms, walk near the water, or feed the squirrels.

8. Everyone in class had to present an oral report, write a term paper, and take a final.

Alfred ✓ 9. We brought a Ouija board, a Scrabble set, and a Boggle game to the party.

10. To earn a decent wage, make a comfortable home, and educate my children—that is my hope.

PART B

Commas with Introductory Phrases, Transitional Expressions, and Parentheticals

✗ Use a comma after most introductory phrases of more than two words:*

> ✓
> 1. *By four in the afternoon,* everybody wanted to go home.
> 2. *After the game on Saturday,* we all went dancing.

*For more work on introductory phrases, see Chapter 14, "Revising for Sentence Variety," Part C.

Use commas to set off transitional expressions:

> 3. Ferns, *for example*, need less sunlight than flowering plants.
>
> 4. Instructors, *on the other hand*, receive a lower salary than assistant professors.

Use commas to set off parenthetical elements:

> 5. *By the way*, where is the judge's umbrella?
>
> 6. Nobody, *it seems*, wants to eat the three-bean salad.

- *By the way* and *it seems* are called parenthetical expressions because they appear to be asides, words not really crucial to the meaning of the sentence. They could almost appear in parentheses: (*By the way*) *where is the judge's umbrella?*

Other common parenthetical expressions are *after all, actually, as a matter of fact,* and *by the way.*

PRACTICE 2   Punctuate the following sentences.

1. Frankly I always suspected that you were a born saleswoman.

2. General Marsh it seems to me trusted only one or two of his advisers.

3. At two o'clock in the morning we were awakened by whippoorwills.

Cathy √ 4. All twelve jurors by the way felt that the defendant was innocent.

5. On every April Fool's Day he tries out a new, dumb practical joke.

6. In fact Lucinda should never have written that poison-pen letter.

7. Close to the top of Mt. Everest the climbers paused for a tea break.

8. To tell the truth that usher needs a lesson in courtesy.

Roy √ 9. Before you leave if you have time take a look at my new CD player.

10. These apples to tell the truth were organically grown in his back yard.

11. During the power blackout people tried to help each other.

12. Near the end of the driveway, a large lilac bush bloomed and brightened the yard.

13. He prefers, as a rule, serious news programs to the lighter sitcoms.

14. To sum up, the committee appointed Mr. Choi to head the investigation.

15. During my three years in Minnesota, I learned how to deal with snow.

PART C

Commas for Appositives

Use commas to set off appositives:*

> 1. Yoko, *our new classmate,* is our best fielder.
>
> 2. *A humorous and charming man,* he was a great hit with my parents.
>
> 3. This is her favorite food, *ketchup sandwiches.*

- Appositive phrases like *our new classmate, a humorous and charming man,* and *ketchup sandwiches* rename or describe nouns and pronouns—*Yoko, he, favorite food.*

> 4. Henry *the Fat* was a great king.
>
> 5. My friend *Bill* owns two stereos.

what's the difference? just one word, no meed for ,

- One-word appositives are generally not set off by commas.

PRACTICE 3   Punctuate the following sentences.

1. Hulk Hogan, the popular wrestler, advises his fans to drink milk and say their prayers.

*For more work on appositives, see Chapter 14, "Revising for Sentence Variety," Part D.

Greg ✓ 2. Cold fruit, especially strawberries, makes a refreshing dessert.

3. David, a resident nurse, hopes to become a pediatrician.

4. I don't trust that tire, the one with the yellow patch on the side.

Robyn ✓ 5. Tanzania, a small African nation, exports cashew nuts.

6. Watch out for Phil, a man whose ambition rules him.

7. Sheila, a well-known nutritionist, lectures at public schools.

8. A real flying ace, Helen will teach a course in sky diving.

9. We support the Center for Science in the Public Interest, a consumer education and protection group.

10. The voters, mostly blue-collar workers, elected the new mayor by a wide margin.

PART D

Commas with Nonrestrictive and Restrictive Clauses

A **relative clause** is a clause that begins with *who, which,* and *that* and that modifies a noun or pronoun. There are two kinds of relative clauses: **nonrestrictive** and **restrictive.***

A **nonrestrictive relative clause** is not essential to the meaning of the sentence:

> 1. Raj, *who is a part-time aviator,* loves to tinker with machines of all kinds.

- *Who is a part-time aviator* is a relative clause describing *Raj.* It is a nonrestrictive relative clause because it is not essential to the meaning of the sentence. The point is that *Raj loves to tinker with machines of all kinds.*

- **Commas** set off the nonrestrictive relative clause.

A **restrictive relative clause** is essential to the meaning of the sentence:

> 2. People *who do their work efficiently* make good students.

*For more work on nonrestrictive and restrictive clauses, see Chapter 14, "Revising for Sentence Variety," Part D.

- *Who do their work efficiently* is a relative clause describing *people*. It is a restrictive relative clause because it is *essential* to the meaning of the sentence. Without it, sentence 2 would read, *People make good students.* But the point is that certain people make good students—*those who do their work efficiently.*

- Restrictive relative clauses *do not* require commas.

PRACTICE 4   Set off the nonrestrictive relative clauses in the following sentences with commas. Note that *which* usually begins a nonrestrictive relative clause and *that* usually begins a restrictive clause. Remember: Restrictive relative clauses are *not* set off by commas.

1. Olive who always wanted to go into law enforcement is a detective in the Eighth Precinct.

2. The tall-masted clipper ships that once sailed the Atlantic are rarely seen nowadays.

3. Polo which is not played much in the United States is very popular in England.

4. A person who always insists upon telling you the truth is sometimes a pain in the neck.

5. Statistics 101 which is required for the business curriculum demands concentration and perseverance.

6. Therese who is from Hawaii recently married Julio who is from Argentina.

7. This small shop sells furniture that is locally handcrafted.

8. His uncle who rarely eats meat consumes enormous quantities of vegetables, fruits, and grains.

9. Pens that slowly leak ink can be very messy.

10. Valley Forge which is the site of Washington's winter quarters draws many tourists every spring and summer.

PART E

Commas for Dates and Addresses

Use commas to separate the elements of an address:

> 1. I live at *300 West Road, Stamford, Connecticut.*
>
> 2. We moved from *10–15 Allen Circle, Morristown, New Jersey,* to *Farland Lane, Dubuque, Iowa.*

Use commas to separate the elements of a date:

> 3. The sociologists arrived in Tibet on *Monday, January 18, 1992,* and plan to stay for two years.
>
> 4. *By June 20, 1994,* I expect to have completed my B.A. in physical education.

✳ Do not use a comma with a single-word address or date preceded by a preposition:

> 5. John DeLeon arrived from Baltimore *in January* and will be our new shortstop this season.

PRACTICE 5   Punctuate the following sentences.

1. On Monday, November 9, 1970, Harold became a father.

   Sallu ✓ 2. My French teacher taught in Senegal from July 15, 1987, to September 1, 1990.

3. The factory's new address is 3001 Hughes Street, Atlanta, Georgia.

   Teresa ✓ 4. All the mail from 20 Riverview, Skokie, Illinois, was mistakenly delivered to 20 Riverview, Chicago, Illinois.

5. A UFO was thought to have landed in the Antarctic on December 31, 1982, but no one was there to verify it.

6. Monday, February 14 is Valentine's Day; I expect flowers from my fiancé, who's on a business trip to Washington, D.C.

7. A new sub shop opened at 300 North Avenue, San Jose, Texas.

8. On Wednesday, January 16, 1975, the weatherman predicted a blizzard.

9. My sister attended both Reed College in Portland, Oregon, and Roosevelt University in Chicago, Illinois.

10. Alexandria, Egypt, was named after Alexander the Great.

PART F

Minor Uses of the Comma

Use a comma after answering a question with *yes* or *no:*

> 1. *No,* I'm not sure about that answer.

Use a comma when addressing someone directly and specifically naming the person spoken to:

> 2. *Alicia,* where did you put my law books?

Use a comma after interjections like *ah, oh,* and so on:

> 3. *Ah,* these artichokes are delicious.

Use a comma to contrast:

> 4. Harold, *not Roy,* is my scuba-diving partner.

PRACTICE 6   Punctuate the following sentences.

1. Yes, London often exports plays and musicals to Broadway.

Juanita ✓ 2. Well, did you call a taxi?

3. The defendant, ladies and gentlemen of the jury, does not even own a red plaid jacket.

4. Cynthia, have you ever camped in the Pacific Northwest?

5. No, I most certainly will not marry you.

6. Oh, I love the meadows in the spring!

Antonette 7. The class feels, Professor Molinor, that your grades are unrealistically high.

8. He said "march," not "swagger."

9. Perhaps, but I still don't think that the carburetor fits there.

10. We all agree, Ms. Crawford, that you are the best jazz bassist around.

**PRACTICE 7
Review**   Proofread the following paragraph for comma errors—either missing commas or commas used incorrectly. Correct the errors above the lines.

The Pyramids of Giza

(1) A wonder of the ancient world, the pyramids of Giza, Egypt, still inspire awe. (2) Built nearly five thousand years ago, the largest of these tombs, was ordered by Khu-fu, a powerful pharaoh of ancient Egypt. (3) The two smaller pyramids nearby belonged to his successors, his son Khafre and his grandson Menkaure. (4) The three pyramids—together with the Sphinx, many temples, and causeways—comprised a ceremonial complex for the dead not far from the Nile River.

(5) We marvel today at the ability of this ancient people to build such colossal structures without the benefit of work animals or machinery, not even the wheel. (6) The Great Pyramid, for instance, is 750 square feet and 480 feet high, roughly the size of Shea Stadium filled in with solid

rock to a height of forty stories. (7) More than 100,000 workers, who were probably peasants forced into service, cut two-and-a-half-ton limestone blocks from quarries on the other side of the Nile, ferried them across the river, and then dragged them up ramps to be fitted exactly in place. (8) Experts estimate that 2.3 million blocks had to be moved over a period of more than twenty years to complete the project.

Danielle → (9) Perhaps the greatest wonder, however, is that these structures have lasted. (10) Countless other buildings, statues, and monuments have been constructed and admired, yet have fallen into ruin since these magnificent structures were built. (11) The pyramids are considered all but indestructible. (12) It has been said, in fact, that they could withstand a direct hit by an atomic bomb.

33

Mechanics

PART A   Capitalization
PART B   Titles
PART C   Direct Quotations
PART D   Minor Marks of Punctuation

PART A

Capitalization

Always capitalize the following: *nationalities, religions, races, countries, cities, months, days of the week, documents, organizations,* and *holidays:*

> 1. The *Protestant* church on the corner will offer *French* and *English* courses starting *Thursday, June 3.*

Capitalize the following *only* when they are used as part of a proper noun: *streets, buildings, organizations, historical events, titles,* and *family relationships:*

> 2. We saw *Professor Rodriguez* at *Silver Hall,* where he was delivering a talk on the *Spanish Civil War.*

Do not capitalize these same words when they are used as common nouns:

> 3. We saw the professor at the lecture hall, where he was delivering a talk on a civil war.

Capitalize geographic locations but not directions:

> 4. The tourists went to the *South* for their winter vacation.
>
> 5. Go south on this boulevard for three miles.

Capitalize academic subjects only if they refer to a specific named and numbered course:

> 6. Have you ever studied psychology?
>
> 7. Last semester, I took *Psychology* 101.

PRACTICE 1   Capitalize wherever necessary in the following sentences. Put a *C* after each correct sentence.

1. She's from australia, but she has lived in boston for years.
            A   B

2. Many people would rather not live on state street, that winding road
                              S   S

    near the waterfront.

3. When senator wong laughed, his assistant felt relieved.
         S   W

④ Next semester, I expect to take english 33, sociology, and history.
                           E

5. Tell the driver to turn north at the next intersection. C
                   N

6. I like going to the northwest in the spring because the weather there

    is so invigorating.
       C   P

7. He took child psychology 70 but found it much more difficult than his

    first course in psychology.
                    W I

8. She attended college in the west indies.
                                P

9. Has anyone seen the professor who teaches philosophy 101?
                    M   D   Y   N   P

⑩ Last summer, I spent memorial day at yellowstone national park.
    T   M   L

11. The truman memorial library is a beautiful building; it houses all of
      P   T

    president truman's papers.

12. No one has seen the judge for a week. C

13. The new manager at general industries corporation is mr. lawrence bungle.

14. Some species of birds spend winters in the south.

15. Everyone who visits New mexico loves it.

PART B

Titles

Capitalize all the words of a title except for short prepositions, short conjunctions, and the articles *the*, *an*, and *a*. But always capitalize the first and last words of the title, no matter what they are:

> 1. I liked *The Color Purple* but found *The House on the River* slow reading.

Underline the titles of long works: *books,** *newspapers, television shows, magazines, plays, record albums, movies, operas,* and *films.*

Put quotation marks around shorter works or parts of longer ones: *articles, short stories, poems, songs, paintings, scenes from plays,* and *chapters from full-length books.*

> 2. Have you read Hemingway's "The Killers" yet?
>
> 3. We are assigned "The Money Market" in *Essentials of Economics* for homework in my marketing course.

- "The Killers" is a short story.

- "The Money Market" is a chapter in the full-length book *Essentials of Economics.*

Do not underline or use quotation marks around the titles on your own papers.

*The titles and parts of sacred books are not underlined and are not set off by quotation marks: Job 5:6, the Koran 1:14, and so on.

PRACTICE 2   Capitalize these titles correctly. Do not underline or use quotation marks in this practice.

      T   F   I
1. the first immigrants
      A T   T
2. a trip through the Netherlands
      M   J   J
3. making jams and jellies
      A D   G
4. a dangerous game
      W   E   A   S   V
5. why every american should vote
      N   P   S   S
6. nuclear power: safe or sorry?
      H   B   S
7. how to build a sailboat
      T   Q   T
8. the quark theory
      S   O
9. starting over
      A B   D   M
10. a boy, a dog, and a murder
      P   W   P
11. parents without partners
      T   V   F
12. the value of friendship
      W   W   D
13. what I would do with $50,000
      T   C   W   W
14. three causes of world war II
      T   F   E
15. the fate of the earth

PRACTICE 3   Wherever necessary, underline or place quotation marks around each title in the sentences below so that the reader will know at a glance what type of work the title refers to. Put a *C* after any correct sentence.

Example   Two of the best short stories in that volume are "Rope" and "The New Dress."

1. Bob Smiley became the host of a new television show, <u>The Gigantic Jackpot</u>.

2. The <u>Kansas City Star</u> often prints articles on fashion. One appeared last week called "Hemlines: Up or Down?"

3. In addition to our text, <u>Introduction to Psychology</u>, Professor Gelato assigned two books, <u>Interpretation of Dreams</u> by Freud and <u>Best Short Stories of the Modern Age</u>.

4. The Orpheum Theater Company is performing <u>The School for Scandal</u> all this month.

5. Our Saturday movie binge included <u>Journey to the Forbidden Planet</u>, <u>Moon Monsters</u>, and seven boxes of popcorn.

6. For helpful information on buying a compact disk player, read "Choosing a Sound System" in this month's <u>Popular Electronics</u>.

7. As part of the wedding ceremony, the preacher read passages from the Bible and from the poetry of Walt Whitman. c

8. The songs on the album <u>Women's Railroad Blues</u> have some wonderfully descriptive titles like "Chicago Bound Blues" and "Mr. Brakeman, Let Me Ride Your Train."

9. I have to write a term paper comparing <u>The House of the Seven Gables</u>, a novel, with "The Raven," a poem.

10. The compact version of the <u>Oxford English Dictionary</u>, including a magnifying glass, costs ninety-five dollars.

PART C

Direct Quotations

Use quotation marks* to enclose the exact words of the speaker:

> 1. He said, "These are the best seats in the house."

- The direct quotation is preceded by a comma or a colon.
- The first letter of the direct quotation is capitalized.
- Periods always go *inside* the quotation marks.

*For more work on direct and indirect quotations, see Chapter 13, "Revising for Consistency and Parallelism," Part D.

> 2. He asked, "Where are my tickets?"
>
> 3. Stewart yelled, "I don't like beans!"

■ Question marks and exclamation points go inside the quotation marks if they are part of the direct words of the speaker.

> 4. "That was meant for the company," he said, "but if you wish, you may have it."
>
> 5. "The trees look magnificent," she exclaimed. "It would be fun to climb them all."

■ In sentence 4, the quotation is one single sentence interrupted by *he said*. Therefore, a comma is used after *he said*, and *but* is not capitalized.

■ In sentence 5, the quotation consists of two different sentences. Thus a period follows *exclaimed*, and the second sentence of the quotation begins with a capital letter.

PRACTICE 4 Insert quotation marks where necessary in each sentence. Capitalize and punctuate correctly.

1. The sign reads don't even think about parking here.

2. Can you direct me to the central bus stop he asked.

3. Alexander Pope wrote to err is human, to forgive divine.

4. Jim wondered why have I been having such good luck lately

5. Well, it takes all kinds she sighed

6. The report stated no one responded to the crisis in time.

7. He exclaimed you look terrific in those jeweled sandals

8. The article said Most American children do poorly in geography.

9. These books on ancient Egypt look interesting he replied but I don't have time to read them now.

10. Although the rain is heavy she said we will continue harvesting the corn.

11. Give up caffeine and get lots of rest the doctor advised.

12. This final is easy he whispered to himself it is a guaranteed *A*.

13. We haven't gone fishing for a month he complained and we really miss it

14. The label warns this product should not be taken by those allergic to aspirin.

15. Red, white, and blue Ronald said are my favorite colors

PART D

Minor Marks of Punctuation

1. The Colon

Use a colon to show that a direct quotation will follow or to introduce a list:*

> 1. This is the opening line of his essay: "The airplane is humanity's greatest invention."
>
> 2. There are four things I can't resist in warm weather: fresh mangoes, a sandy beach, cold drinks, and a hammock.

Use a colon to separate the chapter and verse in a reference to the Bible or to separate the hour and minute:

> 3. This quotation comes from Genesis 1:1.
>
> 4. It is now exactly 4:15 P.M.

---

*Avoid using a colon after any form of the verb *to be* or after a preposition.

2. Parentheses

Use parentheses to enclose a phrase or word that is not essential to the meaning of the sentence:

> 5. Herpetology (the study of snakes) is a fascinating area of zoology.
>
> 6. She left her home town (Plunkville) to go to the big city (Fairmount) in search of success.

3. The Dash

Use a dash to emphasize a portion of a sentence or to interrupt the sentence with an added element:

> 7. This is the right method—the only one—so we are stuck with it.

The colon, parentheses, and the dash should be used sparingly.

PRACTICE 5   Punctuate these sentences with colons, dashes, or parentheses.

1. Calvin asked for the following two light bulbs, a pack of matches, a lead pencil, and a pound of grapes.

2. They should leave by 11 30 P.M.

3. The designer's newest fashions magnificent leather creations were generally too expensive for the small chain of clothing stores.

4. Harvey the only Missourian in the group remains unconvinced.

5. She replied, "This rock group The Woogies sounds like all of the others I've heard this year."

6. If you eat a heavy lunch as you always do remember not to go swimming immediately afterwards.

7. By 9:30 P.M., the new zoologist (a Dr. Smittens) had operated on the elephant.

8. Note these three tips for hammering in a nail: hold the hammer at the end of the handle, position the nail carefully, and watch your thumb.

9. Whenever Harold Garvey does his birdcalls at parties—as he is sure to do—everyone begins to yawn.

10. Please purchase these things at the hardware store: masking tape, thumbtacks, a small hammer, and some sandpaper.

PRACTICE 6
Review
Proofread the following essay for errors in capitalization, quotation marks, colons, parentheses, and dashes. Correct the errors by writing above the lines.

The Passion of Thomas Gilcrease

(1) Thomas Gilcrease, a descendent of Creek Indians, became an instant Millionaire when oil was discovered on his homestead in 1907. (2) He spent most of his fortune collecting objects that tell the story of the American frontier, particularly of the Native American experience. (3) The Thomas Gilcrease Institute of American History and Arts in Tulsa, Oklahoma, is the result of his lifelong passion.

(4) This huge collection—more than 10,000 works of art, 90,000 historical documents, and 250,000 Native American artifacts—spans the centuries from 10,000 B.C. to the 1950s. (5) Awed visitors can view nearly 200 George Catlin paintings of Native American life. (6) They can walk among paintings and bronze sculptures by Frederic Remington with names like "The Coming and Going of the Pony Express" that call up images of the West. (7) Museum-goers can admire Thomas Moran's watercolors that helped persuade Congress to create Yellowstone, the

first national park. (8) In addition, visitors are treated to works by modern Native Americans, such as the display of wood sculptures by the
C
cherokee Willard Stone.

(9) The museum also houses many priceless documents an original
           D   I   ∧
copy of the declaration of independence, the oldest known letter written
                N   W
from the new world, and the papers of Hernando Cortés. (10) A new glass storage area even allows visitors to view the 80 percent of the holdings that are not on display. (11) Thousands of beaded moccasins and buckskin dresses line the shelves, and a collection of magnificent war bonnets hangs from brackets.

(12) When the Gilcrease Museum opened its doors on May 2, 1949, *Life* declared "it is the best collection of art and literature ever assembled on the American frontier and the Indian. (13) Thousands of visitors agree.

Appendix 1

Spelling

PART A   Suggestions for Improving Your Spelling
PART B   Spotting Vowels and Consonants
PART C   Doubling the Final Consonant (in Words of One Syllable)
PART D   Doubling the Final Consonant (in Words of More Than One Syllable)
PART E   Dropping or Keeping the Final *E*
PART F   Changing or Keeping the Final *Y*
PART G   Adding *-S* or *-ES*
PART H   Choosing *IE* or *EI*
PART I   Spelling Lists

PART A   Suggestions for Improving Your Spelling

Accurate spelling is an important ingredient of good writing. No matter how interesting your ideas are, if your spelling is poor, your writing will not be effective.

Some Tips for Improving Your Spelling

- **Look closely at the words on the page.** Use any tricks you can to remember the right spelling. For example, "The *a*'s in *separate* are separated by an *r*," or "*Dessert* has two *s*'s because you want two desserts."

- **Use a dictionary.** Even professional writers frequently check spelling in a dictionary. As you write, underline the words you are not sure of and look them up when you write your final draft. If locating words in the dictionary is a real problem for you, consider a "poor speller's dictionary." Ask your professor to recommend one.

- **Keep a list of the words you misspell.** Look over your list whenever you can and keep it handy as you write.

- **Look over corrected papers for misspelled words** (often marked *sp.*). Add these words to your list. Practice writing each word three or four times.

- **Test yourself.** Use flash cards or have a friend dictate words from your list or from this chapter.

- **Review the basic spelling rules explained in this chapter.** Take time to learn the material; don't rush through the entire chapter all at once.

- **Study the spelling list on pages 451–452,** and test yourself on these words.

- **Read through Appendix 2, "Look-Alikes/Sound-Alikes,"** for commonly confused words (*their, there,* and *they're,* for instance). The practices in that chapter will help you eliminate some common spelling errors from your writing.

PART B   Spotting Vowels and Consonants

To learn some basic spelling rules, you must know the difference between vowels and consonants.

> The **vowels** are *a, e, i, o,* and *u.*
> The **consonants** are *b, c, d, f, g, h, j, k, l, m, n, p, q, r, s, t, v, w, x,* and *z.*
> The letter *y* can be either a vowel or a consonant, depending on its sound:
>
> **daisy**   **sky**

- In each of these words, *y* is a vowel because it has a vowel sound: an *ee* sound in *daisy* and an *i* sound in *sky.*

> **yellow**   **your**

- In both *yellow* and *your, y* is a consonant because it has the consonant sound of *y.*

PRACTICE 1   Write *v* for vowel and *c* for consonant in the space on top of each word. Be careful of the *y.*

Example |

$$\frac{c}{h}\ \frac{v}{o}\ \frac{c}{p}\ \frac{v}{e}\ \frac{c}{d}$$

1. $\frac{c}{h}\ \frac{v}{a}\ \frac{c}{l}\ \frac{c}{l}$

2. $\frac{c}{r}\ \frac{v}{e}\ \frac{c}{l}\ \frac{v}{y}$

3. $\frac{c}{p}\ \frac{v}{e}\ \frac{c}{r}\ \frac{c}{h}\ \frac{v}{a}\ \frac{c}{p}\ \frac{c}{s}$

4. $\frac{c}{y}\ \frac{v}{a}\ \frac{c}{w}\ \frac{c}{n}$

5. $\frac{v}{i}\ \frac{c}{n}\ \frac{c}{s}\ \frac{c}{t}\ \frac{v}{e}\ \frac{v}{a}\ \frac{c}{d}$

6. $\frac{c}{j}\ \frac{v}{u}\ \frac{c}{m}\ \frac{c}{p}$

7. $\frac{c}{q}\ \frac{v}{u}\ \frac{v}{a}\ \frac{c}{l}\ \frac{v}{i}\ \frac{c}{f}\ \frac{v}{y}$

8. $\frac{c}{h}\ \frac{v}{i}\ \frac{c}{d}\ \frac{c}{d}\ \frac{v}{e}\ \frac{c}{n}$

9. $\frac{c}{f}\ \frac{v}{o}\ \frac{c}{r}\ \frac{c}{g}\ \frac{v}{e}$

10. $\frac{c}{b}\ \frac{v}{y}\ \frac{c}{s}\ \frac{c}{t}\ \frac{v}{a}\ \frac{c}{n}\ \frac{c}{d}\ \frac{v}{e}\ \frac{c}{r}$

PART C   Doubling the Final Consonant (in Words of One Syllable)

When you add a suffix or an ending that begins with a vowel (like *-ed, -ing, -er, -est*) to a word of one syllable, double the final consonant *if* the last three letters of the word are *consonant-vowel-consonant* or *c-v-c.*

plan + ed = planned   swim + ing = swimming

thin + est = thinnest   light + er = lighter

- *Plan, swim,* and *thin* all end in *cvc;* therefore, the final consonants are doubled.

- *Light* does not end in *cvc;* therefore, the final consonant is not doubled.

PRACTICE 2 Which of the following words should double the final consonant? Check to see whether the word ends in *cvc.* Then add the suffixes *-ed* and *-ing.*

	Word	Last Three Letters	-ed	-ing
Example	drop	cvc	dropped	dropping
	boil	vvc	boiled	boiling
	1. tan	cvc	tanned	tanning
	2. brag	cvc	bragged	bragging
	3. rip	cvc	ripped	ripping
	4. mail	vvc	mailed	mailing
	5. stop	cvc	stopped	stopping
	6. peel	vvc	peeled	peeling
	7. shift	vcc	shifted	shifting
	8. wrap	cvc	wrapped	wrapping
	9. ask	vcc	asked	asking
	10. chat	cvc	chatted	chatting

PRACTICE 3 Which of the following words should double the final consonant? Check for *cvc.* Then add the suffixes *-er* or *-est.*

	Word	Last Three Letters	-er	-est
Example	wet	cvc	wetter	wettest
	cool	vvc	cooler	coolest
	1. deep	vvc	deeper	deepest
	2. short	vcc	shorter	shortest
	3. fat	cvc	fatter	fattest
	4. slim	cvc	slimmer	slimmest
	5. red	cvc	redder	reddest
	6. green	vvc	greener	greenest
	7. moist	vcc	moister	moistest

8. clean	vvc	cleaner	cleanest
9. dim	cvc	dimmer	dimmest
10. bright	ccc	brighter	brightest

PART D Doubling the Final Consonant (in Words of More Than One Syllable)

When you add a suffix that begins with a vowel to a word of more than one syllable, double the final consonant *if*

(1) the last three letters of the word are *cvc, and*

(2) the accent or stress is on the *last* syllable.

> ✓ **begin + ing = beginning**   **control + ed = controlled**

- *Begin* and *control* both end in *cvc.*

- In both words, the stress is on the last syllable: *be-gin', con-trol'.* (Pronounce the words aloud and listen for the correct stress.)

- Therefore, *beginning* and *controlled* double the final consonant.

>   **listen + ing = listening**   **visit + ed = visited**

- *Listen* and *visit* both end in *cvc.*

- However, the stress is *not* on the last syllable: lis'-ten, vis'-it.

- Therefore, *listening* and *visited do not* double the final consonant.

PRACTICE 4   Which of the following words should double the final consonant? First, check for *cvc;* then check for the final stress. Then add the suffixes -*ed* and -*ing.*

Word	Last Three Letters	-*ed*	-*ing*
Example repel	cvc	repelled	repelling
enlist	vcc	enlisted	enlisting
1. expel	cvc	expelled	expelling
2. happen	cvc	happened	happening
3. polish	vcc	polished	polishing
4. admit	cvc	admitted	admitting
5. offer	cvc	offered	offering
6. prefer	cvc	preferred	preferring
7. commit	cvc	committed	committing
8. pardon	cvc	pardoned	pardoning
9. compel	cvc	compelled	compelling
10. answer	cvc	answered	answering

PART E   Dropping or Keeping the Final *E*

When you add a suffix that begins with a vowel (like *-able, -ence, -ing*), drop the final *e*.

When you add a suffix that begins with a consonant (like *-less, -ment, -ly*), keep the final *e*.

move + ing = moving   **pure + ity = purity**

- *Moving* and *purity* both drop the final *e* because the suffixes *-ing* and *-ity* begin with vowels.

home + less = homeless   **advertise + ment = advertisement**

- *Homeless* and *advertisement* keep the final *e* because the suffixes *-less* and *-ment* begin with consonants.

Here are some exceptions to memorize:

argument	manageable
awful	noticeable
courageous	truly
judgment	simply

PRACTICE 5   Add the suffix shown to each word.

Example | hope + ing = ___hoping___
            | hope + ful = ___hopeful___

1. love + able = ___lovable___
2. love + ly = ___lovely___
3. pure + ly = ___purely___
4. pure + er = ___purer___
5. complete + ing = ___completing___

6. complete + ness = ___completeness___
7. enforce + ment = ___enforcement___
8. enforce + ed = ___enforced___
9. arrange + ing = ___arranging___
10. arrange + ment = ___arrangement___

PRACTICE 6   Add the suffix shown to each word.

Example | come + ing = ___coming___
            | rude + ness = ___rudeness___

1. guide + ance = ___guidance___
2. manage + ment = ___management___
3. dense + ity = ___density___
4. complete + ly = ___completely___
5. motive + ation = ___motivation___

6. sincere + ly = ___sincerely___
7. notice + able = ___noticeable___
8. response + ible = ___responsible___
9. judge + ment = ___judgment___
10. fame + ous = ___famous___

PART F   Changing or Keeping the Final Y

When you add a suffix to a word that ends in -*y*, change the *y* to *i* if the letter before the *y* is a consonant.

Keep the final *y* if the letter before the *y* is a vowel.

happy + ness = happiness   portray + ed = portrayed

- The *y* in *happiness* is changed to *i* because the letter before the *y* is a consonant, *p*.

- The *y* in *portrayed* is not changed because the letter before it is a vowel, *a*.

However, when you add -*ing* to words ending in *y*, always keep the *y*:

copy + ing = copying   delay + ing = delaying

Here are some exceptions to memorize:

day + ly = daily   pay + ed = paid

lay + ed = laid   say + ed = said

PRACTICE 7   Add the suffix shown to each of the following words.

Example | marry + ed = _married_
             | buy + er = _buyer_

1. try + ed = _tried_   6. wealthy + est = _wealthiest_
2. vary + able = _variable_   7. day + ly = _daily_
3. worry + ing = _worrying_   8. duty + ful = _dutiful_
4. pay + ed = _paid_   9. display + s = _displays_
5. enjoy + able = _enjoyable_   10. occupy + ed = _occupied_

PRACTICE 8   Add the suffixes in parentheses to each word.

1. beauty (fy)   _beautify_   4. angry (er)   _angrier_
           (ful)   _beautiful_   (est)   _angriest_
           (es)   _beauties_   (ly)   _angrily_

2. lonely (er)   _lonelier_   5. study (es)   _studies_
           (est)   _loneliest_   (ous)   _studious_
           (ness) _loneliness_   (ing)   _studying_

3. betray (ed)   _betrayed_   6. busy   (ness) _business_
           (ing)   _betraying_   (er)   _busier_
           (al)   _betrayal_   (est)   _busiest_

PART G Adding *-S* or *-ES*

Nouns usually take an *-s* or an *-es* ending to form the plural. Verbs take an *-s* or *-es* in the third person singular (*he*, *she*, or *it*).

Add *-es* instead of *-s* if a word ends in *ch*, *sh*, *ss*, *x*, or *z* (the *-es* adds an extra syllable to the word):

box + es = boxes   **crutch + es = crutches**   **miss + es = misses**

Add *-es* instead of *-s* for most words that end in *o*:

do + es = does   **hero + es = heroes**

echo + es = echoes   **tomato + es = tomatoes**

go + es = goes   **potato + es = potatoes**

Here are some exceptions to memorize:

pianos   sopranos

radios   solos

When you change the final *y* to *i* in a word,* add *-es* instead of *-s:*

fry + es = fries   **marry + es = marries**   **candy + es = candies**

PRACTICE 9 Add *-s* or *-es* to the following nouns and verbs, changing the final *y* to *i* when necessary.

Example | sketch ___sketches___
            | echo ___echoes___

1. watch ___watches___
2. tomato ___tomatoes___
3. reply ___replies___
4. company ___companies___
5. bicycle ___bicycles___

6. piano ___pianos___
7. donkey ___donkeys___
8. dictionary ___dictionaries___
9. boss ___bosses___
10. hero ___heroes___

PART H Choosing *IE* or *EI*

Write *i* before *e*, except after *c*, or in an *ay* sound like *neighbor* or *weigh*.

achieve, niece   **deceive**   **vein**

- *Achieve* and *niece* are spelled *ie*.
- *Deceive* is spelled *ei* because of the preceding *c*.
- *Vein* is spelled *ei* because of its *ay* sound.

*See Part F of this appendix for more on changing or keeping the final *y*.

However, words with a *shen* sound are spelled with an *ie* after the *c:* *ancient, conscience, efficient, sufficient.*

Here are some exceptions to memorize:

either	seize
neither	society
foreign	their
height	weird

PRACTICE 10   Pronounce each word out loud. Then fill in either *ie* or *ei.*

1. bel _i_ _e_ ve
2. _e_ _i_ ght
3. effic _i_ _e_ nt
4. n _e_ _i_ ther
5. cash _i_ _e_ r
6. th _e_ _i_ r
7. ch _i_ _e_ f
8. soc _i_ _e_ ty

9. rec _e_ _i_ ve
10. fr _i_ _e_ nd
11. consc _i_ _e_ nce
12. h _e_ _i_ ght
13. ach _i_ _e_ ve
14. v _e_ _i_ n
15. for _e_ _i_ gn
16. perc _e_ _i_ ve

PRACTICE 11
Review

Test your knowledge of the spelling rules in this appendix by adding suffixes to the following words. If you have trouble, the part in which the rule appears is shown in parentheses.

	Part			Part
1. nerve + ous _nervous_	(E)	11. carry + ing _carrying_	(F)
2. feed + ing _feeding_	(C)	12. tomato + s/es _tomatoes_	(G)
3. beach + s/es _beaches_	(G)	13. admit + ing _admitting_	(D)
4. drop + ed _dropped_	(C)	14. test + er _tester_	(C)
5. hope + ing _hoping_	(E)	15. tasty + est _tastiest_	(F)
6. study + s/es _studies_	(G)	16. sip + ing _sipping_	(C)
7. busy + ness _business_	(F)	17. believe + able _believable_	(E)
8. manage + ment _management_	(E)	18. commit + ment _commitment_	(D)
9. radio + s/es _radios_	(G)	19. deny + al _denial_	(F)
10. occur + ed _occurred_	(D)	20. day + ly _daily_	(F)

PRACTICE 12
Review

Circle the correctly spelled word in each pair.

1. writting, (writing)
2. (receive,) recieve
3. begining, (beginning)
4. greif, (grief)
5. grammer, (grammar)

6. (piece,) peice
7. (resourceful,) resourcful
8. (argument,) arguement
9. (marries,) marrys
10. thier, (their)

PART I Spelling Lists

Commonly Misspelled Words

Here is a list of words that are often misspelled. As you can see, they are words that you might use daily in speaking and writing. The trouble spot, the part of each word that is usually spelled incorrectly, has been put in bold type.

To help yourself learn these words, you might copy each one twice, making sure to underline the trouble spot, or copy the words on flash cards and have someone test you.

1. across	18. doesn't	35. jewelry
2. address	19. eighth	36. judgment
3. answer	20. embarrass	37. knowledge
4. argument	21. environment	38. maintain
5. athlete	22. exaggerate	39. mathematics
6. beginning	23. familiar	40. meant
7. behavior	24. finally	41. necessary
8. calendar	25. government	42. nervous
9. career	26. grammar	43. occasion
10. conscience	27. height	44. opinion
11. crowded	28. illegal	45. optimist
12. definite	29. immediately	46. particular
13. describe	30. important	47. perform
14. desperate	31. integration	48. perhaps
15. different	32. intelligent	49. personnel
16. disappoint	33. interest	50. possess
17. disapprove	34. interfere	51. possible

52. **prefer**	60. ridi**c**ulous	68. **tau**ght
53. pre**jud**ice	61. sep**arat**e	69. temperature
54. privi**lege**	62. sim**ilar**	70. **th**orough
55. pro**bab**ly	63. **since**	71. thought
56. **psy**chology	64. speech	72. ti**red**
57. **pur**sue	65. stren**gth**	73. until
58. ref**ere**nce	66. su**cce**ss	74. wei**gh**t
59. r**hyth**m	67. **sur**prise	75. written

Personal Spelling List

In your notebook, keep a list of words that *you* misspell. Add words to your list from corrected papers and from the exercises in this appendix. First copy each word as you misspelled it, underlining the trouble spot; then write the word correctly. Study your list often. Use this form:

As I Wrote It	**Correct Spelling**
1. _probly_____	probably_____
2. _____	_____
3. _____	_____
4. _____	_____
5. _____	_____

PRACTICE 13
Review

Proofread the following essay for spelling errors. (Be careful: There are misspelled words from both the exercises in this appendix and the spelling list.) Correct any errors by writing above the lines.

Leap Years

                    knowledge
(1) It is common ~~knowlege~~ that a leap year has 366 days, instead of the usual
                                    February
365, and that we add the extra day to ~~Febuary~~. (2) Everyone knows that a leap
      occurs
year ~~occurrs~~ every four years and always in an even-numbered year. (3) How-
                                                    important
ever, many people do not know why leap year is ~~important~~ in our calendar.
                    ancient
(4) The ~~aneeint~~ Roman leader Julius Caesar first addressed the need for a
                                                    length
leap year when his astronomers decided that the ~~lenth~~ of the year was 365 days
and six hours. (5) To make the Roman calendar regular, he declared that

beginning
begining in 46 B.C., most years would be 365 days long, with every fourth year

receiving
recieving an extra day.

mathematics
(6) Caesar's mathmatics did not give the perfect answer because his astron-

omers' year was longer than the actual year by eleven minutes and fourteen sec-

difference
onds. (7) Over time, the diffrence between the calendar year and the true solar

separated
year grew larger. (8) By 1582, ten days seperated them. (9) Finally, Pope Greg-

dropped   ruled
ory XIII droped ten days and rulled that every fourth year would continue to be

divided
a leap year, except for century years that could not be evenly dividded by 400.

(10) That is, 1700, 1800, and 1900 were not leap years, but the year 2000 will be

one.

immediately
(11) Some nations immedietely switched to the new calendar, but England

until
and its colonies in North America did not adopt this version untill 1752. (12)

countries   calendar
Many east European countrys and China did not accept the corrected calender

until this century and lagged thirteen days behind the rest of the world before

they changed.

Appendix 2

Look-Alikes/Sound-Alikes

A/an/and

1. *A* is used before a word beginning with a consonant or a consonant sound.

    a **man**   *a* **house**

    a **union** (*u* in *union* is pronounced like the consonant *y*)

2. *An* is used before a word beginning with a vowel (*a, e, i, o, u*) or silent *h.*

    an **igloo**   *an* **apple**

    an **hour** (*h* in *hour* is silent)

3. *And* joins words or ideas together.

    Edward *and* Ralph are taking the same biology class.

    He is very honest, *and* most people respect him.

PRACTICE 1   Fill in *a, an,* or *and.*

1. The administration building is __an__ old brick house on top of a __a__ hill.

2. __An__ artist __and__ two musicians share that studio.

3. The computer in my office has __an__ amber screen __and__ __a__ hard-disk drive.

4. Joyce __and__ Luis saw __a__ great movie last night.

5. For lunch, Ben ate __a__ ham sandwich, __an__ apple, __and__ two bananas.

Accept/except

1. *Accept* means to receive.

    That college *accepts* only women.   I *accepted* his offer of help.

2. *Except* means other than or excluding.

    Everyone *except* Ron thinks it's a good idea.

PRACTICE 2   Fill in *accept* or *except*.

1. Jan has read all of Shakespeare's comedies ___except___ one.

2. Please ___accept___ my apologies.

3. Unable to ___accept___ defeat, the boxer protested the decision.

4. Sam loves all his courses ___except___ chemistry.

5. ___Except___ for Elizabeth, everyone here speaks fluent Spanish.

Affect/effect

1. *Affect* (verb) means to have an influence on or to change.

   Her father's career as a lawyer *affected* her decision to go to law school.

2. *Effect* (noun) means the result of a cause or an influence.

   Careful proofreading had a positive *effect* on the grades Carl received for his compositions.

3. *Effect* is also a verb that means *to cause*.

   The senate is attempting to *effect* changes in foreign policy.

PRACTICE 3   Fill in *affect* or *effect*.

1. You are mistaken if you think alcohol will not ___affect___ your judgment.

2. Attractive, neat clothing will have a positive ___effect___ on an employment interviewer.

3. The Everglades were drastically ___affected___ by the drought.

4. Hot, humid summers always have the ___effect___ of making me lazy.

5. We will not be able to ___effect___ these changes without the cooperation of the employees and the union.

Buy/by

1. *Buy* means to purchase.

   She *buys* new furniture every five years.

2. *By* means near, by means of, or before.

   He walked right *by* and didn't say hello.

   By sunset, we had finished the harvest.

PRACTICE 4   Fill in *buy* or *by*.

1. You can't __buy__ happiness, but many people try.

2. Lee __buys__ sand __by__ the ton for his masonry business.

3. Please drop __by__ the box office and __buy__ three tickets for Friday night.

4. __By__ __buying__ out his partners, Joe became sole owner of the firm.

5. __By__ the time he is thirty, Emil will have earned his M.A.

Been/being

1. *Been* is the past participle form of *to be*. *Been* is usually used after the helping verbs *have, has,* or *had.*

   I *have been* to that restaurant before.

   She *has been* a poet for ten years.

2. *Being* is the *-ing* form of *to be*. *Being* is usually used after the helping verbs *is, are, am, was,* or *were.*

   They *are being* helped by the salesperson.

   Rhonda *is being* foolish and stubborn.

PRACTICE 5   Fill in *been* or *being*.

1. Have you __been__ to Rib Heaven yet?

2. Pete thinks his phone is __being__ taped.

3. Are you __being__ secretive, or have I __been__ imagining it?

4. Yoko has never __been__ to Omaha!

5. __Being__ a dynamic teacher is Chris's goal.

It's/its

1. *It's* is a contraction of *it is* or *it has*. If you cannot substitute *it is* or *it has* in the sentence, you cannot use *it's*.

   _It's_ a ten-minute walk to my house.   **_It's_ been a nice party.**

2. *Its* is a possessive and shows ownership.

   The kitten rolled playfully on *its* side.

   Industry must do *its* share to curb inflation.

PRACTICE 6   Fill in *it's* or *its.*

1. Put the contact lens in __its__ case, please.

2. __It's__ about time H.T. straightened up the rubble in his room.

3. Dan's truck has a dent in __its__ fender.

4. The medical profession is supposed to be __its__ own watchdog.

5. You know __it's__ cold when the pond has ice on __its__ surface.

Know/knew/no/new

1. *Know* means to have knowledge or understanding.

2. *Knew* is the past tense of the verb *know.*

   Carl *knows* he has to finish by 6 P.M.

   The police officer *knew* the quickest route to the pier.

3. *No* is a negative.

   He is *no* longer dean of academic affairs.

4. *New* means recent, fresh, unused.

   I like your *new* hat.

PRACTICE 7   Fill in *know, knew, no,* or *new.*

1. I __know__ he's __new__ in town, but this is ridiculous.

2. If I __knew__ then what I __know__ now, I wouldn't have made so many mistakes when I was young.

3. Abe __knows__ that he has __no__ chance of winning the marathon.

4. Fran __knew__ when she bought this __new__ chair that it was too big for the room.

5. __No__ , I don't __know__ the way to grandma's house, you hairy weirdo.

Lose/loose

1. *Lose* means to misplace or not to win.

   Be careful not to *lose* your way on those back roads.

   George hates to *lose* at cards.

2. *Loose* means too large, not tightly fitting.

   That shirt is not my size; it's *loose.*

PRACTICE 8   Fill in *lose* or *loose*.

1. When Ari studies in bed, he __loses__ the __loose__ change from his pockets.
2. Several layers of __loose__ clothing can warm you in winter.
3. Although a lion was __loose__ in the zoo, no one panicked.
4. Don't __lose__ any sleep over tomorrow's exam.
5. If you __lose__ that __loose__ screw, the handle will fall off.

Past/passed

1. *Past* is that which has already occurred; it is over with.

   His *past* work has been satisfactory.

   Never let the *past* interfere with your hopes for the future.

2. *Passed* is the past tense of the verb *to pass.*

   She *passed* by and nodded hello.   **The wild geese *passed* overhead.**

PRACTICE 9   Fill in *past* or *passed*.

1. As Jake __passed__ the barn, he noticed a man talking to the reindeer.
2. To children, even the recent __past__ seems like ancient history.
3. Mia __passed__ up the opportunity to see a friend from her __past__.
4. The quarterback __passed__ the ball fifty yards for a touchdown.
5. This Bible was __passed__ down to me by my mother; it contains records of our family's __past__.

Quiet/quit/quite

1. *Quiet* means silent, still.

   The wood are *quiet* tonight.

2. *Quit* means to give up or to stop doing something.

   Last year I *quit* drinking.

3. *Quite* means very or exactly.

   He was *quite* tired after playing handball for two hours.

   That's not *quite* right.

PRACTICE 10   Fill in *quiet*, *quit*, or *quite*.

1. The cottage is a ___quiet___ and beautiful place to study.

2. Nora is ___quite___ dedicated to her veterinary career.

3. Don't ___quit___ yet; you haven't ___quite___ finished the race, but you can do it.

4. Each day when he ___quits___ work, Dan visits a ___quiet___ spot in the park.

5. She made ___quite___ an impression in red fake fur and a blond wig.

Rise/raise

1. *Rise* means to get up by one's own power.
   The past tense of *rise* is *rose*.
   The past participle of *rise* is *risen*.

   The sun *rises* at 6 A.M.

   Daniel *rose* early yesterday.

   He has *risen* from the table.

2. *Raise* means to lift an object or to grow or increase.
   The past tense of *raise* is *raised*.
   The past participle of *raise* is *raised*.

   Raise your right hand.

   She *raised* the banner over her head.

   We have *raised* one thousand dollars.

PRACTICE 11   Fill in the correct form of *rise* or *raise*.

1. The loaves of bread have ___risen___ perfectly.

2. The new mayor ___raised___ his arms in a victory salute.

3. Once the sun has ___risen___, Pete opens the shades and ___raises___ the window.

4. We all ___rose___ as the bride walked down the aisle.

5. The money we have ___raised___ will help the homeless.

Sit/set

1. *Sit* means to seat oneself.
   The past tense of *sit* is *sat*.
   The past participle of *sit* is *sat*.

   Sit up straight!

   He *sat* down on the porch and fell asleep.

   She has *sat* reading that book all day.

2. *Set* means to place or put something down.
The past tense of *set* is *set*.
The past participle of *set* is *set*.

Don't *set* your books on the dining room table.

She *set* the package down and walked off without it.

She had *set* the timer on the stove.

PRACTICE 12   Fill in *sit* or *set*.

1. Please __set__ your briefcase here. Would you like to __sit__ down?

2. Have they __sat__ in on a rehearsal before?

3. Tom __set__ the chair by the window and __sat__ down.

4. Maria __set__ her alarm clock for 6:30 A.M.

5. I wouldn't have __sat__ here if I had known you were returning.

Suppose/supposed

1. *Suppose* means to assume or guess.
The past tense of *suppose* is *supposed*.
The past participle of *suppose* is *supposed*.

Brad *supposes* that the teacher will give him an *A*.

We all *supposed* she would win first prize.

I had *supposed* Dan would bring his trumpet.

2. *Supposed* means ought to or should; it is followed by *to*.

He is *supposed* to meet us after class.

You were *supposed to* wash and wax the car.

Remember: When you mean *ought to* or *should*, always use the *-ed* ending—*supposed*.

PRACTICE 13   Fill in *suppose* or *supposed*.

1. Why do you __suppose__ wolves howl at the moon?

2. I __suppose__ you like heavy metal music.

3. Detective Baker is __supposed__ to address the Citizens' Patrol tonight.

4. Wasn't Erik __supposed__ to meet us at five?

5. Ms. Ita says we're not __supposed__ to guess in computer science class; we're __supposed__ to know.

Their/there/they're

1. *Their* is a possessive and shows ownership.

   They couldn't find *their* wigs.   **Their children are charming.**

2. *There* indicates a direction.

   I wouldn't go *there* again.   **Put the lumber down *there*.**

   There is also a way of introducing a thought.

   There is a fly in my soup.

   There are two ways to approach this problem.

3. *They're* is a contraction: *they* + *are* = *they're*. If you cannot substitute *they are* in the sentence, you cannot use *they're*.

   They're the best tires money can buy.   **If *they're* coming, count me in.**

PRACTICE 14   Fill in *their, there,* or *they're*.

1. Right over ___there___ at the Jean Cocteau Theatre, ___they're___ performing a play by Oscar Wilde.

2. ___They're___ two of the most amusing people I know.

3. ___There___ are two choices you can make, and ___they're___ both risky.

4. Two mail carriers left ___their___ mail bags ___there___ on the post office steps.

5. Is ___there___ a doctor in the house?

6. Two cruisers lost ___their___ way in the storm.

7. ___Their___ house is fun to visit.

8. Don't worry about ___their___ performance in the race because ___they're___ both tough.

Then/than

1. *Then* means afterward or at that time.

   First we went to the theater, and *then* we went out for a pizza and champagne.

   I was a heavyweight boxer *then*.

2. *Than* is used in a comparison.

   She is a better student *than* I.

PRACTICE 15   Fill in *then* or *than*.

1. First Cassandra kicked off her shoes; __then__ she began to dance.

2. Jupiter's diameter is eleven times larger __than__ Earth's.

3. If you're more familiar with this trail __than__ I, __then__ you should lead the way.

4. Fran lived in Chicago __then__; now she lives in Miami.

5. If he is better prepared __than__ you, what will you do __then__?

Through/though

1. *Through* means in one side and out the other or finished.

   The rain came *through* the open window.

   We should be *through* soon.

2. *Though* means although or, used with *as*, means as if.

   ***Though* he rarely speaks, he writes terrific letters.**

   It was as *though* I had never ridden a bicycle before.

PRACTICE 16   Fill in *through* or *though*.

1. Clayton is a Texan __through__ and __through__.

2. Dee usually walks to work, __though__ she sometimes rides the bus.

3. Julio strode __through__ the bank as __though__ he owned it.

4. __Through__ study and perseverance, Charelle earned her degree in three years.

5. I'm not really hungry; I will have an apple, __though__.

To/too/two

1. *To* means toward.

   We are going *to* the stadium.

   To can also be combined with a verb to form an infinitive.

   Where do you want *to go* for lunch?

2. *Too* means also or very.

   Roberto is going to the theater *too*.

   They were *too* bored to stay awake.

3. *Two* is the number 2.

   There are *two* new accounting courses this term.

PRACTICE 17   Fill in *to*, *too*, or *two*.

1. Please take my daughter __to__ the movies __too__.
2. We'd like a table for __two__ with a view of the sea.
3. Dan, __too__, took __two__ hours __to__ complete the exam.
4. Luis went __to__ Iowa State for __two__ semesters.
5. This curry is __too__ hot __to__ eat and __too__ good __to__ resist.

Use/used

1. *Use* means to make use of.
   The past tense of *use* is *used.*
   The past participle of *use* is *used.*

   Why do you *use* green ink?

   He *used* the wrong paint in the bathroom.

   I have *used* that brand of toothpaste myself.

2. *Used* means in the habit of or accustomed to; it is followed by *to.*

   I am not *used to* getting up at 4 A.M.   They got *used to* the good life.

Remember: When you mean *in the habit of* or *accustomed to,* always use the *-ed* ending—*used.*

PRACTICE 18   Fill in *use* or *used.*

1. Marie __used__ to drive a jalopy she bought at a __used__ car lot.
2. We will __use__ about three gallons of paint on this shed.
3. Can you __use__ a __used__ computer?
4. Pam __used__ to __use__ a pick instead of her fingers to strum her guitar.
5. Shall I __use__ contrast or illustration to develop this essay?

Weather/whether

1. *Weather* refers to atmospheric conditions.

   In June, the *weather* in Spain is lovely.

2. *Whether* implies a question.

   Whether or not you pass depends on you.

PRACTICE 19   Fill in *weather* or *whether.*

1. In fine __weather__, we take long walks in the woods.

2. _Whether_____ or not you like Chinese food, you'll love this dish.

3. The _weather_____ person never said _whether_____ or not it would snow.

4. I can't recall _whether_____ you prefer tea or coffee.

5. In 1870 a national _weather_____ service was established.

Where/were/we're

1. *Where* implies place or location.

   Where have you been all day?   **Home is *where* you hang your hat.**

2. *Were* is the past tense of *are*.

   We *were* on our way when the hurricane hit.

3. *We're* is a contraction: *we + are = we're*. If you cannot substitute *we are* in the sentence, you cannot use *we're*.

   We're going to leave now.   **Since *we're* in the city, let's go to the zoo.**

PRACTICE 20   Fill in *where, were,* or *we're*.

1. _We're_____ going to Hawaii, _where_____ the sun always shines.

2. _Were_____ you standing _where_____ we agreed to meet?

3. _We're_____ working out three times a week.

4. There _were_____ two high-rises _where_____ the park used to be.

5. _We're_____ determined to attend college, though we don't yet know _where_____.

Whose/who's

1. *Whose* implies ownership and possession.

   Whose term paper is that?

2. *Who's* is a contraction of *who is* or *who has*. If you cannot substitute *who is* or *who has*, you cannot use *who's*.

   Who's knocking at the window?

   Who's seen my new felt hat with the red feathers?

PRACTICE 21   Fill in *whose* or *who's*.

1. _Whose_____ Miata convertible is this?

2. Tanya, ____who's____ in my history class, will join us for dinner.

3. Janet Jackson, ____whose____ new album was just released, is a star ____who's____ definitely rising.

4. ____Whose____ biology textbook is this?

5. ____Who's____ going to clean the oven?

Your/you're

1. *Your* is a possessive and shows ownership.

   Your knowledge astonishes me!

2. *You're* is a contraction: *you + are = you're*. If you cannot substitute *you are* in the sentence, you cannot use *you're*.

   You're the nicest person I know.

PRACTICE 22   Fill in *your* or *you're*.

1. ____You're____ sitting on ____your____ hat.

2. When ____you're____ ready to begin ____your____ piano lesson, we'll leave.

3. Let ____your____ advisor help you plan ____your____ course schedule.

4. When ____you're____ with ____your____ friends, ____you're____ a different person.

5. If you think ____you're____ lost, why not use ____your____ map?

Personal Look-Alikes/Sound-Alikes List

In your notebook, keep a list of look-alikes and sound-alikes that *you* have trouble with. Add words to your list from corrected papers and from the exercises in this appendix; consider such pairs as adapt/adopt, addition/edition, device/devise, stationery/stationary, and so forth.

First, write the word you used incorrectly; then write its meaning or use it correctly in a sentence, whichever best helps you remember. Now do the same with the word you meant to use.

	Word	**Meaning**
1.	though	means although
	through	I drove through the woods.
2.		

PRACTICE 23
Review

The following essay contains a number of look-alike, sound-alike errors. Proofread for these errors, writing the correct word above the line.

Zora Neale Hurston

(1) Never will ~~their~~ *there* be another person ~~quiet~~ *quite* like Zora Neale Hurston. (2) Brilliant, restless, and unconventional, she was the most influential African-American female writer of the 1930s.

(3) Hurston came from Eatonville, Florida, a completely African-American community with ~~it's~~ *its* own officials and culture. (4) In this all-black world, she learned the rich folklore and love of independence that ~~effected~~ *affected* her future writing. (5) An orphan at fourteen, young Zora worked her way north, attending Howard University in Washington, D.C. (6) In 1925, she moved to New York, becoming the first black woman to graduate from Barnard College. (7) She ~~than~~ *then* studied anthropology at Columbia University.

(8) During the 1930s, Hurston wrote five major works. (9) ~~Too~~ *Two* books explored the folklore of rural black cultures—those of Florida, Alabama, and Louisiana, as well as the voodoo of Haiti and Jamaica. (10) Hurston now saw the folklore of her youth ~~though~~ *through* the trained eye of the social scientist. (11) She also turned her personal and scholarly knowledge into three fine novels. (12) Written in black dialect, her masterpiece, *Their Eyes Were Watching God*, tells the life of Janie, ~~who's~~ *whose* life of struggle leads to self-acceptance. (13) Hurston wrote ~~a~~ *an* autobiography too, as well as many articles, essays, short stories, and plays.

(14) In 1991, *Mule Bone*, one of her plays, finally reached Broadway.

(15) In her writings, Zora Neale Hurston showed the vitality of the African-American ~~passed~~ *past* captured in oral folk tradition and the need of all people to attain emotional and spiritual freedom in ~~there~~ *their* lives.

Reading
Selections

Beauty:
When the Other Dancer Is the Self

Alice Walker

Being physically injured can be terrifying; coming to terms with a permanent disability can be a painful, difficult process. Alice Walker, a noted fiction writer, poet, and author of *The Color Purple*, tells of her feelings and experiences before, during, and after an injury that changed her life.

It is a bright summer day in 1947. My father, a fat, funny man with beautiful eyes and a subversive wit,[1] is trying to decide which of his eight children he will take with him to the county fair. My mother, of course, will not go. She is knocked out from getting most of us ready: I hold my neck stiff against the pressure of her knuckles as she hastily completes the braiding and then beribboning of my hair.

My father is the driver for the rich old white lady up the road. Her name is Miss Mey. She owns all the land for miles around, as well as the house in which we live. All I remember about her is that she once offered to pay my mother thirty-five cents for cleaning her house, raking up piles of her magnolia leaves, and washing her family's clothes, and that my mother—she of no money, eight children, and a chronic earache—refused it. But I do not think of this in 1947. I am two and a half years old. I want to go everywhere my daddy goes. I am excited at the prospect of riding in a car. Someone has told me fairs are fun. That there is room in the car for only three of us doesn't faze[2] me at all. Whirling happily in my starchy frock, showing off my biscuit-polished patent-leather shoes and lavender socks, tossing my head in a way that makes my ribbons bounce, I stand, hands on hips, before my father. "Take me, Daddy," I say with assurance; "I'm the prettiest!"

Later, it does not surprise me to find myself in Miss Mey's shiny black car, sharing the back seat with the other lucky ones. Does not surprise me that I thoroughly enjoy the fair. At home that night I tell the unlucky ones all I can remember about the merry-go-round, the man who eats live chickens, and the teddy bears, until they say: that's enough, baby Alice. Shut up now, and go to sleep.

It is Easter Sunday, 1950. I am dressed in a green, flocked, scalloped-hem dress (handmade by my adoring sister, Ruth) that has its own smooth satin petticoat and tiny hot-pink roses tucked into each scallop. My shoes, new T-strap patent leather, again highly biscuit-polished. I am six years old and have learned one of the longest Easter speeches to be heard that day, totally unlike the speech I said when I was two: "Easter lilies / pure and white / blossom in / the morning light." When I rise to give my

1

2

3

4

1. subversive wit: sarcastic, sharp sense of humor
2. faze: discourage

speech I do so on a great wave of love and pride and expectation. People in the church stop rustling their new crinolines. They seem to hold their breath. I can tell they admire my dress, but it is my spirit, bordering on sassiness (womanishness), they secretly applaud.

"That girl's a little *mess*," they whisper to each other, pleased.   5

Naturally I say my speech without stammer or pause, unlike those   6 who stutter, stammer, or, worst of all, forget. This is before the word "beautiful" exists in people's vocabulary, but "Oh, isn't she the *cutest* thing!" frequently floats my way. "And got so much sense!" they gratefully add ... for which thoughtful addition I thank them to this day.

It was great fun being cute. But then, one day, it ended.   7

I am eight years old and a tomboy. I have a cowboy hat, cowboy boots,   8 checkered shirt and pants, all red. My playmates are my brothers, two and four years older than I. Their colors are black and green, the only difference in the way we are dressed. On Saturday nights we all go to the picture show, even my mother; Westerns are her favorite kind of movie. Back home, "on the ranch," we pretend we are Tom Mix, Hopalong Cassidy, Lash LaRue (we've even named one of our dogs Lash LaRue); we chase each other for hours rustling cattle, being outlaws, delivering damsels from distress. Then my parents decide to buy my brothers guns. These are not "real" guns. They shoot "BBs," copper pellets my brothers say will kill birds. Because I am a girl, I do not get a gun. Instantly I am relegated[3] to the position of Indian. Now there appears a great distance between us. They shoot and shoot at everything with their new guns. I try to keep up with my bow and arrows.

One day while I am standing on top of our makeshift "garage"—   9 pieces of tin nailed across some poles—holding my bow and arrow and looking out toward the fields, I feel an incredible blow in my right eye. I look down just in time to see my brother lower his gun.

Both brothers rush to my side. My eye stings, and I cover it with my   10 hand. "If you tell," they say, "we will get a whipping. You don't want that to happen, do you?" I do not. "Here is a piece of wire," says the older brother, picking it up from the roof; "say you stepped on one end of it and the other flew up and hit you." The pain is beginning to start. "Yes," I say. "Yes, I will say that is what happened." If I do not say this is what happened, I know my brothers will find ways to make me wish I had. But now I will say anything that gets me to my mother.

Confronted by our parents we stick to the lie agreed upon. They place   11 me on a bench on the porch and I close my left eye while they examine the right. There is a tree growing from underneath the porch that climbs past the railing to the roof. It is the last thing my right eye sees. I watch as its trunk, its branches, and then its leaves are blotted out by the rising blood.

I am in shock. First there is intense fever, which my father tries to   12 break using lily leaves bound around my head. Then there are chills: my

3. relegated to: assigned

mother tries to get me to eat soup. Eventually, I do not know how, my parents learn what has happened. A week after the "accident" they take me to see a doctor. "Why did you wait so long to come?" he asks, looking into my eye and shaking his head. "Eyes are sympathetic,[4]" he says. "If one is blind, the other will likely become blind too."

This comment of the doctor's terrifies me. But it is really how I look **13** that bothers me most. Where the BB pellet struck there is a glob of whitish scar tissue, a hideous cataract, on my eye. Now when I stare at people—a favorite pastime, up to now—they will stare back. Not at the "cute" little girl, but at her scar. For six years I do not stare at anyone, because I do not raise my head.

Years later, in the throes[5] of a mid-life crisis, I ask my mother and sister **14** whether I changed after the "accident." "No," they say, puzzled. "What do you mean?"

What do I mean? **15**

I am eight, and, for the first time, doing poorly in school, where I have **16** been something of a whiz since I was four. We have just moved to the place where the "accident" occurred. We do not know any of the people around us because this is a different county. The only time I see the friends I knew is when we go back to our old church. The new school is the former state penitentiary. It is a large stone building, cold and drafty, crammed to overflowing with boisterous,[6] ill-disciplined children. On the third floor there is a huge circular imprint of some partition that has been torn out.

"What used to be there?" I ask a sullen girl next to me on our way **17** past it to lunch.

"The electric chair," says she. **18**

At night I have nightmares about the electric chair, and about all the **19** people reputedly[7] "fried" in it. I am afraid of the school, where all the students seem to be budding criminals.

"What's the matter with your eye?" they ask, critically. **20**

When I don't answer (I cannot decide whether it was an "accident" **21** or not), they shove me, insist on a fight.

My brother, the one who created the story about the wire, comes to **22** my rescue. But then brags so much about "protecting" me, I become sick.

After months of torture at the school, my parents decide to send me **23** back to our old community, to my old school. I live with my grandparents and the teacher they board. But there is no room for Phoebe, my cat. By the time my grandparents decide there *is* room, and I ask for my cat, she cannot be found. Miss Yarborough, the boarding teacher, takes me under her wing, and begins to teach me to play the piano. But soon she marries an African—a "prince," she says—and is whisked away to his continent.

At my old school there is at least one teacher who loves me. She is **24** the teacher who "knew me before I was born" and bought my first baby

4. sympathetic: closely connected
5. throes: a condition of struggle
6. boisterous: rowdy and noisy
7. reputedly: supposedly

clothes. It is she who makes life bearable. It is her presence that finally helps me turn on the one child at the school who continually calls me "one-eyed bitch." One day I simply grab him by his coat and beat him until I am satisfied. It is my teacher who tells me my mother is ill.

My mother is lying in bed in the middle of the day, something I have 25 never seen. She is in too much pain to speak. She has an abscess in her ear. I stand looking down on her, knowing that if she dies, I cannot live. She is being treated with warm oils and hot bricks held against her cheek. Finally a doctor comes. But I must go back to my grandparents' house. The weeks pass but I am hardly aware of it. All I know is that my mother might die, my father is not so jolly, my brothers still have their guns, and I am the one sent away from home.

"You did not change," they say. 26

Did I imagine the anguish of never looking up? 27

I am twelve. When relatives come to visit I hide in my room. My cousin 28 Brenda, just my age, whose father works in the post office and whose mother is a nurse, comes to find me. "Hello," she says. And then she asks, looking at my recent school picture, which I did not want taken, and on which the "glob," as I think of it, is clearly visible, "You still can't see out of that eye?"

"No," I say, and flop back on the bed over my book. 29

That night, as I do almost every night, I abuse my eye. I rant and rave 30 at it, in front of the mirror. I plead with it to clear up before morning. I tell it I hate and despise it. I do not pray for sight. I pray for beauty.

"You did not change," they say. 31

I am fourteen and baby-sitting for my brother Bill, who lives in Boston. 32 He is my favorite brother and there is a strong bond between us. Understanding my feelings of shame and ugliness he and his wife take me to a local hospital, where the "glob" is removed by a doctor named O. Henry. There is still a small bluish crater where the scar tissue was, but the ugly white stuff is gone. Almost immediately I become a different person from the girl who does not raise her head. Or so I think. Now that I've raised my head I win the boyfriend of my dreams. Now that I've raised my head I have plenty of friends. Now that I've raised my head classwork comes from my lips as faultlessly as Easter speeches did, and I leave high school as valedictorian, most popular student, and *queen*, hardly believing my luck. Ironically, the girl who was voted most beautiful in our class (and was) was later shot twice through the chest by a male companion, using a "real" gun, while she was pregnant. But that's another story in itself. Or is it?

"You did not change," they say. 33

It is now thirty years since the "accident." A beautiful journalist comes 34 to visit and to interview me. She is going to write a cover story for her magazine that focuses on my latest book. "Decide how you want to look on the cover," she says. "Glamorous, or whatever."

Never mind "glamorous," it is the "whatever" that I hear. Suddenly **35** all I can think of is whether I will get enough sleep the night before the photography session: if I don't, my eye will be tired and wander, as blind eyes will.

At night in bed with my lover I think up reasons why I should not **36** appear on the cover of a magazine. "My meanest critics will say I've sold out," I say. "My family will now realize I write scandalous books."

"But what's the real reason you don't want to do this?" he asks. **37**

"Because in all probability," I say in a rush, "my eye won't be **38** straight."

"It will be straight enough," he says. Then, "Besides, I thought you'd **39** made your peace with that."

And I suddenly remember that I have. **40**

I remember: **41**

I am talking to my brother Jimmy, asking if he remembers anything **42** unusual about the day I was shot. He does not know I consider that day the last time my father, with his sweet home remedy of cool lily leaves, chose me, and that I suffered and raged inside because of this. "Well," he says, "all I remember is standing by the side of the highway with Daddy, trying to flag down a car. A white man stopped, but when Daddy said he needed somebody to take his little girl to the doctor, he drove off."

I remember: **43**

I am in the desert for the first time. I fall totally in love with it. I am **44** so overwhelmed by its beauty, I confront for the first time, consciously, the meaning of the doctor's words years ago: "Eyes are sympathetic. If one is blind, the other will likely become blind too." I realize I have dashed about the world madly, looking at this, looking at that, storing up images against the fading of the light. *But I might have missed seeing the desert!* The shock of that possibility—and gratitude for over twenty-five years of sight—sends me literally to my knees. Poem after poem comes—which is perhaps how poets pray.

On Sight

I am so thankful I have seen
The Desert
And the creatures in the desert
And the desert Itself.

The desert has its own moon
Which I have seen
With my own eye.
There is no flag on it.

Trees of the desert have arms
All of which are always up
That is because the moon is up
The sun is up
Also the sky
The stars
Clouds
None with flags.

If there *were* flags, I doubt
the trees would point.
Would you?

But mostly, I remember this: 45

I am twenty-seven, and my baby daughter is almost three. Since her   46
birth I have worried about her discovery that her mother's eyes are different from other people's. Will she be embarrassed? I think. What will
she say? Every day she watches a television program called "Big Blue
Marble." It begins with a picture of the earth as it appears from the
moon. It is bluish, a little battered-looking, but full of light, with whitish
clouds swirling around it. Every time I see it I weep with love, as if it is
a picture of Grandma's house. One day when I am putting Rebecca down
for her nap, she suddenly focuses on my eye. Something inside me cringes,
gets ready to try to protect myself. All children are cruel about physical
differences, I know from experience, and that they don't always mean to
be is another matter. I assume Rebecca will be the same.

But no-o-o-o. She studies my face intently as we stand, her inside and   47
me outside her crib. She even holds my face maternally between her dim-
pled little hands. Then, looking every bit as serious and lawyerlike as her
father, she says, as if it may just possibly have slipped my attention:
"Mommy, there's a *world* in your eye." (As in, "Don't be alarmed, or do
anything crazy.") And then, gently, but with great interest: "Mommy,
where did you *get* that world in your eye?"

For the most part, the pain left then. (So what, if my brothers grew   48
up to buy even more powerful pellet guns for their sons and to carry real
guns themselves. So what, if a young "Morehouse man" once nearly fell
off the steps of Trevor Arnett Library because he thought my eyes were
blue.) Crying and laughing I ran to the bathroom, while Rebecca mum-
bled and sang herself off to sleep. Yes indeed, I realized, looking into the
mirror. There *was* a world in my eye. And I saw that it was possible to
love it: that in fact, for all it had taught me of shame and anger and inner
vision, I *did* love it. Even to see it drifting out of orbit in boredom, or
rolling up out of fatigue, not to mention floating back at attention in
excitement (bearing witness, a friend has called it), deeply suitable to my
personality, and even characteristic of me.

That night I dream I am dancing to Stevie Wonder's song "Always"   49
(the name of the song is really "As," but I hear it as "Always"). As I
dance, whirling and joyous, happier than I've ever been in my life,
another bright-faced dancer joins me. We dance and kiss each other and
hold each other through the night. The other dancer has obviously come
through all right, as I have done. She is beautiful, whole and free. And
she is also me. ∎

Discussion and Writing Questions

1. When did the author stop being "cute"? Is she happy about this
   change?

2. Why do you think her family insists that she did not change after the
   shooting?

3. Until her operation at age fourteen, Walker speaks of hating her injured eye. By the end of the essay, she dances with another "dancer," who is "beautiful, whole and free. And she is also me." What makes the author change her mind about her "deformity"?

4. The author uses particular words and phrases to indicate time or chronological order in her narrative. Find the words that indicate time order. At one point in her narrative, she breaks this time order to skip back into the past. In which paragraph does this flashback occur?

Writing Assignments

1. Write about an unpleasant event or experience that resulted in personal growth for you. Your writing need not focus on something as painful as Alice Walker's injury. What is important is how you came to terms with the experience, and what you ultimately learned from it.

2. Tell a story about being thrust into a completely unfamiliar situation. You might describe your reaction to attending a new school, starting a new job, or moving to a new city. Present concrete details of your experience. Organize the story around your most vivid memories, like meeting new classmates for the first time, or your first few days on the new job.

3. Walker says that for a time she hated her blind eye. Do you think that this is a common reaction in people with a physical defect or illness?

In Search of Bruce Lee's Grave

Shanlon Wu

Most young people need heroes to respect or imitate. In this essay, Shanlon Wu discusses the lack of Asian heroes as he grew up in suburban New York in the 1950s. Then he saw his first Bruce Lee movie.

It's Saturday morning in Seattle, and I am driving to visit Bruce Lee's grave. I have been in the city for only a couple of weeks and so drive two blocks past the cemetery before realizing that I've passed it. I double back and turn through the large wrought-iron gate, past a sign that reads: "Open to 9 P.M. or dusk, whichever comes first." 1

It's a sprawling cemetery, with winding roads leading in all directions. I feel silly trying to find his grave with no guidance. I think that my search for his grave is similar to my search for Asian heroes in America. 2

I was born in 1959, an Asian-American in Westchester County, N.Y. **3** During my childhood there were no Asian sports stars. On television, I can recall only that most pathetic of Asian characters, Hop Sing, the Cartwright family houseboy on "Bonanza." But in my adolescence there was Bruce.

I was 14 years old when I first saw "Enter the Dragon," the grand- **4** daddy of martial-arts movies. Bruce had died suddenly at the age of 32 of cerebral edema, an excess of fluid in the brain, just weeks before the release of the film. Between the ages of 14 and 17, I saw "Enter the Dragon" 22 times before I stopped counting. During those years I collected Bruce Lee posters, putting them up at all angles in my bedroom. I took up Chinese martial arts and spent hours comparing my physique with his.

I learned all I could about Bruce: that he had married a Caucasian, **5** Linda; that he had sparred with Kareem Abdul-Jabbar; that he was a buddy of Steve McQueen and James Coburn, both of whom were his pallbearers.

My parents, who immigrated to America and had become professors **6** at Hunter College, tolerated my behavior, but seemed puzzled at my admiration of an "entertainer." My father jokingly tried to compare my obsession with Bruce to his boyhood worship of Chinese folk-tale heroes.

"I read them just like you read American comic books," he said. **7**

But my father's heroes could not be mine; they came from an ancient **8** literary tradition, not comic books. He and my mother had grown up in a land where they belonged to the majority. I could not adopt their childhood and they were wise enough not to impose it upon me.

Although I never again experienced the kind of blind hero worship I **9** felt for Bruce, my need to find heroes remained strong.

In college, I discovered the men of the 442d Regimental Combat Team, **10** a United States Army all-Japanese unit in World War II. Allowed to fight only against Europeans, they suffered heavy casualties while their families were put in internment camps. Their motto was "Go for Broke."

I saw them as Asians in a Homeric epic, the protagonists[1] of a Shake- **11** spearean tragedy; I knew no Eastern myths to infuse them with.[2] They embodied my own need to prove myself in the Caucasian world. I imagined how their American-born flesh and muscle must have resembled mine: epicanthic folds[3] set in strong faces nourished on milk and beef. I thought how much they had proved where there was so little to prove.

After college, I competed as an amateur boxer in an attempt to find **12** my self-image in the ring. It didn't work. My fighting was only an attempt to copy Bruce's movies. What I needed was instruction on how to live. I quit boxing after a year and went to law school.

I was an anomaly[4] there: a would-be Asian litigator.[5] I had always **13** liked to argue and found I liked doing it in front of people even more.

1. protagonists: main characters
2. infuse . . . with: put into
3. epicanthic folds: folds of the upper eyelid skin found in many Asian people
4. anomaly: oddity, unusual person
5. litigator: one who argues legal matters

When I won the first-year moot court competition in law school, I asked an Asian classmate if he thought I was the first Asian to win. He laughed and told me I was probably the only Asian to even compete.

The law-firm interviewers always seemed surprised that I wanted to litigate. **14**

"Aren't you interested in Pacific Rim trade?" they asked. **15**

"My Chinese isn't good enough," I quipped. **16**

My pat response seemed to please them. It certainly pleased me. I thought I'd found a place of my own—a place where the law would insulate[6] me from the pressure of defining my Asian maleness. I sensed the possibility of merely being myself. **17**

But the pressure reasserted itself. One morning, the year after graduating from law school, I read the obituary of Gen. Minoru Genda—the man who planned the Pearl Harbor attack. I'd never heard of him and had assumed that whoever did that planning was long since dead. But the general had been alive all those years—rising at 4 every morning to do his exercises and retiring every night by 8. An advocate of animal rights, the obituary said. **18**

I found myself drawn to the general's life despite his association with the Axis powers. He seemed a forthright, graceful man who died unhumbled. The same paper carried a front-page story about Congress's failure to pay the Japanese-American internees their promised reparation[7] money. The general, at least, had not died waiting for reparations. **19**

I was surprised and frightened by my admiration for General Genda, by my still-strong hunger for images of powerful Asian men. That hunger was my vulnerability manifested,[8] a reminder of my lack of place. **20**

The hunger is eased this gray morning in Seattle. After asking directions from a policeman—Japanese—I easily locate Bruce's grave. The headstone is red granite with a small picture etched into it. The picture is very Hollywood—Bruce wears dark glasses—and I think the calligraphy[9] looks a bit sloppy. Two tourists stop but leave quickly after glancing at me. **21**

I realize I am crying. Bruce's grave seems very small in comparison to his place in my boyhood. So small in comparison to my need for heroes. Seeing his grave, I understand how large the hole in my life has been, and how desperately I'd sought to fill it. **22**

I had sought an Asian hero to emulate.[10] But none of my choices quite fit me. Their lives were defined through heroic tasks—they had villains to defeat and wars to fight—while my life seemed merely a struggle to define myself. **23**

But now I see how that very struggle has defined me. I must be my own hero even as I learn to treasure those who have gone before. **24**

I have had my powerful Asian male images: Bruce, the men of the 442d and General Genda; I may yet discover others. Their lives beckon **25**

6. insulate: protect
7. reparation: payment made to someone who has been wrongly treated
8. manifested: made apparent
9. calligraphy: elegant handwritten lettering
10. emulate: imitate

like fireflies on a moonless night, and I know that they—like me—may have been flawed by foolhardiness and even cruelty. Still, their lives were real. They were not houseboys on "Bonanza." ▪

Discussion and Writing Questions

1. Why did Wu see "Enter the Dragon" so many times?

2. Why did the author need so badly to find heroes? How did his situation differ from that of his parents?

3. Does Wu conclude his search for heroes?

4. This narrative begins in the present, then switches to the past, then ends in the present. Why does the author switch tenses this way?

Writing Assignments

1. The search for a hero is the search for someone who sets an example or encourages you or teaches you. Write a narrative about your search for a hero, either in childhood or in the present day. In your narrative, include who this hero was, what he or she meant to you, and what your search taught you.

2. Discuss how it feels to be a stranger or an outsider. Perhaps you have felt like an outsider because your interests or way of dressing are different from those of your classmates or neighbors; perhaps you have felt left out by your coworkers; or perhaps you have been treated as "different" because of your ethnic group or even your gender.

3. Write about a longing you felt as a child that was important in your development as a person—perhaps to have friends, to play music, or to make your parents happy. Was this longing ever filled? Do you think this longing has helped shape the person who you are today?

A Brother's Murder

Brent Staples

Brent Staples grew up in a rough, industrial city. He left to become a successful journalist, but his younger brother remained. Staples' story of his brother is a reminder of the grim circumstances in which so many young black men of the inner city find themselves today.

It has been more than two years since my telephone rang with the news 1 that my younger brother Blake—just twenty-two years old—had been murdered. The young man who killed him was only twenty-four. Wearing a ski mask, he emerged from a car, fired six times at close range with a massive .44 Magnum, then fled. The two had once been inseparable friends. A senseless rivalry—beginning, I think, with an argument over a girfriend—escalated[1] from posturing,[2] to threats, to violence, to murder. The way the two were living, death could have come to either of them from anywhere. In fact, the assailant had already survived multiple gunshot wounds from an accident much like the one in which my brother lost his life.

As I wept for Blake I felt wrenched backward into events and circumstances that had seemed light-years gone. Though a decade apart, we both were raised in Chester, Pennsylvania, an angry, heavily black, heavily poor, industrial city southwest of Philadelphia. There, in the 1960s, I was introduced to mortality, not by the old and failing, but by beautiful young men who lay wrecked after sudden explosions of violence. The first, I remembered from my fourteenth year—Johnny, brash lover of fast cars, stabbed to death two doors from my house in a fight over a pool game. The next year, my teenage cousin, Wesley, whom I loved very much, was shot dead. The summers blur. Milton, an angry young neighbor, shot a crosstown rival, wounding him badly. William, another teenage neighbor, took a shotgun blast to the shoulder in some urban drama and displayed his bandages proudly. His brother, Leonard, severely beaten, lost an eye and donned a black patch. It went on. **2**

I recall not long before I left for college, two local Vietnam veterans— one from the Marines, one from the Army—arguing fiercely, nearly at blows about which outfit had done the most in the war. The most killing, they meant. Not much later, I read a magazine article that set that dispute in a context. In the story, a noncommissioned officer—a sergeant, I believe—said he would pass up any number of affluent, suburban-born recruits to get hard-core soldiers from the inner city. They jumped into the rice paddies with "their manhood on their sleeves," I believe he said. These two items—the veterans arguing and the sergeant's words—still characterize for me the circumstances under which black men in their teens and twenties kill one another with such frequency. With a touchy paranoia born of living battered lives, they are desperate to be *real* men. Killing is only machismo taken to the extreme. Incursions[3] to be punished by death were many and minor, and they remain so: they include stepping on the wrong toe, literally; cheating in a drug deal; simply saying "I dare you" to someone holding a gun; crossing territorial lines in a gang dispute. My brother grew up to wear his manhood on his sleeve. And when he died, he was in that group—black, male and in its teens and early twenties—that is far and away the most likely to murder or be murdered. **3**

I left the East Coast after college, spent the mid- and late 1970s in Chicago as a graduate student, taught for a time, then became a journalist. Within ten years of leaving my hometown, I was overeducated and "upwardly mobile," ensconced[4] on a quiet, tree-lined street where voices **4**

1. escalated: increased
2. posturing: trying to appear tough
3. incursions: attacks, violations
4. ensconced: settled comfortably

raised in anger were scarcely ever heard. The telephone, like some grim umbilical, kept me connected to the old world with news of deaths, imprisonings and misfortune. I felt emotionally beaten up. Perhaps to protect myself, I added a psychological dimension to the physical distance I had already achieved. I rarely visited my hometown. I shut it out.

As I fled the past, so Blake embraced it. On Christmas of 1983, I traveled from Chicago to a black section of Roanoke, Virginia, where he then lived. The desolate public housing projects, the hopeless, idle young men crashing against one another—these reminded me of the embittered town we'd grown up in. It was a place where once I would have been comfortable, or at least sure of myself. Now, hearing of my brother's forays[5] into crime, his scrapes with police and street thugs, I was scared, unsteady on foreign terrain.[6]

I saw that Blake's romance with the street life and the hustler image had flowered dangerously. One evening that late December, standing in some Roanoke dive among drug dealers and grim, hair-trigger losers, I told him I feared for his life. He had affected the image of the tough he wanted to be. But behind the dark glasses and the swagger, I glimpsed the baby-faced toddler I'd once watched over. I nearly wept. I wanted desperately for him to live. The young think themselves immortal, and a dangerous light shone in his eyes as he spoke laughingly of making fools of the policemen who had raided his apartment looking for drugs. He cried out as I took his right hand. A line of stitches lay between the thumb and index finger. Kickback from a shotgun, he explained, nothing serious. Gunplay had become part of his life.

I lacked the language simply to say: Thousands have lived this for you and died. I fought the urge to lift him bodily and shake him. This place and the way you are living smells of death to me, I said. Take some time away, I said. Let's go downtown tomorrow and buy a plane ticket anywhere, take a bus trip, anything to get away and cool things off. He took my alarm casually. We arranged to meet the following night—an appointment he would not keep. We embraced as though through glass. I drove away.

As I stood in my apartment in Chicago holding the receiver that evening in February 1984, I felt as though part of my soul had been cut away. I questioned myself then, and I still do. Did I not reach back soon enough or earnestly enough for him? For weeks I awoke crying from a recurrent dream in which I chased him, urgently trying to get him to read a document I had, as though reading it would protect him from what had happened in waking life. His eyes shining like black diamonds, he smiled and danced just beyond my grasp. When I reached for him, I caught only the space where he had been. ∎

Discussion and Writing Questions

1. Staples says that he was "introduced to mortality" in Chester, Pennsylvania, in the 1960s (paragraph 2). What does he mean?

---

5. forays: undertakings, trips
6. terrain: ground

2. What does the author mean when he says his brother grew up to "wear his manhood on his sleeve" (paragraph 3)? Does he imply there are other ways of expressing masculinity?

3. Staples speaks of a dream in which he holds a document for his brother to read (paragraph 8). What do you suppose that document might say? What does this dream seem to say about communication between the two brothers?

4. Staples begins his narrative by describing the moment at which he hears of Blake's death. Why does he *start* with this event, instead of moving toward it?

Writing Assignments

1. Write a narrative about a shocking incident that took place in your neighborhood. Like Staples, you may want to start with the incident, and then narrate the smaller events in the story that led up to it. Or you can follow time order and end with the incident.

2. What is the most significant problem facing young people in the inner city today? Is it crime? Drugs? Lack of educational or employment opportunities? Discuss your opinion on this subject.

3. Do you think Brent Staples could have done more to change his brother? Can we really influence others to change their lives?

One More Lesson

Judith Ortiz Cofer

Judith Ortiz Cofer attended Augusta College, Florida Atlantic University, and Oxford University in England. Here she contrasts her memories of holidays in her native Puerto Rico and of later school experiences in Paterson, New Jersey, telling what she learned about love, prejudice, and the power of words. Her essay sheds light, too, on her decision to become a writer.

I remember Christmas on the Island by the way it felt on my skin. The temperature dropped into the ideal seventies and even lower after midnight when some of the more devout Catholics, mostly older women, got up to go to church—*misa del gallo*, they called it; mass at the hour when the rooster crowed for Christ. They would drape shawls over their heads and shoulders and move slowly toward town. The birth of Our Savior was a serious affair in our town.

At Mamá's house, food was the focal point of *Navidad*. There were banana leaves brought in bunches by the boys, spread on the table, where the women would pour coconut candy steaming hot, and the leaves would wilt around the sticky lumps, adding an extra tang of flavor to the already irresistible treat. Someone had to watch the candy while it cooled, or it would begin to disappear as the children risked life and limb for a stolen piece of heaven. The banana leaves were also used to wrap the traditional food of holidays in Puerto Rico: *pasteles*, the meat pies made from grated yucca[1] and plantain[2] and stuffed with spiced meats.

food

Every afternoon during the week before Christmas Day, we would **3** come home from school to find the women sitting around in the parlor with bowls on their laps, grating pieces of coconut, yuccas, plantains, cheeses—all the ingredients that would make up our Christmas Eve feast. The smells that filled Mamá's house at that time have come to mean anticipation and a sensual joy during a time in my life, the last days of my early childhood, when I could absorb joy through my pores—when I had not yet learned that light is followed by darkness, that all of creation is based on that simple concept, and maturity is a discovery of that natural law.

food

It was in those days that the Americans sent baskets of fruit to our **4** barrio[3]—apples, oranges, grapes flown in from the States. And at night, if you dared to walk up to the hill where the mango tree stood in the dark, you could see a wonderful sight: a Christmas tree, a real pine, decorated with lights of many colors. It was the blurry outline of this tree you saw, for it was inside a screened-in-porch, but we had heard a thorough description of it from the boy who delivered the fruit, a nephew of Mamá's, as it had turned out. Only, I was not impressed, since just the previous year we had put up a tree ourselves in our apartment in Paterson.

food

Packages arrived for us in the mail from our father. I got dolls **5** dressed in the national costumes of Spain, Italy, and Greece (at first we could not decide which of the Greek dolls was the male, since they both wore skirts); my brother got picture books; and my mother, jewelry that she would not wear, because it was too much like showing off and might attract the Evil Eye.

Evil Eye or not, the three of us were the envy of the pueblo.[4] Every- **6** thing about us set us apart, and I put away my dolls quickly when I discovered that my playmates would not be getting any gifts until *Los Reyes*—the Day of the Three Kings, when Christ received His gifts—and that even then it was more likely that the gifts they found under their beds would be practical things like clothes. Still, it was fun to find fresh grass for the camels the night the Kings were expected, tie it in bundles with string, and put it under our beds along with a bowl of fresh water.

The year went by fast after Christmas, and in the spring we received **7** a telegram from Father. His ship had arrived in Brooklyn Yard. He gave us a date for our trip back to the States. I remember Mother's frantic packing, and the trips to Mayagüez for new clothes; the inspections of my brother's and my bodies for cuts, scrapes, mosquito bites, and other

1. yucca: a thick-stemmed tropical plant
2. plantain: a banana-like fruit
3. barrio: district or neighborhood
4. pueblo: Spanish for *town*

"damage" she would have to explain to Father. And I remember begging Mamá to tell me stories in the afternoons, although it was not summer yet and the trips to the mango tree had not begun. In looking back I realize that Mamá's stories were what I packed—my winter store.

Father had succeeded in finding an apartment outside Paterson's **8** "vertical barrio," the tenement Puerto Ricans called *El Building*. He had talked a Jewish candy store owner into renting us the apartment above his establishment, which he and his wife had just vacated after buying a house in West Paterson, an affluent suburb. Mr. Schultz was a nice man whose melancholy[5] face I was familiar with from trips I had made often with my father to his store for cigarettes. Apparently, my father had convinced him and his brother, a look-alike of Mr. Schultz who helped in the store, that we were not the usual Puerto Rican family. My father's fair skin, his ultra-correct English, and his Navy uniform were a good argument. Later it occurred to me that my father had been displaying me as a model child when he took me to that store with him. I was always dressed as if for church and held firmly by the hand. I imagine he did the same with my brother. As for my mother, her Latin beauty, her thick black hair that hung to her waist, her voluptuous[6] body which even the winter clothes could not disguise, would have been nothing but a hindrance to my father's plans. But everyone knew that a Puerto Rican woman is her husband's satellite; she reflects both his light and his dark sides. If my father was respectable, then his family would be respectable. We got the apartment on Park Avenue.

Unlike El Building, where we had lived on our first trip to Paterson, **9** our new home was truly in exile. There were Puerto Ricans by the hundreds only one block away, but we heard no Spanish, no loud music, no mothers yelling at children, nor the familiar *¡Ay Bendito!*, that catch-all phrase of our people. Mother lapsed into silence herself, suffering from *La Tristeza*, the sadness that only place induces and only place cures. But Father relished[7] silence, and we were taught that silence was something to be cultivated and practiced.

Since our apartment was situated directly above where the Schultzes **10** worked all day, our father instructed us to remove our shoes at the door and walk in our socks. We were going to prove how respectable we were by being the opposite of what our ethnic group was known to be—we would be quiet and inconspicuous.[8]

I was escorted each day to school by my nervous mother. It was a long **11** walk in the cooling air of fall in Paterson and we had to pass by El Building where the children poured out of the front door of the dilapidated[9] tenement still answering their mothers in a mixture of Spanish and English: "Sí, Mami, I'll come straight home from school." At the corner we were halted by the crossing guard, a strict woman who only gestured her instructions, never spoke directly to the children, and only ordered

5. melancholy: sad
6. voluptuous: having a rounded, full shape
7. relished: enjoyed
8. inconspicuous: hard to notice
9. dilapidated: run-down

us to "halt" or "cross" while holding her white-gloved hand up at face level or swinging her arm sharply across her chest if the light was green.

The school building was not a welcoming sight for someone used to **12** the bright colors and airiness of tropical architecture. The building looked functional. It could have been a prison, an asylum, or just what it was: an urban school for the children of immigrants, built to withstand waves of change, generation by generation. Its red brick sides rose to four solid stories. The black steel fire escapes snaked up its back like an exposed vertebra. A chain-link fence surrounded its concrete playground. Members of the elite safety patrol, older kids, sixth graders mainly, stood at each of its entrances, wearing their fluorescent white belts that criss-crossed their chests and their metal badges. No one was allowed in the building until the bell rang, not even on rainy or bitter-cold days. Only the safety-patrol stayed warm.

My mother stood in front of the main entrance with me and a growing **13** crowd of noisy children. She looked like one of us, being no taller than the sixth-grade girls. She held my hand so tightly that my fingers cramped. When the bell rang, she walked me into the building and kissed my cheek. Apparently my father had done all the paperwork for my enrollment, because the next thing I remember was being led to my third-grade classroom by a black girl who had emerged from the principal's office.

Though I had learned some English at home during my first years in **14** Paterson, I had let it recede deep into my memory while learning Spanish in Puerto Rico. Once again I was the child in the cloud of silence, the one who had to be spoken to in sign language as if she were a deaf-mute. Some of the children even raised their voices when they spoke to me, as if I had trouble hearing. Since it was a large troublesome class composed mainly of black and Puerto Rican children, with a few working-class Italian children interspersed,[10] the teacher paid little attention to me. I re-learned the language quickly by the immersion method.[11] I remember one day, soon after I joined the rowdy class when our regular teacher was absent and Mrs. D., the sixth-grade teacher from across the hall, attempted to monitor both classes. She scribbled something on the chalkboard and went to her own room. I felt a pressing need to use the bathroom and asked Julio, the Puerto Rican boy who sat behind me, what I had to do to be excused. He said that Mrs. D. had written on the board that we could be excused by simply writing our names under the sign. I got up from my desk and started for the front of the room when I was struck on the head hard with a book. Startled and hurt, I turned around expecting to find one of the bad boys in my class, but it was Mrs. D. I faced. I remember her angry face, her fingers on my arms pulling me back to my desk, and her voice saying incomprehensible things to me in a hissing tone. Someone finally explained to her that I was new, that I did not speak English. I also remember how suddenly her face changed from anger to anxiety.

10. interspersed: mixed in
11. immersion method: method of learning a foreign language where the student is surrounded only by speakers of that language

But I did not forgive her for hitting me with that hard-cover spelling book. Yes, I would recognize that book even now. It was not until years later that I stopped hating that teacher for not understanding that I had been betrayed by a classmate, and by my inability to read her warning on the board. I instinctively understood then that language is the only weapon a child has against the absolute power of adults.

I quickly built up my arsenal[12] of words by becoming an insatiable[13]   **15**
reader of books. ■

Discussion and Writing Questions

1. Cofer writes that at some point after her early childhood she "learned that light is followed by darkness" (paragraph 3). What do you suppose she means by this?

2. How does the author seem to feel about her memories of Christmas in Puerto Rico? Is this a different feeling than she seems to have about her memories of Paterson?

3. Why does Cofer title her essay "One More Lesson"? What lesson does she learn? Why do you think she responded to her school experience by becoming a reader (and later, a writer), when another child might have learned to hate school?

4. Cofer uses rich description in this essay. Choose one paragraph that you think contains excellent description. What words and details help you "see" Cofer's young world?

Writing Assignments

1. Compare two places that have been important to you. You may want to concentrate on the people in those two places, or you might discuss the smells and sounds or other physical details of each location. Focus on the most important details.

2. Write about a lesson you learned, especially an experience of prejudice, misunderstanding, or achievement that strongly affected your attitude toward English class, reading, or school.

3. Currently, educators are debating how English should be taught to speakers of foreign languages. Some believe that bilingual education, where students are taught in their native language as well as in English, helps students learn better than the "immersion method" Cofer writes about. Take a stand for bilingual education or for the immersion method. Which do you think is better for students in the long run?

---

12. arsenal: stockpile of weapons
13. insatiable: unable to be satisfied

How to Get the Most out of Yourself

Alan Loy McGinnis

Why are some persons successful and productive while others struggle along unhappily? Alan Loy McGinnis, a psychotherapist, believes that the answer lies in self-image. In this essay, he presents numerous ways people can strengthen their self-image.

Our success at business, sports, friendship, love—nearly every enterprise 1 we attempt—is largely determined by our own self-image. People who have confidence in their personal worth seem to be magnets for success and happiness. Good things drop into their laps regularly, their relationships are long-lasting, their projects are usually carried to completion. To use the imagery of English poet William Blake, they "catch joy on the wing."

Conversely, some people seem to be magnets for failure and unhap- 2 piness. Their plans go awry,[1] they have a way of torpedoing their own potential successes, and nothing seems to work out for them. As a counselor, I see many such persons. Their problems usually stem from a difficulty with self-acceptance. When I am able to help them gain more confidence, often their troubles take care of themselves.

I believe that anyone can change his self-perception. A person with 3 low self-image is not doomed to a life of unhappiness and failure. It *is* possible to get rid of negative attitudes and gain the healthy confidence needed to realize one's dreams. Here's how:

Focus on your potential—not your limitations. When Helen Hayes was 4 a young actress, producer George Tyler told her that, were she four inches taller, she could become one of the great actresses of her time. "I decided," she says, "to lick my size. A string of teachers pulled and stretched till I felt I was in a medieval torture chamber. I gained nary[2] an inch—but my posture was military-straight. I became the tallest five-foot woman in the world. And my refusal to be limited by my limitations enabled me to play Mary of Scotland, one of the tallest queens in history."

Helen Hayes succeeded because she chose to focus on her strong 5 points, not her weak ones.

Many clients tell me that because they are not as smart or good-look- 6 ing or witty as others, they feel inferior. Probably no habit chips away at our self-confidence quite so effectively as that of scanning the people around us to see how we compare. And when we find that someone is indeed smarter, better-looking or wittier, it diminishes our sense of self-worth.

The Hasidic rabbi Zusya was asked on his deathbed what he thought 7 the kingdom of God would be like. "I don't know," he replied. "But one thing I *do* know. When I get there I am not going to be asked, 'Why

1. go awry: go off course
2. nary: not even one

weren't you Moses? Why weren't you David?' I am only going to be asked, 'Why weren't you Zusya? Why weren't you fully you?'"

Devote yourself to something you do well. There is nothing so common **8** as unsuccessful people with talent. Usually the problem lies not in discovering our natural aptitude but in developing that skill.

Young surgeons practice skills for months on end, such as tying knots **9** in a confined space or suturing. The refining of these skills is the surgeon's main method of improving total performance.

Many of us get interested in a field, but then the going gets tough, we **10** see that other people are more successful, and we become discouraged and quit. But it is often the boring, repetitive sharpening of our skills that will ultimately enable us to reach our goals.

Horace Bushnell, the great New England preacher, used to say, **11** "Somewhere under the stars God has a job for you to do, and nobody else can do it." Some of us must find our place by trial and error. It can take time, with dead ends along the way. But we should not get discouraged because others seem more skilled. Usually it is not raw talent but drive that makes the difference.

See yourself as successful. If I could plug into the minds of my patients **12** and listen to the statements they make to themselves, I am convinced that the majority of them would be negative: "I'm running late again—as usual." "My hair looks terrible this morning." "That was a stupid remark I made—she probably thinks I'm a dummy." Since thousands of these messages flash across our brains every day, it is small wonder that the result is a diminished self-image.

One daily exercise for building self-confidence is called "imaging" or **13** "visualization." In order to succeed, you must *see* yourself succeeding. Picture yourself approaching a difficult challenge with poise[3] and confidence. Athletes often visualize a move over and over in their minds; they see themselves hitting the perfect golf or tennis shot. When we burn such positive images into our minds deeply enough, they become a part of the unconscious, and we begin to expect to succeed.

Author and editor Norman Cousins wrote: "People are never more **14** insecure than when they become obsessed with their fears at the expense of their dreams." There is no doubt that if we can envision beneficial things happening, they have a way of actually occurring.

Break away from other people's expectations. It is a liberating step **15** when we decide to stop being what other people want us to be. Although opera singer Risë Stevens performed onstage with great poise, the self-confidence she felt before audiences evaporated in social situations. "My discomfort," she says, "came from trying to be something I was not—a star in the drawing room as well as onstage. If a clever person made a joke, I tried to top it—and failed. I pretended to be familiar with subjects I knew nothing of."

Stevens finally had a heart-to-heart talk with herself: "I realized that **16** I simply wasn't a wit or an intellectual and that I could succeed only as myself. I began listening and asking questions at parties instead of trying

3. poise: a look and feeling of self-assurance, calmness

to impress the guests. When I spoke, I tried to contribute, not to shine. Almost at once I started to feel a new warmth in my social contacts. They liked the real me better."

If we are true to our instincts, most of us will find that we naturally **17** develop certain trademarks. The discovery and expression of that uniqueness is one reason we are on this planet. Resisting conformity and developing some small eccentricities[4] are among the steps to independence and self-confidence.

Build a network of supportive relationships. Many of my clients scram- **18** ble to shore up[5] their self-images with various techniques, overlooking the source from which they will get help most readily—good friendships.

One of the surest ways to improve confidence is to make certain you **19** have lots of love in your life, to go to whatever lengths are necessary to construct a network of sustaining and nurturing relationships. In building such supportive relationships, most of my patients think their problem is in meeting new people. But the answer, really, is in deepening the friendships you presently have.

The extended family can be a major source of support and nurture. A **20** friend who is 45 tells me that visiting her parents in Indiana is always "a mixed bag." She makes connections with some relatives she'd just as soon not see anymore, and she usually has at least one blow-up with her parents. "But it's important to be around my family," she says. "I always come back feeling that I have a clearer idea of who I am, where I came from, and where I want to go."

She is a wise woman. Such connections with our heritage make our **21** identities more secure. As author John Dos Passos said, "A sense of continuity with the generations gone before can stretch like a lifeline across the scary present."

The distribution of talents in this world should not be our concern. Our **22** responsibility is to take the talents we have and ardently parlay[6] them to the highest possible achievement.

When Yoshihiko Yamamoto of Nagoya City, Japan, was six months **23** old, physicians told his parents that he was mentally retarded. With a hearing loss that strangled his speech and an I.Q. that tested very low, Yamamoto faced a bleak future.

But a new special-education teacher, Takashi Kawasaki, took a special **24** interest in the boy. Gradually Yamamoto began to smile in class. He learned to copy the characters from the blackboard and cartoons from magazines. One day, Yamamoto drew an accurate sketch of Nagoya Castle. Kawasaki had the boy transfer his design to a wood block and encouraged him to concentrate on printmaking. Eventually Yamamoto won first prize in an art contest. Today, his work is much sought after.

It is not important that Yoshihiko Yamamoto has limitations. The **25** important thing is that he has capitalized on his potential.

4. eccentricities: unusual or quirky personality traits or behavior
5. shore up: support, strengthen
6. parlay: turn into

Self-confidence, like happiness, is slippery when we set out to grab it for   26
its own sake. Usually it comes as a by-product. We lose ourselves in service or work, friendship or love, and suddenly one day we realize that we
are confident and happy. ■

Discussion and Writing Questions

1. McGinnis discusses several ways of overcoming poor self-esteem.
   What are these ways? Can you think of others he doesn't mention?

2. Which of these ways do you think is the most effective? The least effective? Why?

3. Identify the paragraphs in which McGinnis uses an anecdote, or brief
   story, to illustrate the topic sentence of the paragraph. Choose one or
   two of these paragraphs and illustrate the topic sentence with anecdotes from your own experience.

Writing Assignments

1. Give examples of ways a person might increase physical strength or
   some other capability or skill. For instance, tell what you or your
   friend did to train for a competitive event, such as a track meet or a
   football or basketball game. Use vivid details to make your illustration
   lively and interesting.

2. Write about someone whom you consider successful. What qualities or
   characteristics distinguish this person from others? The person need
   not be someone you know directly; he or she could be a politician, a
   rock star, a local personality, or an athlete. Be sure to choose someone
   about whom you know interesting details, so that your writing will
   engage your reader.

3. Choose one of the methods the author presents for improving self-
   esteem and restate the method as a topic sentence. Then write a paragraph that fully develops that topic sentence. For example, you could
   restate "Break away from other people's expectations" (paragraph 15)
   this way: "In order for me to break away from other people's expectations, I have to concentrate on what *I* want in life." The supporting
   details would then show how you concentrate on what you want.
   Remember to use details that clearly support the topic sentence.

Hunger of Memory

Richard Rodriguez

"The Workers"

Growing up in California as a second-generation Mexican American, Richard Rodriguez wanted to understand the lives of *los pobres*, the poor Mexican laborers he saw around him. In this selection **from *Hunger of Memory*, he tells of taking a summer job as a laborer and of learning about himself in the process.**

Freshman Seminar

1 It was at Stanford, one day near the end of my senior year, that a friend told me about a summer construction job he knew was available. I was quickly alert. Desire uncoiled[1] within me. My friend said that he knew I had been looking for summer employment. He knew I needed some money. Almost apologetically he explained: It was something I probably wouldn't be interested in, but a friend of his, a contractor, needed someone for the summer to do menial[2] jobs. There would be lots of shoveling and raking and sweeping. Nothing too hard. But nothing more interesting either. Still, the pay would be good. Did I want it? Or did I know someone who did?

all short sentences

2 I did. Yes, I said, surprised to hear myself say it.

3 In the weeks following, friends cautioned that I had no idea how hard physical labor really is. ("You only *think* you know what it is like to shovel for eight hours straight.") Their objections seemed to me challenges. They resolved the issue. I became happy with my plan. I decided, however, not to tell my parents. I wouldn't tell my mother because I could guess her worried reaction. I would tell my father only after the summer was over, when I could announce that, after all, I did know what "real work" is like.

4 The day I met the contractor (a Princeton graduate, it turned out), he asked me whether I had done any physical labor before. "In high school, during the summer," I lied. And although he seemed to regard me with skepticism,[3] he decided to give me a try. Several days later, expectant, I arrived at my first construction site. I would take off my shirt to the sun. And at last grasp desired sensation. No longer afraid. At last become like a *bracero*.[4] "We need those tree stumps out of here by tomorrow," the contractor said. I started to work.

5 I labored with excitement that first morning—and all the days after. The work was harder than I could have expected. But it was never as tedious as my friends had warned me it would be. There was too much physical pleasure in the labor. Especially early in the day, I would be most alert to the sensations of movement and straining. Beginning around seven each morning (when the air was still damp but the scent of weeds

---

1. uncoiled: loosened, unwound
2. menial: lowly, lacking status
3. skepticism: doubt
4. *bracero:* a Mexican living and working in the United States for a period of time

good description of work

and dry earth anticipated the heat of the sun), I would feel my body resist the first thrusts of the shovel. My arms, tightened by sleep, would gradually loosen; after only several minutes, sweat would gather in beads on my forehead and then—a short while later—I would feel my chest silky with sweat in the breeze. I would return to my work. A nervous spark of pain would fly up my arm and settle to burn like an ember in the thick of my shoulder. An hour, two passed. Three. My whole body would assume regular movements; my shoveling would be described by identical, even movements. Even later in the day, my enthusiasm for primitive sensation would survive the heat and the dust and the insects pricking my back. I would strain wildly for sensation as the day came to a close. At three-thirty, quitting time, I would stand upright and slowly let my head fall back, luxuriating[5] in the feeling of tightness relieved.

Work smarter not harder

Some of the men working nearby would watch me and laugh. Two or three of the older men took the trouble to teach me the right way to use a pick, the correct way to shovel. "You're doing it wrong, too fucking hard," one man scolded. Then proceeded to show me—what persons who work with their bodies all their lives quickly learn—the most economical way to use one's body in labor.

"Don't make your back do so much work," he instructed. I stood impatiently listening, half listening, vaguely watching, then noticed his work-thickened fingers clutching the shovel. I was annoyed. I wanted to tell him that I enjoyed shoveling the wrong way. And I didn't want to learn the right way. I wasn't afraid of back pain. I liked the way my body felt sore at the end of the day.

It was a good exp. because it wasn't The ONLY way he could make a living About having CHOICES in life

I was about to, but, as it turned out, I didn't say a thing. Rather it was at that moment I realized that I was fooling myself if I expected a few weeks of labor to gain me admission to the world of the laborer. I would not learn in three months what my father had meant by "real work." I was not bound to this job; I could imagine its rapid conclusion. For me the sensations of exertion and fatigue could be savored. For my father or uncle, working at comparable jobs when they were my age, such sensations were to be feared. Fatigue took a different toll on their bodies—and minds.

It was, I know, a simple insight. But it was with this realization that I took my first step that summer toward realizing something even more important about the "worker." In the company of carpenters, electricians, plumbers, and painters at lunch, I would often sit quietly, observant. I was not shy in such company. I felt easy, pleased by the knowledge that I was casually accepted, my presence taken for granted by men (exotics[6]) who worked with their hands. Some days the younger men would talk and talk about sex, and they would howl at women who drove by in cars. Other days the talk at lunchtime was subdued;[7] men gathered in separate groups. It depended on who was around. There were rough, good-natured

6

7

8

9

5. luxuriating: enjoying with deep pleasure
6. exotics: people who are quite unfamiliar
7. subdued: quiet, constrained

workers. Others were quiet. The more I remember that summer, the more I realize that there was no single *type* of worker. I am embarrassed to say I had not expected such diversity. I certainly had not expected to meet, for example, a plumber who was an abstract painter in his off hours and admired the work of Mark Rothko. Nor did I expect to meet so many workers with college diplomas. (They were the ones who were not surprised that I intended to enter graduate school in the fall.) I suppose what I really want to say here is painfully obvious, but I must say it nevertheless: The men of that summer were middle-class Americans. They certainly didn't constitute[8] an oppressed society. Carefully completing their work sheets; talking about the fortunes of local football teams; planning Las Vegas vacations; comparing the gas mileage of various makes of campers—they were not *los pobres*[9] my mother had spoken about.

On two occasions, the contractor hired a group of Mexican aliens. **10** They were employed to cut down some trees and haul off debris. In all, there were six men of varying age. The youngest in his late twenties; the oldest (his father?) perhaps sixty years old. They came and they left in a single old truck. Anonymous men. They were never introduced to the other men at the site. Immediately upon their arrival, they would follow the contractor's directions, start working—rarely resting—seemingly driven by a fatalistic[10] sense that work which had to be done was best done as quickly as possible.

I watched them sometimes. Perhaps they watched me. The only time **11** I saw them pay me much notice was one day at lunchtime when I was laughing with the other men. The Mexicans sat apart when they ate, just as they worked by themselves. Quiet. I rarely heard them say much to each other. All I could hear were their voices calling out sharply to one another, giving directions. Otherwise, when they stood briefly resting, they talked among themselves in voices too hard to overhear.

The contractor knew enough Spanish, and the Mexicans—or at least **12** the oldest of them, their spokesman—seemed to know enough English to communicate. But because I was around, the contractor decided one day to make me his translator. (He assumed I could speak Spanish.) I did what I was told. Shyly I went over to tell the Mexicans that the *patrón*[11] wanted them to do something else before they left for the day. As I started to speak, I was afraid with my old fear that I would be unable to pronounce the Spanish words. But it was a simple instruction I had to convey. I could say it in phrases.

The dark sweating faces turned toward me as I spoke. They stopped **13** their work to hear me. Each nodded in response. I stood there. I wanted to say something more. But what could I say in Spanish, even if I could have pronounced the words right? Perhaps I just wanted to engage them in small talk, to be assured of their confidence, our familiarity. I thought

---

8. constitute: make up
9. *los pobres:* the poor people
10. fatalistic: believing events to be predetermined; yielding to one's fate
11. *patrón:* boss

for a moment to ask them where in Mexico they were from. Something like that. And maybe I wanted to tell them (a lie, if need be) that my parents were from the same part of Mexico.

I stood there.

Their faces watched me. The eyes of the man directly in front of me moved slowly over my shoulder, and I turned to follow his glance toward *el patrón* some distance away. For a moment I felt swept up by that glance into the Mexicans' company. But then I heard one of them returning to work. And then the others went back to work. I left them without saying anything more.

When they had finished, the contractor went over to pay them in cash. (He later told me that he paid them collectively—"for the job," though he wouldn't tell me their wages. He said something quickly about the good rate of exchange "in their own country.") I can still hear the loudly confident voice he used with the Mexicans. It was the sound of the *gringo*[12] I had heard as a very young boy. And I can still hear the quiet, indistinct sounds of the Mexican, the oldest, who replied. At hearing that voice I was sad for the Mexicans. Depressed by their vulnerability. Angry at myself. The adventure of the summer seemed suddenly ludicrous. I would not shorten the distance I felt from *los pobres* with a few weeks of physical labor. I would not become like them. They were different from me. ■

Discussion and Writing Questions

1. Why does the author decide to take the summer construction job?

2. Why does Rodriguez say he didn't mind shoveling the wrong way? As he says this, what does he realize about the men he works with?

3. Why does the experience with the Mexican laborers have such an impact on Rodriguez?

4. Rodriguez might have written his essay using comparison or contrast, discussing his feelings before and after his work on the summer construction crew. Why do you think he chose to write it as a narrative?

Writing Assignments

1. Retell Rodriguez's narrative from the point of view of one of the Mexican laborers. You could retell the story Rodriguez tells about speaking with the men, but this time from *your* point of view as a laborer. Or you could describe a typical day working for the *patrón*, doing various jobs at the construction site.

2. Tell what it is like to do a particular kind of work. You may choose, like Rodriguez, to describe hard, manual labor, or you may have a less

---

12. *gringo:* slang for a person from the United States

[handwritten margin notes:]

After that summer, he was no longer ashamed of his body. Has lectured in ghetto highschools since & notices ghetto girls mimic highfashion models. Bold. Theatrical

From the context of his life. people see his → (darker) complexion & assume he just came from skiing in Switzerland or the man who carries his luggage in NY assumes he's just returned from the Caribbean. "My skin means nothing." He thought disadvantaged life was shown by particular occupation.

★ "It would go differently for me - My long education would favor me"

[margin numbers:] 14 15 16

strenuous form of work in mind. Whatever work you tell about, be sure to describe it in detail, so that your audience can picture exactly what the job involves.

20 min in class writing

3. Rodriguez writes of the labor his father or uncle would have known during a life of hard work. Write about a person of an older generation than yours. What kind of work did he or she do? Consider that person's job opportunities, or lack of them.

Two Views of the River

Mark Twain

Discuss something that has changed for you.

One of the America's foremost humorists and writers, Mark Twain was, for a time, the pilot of a riverboat on the Mississippi. Here he views a river sunset from two perspectives, one as a new pilot and one as an experienced "reader" of the river.

Now when I had mastered the language of this water, and had come to know every trifling[1] feature that bordered the great river as familiarly as I knew the letters of the alphabet, I had made a valuable acquisition.[2] But I had lost something, too. I had lost something which could never be restored to me while I lived. All the grace, the beauty, the poetry, had gone out of the majestic river! I still keep in mind a certain wonderful sunset which I witnessed when steamboating was new to me. A broad expanse of the river was turned to blood; in the middle distance the red hue brightened into gold, through which a solitary log came floating black and conspicuous;[3] in one place a long, slanting mark lay sparkling upon the water; in another the surface was broken by boiling, tumbling rings, that were as many-tinted as an opal; where the ruddy flush was faintest, was a smooth spot that was covered with graceful circles and radiating lines, ever so delicately traced; the shore on our left was densely wooded, and the somber shadow that fell from this forest was broken in one place by a long, ruffled trail that shone like silver; and high above the forest wall a clean-stemmed dead tree waved a single leafy bough that glowed like a flame in the unobstructed splendor that was flowing from the sun. There were graceful curves, reflected images, woody heights, soft distances; and over the whole scene, far and near, the dissolving lights drifted steadily, enriching it every passing moment with new marvels of coloring.

I stood like one bewitched. I drank it in, in a speechless rapture. The world was new to me, and I had never seen anything like this at home. But as I have said, a day came when I began to cease from noting the

1. trifling: small, unimportant
2. acquisition: a gain
3. conspicuous: noticeable

glories and the charms which the moon and the sun and the twilight wrought upon the river's face; another day came when I ceased altogether to note them. Then, if that sunset scene had been repeated, I should have looked upon it without rapture, and should have commented upon it, inwardly, after this fashion: "This sun means that we are going to have wind to-morrow; that floating log means that the river is rising, small thanks to it; that slanting mark on the water refers to a bluff reef which is going to kill somebody's steamboat one of these nights, if it keeps on stretching out like that; those tumbling 'boils' show a dissolving bar and a changing channel there; the lines and circles in the slick water over yonder are a warning that that troublesome place is shoaling up[4] dangerously; that silver streak in the shadow of the forest is the 'break' from a new snag, and he has located himself in the very best place he could have found to fish for steamboats; that tall dead tree, with a single living branch, is not going to last long, and then how is a body ever going to get through this blind place at night without the friendly old landmark?"

No, the romance and beauty were all gone from the river. All the   3 value any feature of it had for me now was the amount of usefulness it could furnish toward compassing the safe piloting of a steamboat. Since those days, I have pitied doctors from my heart. What does the lovely flush in a beauty's cheek mean to a doctor but a "break" that ripples above some deadly disease? Are not all her visible charms sown[5] thick with what are to him the signs and symbols of hidden decay? Does he ever see her beauty at all, or doesn't he simply view her professionally, and comment upon her unwholesome condition all to himself? And doesn't he sometimes wonder whether he has gained most or lost most by learning his trade? ■

Questions for Discussion and Writing

1. Twain says that, in learning about the river, he "had lost something which could never be restored to me while I lived" (paragraph 1). What does he mean?

2. In paragraph 1, Twain discusses a memorable sunset on the river that he witnessed as a young pilot. In paragraph 2, he tells how more knowledge changed his response to that sunset. What kinds of changes have occurred in him? What do these changes mean for him? How can you tell?

3. The author implies that there are tradeoffs in learning about something in depth. What might be the positive effects of such learning?

4. Twain gives *all* of his first impressions of the river, then *all* of his later impressions. Is this plan more effective or less effective than a point-by-point comparison-contrast of each element of the river? Why or why not?

4. shoaling up: becoming shallow
5. sown: implanted

Writing Assignments

1. Twain contrasts his first impression of the Mississippi with a later impression of the same river. Today, we might hear someone describe a river before and after pollution dirtied it or a stretch of countryside before and after the building of a new housing development or landfill. Contrast your memories and your current impressions of something in nature, such as a river or an area of land, or of another setting, such as a neighborhood or a city. Either follow the plan of "Two Views of the River" or follow a point-by-point plan.

2. You've probably heard the saying "You can never go home again." Write a comparison of your feelings about your home before you left it (to attend college, move to your own apartment, go into the military, or marry) with the feelings you experienced the first time you returned. Or write about returning to visit your old home after moving to another. Had anything changed for you about your home? What had changed within you?

3. Write about an experience in which you felt that you lost as much as (or more than) you gained. You may have been in a romantic relationship that went from exciting to dull or even bitter, or perhaps you took a much-anticipated vacation that turned into a nightmare of bad weather and illness.

10 min: Describe a place that you know very well — your private place, a place where you go when you want to get away from everyone & everything.

How to Put Off Doing a Job

Andy Rooney

Andy Rooney is perhaps best known for his humorous commentary on the TV show "60 Minutes," where he explains his views on everything from milk cartons and soap to international affairs. Here he presents—in typical tongue-in-cheek style—his belief in putting off until tomorrow what should be done today.

February is one of the most difficult times of the year to put off doing 1
some of the things you've been meaning to do. There's no vacation coming up, there are no long weekends scheduled in the immediate future; it's just this long, grim February. Don't tell me it's a short month. February is the longest by a week.

Because I have so many jobs that I don't like to do, I've been reviewing 2
the notebook I keep with notes in it for how to put off doing a job. Let's see now, what could I use today?

■ Go to the store to get something. This is one of my most depend- 3
able putter-offers. If I start a job and find I need some simple tool or a piece of hardware, I stop right there. I put on some better clothes, get in the car and drive to the store. If that store doesn't have what I'm

looking for, I go to another. Often I'm attracted to some item that has nothing whatsoever to do with the job I was about to start and I buy that instead. For instance, if I go to the hardware store to buy a new snow shovel so I can clean out the driveway, but then I see a can of adhesive spray that will keep rugs in place on the floor, I'm apt to buy the adhesive spray. That ends the idea I had to shovel out the driveway.

■ Tidy up the work area before starting a job. This has been useful **4** to me over the years as a way of not getting started. Things are such a mess in my workshop, on my desk, in the kitchen and in the trunk of the car that I decide I've got to go through some of the junk before starting to work.

■ Make those phone calls. There's no sense trying to do a job if you **5** have other things on your mind, so get them out of the way first. This is a very effective way of not getting down to work. Call friends you've been meaning to call, or the distant relative you've been out of touch with. Even if someone is in California, Texas or Chicago and you're in Florida, call. Paying for a long-distance call is still easier and less unpleasant than actually getting down to work.

■ Study the problem. It's foolish to jump right into a job before **6** you've thought it through. You might be doing the wrong thing. There might be an easier way to accomplish what you want to do, so think it over carefully from every angle. Perhaps someone has written a how-to book about the job you have in front of you. Buy the book and then sit down and read it. Ask friends who have had the same job for advice about the best way to do it.

Once you've studied the problem from every angle, don't make a quick **7** decision. Sleep on it.

■ Take a coffee break. Although the term "coffee break" assumes **8** that you are drinking coffee in an interim[1] period between stretches of solid work, this is not necessarily so. Don't be bound by old ideas about when it's proper to take a coffee break. If taking it before you get started is going to help keep you from doing the work, by all means take your coffee break first.

■ As a last resort before going to work, think this thing over. Is this **9** really what you want to do with your life? Philosophize. Nothing is better for putting off doing something than philosophizing.[2] Are you a machine, trapped in the same dull, day-after-day routine that everyone else is in? Or are you a person who makes up his or her own mind about things? Are you going to do these jobs because that's what's expected of you, or are you going to break the mold and live the way you feel like living?

Try these as ways for not getting down to work. ■   **10**

Discussion and Writing Questions

1. Why is February one of the hardest months to put off doing things?

1. interim: the time between two events
2. philosophizing: intense thinking about important issues or questions

2. What is Rooney's most dependable means of avoiding work?

3. Do you suppose the author avoids work as much as he seems to claim? Why or why not?

4. This essay gives examples of things a person can do to avoid work. Rooney also uses process to make his point. In which paragraphs is process used?

Writing Assignments

1. Taking a humorous approach, give examples of ways in which someone can put off doing a particular job. You could write about how a teenager avoids doing homework, how a child avoids cleaning his or her bedroom, or how an adult postpones paying taxes, cleaning out the refrigerator, or inviting the in-laws to dinner.

2. Groups of people can avoid unpleasant tasks as easily as individuals. For instance, legislators can refrain from voting on a bill for fear of angering voters. Citizens can avoid taking action on such community problems as the homeless by saying the government can do it. Write about what happens when a group of people postpones action on some important activity. For example, you might discuss delays in caring for the homeless in your town or a college's refusal to look at drug use by athletes. Why do people delay? What might be done to wake them up?

3. The mirror opposite of the person who puts off a job would be someone who energetically bustles around, immediately taking care of all sorts of jobs and errands. Contrast the different personalities of two people you know. For instance, you might discuss a pair of twins, one of whom is almost a hermit, while the other is very sociable. Or talk about the differences between your mountain-climbing aunt and her stay-at-home husband.

Some Thoughts About Abortion

Anna Quindlen

Since the *Roe vs. Wade* Supreme Court decision of 1973, the issue of abortion has gripped the United States as perhaps never before. In this essay, noted *New York Times* columnist Anna Quindlen describes her own mixed feelings about the subject, and at the same time gives persuasive reasons for keeping abortion legal.

It was always the look on their faces that told me first. I was the fresh- 1
man dormitory counselor and they were the freshmen at a women's college where everyone was smart. One of them would come into my room, a golden girl, a valedictorian, an 800 verbal score on the S.A.T.'s, and her

eyes would be empty, seeing only a busted future, the devastation of her life as she knew it. She had failed biology, messed up the math; she was pregnant.

That was when I became pro-choice. **2**

It was the look in his eyes that I will always remember, too. They were **3** as black as the bottom of a well, and in them for a few minutes I thought I saw myself the way I had always wished to be—clear, simple, elemental, at peace. My child looked at me and I looked back at him in the delivery room, and I realized that out of a sea of infinite possibilities it had come down to this: a specific person, born on the hottest day of the year, conceived on a Christmas Eve, made by his father and me miraculously from scratch.

Once I believed that there was a little blob of formless protoplasm[1] **4** in there and a gynecologist went after it with a surgical instrument, and that was that. Then I got pregnant myself—eagerly, intentionally, by the right man, at the right time—and I began to doubt. My abdomen still flat, my stomach roiling with morning sickness, I felt not that I had protoplasm inside, but, instead, a complete human being in miniature to whom I could talk, sing, make promises. Neither of these views was accurate; instead, I think, the reality is something in the middle. And that is where I find myself now, in the middle—hating the idea of abortions, hating the idea of having them outlawed.

For I know it is the right thing in some times and places. I remember **5** sitting in a shabby clinic far uptown with one of those freshmen, only three months after the Supreme Court had made what we were doing possible, and watching with wonder as the lovely first love she had had with a nice boy unraveled[2] over the space of an hour as they waited for her to be called, degenerated[3] into sniping[4] and silences. I remember a year or two later seeing them pass on campus and not even acknowledge each other because their conjoining had caused them so much pain, and I shuddered to think of them married, with a small psyche in their unready and unwilling hands.

I've met fourteen-year-olds who were pregnant and said they could **6** not have abortions because of their religion, and I see in their eyes the shadows of twenty-two-year-olds I've talked to who lost their kids to foster care because they hit them or used drugs or simply had no money for food and shelter. I read not long ago about a teenager who said she meant to have an abortion but she spent the money on clothes instead: now she has a baby who turns out to be a lot more trouble than a toy. The people who hand out those execrable[5] little pictures of dismembered fetuses at abortion clinics seem to forget the extraordinary pain children may endure after they are born when they are unwanted, even hated, or simply tolerated.

I believe that in a contest between the living and the almost living, **7**

1. protoplasm: living matter
2. unraveled: came apart
3. degenerated: became worse
4. sniping: bickering, arguing
5. execrable: disgusting

the latter must, if necessary, give way to the will of the former. That is what the fetus is to me, the almost living. These questions began to plague me—and, I've discovered, a good many other women—after I became pregnant. But they became even more acute after I had my second child, mainly because he is so different from his brother. On two random nights eighteen months apart the same two people managed to conceive, and on one occasion the tumult[6] within turned itself into a curly-haired brunet with merry black eyes who walked and talked late and loved the whole world, and on another it became a blond with hazel Asian eyes and a pug nose who tried to conquer the world almost as soon as he entered it.

8   If we were to have an abortion next time for some reason or another, which infinite possibility becomes, not a reality, but a nullity?[7] The girl with the blue eyes? The improbable redhead? The natural athlete? The thinker? My husband, ever at the heart of the matter, put it another way. Knowing he is finding two children somewhat more overwhelming than he expected, I asked if he would want me to have an abortion if I accidentally became pregnant again right away. "And waste a perfectly good human being?" he said.

9   Coming to this quandary[8] has been difficult for me. In fact, I believe the issue of abortion is difficult for all thoughtful people. I don't know anyone who has had an abortion who has been casual about it. If there is one thing I find intolerable about most of the so-called right-to-lifers, it is that they try to portray abortion rights as something that feminists thought up on a slow Saturday over a light lunch. That is nonsense. I also know that some people who support abortion rights are most comfortable with a monolithic[9] position because it seems the strongest front against the smug and sometimes violent opposition.

10   But I don't feel all one way about abortion anymore, and I don't think it serves a just cause to pretend that many of us do. For years I believed that a woman's right to choose was absolute, but now I wonder. Do I, with a stable home and marriage and sufficient stamina and money, have the freedom to choose abortion because a pregnancy is inconvenient just now? Legally I do have the right; legally I want always to have that right. It is the morality of exercising it under those circumstances that makes me wonder.

11   Technology has foiled[10] us. The second trimester has become a time of resurrection; a fetus at six months can be one woman's late abortion, another's premature, viable[11] child. Photographers now have film of embryos the size of a grape, oddly human, flexing their fingers, sucking their thumbs. Women have amniocentesis[12] to find out whether they are carrying a child with birth defects that they may choose to abort. Before

6. tumult: energetic movement
7. nullity: nonexistence
8. quandary: tough spot, predicament
9. monolithic: unified and solid
10. foiled: tricked, confused
11. viable: able to live
12. amniocentesis: a medical procedure for checking the amniotic fluid in the uterus

the procedure, they must have a sonogram, one of those fuzzy black-and-white photos like a love song heard through static on the radio, which shows someone is in there.

I have taped on my VCR a public television program in which some- 12 how, inexplicably,[13] a film is shown of a fetus *in utero*[14] scratching its face, seemingly putting up a tiny hand to shield itself from the camera's eye. It would make a potent weapon in the arsenal of the antiabortionists. I grow sentimental about it as it floats in the salt water, part fish, part human being. It is almost living, but not quite. It has almost turned my heart around, but not quite turned my head. ▪

Discussion and Writing Questions

1. Quindlen describes two positions she has taken about abortion. What are they?

2. In which paragraph does the author begin to express doubts about abortion? Why does she have these doubts?

3. By the end of her essay, how does Quindlen feel about abortion?

4. What types of proof does the author use in her argument?

Writing Assignments

1. Write on an issue about which you are, like Quindlen, undecided. Choose a topic you know fairly well so that you can present solid arguments for both sides. Be objective, but let your reader know which side you finally find more persuasive.

2. Do you believe that teen-agers should be required to inform their parents before obtaining an abortion? Argue in favor of or against this position.

3. Quindlen first gained experience with the abortion issue as a freshman dorm counselor. Write about a time that you once counseled, or gave advice to, a friend in need. Your friend might have been contemplating an abortion, like some of the young women Quindlen describes. She or he may have been fighting with a mate or having a problem with money, career decisions, or school.

13. inexplicably: unexplainably
14. *in utero:* in the mother's uterus

On Kids and Couples

Francine Klagsbrun

In what ways does a new child change a couple's relationship? Francine Klagsbrun, in her interviews with a number of adults, uncovers many examples—some humorous, some quite serious.

Once a couple have a child, everything in life changes. Raising children **1** may be the most rewarding job in the world, but it is also undoubtedly the most difficult—an "impossible profession," Salvador Minuchin[1] called it. Or in the words of one mother, "With kids, you're damned if you do and you're damned if you don't, meaning you never never know what's right." True, there are hundreds of experts out there telling us in books and articles what's right. The problem is that what's right with one is wrong with the next. Fashions in childrearing change and so does expert advice. In the end, as everyone knows, you and your spouse and your child have to figure out how to handle each other.

Having a child is like getting married: you have to experience it to **2** understand it. As prepared as anybody is, nobody is really prepared, at least not for the first child. The way you eat, the way you play, the way you work, the way you think—they all become different with the arrival of a baby. One of my favorite anecdotes[2] was told to me by a professor who described bringing his wife home from the hospital with their beautiful newborn son. They settled the baby in his sparkling bassinette, played with him for a while, then put on their coats and headed out to get some pizza. Partway through the door his wife cried, "Oh, my God, we left the baby alone," and ran back. They had simply forgotten that a new person had joined their lives and that many years would pass before they could casually leave the house together without thinking about him.

For a couple, a child is an interruption—a constant interruption that **3** needs to be fed, cared for, loved. The baby interrupts the flow between parents, the one-on-one intimacy that had existed before. A third being now becomes a focal point in the marriage; he or she also becomes a medium[3] through whom flow the issues and tensions with which partners themselves may be grappling. In her humorous but serious novel *Heartburn*, about the breakup of her marriage, Nora Ephron describes the effects of having a child this way:

"After Sam was born I remember thinking that no one had ever told **4** me how much I would love my child; now, of course, I realized something no one ever tells you: that a child is a grenade. When you have a baby you set off an explosion in your marriage, and when the dust settles, your marriage is different from what it was." And she goes on: "All those idiotically lyrical articles about sharing childrearing duties never mention

1. Salvador Minuchin: well-known family therapist
2. anecdotes: brief stories
3. medium: the means by which the parents communicate with each other

that, nor do they allude to[4] something else that happens when a baby is born, which is that all the power struggles of the marriage have a new playing field. The baby wakes up in the middle of the night, and instead of jumping out of bed, you lie there thinking: whose turn is it? If it's your turn, you have to get up; if it's his turn, then why is he still lying there asleep while you're awake wondering whose turn it is?"

Among the people I interviewed, arguments were said to center 5 around children more than around any other issue in the marriage. Neither money nor sex nor in-laws nor work was mentioned as often as children as sources of disagreement in a marriage. For some couples, the tensions begin early on, almost as soon as the baby is born. A wife's deep involvement with a newborn baby can make her husband feel left out, almost like a sibling whose mother has abandoned him for the other child, the younger and cuter one. In turn, the husband's sullenness or jealousy can push the wife ever closer to the baby for comfort and emotional support. Even when a husband involves himself in caring for a baby, as so many do now, it may be hard for him to break through the physical and psychological closeness of a mother to her infant, especially if the mother is breast-feeding.

Added to this issue, a certain amount of sexual distancing often takes 6 place after the birth of a child. For a woman, the disinterest may be due to hormonal changes or to the enormous physical satisfaction she gets from holding and cuddling her baby. For both parents, there is the exhaustion and emotional drain of caring for an infant, an exhaustion that may continue even as a baby gets older and certainly as other children arrive. Children's demands and needs tire parents out, and the preoccupation with children in a family can shift interests and energies away from sexual desires. (They shift back again, of course, and many couples help things along by taking time out for themselves—getting a babysitter or a family member to stay with the baby during evenings or weekends while they concentrate on each other.)

Children may inhibit sex also simply because they are *there*, in the 7 next room or, at the most unexpected times, in parents' rooms. A topic of perennial[5] interest among parents is whether to lock their bedroom door so a child cannot enter when they may be making love, and what to say to a child who does see them in the act. In either case, a child's presence in a family may make sex between partners more self-conscious than ever before.

It may also raise career tensions. Many a couple, like Kimberly and 8 Randy, who are cool and confident before a child is born about their ability to handle a child and two careers, find the actuality more difficult than expected. The smoothest-running dual-career families are those that can afford, and find, excellent help to care for home and children. In most others, partners constantly juggle and trade off time with each other. Who takes off from work to take the baby to the pediatrician, later to the dentist? Who stays home with a child when she's sick? And who loses a

---

4. allude to: hint at, refer to
5. perennial: happening again and again

workday to go to a school play (an activity at which no one can substitute for a parent)? "When you're a working mother, you give up everything except your work and your family," said one woman. Working fathers make their sacrifices too, and the sorting out of who does what can generate anxieties in the marriage.

Then there are less expected work issues. For some men, liberation 9 flies out the window when a baby is carried through the door. No matter how accepting they may be of a wife's work or career, once they have a child, they want their wives to be home, if not full time, then much of the time. They may be willing to "help out," and they may agree to hiring an outsider to handle some duties, but they expect, as their fathers expected, the major responsibility to rest with their wives. In such situations, the baby becomes the catalyst for a deeper struggle going on between the couple, the power struggle Nora Ephron describes, but even more, the struggle over roles and work and each spouse's interpretation of the marriage.

"I just think," said one husband to me in front of his wife, "that a 10 baby needs a parent at home. I think one of us needs to be here for him now, and one of us will need to be here later when he gets older and goes off to school and comes home from school."

"Does she have to be the one who's here with the baby? Isn't it pos- 11 sible for you to be here some of the time?" I asked.

"I can't organize my work that way," he answered quickly (he's a den- 12 tist), "but Debbie can find part-time work."

Debbie shrugged. "We're negotiating," she said, as if wanting to stop 13 the conversation before it got pushed into a track from which she knew she would have trouble extricating[6] it. "The problem for me is he makes more money than I do, so I'm on weaker grounds. But we'll work this thing out."

I expect they will, but it will take quite a bit of negotiating. The baby 14 has set in motion other conflicts between them that have to do with how they view themselves and each other. Had it not been for the baby, the dispute might have taken other forms or may not even have arisen for many years. It has arisen now, and the baby became the trigger for setting it off.

Children can be explosives in other areas. The parents of four children 15 portrayed their most heated battles as resulting from the kids' sloppiness and their way of strewing belongings in every room of the house. The husband would shout at the children, and when his wife tried to calm him down, they would get into a brawl of their own in which he would accuse her of being too easy on the children. The longer we spoke, however, the clearer it became to me (and to them too, I believe, although we didn't articulate it) that his anger at the children about their sloppiness was also an expression of his anger at his wife's careless housekeeping. "Gail can leave an open can of tomato sauce in the refrigerator for weeks, until it's covered with green mold, and not even notice," he said with a tight smile. Or "I've had friends come to visit and they go into the kitchen to

---

6. extricating: getting out of a difficult situation

see if the oven is as dirty as I told them it is. And it is." Or "I'm used to seeing cobwebs wherever I look in this house." Instead of shouting directly at his wife about her habits, which may be too threatening to their relationship, he detours his anger through the kids. She responds by defending the children, which is also a way of defending herself, and both avoid an open battle around the things they dislike most about each other.

Children are sometimes used more openly as an excuse to cover up for 16 difficulties between parents. A spouse who wants to avoid sex, for example, may use the excuse that the children will hear, and then will complain that kids interfere with sex in marriage. In more serious situations, children become scapegoats[7] for the angers and disappointments of mates. The parents may blame the child for everything that is wrong between them—"If Tommy weren't doing so badly in school, we would have no problems in this family"—refusing to recognize that Tommy's difficulties may be not the cause but the result of family troubles. ∎

Discussion and Writing Questions

1. Klagsbrun describes several kinds of conflict that can arise between people when they have a child. What are they? Can you think of others that she doesn't mention?

2. The author points out that the child "becomes a medium" for a couple's issues and tensions (paragraph 3). What does she mean?

3. Which of the examples do you think is the most serious? Why?

4. Not every topic sentence of this essay supports the thesis statement directly, yet the essay is well organized. How does Klagsbrun develop her thesis? That is, how does she organize her essay?

Writing Assignments

1. As this reading selection illustrates, we all face stress in our lives: parenthood, job stress, family pressures. How we handle stress is important for our happiness and health. Write about effective ways of handling stress. You may want to give examples of techniques that have worked for you, such as getting some exercise, talking with a friend, or meditating on a peaceful scene.

2. Discuss how you balance two or more demands on your time. You might write about having a family and attending school or juggling family, school, and a job, for example. You might narrate a particular morning you remember as you prepared your child for school while getting yourself dressed. Or you may write about the process of a daily routine.

---

7. scapegoats: people who take the blame unfairly for others

3. The author says that you have to experience the birth of a child in order to understand that event (paragraph 2). What event from your own life would you characterize this way? Perhaps you feel that you didn't really know what "going to college" was all about until you attended college. Or maybe you changed your notion of the ideal romance after you really fell in love. Try to retell the experience so vividly that the reader will be able to understand it.

Do You Know Who Your Friends Are?

Larry Letich

Larry Letich observes that many men over thirty spend more time caring for their lawns than they do nurturing friendships with one another. Arguing that men know little about building friendships, he gives reasons why he believes this is true and then suggests practical steps to help men out of the isolation trap.

You gotta have frieeends," sang Bette Midler. But most men past the age 1 of 30 don't have friends—not really. They have colleagues and work buddies, golf partners and maybe a "couple" friend or two, where the bond is really between the wives. If they say they *do* have a best friend, often it turns out to be an old friend whom they see or speak to once every few years.

Sadly, for most men in our culture, male friendship is a part of their 2 distant past. One man spoke for many at a recent men's conference in Montclair, N.J., when he lamented, "I haven't made a new friend in 25 years."

Why is this so? All sorts of theories are thrown around, from "homo- 3 phobia"[1] to the absurd idea that men are biologically geared to competitiveness, which precludes[2] friendship. But the major reason for the shortage of true friendship among men in America is that our culture discourages it.

Male friendship is idealized in the abstract (think of *Butch Cassidy* 4 *and the Sundance Kid* and numerous other "buddy movies"), but if a man manages to have any true emotional attachment to another man, a lot of subtle pressures are placed on him to eliminate it. The most obvious time this happens is when a man gets married (especially if he's still in his 20s). Think of the impression that comes to mind from a thousand movies and TV shows about the guy who "leaves his wife" for the evening to "go out with the guys." Invariably, the other guys are shown as both imma-ture *and* lower-class, losers who'll never amount to anything in life. The

1. homophobia: irrational fear and hatred of homosexuals
2. precludes: prevents

message is clear—no self-respecting middle-class man hangs out regularly with his friends.

In fact, friendship between men is rarely spoken of at all. Instead, we hear about something called male bonding, as if all possible non-sexual connection between men is rooted in some crude, instinctual impulse. More often than not, male friendship, reduced to male bonding, is sniggered at as something terribly juvenile and possibly dangerous. **5**

This denigration[3] of male friendship fits well into . . . capitalism. The decline in blue-collar jobs and the great white-collar work speed-up of the 1980s made no man's job safe. And money—not the richness of a man's relationship with family, friends, and community—became even more so the universally accepted value of a man's worth. **6**

In this system, men . . . are put in the position of constantly, and often ruthlessly, competing with all other men for the limited number of positions higher up the ladder—or even to hold onto their jobs at all. Men are encouraged not to trust one another, and are frankly told never to band together. (For example, in most places it is a serious faux pas,[4] and often a dismissable offense, simply to tell a fellow worker what you make for a living; supposedly it is "bad for morale.") Naturally, this keeps men—and women, too—constantly knocking themselves out for the next promotion rather than demanding real changes, like cutting the CEO's[5] million-dollar salary down to size. **7**

Given the kind of sterile, high-pressure work environments men are expected to devote themselves to, it's not surprising that the ideal American man is supposed to feel little or no passion about anything. As Robert Bly[6] has pointed out, the most damaged part of the psyche[7] in modern man is the "lover," meaning not just the ability to make love, but the ability to love life, to feel, to be either tender or passionate. But passion—and with it the capacity for intimacy—is absolutely essential for friendship. **8**

It's also not surprising that our society's ideal man is not supposed to have any emotional needs. Since few men can actually live up to that ideal, it's considered acceptable, even laudable,[8] for him to channel all his emotional needs in one direction—his wife and children. A man who has any other important emotional bonds (that are not based on duty, such as an ailing parent) is in danger of being called neglectful, or irresponsible, or weak, because forging emotional bonds with others takes time—time that is supposed to be spent "getting ahead." **9**

Small wonder that the only friendships allowed are those that serve a "business" purpose or those that can be fit effortlessly into one's leisure time. Maintaining one's lawn is more important than maintaining one's friendships. In keeping with this, there are no rituals and no respect given **10**

3. denigration: undervaluing
4. faux pas: French for a social error, mistake
5. CEO's: Chief Executive Officer's
6. Robert Bly: a poet who writes and lectures about men's issues
7. psyche: the deep self
8. laudable: worthy of praise

a man's friendships. When was the last time you heard a grown man talk proudly about his best friend?

Despite all these obstacles, it *is* possible to develop a real male friend- **11** ship—the kind men remember from their childhood, high school, college, or military days—after the age of 30. My best friend today, with whom I share a deep and abiding[9] bond, is a man I met five years ago when I was 30. But to forge real male friendships requires a willingness to *recognize* that you're going against the grain, and the *courage* to do so. And it requires the sort of conscious, deliberate campaign worthy of a guerrilla leader. Here are step-by-step guerrilla[10] tactics to forge, maintain, and deepen male friendships in a hostile environment:

1. First you have to want it. Sounds simple and obvious, but isn't. **12** You have to want it badly enough to work at getting it, just as you would a job or a sexual relationship. Right away, this causes anxiety, because it goes against the male self-sufficiency myth. You have to remind yourself *often* that there's nothing weird or effeminate[11] about wanting a friend. Let your wife and children know about your quest.[12] It's good for your sons, especially, to know what you're trying to do. They might even have some good suggestions!

2. Identify a possible friend. Men in men's groups and others who **13** seem in some way to be questioning society's view of masculinity and success are possible candidates. Don't look for men so upstanding and "responsible" they never have a second to themselves. Stuart Miller, author of the book *Men & Friendship*, suggested in a recent interview reconnecting with your old friends from childhood or adolescence.

3. Be sneaky. Once you've identified the guy you want to make your **14** friend, do you say, "Hey, I want to be your friend, let's do lunch?" No. One of you will probably soon get threatened and pull away. Instead, get involved in a project with him, preferably non-work-related. For my best friend Mike and me, it was a newsletter we were working on. You need structured time just to be together, feel each other out, and get used to each other without the pressure of being "friends."

4. Invite him to stop for a beer or a cup of coffee. Ask personal **15** questions. Find out about his wife, his children, his girlfriend, his job. Find out what's really bugging him in his life. Look for common likes and dislikes. And risk being personal about yourself as well. Do this several times, each time risking a little more honesty.

5. Call just to get together after a few months of this. Arrange to **16** get together at least once a month, even if only for a few hours. Expect to always be the caller and arranger, especially in the beginning.

6. Sit down and talk about your friendship. It may take some time **17** to reach this point. But while it's typical for men to leave things unsaid, this step is crucial. In a society that treats friendships as replaceable, you

9. abiding: lasting
10. guerrilla: a revolutionary or patriotic fighter
11. effeminate: feminine-seeming
12. quest: pursuit

have to go against the tide by declaring the value of this special friendship between you. Only then will it survive life's stresses, such as a serious disagreement or one of you moving away. ▪

Discussion and Writing Questions

Describes the process of making a friend

1. Do you agree with the author that men over thirty have few, if any, good friendships? Why or why not?

2. Letich talks about "all sorts of theories" (paragraph 3) that explain men's lack of involvement with other men. Why do you think men might find it difficult to make and maintain friendships?

3. Do you agree with the author that passion is necessary for a friendship? Why or why not?

4. Do you think that Letich's methods for making friends would work for you? Why or why not?

Writing Assignments

1. Write about man-to-man friendships and friendships between women, comparing or contrasting. Are the two types of friendships alike or dissimilar? How?

2. Examine a particular friendship you have had (or still have). What was (or is) special about your friendship? You may want to write about an incident that you feel best illustrates this friendship.

3. Argue for or against giving your all to "getting ahead." Do the benefits of hard work (money, security, status, and so on) outweigh the disadvantages (lack of time, pressure, loneliness, and so on)? Is "getting ahead" worth the time and effort it takes?

Living with My VCR

Nora Ephron

Nora Ephron writes about many topics, often with humor. In this essay, she describes her compli- cated feelings about an item many of us take for granted: the video-cassette recorder, or VCR.

When all this started, two Christmases ago, I did not have a video-cas- 1
sette recorder. What I had was a position on video-cassette recorders. I was against them. It seemed to me that the fundamental idea of the VCR—which is that if you go out and miss what's on television, you can always watch it later—flew in the face of almost the only thing I truly

believed—which is that the whole point of going out is to miss what's on television. Let's face it: Part of being a grown-up is that every day you have to choose between going out at night or staying home, and it is one of life's unhappy truths that there is not enough time to do both.

Finally, though, I broke down, but not entirely. I did not buy a video-cassette recorder. I rented one. And I didn't rent one for myself—I myself intended to stand firm and hold to my only principle. I rented one for my children. For $29 a month, I would tape "The Wizard of Oz" and "Mary Poppins" and "Born Free," and my children would be able to watch them from time to time. In six months, when my rental contract expired, I would reevaluate. **2**

For quite a while, I taped for my children. Of course I had to subscribe to Home Box Office and Cinemax in addition to my normal cable service, for $19 more a month—but for the children. I taped "Oliver" and "Annie" and "My Fair Lady" for the children. And then I stopped taping for the children—who don't watch much television, in any case—and started to tape for myself. **3**

I now tape for myself all the time. I tape when I am out, I tape when I am at home and doing other things, and I tape when I am asleep. At this very moment, as I am typing, I am taping. The entire length of my bedroom bookshelf has been turned over to video cassettes, mostly of movies; they are numbered and indexed and stacked in order in a house-hold where absolutely nothing else is. Occasionally I find myself browsing through publications like Video Review and worrying whether I shouldn't switch to chrome-based videotape or have my heads cleaned or upgrade to a machine that does six or seven things at once and can be set to tape six or seven months in advance. No doubt I will find myself shopping at some Video Village for racks and storage systems especially made for what is known as "the serious collector." **4**

How this happened, how I became a compulsive[1] videotaper, is a mystery to me, because my position on video-cassette recorders is very much the same as the one I started with. I am still against them. Now, though, I am against them for different reasons: Now I hate them out of knowledge rather than ignorance. The other technological break-throughs that have made their way into my life after my initial pigheaded opposition to them—like the electric typewriter and the Cuisinart—have all settled peacefully into my home. I never think about them except when I'm using them, and when I'm using them I take them for granted. They do exactly what I want them to do. I put the slicing disk into the Cuisinart, and damned if the thing doesn't slice things up just the way it's supposed to. But there's no taking a VCR for granted. It squats there, next to the television, ready to rebuke[2] any fool who expects something of it. **5**

A child can operate a VCR, of course. Only a few maneuvers are required to tape something, and only a few more are required to tape something while you are out. You must set the timer to the correct time you wish the recording to begin and end. You must punch the channel **6**

---

1. compulsive: obsessive, driven
2. rebuke: scold

selector. You must insert a videotape. And, on my set, you must switch the "on" button to "time record." Theoretically, you can then go out and have a high old time, knowing that even if you waste the evening, your video-cassette recorder will not.

Sometimes things work out. Sometimes I return home, rewind the **7** tape, and discover that the machine has recorded exactly what I'd hoped it would. But more often than not, what is on the tape is not at all what I'd intended; in fact, the moments leading up to the revelation of what is actually on my video-cassettes are without doubt the most suspenseful of my humdrum³ existence. As I rewind the tape, I have no idea of what, if anything, will be on it; as I press the "play" button, I have not a clue as to what in particular has gone wrong. All I ever know for certain is that something has.

Usually it's my fault. I admit it. I have mis-set the timer or channel **8** selector or misread the newspaper listing. I have knelt at the foot of my machine and methodically, carefully, painstakingly set it—and set it wrong. This is extremely upsetting to me—I am normally quite competent when it comes to machines—but I can live with it. What is far more disturbing are the times when what has gone wrong is not my fault at all but the fault of outside forces over which I have no control whatsoever. The program listing in the newspaper lists the channel incorrectly. The cable guide inaccurately lists the length of the movie, lopping⁴ off the last 10 minutes. The evening's schedule of television programming is thrown off by an athletic event. The educational station is having a fund-raiser.

You would be amazed at how often outside forces affect a video-cas- **9** sette recorder, and I think I am safe in saying that video-cassette recorders are the only household appliances that outside forces are even relevant to. As a result, my video-cassette library is a raggedy collection of near misses: "The Thin Man" without the opening; "King Kong" without the ending; a football game instead of "Murder, She Wrote"; dozens of PBS auctions and fundraisers instead of dozens of episodes of "Masterpiece Theater." All told, my success rate at videotaping is even lower than my success rate at buying clothes I turn out to like as much as I did in the store; the machine provides more opportunities per week to make mistakes than anything else in my life.

Every summer and at Christmastime, I re-evaluate my six-month **10** rental contract. I have three options: I can buy the video-cassette recorder, which I would never do because I hate it so much; I can cancel the contract and turn in the machine, which I would never do because I am so addicted to videotaping; or I can go on renting. I go on renting. In two years I have spent enough money renting to buy two video-cassette recorders at the discount electronics place in the neighborhood, but I don't care. Renting is my way of deluding⁵ myself that I have some power over my VCR; it's my way of believing that I can still some day reject the

3. humdrum: boring, ordinary
4. lopping: cutting
5. deluding: fooling

machine in an ultimate way (by sending it back)—or else forgive it (by buying it)—for all the times it has rejected me.

In the meantime, I have my pathetic but ever-expanding collection of 11 cassettes. "Why don't you just rent the movies?" a friend said to me recently, after I finished complaining about the fact that my tape of "The Maltese Falcon" now has a segment of "Little House on the Prairie" in the middle of it. Rent them? What a bizarre suggestion. Then I would have to watch them. And I don't watch my videotapes. I don't have time. I would virtually have to watch my videotapes for the next two years just to catch up with what my VCR has recorded so far; and in any event, even if I did have time, the VCR would be taping and would therefore be unavailable for use in viewing.

So I merely accumulate video-cassettes. I haven't accumulated any- 12 thing this mindlessly since my days in college, when I was obsessed with filling my bookshelf, it didn't matter with what; what mattered was that I believed that if I had a lot of books, it would say something about my intelligence and taste. On some level, I suppose I believe that if I have a lot of video-cassettes, it will say something—not about my intelligence or taste, but about my intentions. I intend to live long enough to have time to watch my videotapes. Any way you look at it, that means forever. ▪

Discussion and Writing Questions

1. Why does Ephron seem to have a love-hate relationship with her VCR?

2. Does the author indicate why she changed from (1) a person who refused to buy a VCR to (2) a person who taped movies "for the children" to (3) a person who taped compulsively?

3. Why do you suppose a person might become addicted to taping movies, watching TV, buying tools or gadgets, or engaging in some other, similar activity?

4. How do you know that this essay is not written with complete seriousness? Give examples of sentences and paragraphs from the essay that suggest the author has a humorous attitude toward her subject.

Writing Assignments

1. Have you had an experience like Ephron's in which you moved from completely resisting something to completely embracing it? Or perhaps you've had the opposite experience, where you enjoyed and accepted something at first but later rejected it. Discuss your experience. Try to show your reader just how you changed.

2. Write about the merits or drawbacks of a particular kind of technology. Like Ephron, you might choose to write about an item found in the home: the microwave, electric shaver, or pocket calculator. Or you

may want to discuss a larger social issue: the reliance of modern medicine on drugs and surgery, the safety concerns associated with nuclear energy, or the effects on viewers of live television coverage of natural or human-caused disasters.

3. Using process, explain the steps to take in using a certain machine. You might write about operating a strange or difficult machine or one you know well. Write a humorous essay if you wish.

A Life Defined by Losses and Delights

Nancy Mairs

Nancy Mairs contracted multiple sclerosis (MS) when she was twenty-nine. In this essay, she defines who she is and is not in terms of this disease, as she describes the enormous impact MS has made on her life.

I am a cripple. I choose this word to name me. I choose from among several possibilities, the most common of which are "handicapped" or "disabled." I made the choice a number of years ago, unaware of my motives for doing so. People—crippled or not—wince at the world "cripple," as they do not at "handicapped" or "disabled." Perhaps I want them to wince. I want them to see me as a tough customer, one to whom the fates/gods/viruses have not been kind, but who can face the truth of her existence squarely. As a cripple, I swagger.

carlin

"Cripple" seems to me a clean word, straightforward and precise. As a lover of words, I like the accuracy with which it describes my condition: I have lost the full use of my limbs. "Disabled," by contrast, suggests any incapacity, physical or mental. And I certainly don't like "handicapped," which implies that I have deliberately been put at a disadvantage, by whom I can't imagine, in order to equalize chances in the great race of life. These words seem to me to be moving away from my condition, to be widening the gap between word and reality. Most remote is the recently coined euphemism[1] "differently abled," which strikes me as pure verbal garbage designed, by its ability to describe anyone, to describe no one.

What's wrong w/ word handicapped ?

I haven't always been crippled, a fact for which I am grateful. To be whole of limb is, I know from experience, infinitely more pleasant and useful than to be crippled; and if that knowledge leaves me open to bitterness at my loss, the physical soundness I once enjoyed (though I did not enjoy it half enough) is well worth the occasional stab of regret.

When I was 28 I started to trip and drop things. What at first seemed my natural clumsiness soon became too pronounced to shrug off. I consulted a neurologist, who told me that I had a brain tumor. About a year

1. euphemism: a word or phrase used instead of an offensive word or phrase

and a half later I developed a blurred spot in one eye. I had, at last, the episodes requisite for a diagnosis: multiple sclerosis. I have never been sorry for the doctor's initial misdiagnosis, however. For almost a week, until the negative results of the tests were in, I thought that I was going to die right away. Every day for the past nearly 10 years, then, has been a kind of gift. I accept all gifts.

Multiple sclerosis is a chronic degenerative disease of the central nervous system; during its course, which is unpredictable and uncontrollable, one may lose vision, hearing, speech, and ability to walk, control of bladder and/or bowels, strength in any or all extremities, sensitivity to touch, vibration, and/or pain, potency, coordination of movements—the list of possibilities is lengthy and, yes, horrifying. One may also lose one's sense of humor. That's the easiest to lose and the hardest to survive without.

In the past 10 years, I have sustained some of these losses; my disease has been slowly progressive. My left leg is now so weak that I walk with the aid of a brace and a cane. I no longer have much use of my left hand. Now my right side is weakening as well. Overall, though, I've been lucky so far; the terrain left me has been ample enough to continue many activities that absorb me: writing, teaching, raising children and plants and snakes, reading, speaking publicly about MS and depression, even playing bridge with people honorable enough to let me scatter cards without sneaking a peek.

Lest[2] I begin to sound like Pollyanna, however, let me say that I don't like having MS. I hate it. My life holds realities—harsh ones, some of them—that no right-minded human being ought to accept without grumbling: One of them is fatigue. I know of no one with MS who does not complain of bone-weariness; I wake up in the morning feeling the way most people do at the end of a bad day, and I take it from there.

I am lucky that my predilections[3] were already solitary, sedentary,[4] and bookish. I am a superb, if messy, cook. I play a fiendish game of Scrabble. I like to sit on my front steps with my husband as we make sure that the sun gets down once more behind the sharp childish scrawl of the Tucson Mountains.

This lively plenty has its bleak complement, of course, in all the things I can no longer do. I will never run, except in dreams, and I can no longer pick up babies, play piano, braid my hair. I am immobilized by acute attacks of depression, which may or may not be related to MS.

These two elements, the plenty and the privation,[5] are never pure, nor are the delight and wretchedness that accompany them. The most important struts in the framework of my existence, of course, are my husband and children. Dismayingly few marriages survive the MS test, and why should they? Most 22- and 19-year-olds, like George and me, can vow in clear conscience, after a childhood of chicken pox and summer colds, to keep one another in sickness and in health so long as they both shall live.

2. lest: out of fear that
3. predilections: interests, inclinations
4. sedentary: pertaining to sitting or not being active
5. privation: lack

Not many are equipped for the dismay, the extra work, the boredom that a degenerative disease can insinuate[6] into a relationship. Children experience similar stresses when faced with a crippled parent, and they are more helpless, since parents and children can't usually get divorced. Deprived of legal divorce, the child can at least deny the mother's disability, even her existence, forgetting to tell her about recitals and PTA meetings, never inviting friends to the house. Many do.

But I've been limping along for 10 years now, and so far George and   **11**
the children are still at my left elbow, holding tight. Anne and Matthew vacuum floors and dust furniture and rake up dog droppings with just enough grumbling so I know that they don't have brain fever. And far from hiding me, they're forever welcoming gaggles[7] of friends while I'm wandering through the house in Anne's filmy pink baby doll pajamas. And they all yell at me, laugh at some of my jokes, in short, treat me as an ordinary human being. I think they like me. Unless they're faking. . . .

Faking. There's the rub. Tugging at the fringes of my consciousness   **12**
always is the terror that people are kind to me only because I'm a cripple. My mother almost shattered me once, with that instinct mothers have for striking blows along the fault-lines of their children's hearts, by telling me, in an attack on my selfishness, "We all have to make allowances for you, of course, because of the way you are." She was awfully angry but at the time I felt my worst fear, suddenly realized. I could bear being called selfish: I am. But I couldn't bear the corroboration[8] that those around me were doing what I'd always suspected them of doing, professing fondness while silently putting up with me because of the way I am. A cripple. I've been a little cracked ever since.

Along with this fear comes a relentless pressure to please. Part of the   **13**
pressure arises from social expectations. In our society, anyone who deviates[9] from the norm had better find some way to compensate. Like fat people, who are expected to be jolly, cripples must bear their lot meekly and cheerfully. A grumpy cripple isn't playing by the rules. And much of the pressure is self-generated. Early on I vowed that, if I had to have MS, by God I was going to do it well. This is a class act, ladies and gentlemen.

Because I hate being crippled, I sometimes hate myself for being a   **14**
cripple. Over the years I have come to expect—even accept—attacks of violent self-loathing. Physical imperfection, even freed of moral disapprobation,[10] still defies and violates the ideal, especially for women, whose confinement in their bodies as objects of desire is far from over. Today's ideal woman, who lives on the glossy pages of dozens of magazines, seems to be between the ages of 18 and 25; her hair has body, her underarms are dry; she has a career but is still a fabulous cook, especially of meals that take less than 20 minutes to prepare; she jogs, swims, plays tennis, sails, but does not bowl. Though usually white and often blonde, she may

[handwritten margin note: worries that people are just being nice because she's crippled]

[handwritten margin note]

6. insinuate: work slowly into
7. gaggles: groups
8. corroboration: confirmation, assurance
9. deviates: turns away from, does not conform
10. disapprobation: blame, condemnation

be black, Hispanic, Asian, or Native American, so long as she is unusually sleek. She may be old, provided she is selling a laxative or is Lauren Bacall. But she is never a cripple.

At my age, however, I don't spend much time thinking about my 15 appearance. The burning egocentricity of adolescence, which assures one that all the world is looking all the time, has passed; I'm also too old to believe in the accuracy of self-image. The self-loathing I feel is neither physically nor intellectually substantial. What I hate is not me but a disease.

I am not a disease.   16

And a disease is not—at least not single-handedly—going to deter- 17 mine who I am.

I learned that one never finishes adjusting to MS. One does not, after 18 all, finish adjusting to life, and MS is simply a fact of my life—not my favorite fact, of course—but as ordinary as my nose and my yellow Mazda station wagon. It may at any time get worse, but no amount of worry can prepare me for a new loss. My life is a lesson in losses. I learn one at a time.

The absence of a cure often makes MS patients bitter toward their 19 doctors. Doctors are, after all, the priests of modern society whose business is to heal. Doctors too think of themselves as healers, and for this reason many have trouble dealing with MS patients, whose disease in its intransigence[11] defeats their aims and mocks their skills. Too few doctors, it is true, treat their patients as whole human beings, but the reverse is also true. I have always tried to be gentle with my doctors, who often have more at stake in terms of ego than I do. I may be frustrated by the incurability of my disease, but I am not diminished by it, and they are.

This gentleness is part of the reason I'm not sorry to be a cripple. I 20 didn't have it before. It has opened my life enormously.

If a cure were found, would I take it? In a minute. I may be a cripple, 21 but I'm only occasionally a loony and never a saint. Anyway, in my brand of theology God doesn't give bonus points for a limp. ▪

Discussion and Writing Questions

1. Why does the author call herself "a cripple" (paragraph 1)? Why does she prefer that word to any other currently in use?

2. How limiting does Mairs find MS to be? Does she find any positive aspects to having the disease?

3. Why does the author worry so much that underneath their helpfulness people might just feel sorry for her? Do you think this is a common concern among people in her situation?

4. In which paragraphs does the author present definitions? What words does she define?

11. intransigence: stubbornness

Writing Assignments

1. Write about a personality trait or a physical fact that you believe defines who you are. For instance, you may see yourself as "fun-loving," "people-pleasing," "overweight," or "athletic." Define this trait for the reader and describe its importance in your life.

2. Use comparison and contrast to write about the good that can arise from a bad situation. First, state the problem itself (like an illness, an accident, being fired from a job, or running out of money while taking a trip). Then discuss the good that came out of it.

3. Mairs discusses how having an illness has clarified for her what she enjoys most in her life. Is there an activity you feel you couldn't do without? Describe this activity and explain why you would always want to be able to pursue it.

Three Types of Resistance to Oppression

Martin Luther King, Jr.

Martin Luther King, Jr., the great civil rights leader of the 1960s, studied the teachings of Mahatma Gandhi, the spiritual leader who struggled for Indian independence from British rule. Gandhi, and King after him, preached nonviolent resistance as a means of achieving social goals.

Oppressed people deal with their oppression in three characteristic ways. 1 One way is acquiescence:[1] the oppressed resign themselves to their doom. They tacitly[2] adjust themselves to oppression, and thereby become conditioned to it. In every movement toward freedom some of the oppressed prefer to remain oppressed. Almost 2800 years ago Moses set out to lead the children of Israel from the slavery of Egypt to the freedom of the promised land. He soon discovered that slaves do not always welcome their deliverers. They become accustomed to being slaves. They would rather bear those ills they have, as Shakespeare pointed out, than flee to others that they know not of. They prefer the "fleshpots of Egypt" to the ordeals of emancipation.

There is such a thing as the freedom of exhaustion. Some people are 2 so worn down by the yoke of oppression that they give up. A few years ago in the slum areas of Atlanta, a Negro guitarist used to sing almost daily: "Ben down so long that down don't bother me." This is the type of negative freedom and resignation that often engulfs the life of the oppressed.

But this is not the way out. To accept passively an unjust system is 3

1. acquiescence: acceptance
2. tacitly: quietly, implicitly

to coöperate with that system; thereby the oppressed become as evil as the oppressor. Noncoöperation with evil is as much a moral obligation as is coöperation with good. The oppressed must never allow the conscience of the oppressor to slumber. Religion reminds every man that he is his brother's keeper. To accept injustice or segregation passively is to say to the oppressor that his actions are morally right. It is a way of allowing his conscience to fall asleep. At this moment the oppressed fails to be his brother's keeper. So acquiescence—while often the easier way—is not the moral way. It is the way of the coward. The Negro cannot win the respect of his oppressor by acquiescing; he merely increases the oppressor's arrogance and contempt. Acquiescence is interpreted as proof of the Negro's inferiority. The Negro cannot win the respect of the white people of the South or the peoples of the world if he is willing to sell the future of his children for his personal and immediate comfort and safety.

4   A second way that oppressed people sometimes deal with oppression is to resort to physical violence and corroding hatred. Violence often brings about momentary results. Nations have frequently won their independence in battle. But in spite of temporary victories, violence never brings permanent peace. It solves no social problem; it merely creates new and more complicated ones.

5   Violence as a way of achieving racial justice is both impractical and immoral. It is impractical because it is a descending spiral ending in destruction for all. The old law of an eye for an eye leaves everybody blind. It is immoral because it seeks to humiliate the opponent rather than win his understanding; it seeks to annihilate rather than to convert. Violence is immoral because it thrives on hatred rather than love. It destroys community and makes brotherhood impossible. It leaves society in monologue rather than dialogue. Violence ends by defeating itself. It creates bitterness in the survivors and brutality in the destroyers. A voice echoes through time saying to every potential Peter, "Put up your sword." History is cluttered with the wreckage of nations that failed to follow this command.

6   If the American Negro and other victims of oppression succumb[3] to the temptation of using violence in the struggle for freedom, future generations will be the recipients of a desolate[4] night of bitterness, and our chief legacy to them will be an endless reign of meaningless chaos. Violence is not the way.

7   The third way open to oppressed people in their quest for freedom is the way of nonviolent resistance. Like the synthesis in Hegelian[5] philosophy, the principle of nonviolent resistance seeks to reconcile the truths of two opposites—acquiescence and violence—while avoiding the extremes and immoralities of both. The nonviolent resister agrees with the person who acquiesces that one should not be physically aggressive toward his opponent; but he balances the equation by agreeing with the person of violence that evil must be resisted. He avoids the nonresistance

3. succumb: give in
4. desolate: empty, barren
5. Hegelian: pertaining to the nineteenth-century German philosopher Georg Hegel

of the former and the violent resistance of the latter. With nonviolent resistance, no individual or group need submit to any wrong, nor need anyone resort to violence in order to right a wrong.

It seems to me that this is the method that must guide the actions of the Negro in the present crisis in race relations. Through nonviolent resistance the Negro will be able to rise to the noble height of opposing the unjust system while loving the perpetrators of the system. The Negro must work passionately and unrelentingly for full stature as a citizen, but he must not use inferior methods to gain it. He must never come to terms with falsehood, malice,[6] hate, or destruction. **8**

Nonviolent resistance makes it possible for the Negro to remain in the South and struggle for his rights. The Negro's problem will not be solved by running away. He cannot listen to the glib[7] suggestion of those who would urge him to migrate en masse[8] to other sections of the country. By grasping his great opportunity in the South he can make a lasting contribution to the moral strength of the nation and set a sublime example of courage for generations yet unborn. **9**

By nonviolent resistance, the Negro can also enlist all men of good will in his struggle for equality. The problem is not a purely racial one, with Negroes set against whites. In the end, it is not a struggle between people at all, but a tension between justice and injustice. Nonviolent resistance is not aimed against oppressors but against oppression. Under its banner consciences, not racial groups, are enlisted. **10**

If the Negro is to achieve the goal of integration, he must organize himself into a militant and nonviolent mass movement. All three elements are indispensable. The movement for equality and justice can only be a success if it has both a mass and militant character; the barriers to be overcome require both. Nonviolence is an imperative in order to bring about ultimate community. **11**

A mass movement of militant quality that is not at the same time committed to nonviolence tends to generate conflict, which in turn breeds anarchy.[9] The support of the participants and the sympathy of the uncommitted are both inhibited by the threat that bloodshed will engulf the community. This reaction in turn encourages the opposition to threaten and resort to force. When, however, the mass movement repudiates[10] violence while moving resolutely[11] toward its goal, its opponents are revealed as the instigators[12] and practitioners of violence if it occurs. Then public support is magnetically attracted to the advocates of nonviolence, while those who employ violence are literally disarmed by overwhelming sentiment against their stand. ■ **12**

6. malice: ill will
7. glib: unthinking, too easy
8. en masse: as a group, all together
9. anarchy: lawlessness
10. repudiates: rejects
11. resolutely: with determination
12. instigators: people who start something

[handwritten margin notes:]
on board
— accept
passively
violently
— nonviolent resistance

Discussion and Writing Questions

1. According to King, what are the three ways that oppressed people respond to their oppression?

2. What does the author mean by "the freedom of exhaustion" (paragraph 2)?

3. King writes of violence as leaving society in "monologue rather than dialogue" (paragraph 5). What does he mean by this?

4. Does King present the three types of resistance to oppression in any particular order? Least to most important? Most to least? Neither of these? Explain your reasoning.

Writing Assignments

1. Classify three different types of love, hate, or friendship that someone can experience. The categories for love might be spiritual love, romantic love, and friendly love, for example. Make sure that each of your categories relates directly to your thesis statement.

2. Discuss the differences between a person who gives in to hardship (illness, poverty, or some other difficulty) and one who refuses to give in. How are the two people different?

[handwritten margin note:] *in class writing*

3. Since the time of the civil rights movement, many obstacles to achieving racial equality in this country have been removed. On the other hand, inequalities in employment, housing, educational opportunities, and health care still exist. Discuss your views on the state of racial equality.

[handwritten note:] Argue that injustices still occur & use facts, examples & consider the opposition. (Introduce, Body, Concl.)

Acknowledgments *(continued from copyright page)*

Pages 474–477—"In Search of Bruce Lee's Grave" by Shanlon Wu. Copyright © 1990 by The New York Times Company. Reprinted by permission.

Pages 477–479—"A Brother's Murder" by Brent Staples. Copyright © 1986 by The New York Times Company. Reprinted by permission.

Pages 480–484—"One More Lesson," by Judith Ortiz Cofer, reprinted with permission from the publisher, from *Silent Dancing: A Partial Remembrance of a Puerto Rican Childhood* (Houston: Arte Publico Press-University of Houston, 1991).

Pages 485–488—"How to Get the Most out of Yourself" by Alan Loy McGinnis. Reprinted from CONFIDENCE by Alan Loy McGinnis, copyright © 1987 Augsburg Publishing House. Used by permission of Augsburg Fortress, and from the March 1988 Reader's Digest.

Pages 489–492—"Hunger of Memory" from HUNGER OF MEMORY by Richard Rodriguez. Copyright © 1982 by Richard Rodriguez. Reprinted by permission of David R. Godine, Publisher.

Pages 495–496—"How to Put Off Doing a Job" by Andy Rooney. Reprinted by permission of The Putnam Publishing Group and Andrew A. Rooney, Writer, from WORD FOR WORD by Andy Rooney. Copyright © 1986 by Essay Productions, Inc.

Pages 497–500—"Some Thoughts About Abortion" by Anna Quindlen. From LIVING OUT LOUD by Anna Quindlen. Copyright © 1987 by Anna Quindlen. Reprinted by permission of Random House, Inc., and International Creative Management.

Pages 501–504—"On Kids and Couples" by Francine Klagsbrun. From MARRIED PEOPLE: STAYING TOGETHER IN THE AGE OF DIVORCE by Francine Klagsbrun. Copyright © 1985 by Francine Klagsbrun. Used by permission of Bantam Books, a division of Bantam Doubleday, Dell Publishing Group, Inc., and The Charlotte Sheedy Agency, Inc.

Pages 505–508—"Do you know who your friends are?," by Larry Letich, Special to *Utne Reader*, May/June 1991, pp. 85–87. Reprinted by permission of Lens Publishing Co., and the author.

Pages 508–511—"Living with My VCR" by Nora Ephron. Reprinted by permission of International Creative Management, Inc. Copyright © 1985 by Nora Ephron.

Pages 512–515—"A Life Defined by Losses and Delights" by Nancy Mairs. Reprinted by permission, Nancy Mairs, "On Being a Cripple," from *Plaintext*, Tucson: The University of Arizona Press. Copyright 1986 by the Arizona Board of Regents.

Pages 516–519—"Three Types of Resistance to Oppression" from STRIDE TOWARD FREEDOM by Martin Luther King, Jr. Copyright © 1958 by Martin Luther King, Jr. Copyright renewed 1986 by Coretta Scott King, Dexter King, Martin Luther King III, Yolanda King and Bernice King. Reprinted by permission of HarperCollins Publishers.

Index

A/an/and, 454
Accept/except, 454–455
Action verbs, 315
Active voice, 376–377
Addresses, punctuation for, 429–430
Adjectives, 409–414
  bad/worse/worst, 410
  changing into adverbs, 410
  comparatives of, 411–412
  definition of, 409
  good/better/best, 414–415
  past participles as, 378–380
  superlatives of, 411–412
Adverbial conjunctions. *See*
  Conjunctive adverbs
Adverbs, 409–414
  badly/worse/worst, 410
  beginning sentence with, 185–186
  and commas, 185, 327
  comparatives of, 411–412
  conjunctive, 327–328
  definition of, 409
  superlatives of, 411–412
  well/better/best, 414
Affect/effect, 455
Agreement, subject-verb, 346–348
  with collective noun, 386
  with *here* and *there*, 353–354
  with irregular verbs, 348–350
  in past tense, 363
  in questions, 354
  in relative clauses, 355
  in separation of subject and
    verb, 352–353
  special singular subjects in, 351–352
Answering the opposition, in
  persuasive paragraphs, 144,
  145, 148, 150
Antecedents, 389–397
  agreement with pronouns, 390–394
  clarity of reference to, 394–395
  collective nouns as, 393–394

definition of, 389
indefinite pronouns as, 391–392
special singular, 392–393
Apostrophe
  for contractions, 417–418
  and omitted numbers, 421
  for ownership, 418–419
  in pluralization, 420
  in time expressions, 420
Appositives, 199–203
  commas with, 200, 202, 426–427
Audience, 3–4, 22
  consideration of, in persuasive
    paragraph, 145–146
  revising for, 31–32
Authority, referring to in
  persuasive paragraphs, 144,
  145, 148

Bad/badly, 410, 414–415
Been/being, 456
Better/best, 414–415
Bible chapter and verse,
  punctuating, 439
Body
  of essay, 238, 246–253
  of paragraph, 17–18, 27
Brainstorming, 8–9, 22, 27, 29, 36,
  246
Budgeting time, 297–299
Buy/by, 455–456

Can/could, 364–365
Capitalization, 433–437
  in direct quotations, 437, 438
Case
  with *and*, 398
  in comparisons, 399–400
  in compound constructions, 398–399
  objective, 397–398, 399, 400
  possessive, 397, 398, 399
  subjective, 391–392, 397, 399, 400
Category (class), definition by, 103–105

Chronological (time) order. *See*
  Order of ideas
Class (category), definition by, 103–105
Classification essay, 283–285
Classification paragraph, 132–140
Clauses
  conjunctions and conjunctive
    adverbs showing relationship
    between, 319, 327
  defined, 318
  dependent (subordinate), 321–325, 329, 338
  independent, 318–321, 325–326,
    327–328, 329, 330
  parallelism of, 169–170
  relative, 203–208, 340, 355, 427–428
  restrictive and nonrestrictive,
    204–205, 427–428
Clichés, 223–224
Climax order. *See* Order of ideas
Clustering (mapping) ideas, 9–10
Coherence
  of essay, 253–254
  of paragraph, 40–62
Collective nouns
  as antecedents of pronouns, 393–394
  verb agreement with, 386–387
Colon, 439–440
  avoidance of use, 439*n*
  with direct quotations, 437, 439
Comma
  for addresses, 429–430
  with adverbs, 185, 327
  with answers to questions, 430
  with appositives, 200, 202, 426–427
  and compound predicates, 190
  with conjunctive adverbs, 327
  to contrast, 430
  with coordinating conjunctions,
    318, 319
  with dates, 429–430

Comma (*cont.*)
  with direct address, 430
  with direct quotations, 437, 438
  general rule for using, 185
  with *-ing* modifiers, 193
  with interjections, 430
  after introductory phrases, 193,
    196, 424–426
  with nonrestrictive clauses, 427
  with parenthetical expressions,
    425
  with past participial modifier,
    196
  with prepositional phrases, 188
  with relative clauses, 204, 205,
    206, 427
  with series of items, 423–424
  with subordinating conjunctions,
    321
  with transitional expressions,
    425
Command. *See* Imperative
    sentence
Comma splices, avoidance of, 334–
    338
Comparatives
  of adjectives and adverbs, 411–
    412
  of *bad/badly*, 414–415
  of *good/well*, 414–415
  with *more*, 412
Comparison-contrast essay, 281–
    283
Comparison-contrast paragraph,
    109, 127–131
Comparison paragraph, 118
Comparisons
  in essay questions, 303
  with figurative language, 225–
    227
  pronouns in, 399–400
  with *than*, 461
Compound constructions
  case in, 398–399
  compound predicate, 190–192
  compound subject, 312, 398
  definition of, 398
Concise language, 219–223
Conclusion, of essays, 239, 250,
    293–294, 295
Conjunctions
  coordinating, 318–321, 329
  subordinating, 321–325, 329–330,
    338
Conjunctive adverbs, 327–328
Consistency
  of number, 163–164, 166

  of person, 165–168
  of quotations, 175–179
  of tense, 158–163
Consonants, 444–448
  doubling final, 444–446
Contractions
  apostrophe for, 417–418
  and look-alikes/sound-alikes,
    456–457, 461, 464, 465
  with pronouns, 417, 419
  of *was* and *were*, 363
Contrast, comma showing, 430
Contrast-comparison essay, 281–
    283
Contrast-comparison paragraph,
    109, 127–131
Contrast paragraph, 114–118
Coordinating conjunctions, 318–
    321, 329
  punctuation with, 318, 319
Coordination, 318–321
  with conjunctive adverbs, 327–
    328, 329
  with coordinating conjunction,
    318–321, 329
  with semicolons, 325–326, 329

Dash, 440
Dates, punctuation for, 429–430
Declarative sentence, 183
Definition
  for essay question, 303
  by negation, 105
Definition essay, 278–280
Definition paragraph, 102–113
  single-sentence, 102–107
Dependent (subordinate) clauses,
    321–325, 329, 338, 355
Descriptive essay, 274–276
Descriptive paragraph, 81–91
  in essay question, 300
Descriptive words
  adjectives, 409–414
  adverbs, 409–414
  appositives as, 199–203
  -ing modifiers as, 192–195
  after linking verbs, 315
Dictionary, use of (in spelling), 443
Direct address, comma with, 430
Direct question, 438. *See also*
    Questions
Direct quotations, 175–179
  beginning essay, 292
  punctuation and capitalization
    of, 175, 437–439
Discourse, consistency of, 175–179

Each
  as special singular antecedent,
    392
  verb with, 351
-ed/-d endings, 358, 360, 368
  doubling consonant before, 444–
    445
Effect/affect, 455
ei/ie spelling, 449–450
Either/neither
  as special singular antecedent,
    392
  verb with, 351
-er/-est endings, 412
  doubling consonant before, 444–
    445
Essay questions, 300–309
  choosing pattern for, 303–305
  topic sentence or thesis
    statement for, 305–307
Essays, 238–267
  body of, 238, 246–253
  brainstorming ideas for, 246
  budgeting time for, 297–299
  conclusion of, 239, 250, 293–294,
    295
  definition of, 238
  final draft of, 261, 264–265
  first draft of, 260, 261–263
  introduction of, 238, 289–292
  linking of paragraphs in, 255–
    260
  narrowing topic in, 290
  order of paragraphs in, 253–255
    (*see also* Order of ideas)
  plan for, 244, 247, 249–250, 265,
    271, 275, 285, 287
  proofreading, 261, 265
  revising, 260–261, 262–264
  short, 260–265
  thesis statement of, *see* Thesis
    statement (of essays)
  title of, 294–296
  topic sentence in, 240, 246, 247,
    248–253, 271, 285, 287
  transition in, 257–258
Essays, types of
  classification, 283–285
  comparison or contrast, 281–283
  definition, 278–280
  descriptive, 274–276
  illustration, 269–271
  narrative, 271–274
  persuasive, 285–288
  process, 276–278
-es/-s endings, 346, 382, 383, 384,
    449

-*est* endings. *See -er/-est* endings
Exact language, 213–219, 243–244, 394–395
Examples, in persuasive paragraphs, 144, 145, 148, 149, 241, 249.
    See also Illustration
Except/accept, 454–455
Exclamation point, with quotation marks, 438
Exclamations, 183, 184
Explanation (process) paragraph, 92, 94–101
    in essay question, 300

Facts, in persuasive paragraphs, 144, 148
-*f/-fe* endings, plural of, 383
Figurative language, 225–227
Final *e* words, suffixes with, 447
Final *y* words, suffixes with, 412, 448
First draft
    of essay, 260, 261–263
    of paragraph, 3, 31, 231, 232–233
Fragments, sentence, 338–344
Freewriting, 5–7, 22, 36. *See also* Brainstorming
Fresh language, 223–225

Good/well, 414–415

Helping verbs, 316, 340, 368, 456
Here, sentences beginning with, 353–354
How-to (process) essay, 276–278
How-to (process) paragraph, 92–94, 96–101, 249
Hyphenated nouns, plural of, 383

Ideas
    brainstorming, 8–9, 22, 27, 29, 36, 246
    joining, 190–207
    key, repetition of, 51, 255–256
    order of, *see* Order of ideas
    parallel, 169–170
    and prewriting, 2, 3, 5–13
    selecting, dropping, and arranging, 29–31, 36
    subordinate, in relative clauses, 203
    surprising, in introductory statement, 290–291
    See also Topic (subject)

ie/ei spelling, 449–450
Illustration
    defined, 64
    for essay question, 303
    See also Examples
Illustration essay, 269–271
Illustration paragraph, 64–72
Imperative sentence, 183, 184
Indefinite pronoun, 165, 391–392
Independent clauses
    and conjunctive adverbs, 327–328, 329
    coordinating conjunctions to join, 318–321, 329
    definition of, 318
    semicolons joining, 325–326, 329
Indirect quotations, 175–179
Infinitives, pronouns as subjects of, 397
-*ing* ending, doubling consonant before, 444–445
-*ing* modifiers, 192–195
-*ing* verbs (present participles), 340
Instruction words, 303–304
Intensive pronouns, 401–402
Interjections, comma with, 430
Introduction, of essay, 238, 289–292
Introductory phrases, 187–189
    comma following, 193, 196, 424–426
Irregular verbs
    lists of, 360–361, 370–372
    past participles of, 369–378
    in past tense, 360–365
    in present tense, 348–350
    See also To be, To do, To have
It's/its, 456–457

Joining ideas
    with appositives, 199–203
    with compound predicates, 190–192
    with conjunctive adverbs, 327–328
    with coordinating conjunctions, 318–321, 329
    with -*ing* modifiers, 192–195
    with past participial modifiers, 196–199
    with relative clauses, 203–208
    with semicolons, 325–326, 329
    with subordinating conjunctions, 321–325, 329–330, 338
Journal, keeping a, 12–13

Key words and ideas
    repetition of, 51–54, 255–256
    of topic sentence, 29
Know/knew/no/new, 457

Language, fresh, 223–225
Linking paragraphs, 255–260
Linking verbs, 315–316, 378–379
Logical sequence. *See* Order of ideas
Long sentences, 181, 182
Look-alikes/sound-alikes, 454–466
    a/an/and, 454
    accept/except, 454–455
    affect/effect, 455
    been/being, 456
    buy/by, 455–456
    it's/its, 456–457
    know/knew/no/new, 457
    lose/loose, 457–458
    past/passed, 458
    quiet/quit/quite, 458–459
    rise/raise, 459
    sit/set, 459–460
    suppose/supposed, 460
    their/there/they're, 461
    then/than, 461–462
    through/though, 462
    to/too/two, 462–463
    use/used, 463
    weather/whether, 463–464
    where/were/we're, 464
    whose/who's, 464–465
    your/you're, 465
Lose/loose, 457–458
-*ly* endings, 410

Mapping (clustering) ideas, 9–10
Metaphors, 226–227
Modifiers
    adjectives as, 409, 414
    adverbs as, 409, 414
    -*ing*, 192–195
    past participial, 196–199
More/most, 412
Myself, incorrect use of, 399, 402

Narrative, 66–67
Narrative essay, 271–274
Narrative paragraph, 73–80
Negation, definition by, 105
No/new/know/knew, 457
Nonrestrictive relative clauses, 204–205, 427–428
Nouns, 382–388
    capitalization of, 433–437
    collective, 386, 393–394

Nouns (*cont.*)
   hyphenated, plural of, 383
   singular and plural, 163–164, 166,
     382–386, 449
Number
   apostrophe for omitted, 421
   consistency of, 163–164, 166
   of pronoun, 390

Objective case, pronouns in, 397–
   398, 399, 400
Objects
   of prepositions, 187, 313–314, 397,
     398
   pronouns as, 397–398, 399, 400
Of, signal words with, 386
One (of)/ every one (of), as special
   singular antecedents, 392
Opposition, answering (in
   persuasive paragraph), 144,
   145, 148, 150
Order of ideas, 30, 84
   climax, 40, 47–50, 253
   logical, 135, 250, 253, 254, 278,
     285
   space, 40, 44–47, 83, 253, 276
   time (chronological), 40–44, 67,
     74, 75, 93, 96, 253
Order of paragraphs (in essay),
   253–255
Ownership
   apostrophe showing, 419
   pronouns showing, 398, 456, 461,
     464, 465

Paragraph groups, 246–247
Paragraphs
   basic, how to write, 39 (*see also*
     Writing process)
   body of, 17–18, 27
   brainstorming ideas for, 8–9, 22,
     27, 29, 36
   coherence of, 40–62
   definition and format of, 16–17
   final draft of, 36
   first draft of, 3, 31, 231, 232–233
   linking, 255–260
   narrowing/limiting the topic for,
     22, 25, 36, 242, 245
   order of (in essay), 253–255 (*see
    also* Order of ideas)
   planning, 248–249
   revising, 31–35, 36, 230–235
   selecting, dropping, and
     arranging ideas for, 29–31, 36
   topic sentence of, *see* Topic
     sentence

Paragraph, types of
   classification, 132–140
   comparison, 118
   comparison-contrast, 109, 127–
     131
   contrast, 114–118
   definition, 102–113
   description, 81–91
   explanation, 92, 94–101
   how-to, 92–94, 96–101, 249
   illustration, 64–72
   narration, 73–80
   persuasive, 109, 141–155
   process, 92–101, 249
Parallelism (parallel structure),
   158, 169–175
Parentheses, 440
Parenthetical expressions, 425
Participles, past. *See* Past
   participles
Participles, present (*-ing* verbs),
   340
Passive voice, 376–378
Past participial modifiers, 196–199
Past participles
   as adjectives, 378–380
   of irregular verbs, 369–378
   in passive voice, 376–378
   in past perfect tense, 375–376
   of regular verbs, 368–369
Past/passed, 458
Past perfect tense, 375–376
Past tense
   can/could, 364–365
   of irregular verbs, 360–365
   of regular verbs, 358–359
   and tense consistency, 158–159
   of *to be*, 363–364
   will/would, 364–365
Peer editing, 261
Perfect tenses
   past, 375–376
   present, 374–375
Period, quotation marks with, 437,
   438
Person
   consistency of, 165–168
   of pronoun, 390
Persuasive essay, 285–288
Persuasive paragraph, 109, 141–
   155
Phrases
   as antecedents, 389
   appositive, 426
   introductory, 187–189
   introductory, comma following,
     193, 196, 424–426

   parallelism of, 169–170
   prepositional, 187–189, 313–314
Plural nouns, 382–386, 449
   and consistency of number, 163–
     164, 166
Plurals, apostrophe used in, 420
Possessive
   apostrophe with, 420
   its as, 456
   their as, 461
   your as, 465
Possessive case, pronouns in, 397,
   398, 399, 420, 456, 461, 464, 465
Predicate, compound, 190–192
Predicting consequences, in
   persuasive paragraphs, 144,
   145, 148, 149
Prepositional phrases
   beginning sentence with, 187–189
   identifying, 313–314
Prepositions, 187, 313, 314, 405–407
   colon use with, 439*n*
   objects of, 187, 313–314, 397, 398
Present participles (*-ing* verbs), 340
Present perfect tense, 374–375
Present tense
   of irregular verbs, 348–350
   and tense consistency, 158–159
   of *to be*, 348–349
   of *to do*, 348–349
   of *to have*, 348–349
Prewriting, 2, 3, 5–13
Process essay, 276–278
Process (how-to, explanation)
   paragraph, 92–101, 249
   in essay question, 300
Pronouns, 389–403
   agreement with antecedents,
     390–394
   ambiguous, 394–395
   antecedents of, 389–397
   and collective nouns, 393–394
   after comparisons, 399–400
   change of, in indirect vs. direct
     discourse, 176
   in compound constructions, 398–
     399
   consistency of, 163–164
   contractions of, 418, 420
   definition of, 389
   indefinite, 165, 391–392
   in objective case, 397–398, 399,
     400
   in possessive case, 397, 398, 399,
     420, 456, 461, 464, 465
   reflexive or intensive, 401–402
   repetitious, 395

Pronouns (*cont.*)
   with *-self/-selves*, 401–402
   with special singular
      antecedents, 392–393
   in subjective case, 391–392, 397,
      399, 400
   substitution of, 52–53
   vague, 394–395
   who/whom, 400–401
Proofreading, 2, 3, 36, 230, 261, 265
Punctuation
   apostrophe, 417–421
   colon, 437, 439–440
   comma, *see* Comma
   with conjunctive adverbs, 327
   with coordinating conjunctions,
      318, 319
   dash, 440
   of direct and indirect discourse,
      175, 176, 437–439
   exclamation point, 438
   parentheses, 440
   period, 437, 438
   with prepositions, 439*n*
   question marks, 438
   quotation marks, 435, 437–439
   with relative clauses, 204–205,
      206, 427–428
   semicolon, 325–326, 329
   with subordinating conjunctions,
      321
Purpose, 4, 22

Question mark, and quotation
     marks, 438
Questions
   agreement in, 354
   asking (in getting started
      writing), 10–12, 22, 28
   comma with answer to, 430
   direct, 438
   essay, 300–309
   essay ending with, 294
   reporter's six, 11
   rhetorical, 183
   and sentence variety, 183
   and subject-verb agreement,
      354
Quiet/quit/quite, 458–459
Quotation marks, 437–439
   with titles, 435
Quotations
   capitalization in, 437, 438
   consistency of, 175–179
   direct, 175–179, 292, 437–439
   indirect, 175–179
   punctuation of, 435, 437–439

Reader. *See* Audience
Reflexive pronouns, 401–402
Regular verbs
   past participles of, 368–369
   in past tense, 358–359
Relative clauses, 203–208
   agreement in, 355
   nonrestrictive, 204–205, 427–428
   punctuation with, 204–205, 206,
      427–428
   restrictive, 205, 427–428
   as sentence fragments, 340
   subject-verb agreement and, 352
   as subordinate clauses, 355
Repetition
   avoidance of (wordiness or
      vagueness), 219, 220, 395
   of important (key) words or
      ideas, 51–54, 255–256
Restrictive relative clauses, 205,
     427–428
Revising, 2, 3
   for consistency and parallelism,
      158–180
   of essays, 260–261, 262–264
   for language awareness, 213–229
   of paragraphs, 31–35, 36, 230–235
   for sentence variety, 181–212
Rhetorical question, 183
Rise/raise, 459
Runs-ons, avoidance of, 334–338

-self/-selves, 401–402
Semicolons, joining independent
     clauses, 325–326, 329
Sentence(s)
   beginning with *there* or *here*,
      353–354
   comma-spliced, 334–338
   complete, 23, 338–341
   declarative, 183
   definitions, single-sentence, 102–
      107
   imperative (command), 183, 184
   linking of, 51–52
   long and short, 181–183
   order of (time, space, climax),
      see Order of ideas
   parallelism in, 169–170
   run-on, 334–338
   simple, 312–317, 318
   topic, *see* Topic sentence
   transitional, 257–258
   variety of (revising for), 181–212
Sentence fragments, 338–344
Separation of subject and verb,
     352–353

Series, comma used with words in,
     423–424
Short sentences, 181, 182
Signal words, for singular and
     plural nouns, 385–386
Similes, 225–227
Simple sentences, 312–317, 318
Singular nouns, 382–386
   and consistency of number, 163–
      164, 166
Singular subjects
   pronouns and, 391, 392–393
   special, 351–352, 392–393
Sit/set, 459–460
Sound-alikes. *See* Look-alikes/
     sound-alikes
Space order. *See* Order of ideas
Specificity, 243. *See also* Exact
     language
Spelling, 443–453
   commonly misspelled words (list
      of), 451–452
   consonants in, 444–448
   doubling final consonant in, 444–
      446
   final *e* in, 447
   final *y* in, 412, 448
   ie/ei, 449–450
   improving your, 443–444
   of plural nouns, 449
   suffixes in, 444–448
   syllables in, 444, 446
   vowels in, 444
   See also Look-alikes/sound-
     alikes
Subject (of sentence)
   agreement of, with verb, 346–
     356, 386–387
   compound, 312
   with compound predicates, 190
   defining and identifying, 312–313
   of infinitive, 397
   pronoun as, 391–392, 397, 399,
     400
   in questions, 354
   and sentence fragments, 338–344
   in sentences beginning with
     there and *here*, 353–354
   separated from verb, 352–353
   singular and plural, 391, 392–393
   special singular, 351–352, 392–
     393
Subject (of writing). *See* Topic
Subjective case, pronouns in, 391–
     392, 397, 399, 400
Subordinate (dependent) clauses,
     321–325, 329, 338, 355

Subordinate idea, in relative
    clause, 203
Subordinating conjunctions, 321–
    325, 329–330, 338
    punctuation with, 321
Subordination, with subordinating
    conjunctions, 321–325, 329–330
Substitution of pronouns and
    synonyms, 51, 52, 53–57
Suffixes
    beginning with consonants, 446,
        447, 448
    beginning with vowels, 444–445,
        447, 448
    -es/-s, 346, 382, 383, 384, 449
    after final consonants, 448
    after final e, 447
    after final y, 448
Superlatives
    of adjectives and adverbs, 411–
        412
    of bad/badly, 414–415
    of good/well, 414–415
    with most, 412
Support, revising for, 32–33
Suppose/supposed, 460
Surprise beginning, 290–291
Syllables, in spelling, 444, 446
Synonyms, 53–57
    definition by, 102–103

Tense
    consistency of, 158–163
    in direct and indirect discourse,
        175–176
    past, 158–159, 358–365
    past perfect, 375–376
    present, 158–159
    present perfect, 374–375
That, who or which clauses, 204–
    208, 340, 355
Their/there/they're, 461
Then/than, 461–462
There, sentences beginning with,
    353–354
Thesaurus
    definition of, 215n
    use of, 54
Thesis statement (of essay), 238,
    240, 241–245, 248–249, 250, 254
    in answering essay question,
        305–307
    classification essay, 284, 285
    comparison or contrast essay,
        282
    definition essay, 279
    descriptive essay, 275
    illustrative essay, 270–271, 290

key words or ideas repeated,
    255–256
    narrative essay, 273
    persuasive essay, 287
    process essay, 277–278
    single-statement, 289–290
    and title of essay, 295
Through/though, 462
Time (chronological) order. See
    Order of ideas
Time expressions
    apostrophe in, 420
    colon in, 439
Titles, 23
    capitalization and underlining
        of, 435–437
    essay, 294–296
    quotation marks for, 435
To be
    been/being, 456
    colon use with, 439n
    as helping verb, 339
    as linking verb, 315
    in passive voice, 376–378
    and past participial modifiers,
        196
    past tense of, 363–364
    present tense of, 348–349
    and subject-verb agreement, 353,
        354
To do, present tense of, 348–349
To have
    as helping verb, 316, 368, 372–
        373, 456
    in past perfect tense, 375–376
    in present perfect tense, 374–375
    present tense of, 348–349
Topic (subject)
    choice of, 3
    narrowing/limiting, 22, 25, 36,
        242, 245, 290
    See also Ideas
Topic sentence, 17–30, 33–35, 36
    in answering essay question,
        305–307
    of classification paragraph, 132–
        133, 134, 138
    of comparison-contrast
        paragraph, 128
    of comparison paragraph, 118
    of contrast paragraph, 114–115,
        116
    definition of, 17–18
    of definition paragraph, 108, 109
    of descriptive paragraph or
        essay, 81, 82, 83, 85–89, 275
    in essays, 240, 246, 247, 248–253,
        271, 285, 287

of how-to (process) paragraph,
    92, 93
    how to write, 23
    of illustrative paragraph, 64, 65–
        66, 71, 72
    key word or words of, 29
    limiting, 25
    of narrative paragraph, 73, 74
    of persuasive paragraph, 141–
        142, 143–144
    of process paragraph, 92, 94, 98–
        100
    thesis statement including, 240,
        241, 249–250, 254
To/too/two, 462–463
Transitional expressions, 57–61
    for classification, 135
    commas with, 425
    for comparison, 119
    for contrast, 119
    and definition paragraphs, 109
    in descriptive paragraphs, 83–
        84
    for illustration, 67–68
    indicating place, 84
    for linking paragraphs, 257
    for narratives, 75
    for persuasion, 144
    for process, 96
Transitional sentences, 257–258
Triteness, avoidance of, 223–225

Underlining (titles), 435–437
Unity, revising for, 33–35
Use/used, 463

Vagueness of language, 213–219,
    243–244, 394–395
Verbs
    action, 315
    with active voice, 376–377
    agreement of, with subject, 346–
        356, 386–387
    in compound predicates, 190
    consistency of tense of, 158–163
    defining and identifying, 315–
        317
    with -ed/-d endings, 358, 360,
        368, 444–445
    with -es/-s endings, 346, 449
    helping, 316, 340, 368, 456
    infinitives of, 397
    -ing (present participle), 340
    irregular, 348–350, 360–365, 369–
        378
    linking, 315–316, 378–379
    of more than one word, see
        helping, above

Verbs (*cont.*)
objects of, 397–398
with passive voice, 376–378
and past participial modifiers, 196–197
past participles of, 369–380
past perfect tense of, 375–376
past tense of, 358–365
present perfect tense of, 374–375
present tense of, 348–350
in questions, 354
regular, 358–359, 368–369
and sentence fragments, 338–344
separation of, from subject, 352–353
singular, special constructions requiring, 351–352
troublesome, *see* irregular, *above*
Verb tense. *See* Tense
Voice, active and passive, 376–378

Vowels, 444
suffixes beginning with, 444–445, 447, 448

Was/were, contractions of, 363
Weather/whether, 463–464
Well/good, 414–415
Where/were/we're, 464
Who or *what* word, 312. *See also* Subject (of sentence)
Who, what, where, when, why, how (reporter's six questions), 11
Who, which or *that* clauses, 204–208, 340, 355
Who/whom, 400–401
Whose/who's, 464–465
Will/would, 364–365
Wordiness, avoidance of, 219–223
Worse/worst, 414
Writing process
for basic paragraph, 39

budgeting time in, 297–299
for classification paragraph, 139–140
for contrast or comparison paragraph, 125–126, 130
defined, 2–3
for definition paragraph, 112–113
for descriptive paragraph, 89–90
for essay, 238–267
final draft, 36
first draft, 3, 31, 231, 232, 260, 261–263
for illustration paragraph, 71–72
for narrative paragraph, 79
for persuasive paragraph, 154
for process paragraph, 100
revising, 2, 3, 31–35, 36, 158–229, 230–235
See also Essays; Paragraphs

Your/you're, 465

Rhetorical Index

The following index first classifies the paragraphs and essays in this text according to rhetorical mode and then according to rhetorical mode by chapter. (Those paragraphs with built-in errors for students to correct are not included.)

Rhetorical Modes

Illustration

Memphis in the late forties, 19
Mrs. Prym, our town's eccentric, 48
Louis Pasteur is honored, 48
I have always considered my father, 53
Hollywood has long depended, 55
More important perhaps, 62
Many famous athletes, 65
Miniaturized versions of many products, 66
Little things that happened, 67
Artists, by choice and by repute, 68
Rules and governments, 68
Acting to Save Mother Earth, 269–270
All last week, fourth-grade teacher, 290
How to Get the Most out of Yourself (Alan Loy McGinnis), 485–489
How to Put Off Doing a Job (Andy Rooney), 495–497
Some Thoughts About Abortion (Anna Quindlen), 497–500
On Kids and Couples (Francine Klagsbrun), 501–505

Narration

It was the most astonishing strikeout, 41
[Harriet] Tubman was born into slavery, 41
Last September, I watched, 74
Walt Disney might be the only, 75–76
Maya Lin's Vietnam War Memorial, 272–273
Beauty: When the Other Dancer Is the Self (Alice Walker), 468–474

In Search of Bruce Lee's Grave (Shanlon Wu), 474–477
A Brother's Murder (Brent Staples), 477–480
One More Lesson (Judith Ortiz Cofer), 480–484
Hunger of Memory (Richard Rodriguez), 489–493
Do You Know Who Your Friends Are? (Larry Letich), 505–508
Living with My VCR (Nora Ephron), 508–512

Description

Gran, you started me, 7
We lived on the top floor, 44
On my right a woods, 45
On September 10, 1990, 54
Rocky Mountain bighorn sheep, 55
Mrs. Zajac seemed to have, 62
On November 27, 1922, when archaeologist, 82
The tension builds, 161
The sculptor built the creation, 161
I recall being told, 182
Little Richard, the King of Rock 'n' Roll, 209
Fishing aboard George's 27-foot Silverton, 214
One night a moth, 228
Visiting my grandparents, 233–234
I wanted all of it, 256
Disney's Perfect World, 274–275
Beauty: When the Other Dancer Is the Self (Alice Walker), 468–474
One More Lesson (Judith Ortiz Cofer), 480–484
Hunger of Memory (Richard Rodriguez), 489–493

Two Views of the River (Mark Twain), 493–495
A Life Defined by Losses and Delights (Nancy Mairs),
   512–516

Process

The technique of coastal whaling, 52
Learning to make a budget, 93
Many experts believe, 94
You are sitting in a restaurant, 96
In order to give my best performance, 232
How to Prepare for a Final Exam, 276–277
How to Put Off Doing a Job (Andy Rooney), 495–497
Do You Know Who Your Friends Are? (Larry Letich),
   505–508
Living with My VCR (Nora Ephron), 508–512

Definition

A grand jury is an investigative body, 52
Ambivalence can be defined, 108
A feminist is *not* a man-hater, 110
Induction is reasoning, 111
Winning, 279
How to Get the Most out of Yourself (Alan Loy
   McGinnis), 485–489
A Life Defined by Losses and Delights (Nancy Mairs),
   512–516

Comparison and Contrast

On April 8, 1982, Captain, 55
Zoos in the past, 58
Although black bass and striped bass, 115, 117
Although separated by many years in age, 118
Two different groups of black musicians, 120
Although contemporary fans, 127
No meal eaten in the Middle East, 128–129
In a democracy we are all, 169
He was a large, juicy man, 226
Two Childhoods, 281–282
Most people believe, 291
One More Lesson (Judith Ortiz Cofer), 480–484
Two Views of the River (Mark Twain), 493–495

Classification

Traditional musical instruments, 133
Commercial wool is divided, 135

The Potato Scale, 283–284
Three Types of Resistance to Oppression (Martin
   Luther King, Jr.), 516–519

Persuasion

Health care will continue to be, 18
Eating sugar can be worse, 18–19
Passengers should refuse to ride, 142
The Comtrex Corporation should provide, 146
Automatic sprinkler systems, 147
The salesperson is crucial, 167
One positive result of the rising crime rate, 182
Why did I become a cab driver? 183
Try to imagine using failure, 184
Making a Difference, 239–240
Keeping Older Workers on the Job, 286–287
Few Americans stay put, 290
Millions of law-abiding Americans, 291
"I get a little weary," 292
Finally, riding with others, 293
What the reader would strive for, 293
Illness related to, 294
How to Get the Most out of Yourself (Alan Loy
   McGinnis), 485–489
Some Thoughts About Abortion (Anna Quindlen), 497–
   500
Do You Know Who Your Friends Are? (Larry Letich),
   505–508
A Life Defined by Losses and Delights (Nancy Mairs),
   512–516
Three Types of Resistance to Oppression (Martin
   Luther King, Jr.), 516–519

Mixed Modes

Boy, I wish, 6
I allow the spiders, 17
The summer picnic gave ladies, 18
Pete's sloppiness, 36
The blues is the one truly American, 61
Bottle Watching, 241
The house where I grew up, 257
With his restaurant forced to close, 258
Banking in Computer Wonderland, 258–259
Portrait of a Bike Fanatic, 264–265

Rhetorical Modes by Chapter

2 Gathering Ideas

Description

Gran, you started me, 7

Mixed Modes

Boy, I wish, 6

3 The Process of Writing Paragraphs

Illustration

Memphis in the late forties, 19

Persuasion

Health care will continue to be, 18
Eating sugar can be worse, 18–19

Mixed Modes

I allow the spiders, 17
The summer picnic gave ladies, 18
Pete's sloppiness, 36

4 Achieving Coherence

Illustration

Mrs. Prym, our town's eccentric, 48
Louis Pasteur is honored, 48
I have always considered my father, 53
Hollywood has long depended, 55
More important, perhaps, 62

Narration

It was the most astonishing strikeout, 41
[Harriet] Tubman was born into slavery, 41

Description

We lived on the top floor, 44
On my right a woods, 45
On September 10, 1990, 54
Rocky Mountain bighorn sheep, 55
Mrs. Zajac seemed to have, 62

Process

The technique of coastal whaling, 52

Definition

A grand jury is an investigative body, 52

Comparison and Contrast

On April 8, 1982, Captain, 55
Zoos in the past, 58

Mixed Modes

The blues is the one truly American, 61

5 Illustration

Illustration

Many famous athletes, 65
Miniaturized versions of many products, 66
Little things that happened, 67
Artists, by choice and by repute, 68
Rulers and governments, 68

6 Narration

Narration

Last September, I watched, 74
Walt Disney might be the only, 75–76

7 Description

Description

On November 27, 1922, when archaeologist, 82

8 Process

Process

Learning to make a budget, 93
Many experts believe, 94
You are sitting in a restaurant, 96

9 Definition

Definition

Ambivalence can be defined, 108
A feminist is *not* a man-hater, 110
Induction is reasoning, 111

10 Comparison and Contrast

Comparison and Contrast

Although black bass and striped bass, 115, 117
Although separated by many years in age, 118
Two different groups of black musicians, 120
Although contemporary fans, 127
No meal eaten in the Middle East, 128–129

11 Classification

Classification

Traditional musical instruments, 133
Commercial wool is divided, 135

12 Persuasion

Persuasion

Passengers should refuse to ride, 142
The Comtrex Corporation should provide, 146
Automatic sprinkler systems, 147

13 Revising for Consistency and Parallelism

Description

The tension builds, 161
The sculptor built the creation, 161

Comparison and Contrast

In a democracy we are all, 169

Persuasion

The salesperson is crucial, 167

14 Revising for Sentence Variety

Description

I recall being told, 182
Little Richard, the King of Rock 'n' Roll, 209

Persuasion

One positive result of the rising crime rate, 182
Why did I become a cab driver? 183
Try to imagine using failure, 184

15 Revising for Language Awareness

Description

Fishing aboard George's 27-foot Silverton, 214
One night a moth, 228

Comparison and Contrast

He was a large, juicy man, 226

16 Putting Your Revision Skills to Work

Description

Visiting my grandparents, 233–234

Process

In order to give my best performance, 232

17 The Process of Writing an Essay

Description

I wanted all of it, 256

Persuasion

Making a Difference, 239–240

Mixed Modes

Bottle Watching, 241
The house where I grew up, 257
With his restaurant forced to close, 258
Banking in Computer Wonderland, 258–259
Portrait of a Bike Fanatic, 264–265

18 Types of Essays

Illustration

Acting to Save Mother Earth, 269–270

Narration

Maya Lin's Vietnam War Memorial, 272–273

Description

Disney's Perfect World, 274–275

Process

How to Prepare for a Final Exam, 276–277

Definition

Winning, 279

Comparison and Contrast

Two Childhoods, 281–282

Classification

The Potato Scale, 283–284

Persuasion

Keeping Older Workers on the Job, 286–287

19 The Introduction, the Conclusion, and the Title

Illustration

All last week, fourth-grade teacher, 290

Comparison and Contrast

Most people believe, 291

Persuasion

Few Americans stay put, 290
Millions of law-abiding Americans, 291
"I get a little weary," 292
Finally, riding with others, 293
What the reader would strive for, 293
Illness related to, 294

Rhetorical Modes in the Reading Selections

Illustration

How to Get the Most out of Yourself (Alan Loy McGinnis), 485–489
How to Put Off Doing a Job (Andy Rooney), 495–497
Some Thoughts About Abortion (Anna Quindlen), 497–500
On Kids and Couples (Francine Klagsbrun), 501–505

Narration

Beauty: When the Other Dancer Is the Self (Alice Walker), 468–474
In Search of Bruce Lee's Grave (Shanlon Wu), 474–477
A Brother's Murder (Brent Staples), 477–480
One More Lesson (Judith Ortiz Cofer), 480–484
Hunger of Memory (Richard Rodriguez), 489–493
Do You Know Who Your Friends Are? (Larry Letich), 505–508
Living with My VCR (Nora Ephron), 508–512

Description

Beauty: When the Other Dancer Is the Self (Alice Walker), 468–474
One More Lesson (Judith Ortiz Cofer), 480–484
Hunger of Memory (Richard Rodriguez), 489–493
Two Views of the River (Mark Twain), 493–495
A Life Defined by Losses and Delights (Nancy Mairs), 512–516

Process

How to Put Off Doing a Job (Andy Rooney), 495–497

Do You Know Who Your Friends Are? (Larry Letich), 505–508
Living with My VCR (Nora Ephron), 508–512

Definition

How to Get the Most out of Yourself (Alan Loy McGinnis), 485–489
A Life Defined by Losses and Delights (Nancy Mairs), 512–516

Comparison and Contrast

One More Lesson (Judith Ortiz Cofer), 480–484
Two Views of the River (Mark Twain), 493–495

Classification

Three Types of Resistance to Oppression (Martin Luther King, Jr.), 516–519

Persuasion

How to Get the Most out of Yourself (Alan Loy McGinnis), 485–489
Some Thoughts About Abortion (Anna Quindlen), 497–500
Do You Know Who Your Friends Are? (Larry Letich), 505–508
A Life Defined by Losses and Delights (Nancy Mairs), 512–516
Three Types of Resistance to Oppression (Martin Luther King, Jr.), 516–519

Evergreen with Readings
Fourth Edition

To the instructor:

One of the best ways to improve the next edition of our textbook is to get reactions and suggestions from you, the instructor. You have worked with *Evergreen with Readings*, Fourth Edition, and we want to know what you like about the book and what can be improved. Please answer the questions below. Tear out this page and mail it to

Susan Fawcett and Alvin Sandberg
c/o Marketing Services
College Division
Houghton Mifflin Company
One Beacon Street
Boston, MA 02108

Be honest and specific in your comments. Tell us both what is good about *Evergreen with Readings* and what could be better. Thank you.

1. Overall, how would you rate *Evergreen with Readings?* (Check one.)
   ☐ excellent   ☐ average
   ☐ good   ☐ poor

2. Which chapters did you find especially helpful? Why? _____

_____

_____

_____

3. Which chapters did you find least helpful? Why? _____

_____

_____

_____

4. Were any chapters too difficult or confusing for your students? Which ones? _____

_____

_____

5. Do any chapters need more explanation or practices? Which ones and why? _____

_____

_____

6. What material would you like to see added to or deleted from future editions of *Evergreen with Readings?* _____

_____

_____

_____

7. Do you have any additional reactions to *Evergreen with Readings?* __

_____

_____

_____

8. How can we improve the Instructor's Annotated Edition? _____

_____

_____

_____

9. Please rate the Reading Selections.

	Excel-lent	Good	Fair	Poor	Didn't read
Beauty: When the Other Dancer Is the Self	☐	☐	☐	☐	☐
In Search of Bruce Lee's Grave	☐	☐	☐	☐	☐
A Brother's Murder	☐	☐	☐	☐	☐
One More Lesson	☐	☐	☐	☐	☐
How to Get the Most out of Yourself	☐	☐	☐	☐	☐
Hunger of Memory	☐	☐	☐	☐	☐
Two Views of the River	☐	☐	☐	☐	☐
How to Put Off Doing a Job	☐	☐	☐	☐	☐
Some Thoughts About Abortion	☐	☐	☐	☐	☐
On Kids and Couples	☐	☐	☐	☐	☐
Do You Know Who Your Friends Are?	☐	☐	☐	☐	☐
Living with My VCR	☐	☐	☐	☐	☐
A Life Defined by Losses and Delights	☐	☐	☐	☐	☐
Three Types of Resistance to Oppression	☐	☐	☐	☐	☐